MW00826752

The Mormon Menace

The Mormon Menace

Violence and Anti-Mormonism
in the Postbellum South

Patrick Q. Mason

UNIVERSITY PRESS

2011

OXFORD
UNIVERSITY PRESS

Oxford University Press, Inc., publishes works that further
Oxford University's objective of excellence
in research, scholarship, and education.

Oxford   New York
Auckland   Cape Town   Dar es Salaam   Hong Kong   Karachi
Kuala Lumpur   Madrid   Melbourne   Mexico City   Nairobi
New Delhi   Shanghai   Taipei   Toronto

With offices in
Argentina   Austria   Brazil   Chile   Czech   Republic   France   Greece
Guatemala   Hungary   Italy   Japan   Poland   Portugal   Singapore
South Korea   Switzerland   Thailand   Turkey   Ukraine   Vietnam

Copyright © 2011 by Oxford University Press, Inc.

Published by Oxford University Press, Inc.
198 Madison Avenue, New York, New York 10016

www.oup.com

Oxford is a registered trademark of Oxford University Press

All rights reserved. No part of this publication may be reproduced,
stored in a retrieval system, or transmitted, in any form or by any means,
electronic, mechanical, photocopying, recording, or otherwise,
without the prior permission of Oxford University Press.

Library of Congress Cataloging-in-Publication Data
Mason, Patrick Q.
The Mormon menace : violence and anti-Mormonism in the postbellum South / Patrick Q. Mason.
   p.   cm.
Includes bibliographical references (p.).
ISBN 978-0-19-974002-4 (hardcover)
1. Church of Jesus Christ of Latter-day Saints—Southern States—History. 2. Mormons—Persecutions—
Southern States—History. 3. Southern States—Church history. I. Title.
BX8615.S88M37   2010
289.3'7509034—dc22   2010012907

1 3 5 7 9 8 6 4 2

Printed in the United States of America
on acid-free paper

To Melissa
and
my father,
who never got to read this book
but in many ways inspired it

Contents

Acknowledgments

It is with great pleasure that I acknowledge and thank a number of institutions and people who assisted in the formulation, research, writing, and production of this book.

This project began as a dissertation at the University of Notre Dame. I am grateful to my committee members—Scott Appleby, Gail Bederman, George Marsden, John McGreevy, and Richard Pierce—who provided critiques and guidance that helped me conceptualize how to transform my inchoate mass of research findings into a book. They are among the most influential teachers I have had.

Financial assistance from the following institutions and awards supported the research and writing of this book: the University of Notre Dame history department; the University of Notre Dame Zahm Research Travel Fund; the American Historical Association Albert J. Beveridge Grant for Research in the History of the Western Hemisphere; the Southern Jewish Historical Society Dissertation Grant Program; the American University in Cairo Summer Research Grant; and the Kroc Institute for International Peace Studies; and the Institute for Scholarship in the Liberal Arts at Notre Dame.

This book could not have been written without the invaluable resources and support of the following libraries and archives, and the assistance of their knowledgeable librarians and archivists: Ron Watt, Jeffrey Johnson, and Larry Skidmore at the Church History Library and Archives, The Church of Jesus Christ of Latter-day Saints, Salt Lake City, Utah; David Whittaker at the L. Tom Perry Special Collections Library, Harold B. Lee Library, Brigham Young University, Provo, Utah; the Manuscripts Division, J. Willard Marriott Library, University of Utah, Salt Lake City; the Center for Jewish History, New York City; Eleanor Yadin at the Dorot Jewish Division, New York Public Library, New York City; Vince McGrath at the Tennessee State Library and Archives, Nashville; Bill Sumner at the Southern Baptist Historical Library and Archives, Nashville; the Manuscripts Department, University Library, University of North Carolina at Chapel Hill; the Rare Book, Manuscript and Special Collections, Perkins Library, Duke University, Durham, North Carolina; Dale Rosengarten at the Special Collections Department, College of

Charleston Libraries, South Carolina; Brian Fahey at the Charleston Diocesan Archives; Harlan Green at the South Carolina History Room, Charleston Public Library; the South Carolinian Library, University of South Carolina, Columbia; the South Carolina Archives & History Center, Columbia; Sandy Berman at the William Breman Jewish Heritage Museum, Atlanta, Georgia; the Georgia Archives, Morrow; the Alabama Department of Archives and History, Montgomery; the Mississippi Department of Archives and History, Jackson; the Hill Memorial Library, Louisiana State University Libraries, Baton Rouge; Art Carpenter and Joan Gaulene at the Special Collections and Archives, Loyola University, New Orleans; Special Collections Division, Howard-Tilton Memorial Library, Tulane University, New Orleans; Cathy Kahn at the Touro Infirmary Archives, New Orleans; Chris Anderson at the Methodist Library, United Methodist Archives Center, Drew University, Madison, New Jersey; and Rare and Special Collections, Princeton University Library, Princeton, New Jersey. Of course, the arguments, conclusions, and any errors in this book are entirely my own responsibility, and do not represent the LDS Church or any of the institutions that provided me with financial support or research materials.

I was fortunate to have two outstanding institutional homes during the writing of this book. The history department at the American University in Cairo was an ideal place to begin my career. I am grateful to David Blanks and Ann Lesch for recruiting me and then providing incredible support and nurturing leadership at every turn, and for colleagues in the department and beyond who were the very picture of collegiality. My students at AUC provided daily intellectual stimulation, good company, and inspiration. I miss you all—though not the traffic and pollution! The Joan B. Kroc Institute for International Peace Studies at the University of Notre Dame is an admirable community of scholars putting top-flight, cutting-edge research at the service of core human values and in the pursuit of greater human flourishing. I appreciate being in a place where we can talk in sophisticated ways about the world not only as it is but also as it should be.

Special thanks are in order for a number of individuals for their support. Marjorie Graves, local historian of Lewis County, Tennessee, escorted me to the site of the Cane Creek killings and then taught me how to dowse for graves (it really works!). Mark Bauman, editor of *Southern Jewish History*, guided me through that literature and gave invaluable editorial comments on the material that appears here as part of chapter 9. Thanks also to Cynthia Read, Charlotte Steinhardt, Brian Desmond, and the entire editorial and production team at Oxford University Press. I subjected a number of family, friends, and colleagues to drafts of various chapters, and their feedback made this a much better book. Many thanks in this respect to Melissa Mason,

Matt Mason, Richard Bushman, John Turner, Ron Walker, members of the Colloquium on Religion and History at the University of Notre Dame, and especially Matt Grow and Dallin Lewis. I am particularly grateful to Scott Appleby, who over the past few years has been a valued teacher, adviser, colleague, and friend. I am lucky to have had the camaraderie of many good friends and colleagues at Notre Dame who have inspired me in various ways over the past decade, including Bryan Smith, Matt Grow, Cody Christopherson, John Young, Darren Dochuk, John Turner, Tommy Kidd, Matt Loveland, John Crawford, and especially Mike DeGruccio. I have been blessed with a wonderful community in South Bend and beyond who provided crucial distractions via Sunday dinners, fantasy baseball, and late nights discussing religion, politics, music, Notre Dame football, and everything else that matters (and a few things that don't).

As is customary, my most sincere thanks comes last for those who mean the most. Every year that passes makes me more appreciative for how my parents, Mike and LeAnn Mason, raised four boys who ended up as well-adjusted human beings without (significant) criminal records. I am grateful for their wisdom, integrity, generosity, unfailing encouragement and support, and most of all love. I can only hope to equal their accomplishments as I attempt to raise my own children: Finn, whose smile lights up a room, whose laugh is infectious, and whose joy and energy know no bounds; and the twins, Everett and Lucia, whose greatest contributions to this project were waiting long enough for me to finish but coming soon enough to provide a deadline. Appreciation most of all goes to and for my wife Melissa, who enriches my life in every way. You make me a happier, better person, and I love you.

The Mormon Menace

1

Introduction

In September 1856, Elder Parley P. Pratt, an apostle and one of the most famed missionaries of the Church of Jesus Christ of Latter-day Saints, bid farewell to his family and embarked on a mission to the eastern United States. Over the next few months he traveled to St. Louis, Cincinnati, Philadelphia, and New York, preaching and meeting with small branches of the church along the way. He reflected on the "ignorant, blind and impenetrable" state of the people who rejected his message, and observed that "the whole country is being overwhelmed with the most abominable lying, mockery, and hatred of the Saints, and with all manner of corruption."[1] This "hatred of the Saints" took on a particularly personal flavor in March 1857 when Pratt discovered that Hector McLean was in hot pursuit with a vow to kill him.

Pratt and McLean had met three years earlier, while Pratt was in San Francisco presiding over the LDS Church's Pacific mission. McLean's wife, Eleanor, had been baptized Mormon in 1854 with her husband's permission, but his displeasure with her newfound faith steadily intensified thereafter, driving an unbridgeable wedge into a marriage already troubled by his alcoholism and occasional physical abuse. Eleanor distanced herself from her husband even as she grew closer to the church and to Pratt, whose home she visited frequently to assist him and his ailing wife. In 1855, after Hector sent their children to live with her parents in New Orleans so as to shield them from further indoctrination in Mormonism, Eleanor decided to leave her husband and San Francisco. She traveled first to New Orleans, where she made an unsuccessful attempt to recover her children. Empty-handed, Eleanor made her way to Salt Lake City, where in November 1855, in a ceremony officiated by Brigham Young, she was "sealed" to Parley Pratt as his twelfth wife, despite the fact that she was never legally divorced from Hector.

When Pratt left for his mission, Eleanor traveled to New Orleans again and, under false pretenses, retrieved her children and began her return trip to Utah in a wagon train. Her parents alerted Hector, who rushed east to find his children and exact revenge on his estranged wife and her new husband. Informed about Pratt's whereabouts, perhaps by Mormon dissenters, McLean followed his trail to St. Louis, but Pratt narrowly escaped to Indian Territory (modern-day

Oklahoma), where he hoped to rendezvous with Eleanor and the children. Tipped off by numerous informers along the way, McLean finally tracked down Eleanor, rode up to her wagon, grabbed the children, and galloped off. Law enforcement officers apprehended Eleanor and Parley soon after, and escorted them to Van Buren, Arkansas, to appear before U.S. commissioner Judge John Ogden. After hearing Eleanor's impassioned and forthright narration of McLean's abusive behavior toward her, Ogden released her without further charges, though not before peppering her with several questions about the condition of women in Utah. When Pratt appeared in the overcrowded courtroom for his hearing, McLean pulled his gun and threatened to kill the Mormon elder on the spot. Restrained by court officials, McLean put down his firearm and read a litany of charges against Pratt, successfully riling up the onlookers but having no effect on Judge Ogden, who apparently had lost sympathy for Hector after hearing Eleanor's story. The judge postponed the trial until the next day, a ruse meant to put off McLean while Pratt could be secretly released, the court finding no prosecutable charges against him.

Pratt was kept in jail overnight for his own protection. Early the next morning, Wednesday, May 13, 1857, Judge Ogden woke Pratt, delivered his horse, and offered him a knife and pistol, which Pratt refused before riding away. McLean soon discovered that Pratt had escaped and immediately gave chase, recruiting two other local roughs to assist in his manhunt. The small posse caught up with Pratt about twelve miles north of Van Buren. McLean emptied his pistol shooting at Pratt, but missed repeatedly. He closed in on the exhausted Pratt, stabbed him twice in the chest, and then rode away. Several minutes later McLean returned, dismounted, and fired his gun point blank into Pratt's neck as the Mormon apostle laid helpless on the ground. A local man who witnessed the episode gathered some of his neighbors and listened as Pratt gave his final testimony of Joseph Smith and the truth of Mormonism. With his final breaths, Pratt gasped, "I am dying a martyr to the faith."[2]

Latter-day Saints immediately echoed Pratt's self-assessment. The British LDS periodical *Millennial Star* commenced its nearly full-issue coverage of the murder by announcing, "Another Martyr has fallen."[3] Church publications and devotional works ever since have reconfirmed Pratt's status in the Mormon pantheon as one of the church's great martyrs.[4] To Hector McLean, however, Parley Pratt was a seducer, adulterer, and apostle of depravity who had deeply dishonored him and thus deserved his fate. Prevailing local sentiment concurred. Two days after the killing, the *Arkansas Intelligencer* published a candid report detailing Pratt and McLean's relationship and the events surrounding Pratt's death. It concluded, however, by expressing sympathy with Hector McLean for "the unfortunate condition in which Mormon villainy and fanaticism has placed him."[5] In the eyes of other southerners, the real victim was McLean, not Pratt.

As a native of the nineteenth-century South, Hector McLean was deeply rooted in the system of beliefs, attitudes, behaviors, and relationships that scholars refer to in shorthand as "honor." In the nineteenth century, honor was a defining concept for most Americans, holding particular sway in the South and West. Honor was a socially constructed characteristic in which the collective estimation of the community dictated the social reputation of each individual. As opposed to virtue or integrity, which could be possessed by an individual regardless of social opinion, honor was not gained by adhering to abstract concepts of law or righteousness, but rather by understanding local values and behaving in accordance with them. Honor was about who you were as well as what you did; a man was defined as much by his family's reputation as by his own merits. Although it affected other groups such as blacks and women, honor in particular pervaded the southern white male self-image, and in many ways acted as the glue that held together nineteenth-century southern culture.[6]

When a man's honor was impugned, it was imperative that he confront the transgressor in order to save face; turning the other cheek was not a compelling masculine value in the honor-bound South. In serious cases, violence against the offender was often the only way to restore lost honor. Many Americans, particularly men, perceived as cowardice the English common law's prescription of retreat in the face of a threat. As Justice Oliver Wendell Holmes remarked in regard to a case of lethal self-defense, "a man is not born to run away."[7] No insult to a man's honor was more egregious, and thus more deserving of a violent response, than a serious imputation on the character of a close female relative, including mothers and sisters but most especially wives and daughters. Sexual deviance involving a man's wife, whether via consensual adultery or coercive rape, required swift and thorough retribution, as it not only undermined the sacred institution of marriage but also assaulted the man's mastery over his household and thus a central aspect of his honor. In such a case, as Bertram Wyatt-Brown observes, "Unpleasant though violence was, the most socially approved course for a husband with a wayward mate was to take the law into his own hands. Even judicial experts all but suggested that physical retort was the proper means of restoring lost honor."[8] The law did not technically sanction such violence, but most states and juries, acting under what historians have called "the unwritten law," were loath to prosecute, let alone convict, an aggrieved husband who killed his wife's seducer; Hector McLean, for instance, was never even tried for the murder of Parley Pratt.[9] The violent enforcement of honor was thus a powerful means of social control in which both southern law and custom asserted that the family, particularly the wife and her sexuality, was the exclusive preserve of the male head of household.

Restoring honor demanded punishment of the transgressor, and if the courts failed to do their duty in prosecuting seducers—as they increasingly did in the nineteenth century—then individual citizens had the duty to uphold law and justice by meting out their own chastisement. This logic motivated the wave of extralegal violence that swept over America, and particularly the South and West, in the nineteenth century. Vigilantes knew they worked outside the restraints of the law—that was precisely the point. They considered their extralegal actions to be justified, and thus not illegal in the higher sense, because they maintained social order, preserved true democracy, and purged their communities of unwanted elements. In antebellum America, and continuing well beyond the Civil War in the frontier West and much of the South, the voice of the people often manifested itself in violent extralegal action that superseded regularly constituted law and government on behalf of the perceived common good. In this way, as historian Richard Maxwell Brown has emphasized, nineteenth-century vigilante movements were typically "socially conservative," seeking to defend the "traditional structure and values of the local community against the threatening presence of the criminal and disorderly." Often including leading citizens of the community, such as politicians, judges, lawyers, and businessmen, vigilantism worked to strengthen, not alter or overthrow, the existing norms and values of society in which the elites maintained the power. The raison d'etre of a typical vigilante movement was not revolution, but rather reification of the status quo.[10]

Nineteenth-century vigilantes targeted a variety of criminals, social deviants, and ne'er-do-wells, including horse thieves, adulterers, murderers, abolitionists, and of course Indians and insurrectionary slaves. Some employed extralegal violence against those guilty of "religious unconventionality," a category under which Mormons indubitably fell.[11] Ever since Joseph Smith founded the Latter-day Saint movement in 1830, Americans placed Mormons alongside other undesirables such as Catholics and Masons, viewing their organizations as subversive groups that were fundamentally anti-American in their ideologies, goals, and structures.[12] In his analysis of nineteenth-century anti-Mormon rhetoric and literature, Terryl Givens has demonstrated that because the founding principles of the nation sheltered religious diversity, those who opposed Mormonism generally framed their objections as social, cultural, and political arguments rather than focusing on theological difference, which was (presumably) protected under the First Amendment.[13] Indeed, religious historian William Hutchison contends that even in the religiously explosive antebellum period, Americans traditionally tolerated radical beliefs but not radical behavior, that "manner" meant more than "matter."[14]

The Latter-day Saints' peculiar institution of plural marriage provided more than enough objectionable "manner" as well as "matter" to inspire the transformation of anti-Mormonism from a relatively localized phenomenon into a veritable national pastime. Mormonism may have constituted a heresy to traditional Christians in the 1830s and 1840s, and a threat to the political and economic power of non-Mormon settlers in certain Ohio, Missouri, and Illinois communities, but it barely registered on the national radar during the Joseph Smith era. Mormonism only became a national concern in the 1850s after the establishment of what outsiders saw as a Mormon theocracy in Utah Territory and the Mormons' 1852 public announcement of plural marriage. What had begun as one of any number of small sects emerging out of the American frontier's spiritual hothouse now seemed to challenge from within the United States' cherished institutions of republican government, the rule of law, and Christian marriage. In 1856, the newly formed Republican Party declared the eradication of polygamy part of its official platform, and James Buchanan sent the U.S. Army against the Mormons in the so-called Utah War of 1857–58. The LDS Church had indeed leapt "out of obscurity," although perhaps not in quite so positive a sense as Joseph Smith's 1831 revelation had predicted.[15]

Polygamy in particular doomed Mormons to the basest representations in the popular imagination. Moralistic and voyeuristic commentators nationwide derided plural marriage as "an institution founded in the lustful and unbridled passions of men, devised by Satan himself to destroy purity and authorize whoredom." Critics called the LDS Church a "society for the seduction of young virgins," and dubbed Salt Lake City "the biggest whorehouse in the world."[16] Latter-day Saints proved remarkably perseverant, even defiant, in the face of such sustained opposition from virtually every segment of American government and society, but placing themselves so far outside the religious, cultural, and political mainstream had its costs. Not the least of these costs was the assassination of Parley Pratt, whose murder was a symptom of the broader cultural processes of honor, the unwritten law, and extralegal violence, all influenced by the nation's revulsion with Mormon polygamy.

Though aiming to regulate the behavior of minorities and social deviants, sometimes the culture of honor and vigilantism led to irreversible miscarriages of the justice the vigilantes sought to enforce. The most dramatic example of this, in the context of southern anti-Mormonism, came in Pine Bluff, Tennessee, in 1899. Six Mormon elders were holding an evening meeting in a schoolhouse, when a mob of over one hundred men stormed the building. They threw eggs and rocks through the windows and "almost demolished" the structure. Pandemonium reigned as the panicked crowd fled amidst a hail of bullets flying "thick and fast." Two missionaries hurried out of the building, with a twelve-year old girl, May Harden, courageously accompanying them as a kind of human shield. The vigilantes had set up an ambush outside with the hope of catching the elders as they were flushed from the building. They fired as soon as the missionaries appeared but hit the girl instead, instantly killing her. May Harden's brothers, vowing to avenge her death, quickly put bloodhounds on the trail of the killers. One of the vigilantes who had lain in wait for the elders was Baxter Vinson, a prominent young farmer and superintendent of a local Protestant Sunday school. Racked with guilt that he had fired the shot that killed the girl, Vinson wrote a remorseful confession in which he claimed her death was a horrible accident. As the hounds reached his home, and in view of his family and the assembled posse, Vinson picked up a knife and gun and simultaneously slit his throat and shot himself in the head.[17] Vinson had killed the very person— an innocent southern girl—he was presumably protecting through his resort to extralegal violence. So ashamed was he at the unintended consequences of his actions, he apparently believed that suicide was the only solution to such an egregious breach of honor.

The problem with vigilante justice, as many law enforcement officers and politicians pointed out throughout the nineteenth century, was that it could take on a life of its own and extinguish the fragile flame of democracy that initially sparked it. In its celebration of democracy and the common man, Jacksonian American culture virtually sanctified the vox populi, raising the question of whether the new nation was governed by the people or by law. In the name of the ascendant will of the people, as historian Michael Feldberg observed, nineteenth-century majorities "used extralegal violence or intimi- dation to compel acquiescence from weak or unpopular minorities, or to punish them for their beliefs or their behavior," especially when the courts and public authorities did not fulfill the desire of the general populace to suppress those minorities.[18] One skeptic of the utility and morality of vigilan- tism was a young Illinois lawyer named Abraham Lincoln. Following the mob murder of antislavery newspaper editor Elijah Lovejoy in 1837, Lincoln delivered a public speech called "The Perpetuation of Our Political Institu- tions," in which he warned that "there is even now something of ill-omen amongst us. I mean the increasing disregard for law which pervades the country; the growing disposition to substitute the wild and furious passions, in lieu of the sober judgments of the courts; and the worse than savage mobs, for the executive ministers of justice."[19] In worrying that extralegal majori- tarian violence would replace the rule of law, Lincoln tacitly acknowledged that vigilantism represented the fiercest and most unruly manifestation of the democratic impulse. As historian David Grimsted shrewdly observed in his study of Jacksonian riots, extralegal violence in the redressing of per- ceived threats to the community "is not antithetical to, or abnormal in, a democracy but a result of very basic tendencies and tensions within it." Riots and vigilantism thus pose "in stark form many of the deepest dilemmas a democracy faces."[20]

Parley Pratt's murder thus occurred at the nexus of a number of powerful forces that shaped nineteenth-century America, and particularly the South. Victorian morality combined with a southern culture of honor and patriarchy to create an idealized nation of peaceful Christian homes and loving marriages, with pure women entirely and gratefully dependent on the strong protection of their husbands. Any breaches to the sanctity of the home, and especially the marriage bed, constituted an assault on the man's honor and the very moral foundations of society. When the law failed to protect the vulnerable or deliver swift and full justice when wrongs had been done, community norms established by the voice of the people could be mobilized through extralegal violence. In the antebellum period, Missourians and Illinoisans resisted the political and economic power of Mormonism by deploying vigilantism as the ultimate check on deviant behavior, thus guaranteeing that the will of the people—or at least the most forceful among them—would reign supreme. Polygamy represented an even greater danger than theocracy in the minds of most nineteenth-century Americans, as it imperiled the Christian home that formed the bedrock of society. The federal government took action throughout the last half of the nineteenth century to address the problem of Mormon plural marriage writ large. Christian churches around the country preached against Mormonism, made antipolygamy a centerpiece of moral reform efforts, and undertook missions and established schools in Utah to reclaim and educate wayward souls. But for Hector McLean, and many other southerners who feared that Mormonism stood poised to swallow up their wives and children, only decisive, violent action against the religion's agents could protect families, restore lost honor, and preserve social order. This book is the story of how southerners, in the generation after Parley Pratt's murder, encountered and then countered the perceived Mormon menace in their midst.

There are two basic truisms about the late nineteenth-century South: first, that it was religious; and second, that it was violent. The statistics on the remarkable religious growth in the region following the Civil War are telling. Between 1850 and 1890, the Southern Baptist Convention alone experienced a 374 percent increase in total membership, a five-to-sixfold explosion in adherents (those who regularly attended services but were not necessarily full members), and a building boom of somewhere between two-and-a-half to four times as many churches.[21] If the early nineteenth century represented "the beginnings of the Bible Belt," then surely the last quarter of the century was when the belt was tightly fastened.[22] Religion was pervasive, even unavoidable, throughout the region; as historian Edward Ayers observed of the New South, "Even those filled with doubt or disdain could not escape the images, the assumptions, the power of faith."[23]

At the same time that religion, and especially evangelical Protestantism, was solidifying its hold on the South, the whole region also seemed to be awash in violence. The quantity and intensity of southern violence, already a distinguishing feature of the region in the antebellum period, swelled in the decades following the Civil War. Violence was a strategic political tool frequently employed during the years of Reconstruction and Redemption. Although used by both races while posturing for power in the transitional postwar society, violence was most effectively utilized by white Democrats to drive both Republicans and blacks out of power, to end any aspirations by poor white and black farmers to change the structures of society, and to reinforce white elites' supremacy by creating the laws and structures that led to Jim Crow and the Solid South.[24] By the last two decades of the century, lynching became a trademark of the region. Originally a means of frontier justice common in many parts of the country, by the 1890s "lynching had become primarily a southern and racial affair."[25] Between the end of Reconstruction and the beginning of the Great Depression, southern mobs lynched at least 2,462 African Americans, according to one recent count; another reliable estimate puts the figure at 3,220.[26] Those numbers do not include "legal lynchings" (state-sponsored executions after summary judgments by judges or juries) and Reconstruction-era violence, which together would considerably increase the totals.[27] From 1889 to 1899, the decade in which the racial terror peaked, an average of at least 187.5 African Americans per year were lynched, more than one every other day.[28] Surveying this veritable bloodbath, distinguished historian C. Vann Woodward suggested that violence was even more characteristic of the New South than the Old, and that the region was "one of the most violent communities of comparable size in all Christendom."[29]

Mormonism entered the South early in the movement's history. Within a decade of the founding of the Church of Jesus Christ of Latter-day Saints in 1830, Mormon elders actively proselytized in a number of southern states, concentrating primarily in Kentucky, Tennessee, and Virginia, but with forays into the Carolinas, Georgia, Alabama, and Mississippi as well. The missionary effort in the antebellum South was sporadic and not well organized, with the relatively limited number of missionaries (also called elders) operating in small circuits, much like Methodist itinerants. Those with family or other roots in the region often focused on bringing their message of the restored gospel to relatives, thus working among kinship lines that typified patterns of early conversions to Mormonism. Missionary labor in the antebellum South provided formative experiences for a number of men who would later become prominent leaders within the nineteenth-century church, including future apostles Jedediah M. Grant and George A. Smith, as well as the eventual fourth president of the church, Wilford Woodruff; indeed, of the first twenty-three LDS apostles, eleven spent time on missions south of the Ohio River. Historians estimate that the antebellum South hosted some 230 missionaries and produced at least 1,300 converts, many of whom eventually left the region to gather with the Saints in Nauvoo, Illinois, or in the Great Basin.[30]

The LDS Church suspended missionary work in the South during the Civil War, resuming it immediately thereafter in only limited fashion.[31] A more concerted effort began in the mid-1870s with the formal establishment of the Southern States Mission. Based on available records, from 1867 to 1898 the church sent over 900 missionaries to the South, representing a significant share of its domestic missionary strength. Once in the South, the mission leadership assigned elders to labor in a particular region, or conference, usually in pairs. Missionaries typically traveled "without purse or scrip," relying on the hospitality of local residents, both members and non-members of the church. In their diaries and letters home, missionaries recorded hardship and hunger as well as friendship and acts of compassion. Most enjoyed some success, as defined in convert baptisms. In one five-year stretch for which detailed statistics are available (August 1884 to August 1889), church membership in the entire South averaged 1,200, with a total of 1,330 new converts baptized. In that same period, some 630 southern converts emigrated west, usually to the San Luis Valley in south-central Colorado.[32] Exact statistics were not kept, particularly in the 1870s and early 1880s, but it seems fair to say the South was a fruitful field of labor for the Latter-day Saints, producing thousands of converts in the last quarter of the nineteenth century.

Historians of the late nineteenth-century South have only skimmed the LDS experience. To some extent this is understandable, given the Mormons' relatively small numbers and lack of significant concentration in any one particular area of the South, expedited by the emigration of at least half of those who did convert. Passing references to anti-Mormon vigilantism do appear in some treatments of southern violence, but in general the literature on the postbellum South has neglected the presence of Mormons and the role of anti-Mormonism in the region.[33] A few scholars have published a handful of articles on specific topics such as the establishment of a Mormon enclave among the Catawba Indian tribe in South Carolina, or the southern "folkways" observed by LDS missionaries in their travels, but no professional historian has endeavored to write a full-scale history of Mormonism in the South.[34]

This book does not attempt to provide such a comprehensive narrative, although primary sources that would allow for such a history to be written abound.[35] *The Mormon Menace* is less about the experience of Mormons in the South than the reaction of southerners to their presence. My analysis is concerned primarily with the attitudes and actions of southerners as they perceived and then responded to Mormon proselytizing in their region and to the challenges that Mormonism—particularly polygamy—posed for their homes and communities, the republic, and Christian civilization writ large. For the most part, Mormons appear here more as objects than subjects. I am fortunate to have had a wealth of sources—missionary diaries and correspondence, newspapers, and the Southern States Mission Manuscript History housed at the LDS Church Archives—that chronicle, often in close detail, episodes of anti-Mormon hostility from the victims' perspective, a boon not always available to scholars of violence. Nevertheless, I do not attempt a history of Mormons in the South per se. Most missionaries on most days were not running from murderous mobs but rather walking country roads looking for a bite to eat, a place to sleep, and ideally someone who would listen to them. Although anti-Mormonism was a constant feature of southern and national culture throughout the last quarter of the century, it did not dictate every interaction between Latter-day Saints and "Gentiles," as they called all non-Mormons. LDS elders frequently recorded shows of hospitality from southerners, often in the same communities where they encountered violent opposition. Any full account of the Mormon experience in the South would detail this broad range of relations and not focus so exclusively on conflict as I do here.

The purpose of this book is to narrate and then understand late nineteenth-century southern anti-Mormonism, both on its own terms and in its significance for broader narratives about southern, religious, and American

Figure 1.1 "A Familiar Scene." Elders W. J. Strong and M. A. Beckstead, missionaries in the LDS Church's Southern States Mission, rest near railroad tracks in southern Alabama. *Southern Star* vol. 1 (Chattanooga: "Southern States Mission, 1899), 64. Courtesy of L. Tom Perry Special Collections, Harold B. Lee Library, Brigham Young University, Provo, Utah.

history. Given their statistically inconsequential presence in the South, relative to the total population, Mormons might have been ignored—as they have been in the historiography. The consistently vitriolic reactions to Mormonism by southerners suggest, however, that the religion's significance for the postbellum South was disproportionate to its numerical weakness. As historian Laurence Moore observes of the movement more broadly, "If sustained controversy denotes cultural importance, then Mormons were as significant as any other religious group in nineteenth-century America." My analysis follows Moore's general argument that the margins define the center, and that we can best understand southern and national culture by examining "contests between groups who revere different cultural symbols and who have different perspectives on shared cultural symbols."[36] The depth, persistence, and violence of southerners' antagonism toward Mormonism are historical facts that bear examination. One might assign blame for their hostility to a general penchant for violence in the South.[37] Such a general explanation, however, does not explain the paucity of violence between different groups of evangelical Protestant southerners who otherwise issued furious denunciations of one another from the pulpit and in their denominational newspapers, or the relative (and somewhat surprising) lack of violence by Protestants against other unpopular religious minorities in the postbellum South such as Jews and Catholics. Mormonism was unique in the way it inspired southerners to set aside general norms of civility and religious tolerance as they sought the eradication of the Mormon presence from their own communities and the destruction of the religion more broadly.

Anti-Mormonism was not the exclusive preserve of the South; indeed, it was one of the truly national phenomena of the last quarter of the nineteenth century.[38] Residents of the former Confederacy expressed their own distinctive form of hostility to Mormonism, however. Southerners victimized Latter-day Saint missionaries and converts in well over three hundred documented cases of violence in the last quarter of the nineteenth century. These episodes occurred in every southern state, and fairly consistently throughout the period. Organized efforts by vigilantes targeted hundreds of LDS missionaries and converts with the purpose of ridding southern communities of their small but apparently menacing presence. Southern "regulators," sometimes acting individually but usually in groups, whipped, kidnapped, and forcibly expelled Mormons from towns or even their own homes. Most of the time vigilantes applied nonlethal force, but the violence did turn deadly in a handful of occasions. While anti-Mormon violence paled in comparison to racial and political violence targeting African Americans, it far exceeded the combined number of attacks against all other religious outsiders in the South, including Jews and Catholics, during this period. The frequency and intensity of violence was a distinguishing characteristic of southern anti-Mormonism in this period. One missionary contrasted the treatment of elders in the South versus the North this way: "the Southerner sallies out against the 'Mormon' Elder with hickory withes, knives and pistols. In the Northern States [anti-Mormon hostility] is of a milder nature, as being rotten-egged, tarred and feathered, etc."[39]

Violence represented the most extreme form of a broader anti-Mormon sentiment that suffused the postbellum South. By the mid-1880s, virtually every segment of southern society—politicians, law enforcement officers, clergymen, the press, women's organizations, the business community, and ordinary farmers—had mobilized against the Mormon threat. This hostility culminated in a regional anti-Mormon rhetoric that found voice in sermons, newspapers, and pamphlets. In 1881 John Morgan, president of the Southern States Mission, noted that contemporary newspapers were "teeming with articles in regard to the Latter-day Saints," that "ministers preach about us from their stands, and lawyers have to allude to us from the forum." Indeed, Morgan concluded, "to-day 'Mormonism' is a living question in the United States . . . the 'Mormon' iron is red-hot."[40]

The southern anti-Mormon campaign coincided with the national crusade to eliminate polygamy, and the entire LDS Church if need be.[41] Prior to the Civil War, most southern Democratic politicians opposed national anti-polygamy legislation, fearful of the precedent it would create for federal intervention against slavery. With a few notable exceptions, however, most southerners came to enthusiastically support the antipolygamy measures adopted by the federal government in the 1880s, and southern state legislatures passed further statutes bent on suppressing the spread of Mormonism and polygamy. Moral outrage trumped political and sectional hatreds, as southerners even went so far as to heartily endorse the antipolygamy policies of a succession of Republican presidents beginning with Rutherford Hayes. In this way, anti-Mormonism provided one set of bonds that helped reforge national unity after the Civil War and Reconstruction, and gave southerners common cause with northern reformers and politicians who had been their bitter enemies only a few years earlier. Although they would not completely surrender their commitments to localism and popular sovereignty, southerners embraced the imposition of coercive federal power on domestic arrangements in Utah, representing a small but significant step in reconciling the former Confederacy with the newly expanded power of the federal government.

The most violent forms of southern anti-Mormonism targeted LDS missionaries, who personified Mormonism's unorthodox religious beliefs and social customs. The fact that most of these missionaries were born in the North, West, or abroad did not ease their position among white southerners who in the late 1860s and 1870s had railed against the evils of non-native political, military, business, and religious intruders in the region. More seriously, however, southerners saw missionaries not just as religious carpet-baggers but as seducers intent on wrecking homes and enticing women to join them in the West, where they would become veritable slaves in the Mormons' degraded polygamous society. Anxious rhetoric about the Mormon seducer paralleled in many ways the contemporary hyperbolic fear that southern white men displayed toward the mythical "black beast rapist." Southern anti-Mormons thus considered the extralegal violence they conducted toward Mormon elders as a socially conservative, and justifiable, defense of community from the intrusion of outsiders. It also reflected late nineteenth-century cultural ideals in which the protection of innocent and helpless white women represented a central defining point of southern manhood. Although southern Protestants complained about the heterodox teachings of Mormonism, it was sexual and social rather than theological anxieties that primarily sparked southerners' violent reactions to the presence of Mormon missionaries in their communities. In this regard the southern anti-Mormon experience was situated at the intersection of gender, religion, and violence in the South.

The conflict between southerners and Mormons centered more on orthopraxis than orthodoxy, strictly speaking, and thus tested the extent of southerners' commitment to religious freedom. Like the U.S. Supreme Court in its landmark decision in *Reynolds v. U.S.* (1879), most southerners admitted Mormons' right to believe whatever they wanted but ferociously attacked the practice of plural marriage. Some southerners reconciled their homage to the constitutional principle of religious liberty with their attacks on Mormons by arguing that the Mormon movement was not a religion but rather an elaborate scheme designed to bed women. In this view, Mormons were not only spiritually deceived but criminal, and therefore forfeited their constitutional rights. Authentic religion could not embrace such a dissolute system as polygamy, and so Mormonism did not qualify for the protections afforded to religions in America.

Latter-day Saints, of course, perceived the situation quite differently. In their view, they were the righteous bearers of glad tidings to a people benighted under the cloak of false religion. Although they did not actively preach polygamy as part of their introduction of the "first principles" of the gospel to potential southern converts, neither were they ashamed of their doctrine of "celestial marriage," and they were quick to defend the system from its many critics. Mormons regarded themselves as victims and saw southerners—particularly evangelical Protestant clergymen—as their assailants. Inverting the standard rhetoric about the evils of polygamy, Mormons claimed the moral high ground, both in terms of religious truth and the virtues of their marriage practices. They located the origins of plural marriage in their own unique revelation, but justified their practice of it by a more universal appeal to the First Amendment guarantee of religious free exercise. Mormon apologists argued that in fighting for the freedom to practice plural marriage as part of their religion, the Saints were defending "the principle by which every church enjoys freedom of worship, freedom to control its own concerns and to propagate its doctrines." Whether "by lawless mobs or through legal means," anti-Mormons sought to destroy religious liberty. The Saints, on the other hand, patiently suffering "wrong at the hands of political tricksters, deprivation under the lash of spoilers and death from the hatred of blinded sectarians," championed religious freedom and thus "stood manfully for principles that must endure forever."[42]

Southern vigilantism provided both a challenge and an opportunity for Mormonism. The pragmatic Mormon response, especially during particularly violent times, was to avoid open confrontation, as suggested by LDS leaders in their official correspondence with missionaries.[43] The cosmological response was an appeal to the persecution and martyrdom tradition that had a history as long as the religion itself, with Latter-day Saints casting themselves as innocent lambs before the slaughter who would ultimately be vindicated by the judgments of a just God avenging His people. The pragmatic approach almost certainly kept the violence from becoming even more widespread, as many missionaries shunned conflict whenever possible; the cosmological perspective allowed the Latter-day Saints, both as individuals and as a group, to interpret and cope with the rhetorical and actual violence, focusing on how their immediate plight would lead to ultimate glory and redemption. Mormons believed that opposition was a sign of success, that the "mobocratic feeling against the Elders is very strong" precisely because "the brethren have succeeded in making some converts."[44] While a non-Mormon newspaper despaired that "Mormonism flourishes under forcible opposition," Latter-day Saints adopted a martyr's view that the concerted efforts of violent southerners to stamp them out would only further their cause and hasten their triumph.[45] This oppositional identity was an essential aspect of nineteenth-century Mormonism that helped the new religion define itself and ultimately not only survive but succeed. As Laurence Moore suggests, "It is difficult to imagine a successful Mormon church without suffering, without the encouragement of it, without the memory of it. Persecution arguably was the only possible force that would have allowed the infant church to prosper."[46]

Recent treatments of nineteenth-century anti-Mormonism—most notably Terryl Givens's groundbreaking examination of the Mormon image in popular fiction and Sarah Barringer Gordon's expert legal history of the national antipolygamy crusade—have squarely situated the phenomenon in relation to the centers of cultural power in nineteenth-century America. As Givens and Gordon demonstrate, much of the hostility to Mormonism, and especially polygamy, was located in the publishing houses of New York, Boston, and Philadelphia and the corridors of power in Washington.[47] Mob violence, which typified the antebellum Mormon experience particularly in Missouri and Illinois, had gradually disappeared throughout much of the country by the mid- to late-nineteenth century. This came as a result of a number of factors, including the gradual professionalization of police forces in cities and a rising emphasis on law and order that subverted older notions of popular justice. The South loomed as the primary exception to this set of processes, as vigilantism remained an active and largely accepted form of citizen-based punishment in most southern communities well into the twentieth century. Though southern mobs most often targeted black men perceived as political threats to the power of white men or sexual threats to the purity of white women, they also focused their ire on Mormons. In overlooking the South we run the risk of transforming late nineteenth-century anti-Mormonism into a purely intellectual, legal, and cultural phenomenon. It was all of those things, but it was also violent. Indeed, the South is the one region of the country in the postbellum period that allows for an examination of the full array of methods, including extralegal violence, employed by Mormonism's opponents in their quest to remove the stain of polygamy from the nation. Southern anti-Mormonism touched on and contributed to some of the most important cultural and political discussions of the age, including debates over modern American notions of the nature of religion and its role in society, the limits of religious freedom, the construction and application of gender norms, state regulation of domestic affairs such as marriage, and the contest between popular sovereignty and the rule of law.

Two disclaimers regarding the book's scope are necessary. First, when referring to Mormons' interactions with southerners, or southerners' participation in anti-Mormon activities, with very few exceptions I am speaking of white southerners. I do not typically include the necessary racial qualifier throughout the book, precisely because my near-universal usage here refers to whites. To conflate "southernness" with "whiteness" is normatively biased and historically inaccurate, but the southerners in my study are almost all white for a specific historical reason: Mormon missionaries restricted their proselytizing to whites. A newspaper article reporting on late nineteenth-century LDS missionary work in the South observed that the Mormons "pay little or no attention to the negroes, although the latter flock to the meetings in large numbers, attracted by the novelty. While they do not oppose their presence, the Mormons do not attempt to baptize them or make any effort for their conversion."[48] The author exaggerated African American attendance at most Mormon preaching engagements in the South but otherwise adeptly captured the racial dynamics at work. Mormons shared the racial viewpoints of most other nineteenth-century white American Christians, supposing that the black race descended from the cursed lineage of Noah's son Ham. As a result, the LDS Church banned black men from being ordained to priesthood office—a privilege extended to all other faithful Mormon men—and barred all blacks (male and female) from entering the church's temples and participating in the sacred rituals performed therein, including eternal marriages and proxy baptisms for their deceased ancestors. Mormonism's exclusivist practices continued until the last quarter of the twentieth century, when in 1978 the church leadership revoked the long-standing racial policy and opened priesthood ordination to "all worthy males" and temple rituals to all faithful members regardless of race.[49] My failure to denote my principal subjects as white merely reflects the nature of most Mormon interactions in the South, and is a conscious decision to avoid redundancy.

The second disclaimer regards the chronological scope of *The Mormon Menace*. My period of study is the last quarter of the nineteenth century. A number of factors contribute to this discrete periodization. Because polygamy was the decisive factor in southern anti-Mormonism, particularly in its activist and not merely theological forms, I am limited to the polygamy period of Mormon history, from the practice's public announcement in 1852 to its official repudiation first in 1890 and then definitively in 1904. Mormon proselytization in the South was relatively sporadic prior to the Civil War, so with the exception of the illustrative example of the Parley Pratt murder in 1857, I focus primarily on the postbellum period, particularly the years following the formal constitution of the Southern States Mission in 1875. Furthermore, the generation following Reconstruction was arguably the most violent in southern history, particularly in regards to extralegal violence. A study examining the intersections of polygamy, Mormon proselytism, and southern violence thus naturally limits itself to the period spanning 1875 to roughly the turn of the twentieth century. When the practice, and thus fear, of Mormon polygamy abated, so did the most coercive forms of southern anti-Mormonism.

Despite the explosion in both religious adherence and social violence in the late nineteenth-century South, the interplay of religion and violence in the region has traditionally received relatively limited scholarly notice. Recent years have brought some welcome attention to this area. Scholars such as Donald Mathews and Orlando Patterson have adopted theories and methodologies from religious studies and anthropology in their innovative analyses of southern lynching. Other historians, including Ted Ownby, Paul Harvey, and Steven Hahn, have similarly given the themes of religion and violence prominent roles in their treatments of the postbellum South. Most of this insightful work, however, focuses almost exclusively on the African American community and race relations.[50] This book introduces new actors and themes into the study of religion and violence in the nineteenth-century South, and in southern history more broadly. By contrast, most previous studies of southern anti-Mormonism have either focused only on a single episode or have been otherwise limited in scope and historical analysis.[51] A thorough examination of southern anti-Mormonism illuminates the religious dimensions of violence in the late nineteenth-century South, as well as the boundaries of religious legitimacy and liberty in the late nineteenth-century United States. *The Mormon Menace* thus bridges the historical literatures on anti-Mormonism, the experience of religious outsiders in America, extralegal violence, and postbellum southern religion, politics, and culture, and contributes to the evolving scholarship exploring the complicated relationship of religion and violence.

Chapters 2 and 3 provide case studies of the two most prominent examples of postbellum southern anti-Mormon violence: the 1879 murder of Joseph Standing, and the 1884 "massacre" at Cane Creek, Tennessee. Narratives of the episodes are intermixed with analysis of the prevailing cultural forces—national, regional, and local—that precipitated the conflict. These chapters introduce many of the themes that will appear in subsequent chapters, namely allegations of LDS missionaries' licentiousness, religious competition introduced by active Mormon proselytization, and the range of southerners' reactions to the Mormon presence in their communities.

Chapters 4 and 5 constitute an extended essay arguing that polygamy—even the very image and suspicion of it—was the primary motivation behind southern anti-Mormonism. Southerners' perceptions about polygamy and Mormon missionaries are analyzed in chapter 4, whereas their concrete responses to the Mormons' proselytism and peculiar marital institution are examined in the following chapter. Polygamy provided the major animus between southerners and Mormons, but not the only one, as demonstrated in chapter 6. In a series of publications ranging from newspaper articles to pamphlets to lengthy tomes, southerners also targeted LDS doctrine and the church's theocratic politics. Its critics claimed that Mormonism's unholy trinity of polygamy, heterodoxy, and theocracy threatened the very foundations of Christian society in the South, and in the nation at large. Opposition to Mormon doctrine and politics, while not directly leading to violence, helped southerners justify behaviors that were primarily construed as a defense against Mormon licentiousness. By highlighting the dangerously heterodox nature of Mormon theology and politics, anti-Mormons further marginalized the religion and its members to the point at which violence and coercive legislation against it became not only tolerated but virtually mandated.

Chapter 7 quantifies and describes the general contours and patterns of the more than three hundred episodes of southern anti-Mormon violence and explores the ways in which they were rooted in a particular set of interactions between Mormonism and postbellum southern culture. The geographical and historical setting of the violence provides a context for understanding the many forms it took, and how it drew from the long tradition of American vigilantism that thrived in the Jim Crow South even as it was dying out in the rest of the country. The locus of analysis shifts in chapter 8 from the South to the West, to explore the contribution of southern anti-Mormonism to LDS identity. The South, though being on the geographical and demographic margins of the religion, loomed prominently in the late nineteenth-century Mormon mind. Southern violence fed a Mormon oppositional identity based largely on narratives of persecution, which not only infringed upon the Latter-day Saints' constitutional rights of religious liberty but also threatened their very existence as a church and as a people. Thus, conflict in the church's southern hinterland deeply affected Mormon identity in the western heartland.

The final chapter offers concluding thoughts on how and why southern violence targeted religious outsiders who were seen as disrupting or sinning against the dominant social order. Brief excursions into the experiences of Jews and Catholics in the postbellum South add comparative perspective to southern anti-Mormonism and religious violence more broadly. While southern Jews and Catholics accommodated themselves to prevailing cultural norms, nineteenth-century Latter-day Saints consciously elevated their distinctive sense of Mormon peoplehood. Competing Mormon and southern notions of peoplehood led to significant, and often violent, conflict in the last quarter of the nineteenth century. The stark imbalance of power between itinerant Mormon missionaries representing a nationally reviled faith and white southerners who controlled virtually all the levers of power in their communities and states meant that the violence was typically one-sided. Latter-day Saints struggled valiantly to preserve their distinctiveness. In the end, however, the forces opposing them, in the South and in the nation, were too great, and they, like other minority groups in nineteenth-century America, were forced to wave the white flag of accommodation in self-preservation.

2

The Lustful Lout

The Murder of Joseph Standing

On July 18, 1879, Joseph Standing, a seasoned Latter-day Saint missionary in the church's Southern States Mission, wrote a casual letter to a friend in Centerville, Utah. He complained of the "simply awful" summer heat in northern Georgia, which wilted not only the local crops but also the missionaries, whose work had them doing "considerable walking" from house to house and town to town. Standing reported having "some success" in his proselytizing efforts, but that most of the people he met were "prejudiced" against the Mormon faith, members of the local Protestant clergy being the worst offenders. With unveiled bitterness, he asked, "How would you like it after having preached to have two preachers get up and lie about you and shake their fists nearly in your face, and that before an audience of 150 people?"[1]

Three days later, Standing lay dead, his body mutilated from repeated bullet wounds to the face and neck. Everyone knew who had committed the awful crime—the murderers made no attempt to conceal their identity during or after the shooting. A coroner's jury immediately identified the perpetrators by name, and a public trial was held. Still, no one was ever convicted for the murder, and Mormons were left hoping that God would avenge what they or the courts could not.[2]

Joseph Standing, twenty-four years old at the time of his death and a native of Salt Lake City, first served a mission for his church in Tennessee in 1875–76. He was called to resume his missionary labors in the South in early 1878, this time assigned to northern Georgia, where he organized the first branch of the LDS Church in Varnell's Station (also known as Varnell) later that same year. Well-liked and faithful, he was entrusted with the responsibility of presiding over the fledgling Georgia Conference of the church in May 1879, and became well known in the region to Mormons and non-Mormons alike.[3] Standing's missionary companion since the late spring was Rudger Clawson. The twenty-two year old son of a polygamous marriage (his mother was the second wife of four), Clawson had ten direct siblings and another thirty-one stepbrothers and stepsisters. As the surviving witness of

Figure 2.1 Photograph of Rudger Clawson and Joseph Standing (seated), ca. 1879. Courtesy of the Church History Library, The Church of Jesus Christ of Latter-day Saints, Salt Lake City, Utah.

the Standing murder he enjoyed minor celebrity status in Utah, but his real rise to prominence came five years later, when he became the first prisoner for polygamy under the 1882 Edmunds Act, which declared polygamy a felony. After his conviction was upheld by the U.S. Supreme Court, Clawson triumphantly paid a fine of $800 and served a four-year prison sentence. A beloved champion of the faith, he was ordained one of the church's twelve apostles in 1898 and served in that leadership position until his death in 1943.[4]

Throughout the early summer of 1879 Elders Standing and Clawson had been preaching in Dalton, Georgia, the seat of Whitfield County. In July the elders were invited to a district conference being held in Rome, some thirty-five miles to the south, and Standing suggested that on their way they visit the members of the church in Varnell. When they arrived at the home of a Mormon family, the elders were shocked at the cold reception they received. It was nine o'clock in the evening and the family had always been friendly on previous visits, but this time they refused to shelter the missionaries. According to Clawson's later reminiscence, the woman at the door told them, "You cannot remain because the mob in this place has threatened your life. They have said that if they ever get hold of you they will kill you. If they know you are here, and possibly they do know it, they will be out tonight in search of you." She reiterated, "You cannot remain."[5]

Unnerved after being turned away by their friends, the missionaries became particularly anxious when they recalled a dream that Standing had some months earlier that was eerily similar to the reception they had just experienced.[6] This premonition hanging heavily in their hearts as darkness approached, the two missionaries finally found lodging for the night with Henry Holston, a local non-Mormon friendly to the elders. Holston informed them that the region was brimming with "threats of mobbing, whipping and even killing the Elders." He expected to "get into trouble on account of entertaining them," but promised, in the best tradition of southern hospitality, to defend them so long as they stayed under his roof. Standing rested uneasily that night, keeping an iron bar beside his bed for self-defense. As he contemplated their situation, he confided to Clawson that he had "an intense horror of being whipped" and would "rather die than be subjected to such an indignity."[7]

The next morning, July 21, Standing and Clawson left the secure confines of Holston's home. They had not gone far down the densely wooded road when they suddenly came upon a dozen undisguised men, three on horseback and the others on foot, "armed to the teeth with clubs, pistols and guns." Tensions mounted as the parties faced each other. After a brief pause, the gang "took off their hats and swung them over their heads with an awful yell and came charging down" toward the elders, shouting, "We've got them, we've got them!" Once apprehended, the missionaries were forced to march down the road. Being in no hurry to get to his unknown destination, Clawson slowed his pace and was struck in the back of the head. Indignant, Standing demanded to know of the mob under what authority they had accosted the elders, asserting that the United States was a country of religious liberty and that the elders had done nothing illegal. He was gruffly answered, "There is no law in Georgia for Mormons, and the Government is against you."[8]

Standing apparently did not mount a counterargument. Indeed, for Mormons in 1879, it certainly would have seemed that the United States government was against them—and with good reason. Earlier that year, the Supreme Court had ruled against the LDS Church in the case of *Reynolds v. United States*. The unanimous decision, written by Chief Justice Morrison Waite, was the first high court ruling to interpret, and then fix, the specific meaning of the free exercise provision of the First Amendment. Essentially, as legal historian Sarah Gordon describes, the Court "decided that the establishment and free exercise clauses would not protect local difference in domestic relations." In other words, Mormons could not claim that their alternative form of marriage was protected under the First Amendment as an expression of religious belief. This struck a major blow to Latter-day Saints' resistance to the imposition of federal authority over their peculiar practice of plural marriage, which they had defended as an essential consti- tutional right.[9] President Rutherford B. Hayes had been outspoken in his opposition to polygamy and had asked Congress to strengthen existing federal antipolygamy statutes. Although Congress would not pass such legis- lation for another three years, Hayes' call to action helped spark the resurgent national antipolygamy crusade that peaked in the 1880s. Hayes even briefly made anti-Mormonism a minor feature of his foreign policy, when his administration unsuccessfully requested several European governments to prevent Mormon converts from immigrating to the United States.[10] All this combined with the increasingly strident voices from around the country denouncing Mormonism, made it easy for a Mormon in 1879 to feel that the United States was against him, or for an anti-Mormon vigilante to assume the same.

The mob's statement that there was "no law in Georgia for the Mormons" would also have rung true in Standing's ears. Latter-day Saints in the South had become accustomed to occasionally rough treatment, and missionaries in particular knew they could expect determined opposition in many southern communities. Nevertheless, the harassment of Mormon elders and converts in Whitfield County, and especially Varnell, had become so unrelenting that in early 1879 Standing had written to Governor Alfred H. Colquitt asking for redress. He reported that numerous Mormon elders had "been obliged at times to flee for their lives," as armed mobs of up to fifty men had "come out against them," and had even forcibly entered local church members' homes in search of the missionaries. Asserting that all citizens had "the right to worship God according to the dictates of conscience," Standing requested that the gov- ernor provide at least a "word or line" in support of religious toleration, so that the missionaries "could then travel without fear of being stoned or shot." Governor Colquitt, whom a southern religious periodical described in July 1879 as a "Christian Magistrate" presiding over a "Methodist Commonwealth," declined to answer. Instead, the only response Standing received was from the governor's secretary, J. W. Warren, who affirmed the importance of reli- gious freedom and agreed that government authorities existed for the purpose of guaranteeing such rights. He conveyed the governor's "regrets" and prom- ised that the state prosecuting attorney would be informed of the situation.[11] No further steps were taken, and no protections were extended to the local Mormon community. The only real value of Standing's letter proved to be its prophetic quality.

Unprotected by the law and vilified by the nation, Standing and Clawson continued on their forced march until the group stopped at a spring just off the road while the three horsemen rode off to find "a more secluded place for the punishment of the Elders." It appears that the mob's intention was not to murder the missionaries but to whip and abuse them before dispatching them out of the county on a train. Their leader, James Fawcett, implied their immediate aims were not lethal when he threatened, "I want you to understand that if after to-day you ever come back to this part of the country, we will hang you up by the neck."[12] Years later, Clawson confirmed this assessment when he wrote that he believed "they intended to give us a severe whipping" to impress upon the two elders the seriousness of previous demands that the missionaries leave the region. For nearly an hour, the captives and their captors sat by the spring waiting for the scouting party to return. In the meantime, the posse harangued the elders and "charged [them] with many crimes." The alleged "catalog of offences" was long, but the mob's primary accusation was that the missionaries had come to Georgia "for the purpose of stealing their wives and daughters and taking them to Utah."[13]

The three horsemen finally returned from their scouting trip and bade the elders, at rifle point, to follow them. Suddenly, Standing grabbed a pistol from a nearby guard and pointed it at the horsemen, demanding that they surrender. Just as he did, another one of the vigilantes stood and fired into Standing's face. The missionary "reeled twice and fell with scarcely a groan." All eyes turned toward Clawson. One of the vigilantes gave the order to "shoot that man." As Clawson looked "down the gun barrels of the murderous mob," he calmed himself, folded his arms, and firmly said, "Shoot." The guns remained silent, the assailants apparently unable to bring themselves to shoot both missionaries, and the order to fire was countermanded.[14]

Having faced down his would-be killers, Clawson stepped over to the spot where Standing had fallen to discover that the shots had not immediately killed his companion. Despite lying unconscious with "a great, gaping bullet wound" in his forehead and his right eye being shot out, Standing was "breathing heavily," with "the death rattle" in his throat. As the stunned group stared down at the dying man, realizing he was "beyond all earthly help," one of the assailants murmured, "Oh, isn't this terrible, isn't this terrible that he should have shot himself." The other members of the gang "took up the ingenious subterfuge" and tried to convince Clawson that Standing "had accidentally killed himself while bringing his weapon into position." Thinking fast, Clawson, who knew the suggestion of suicide was "ridiculous," took advantage of the situation to secure his own escape. He played along with the charade by agreeing that "Yes, it is terrible; it is a terrible tragedy," earnestly adding that either one of them must get help for the dying man or they must let him go. After what must have seemed like an interminable pause, the posse released Clawson. As he walked back toward the road he took care not to run, confident that any demonstration of fear would have only earned him a bullet in the back.[15]

Clawson hurried the two miles down the road to fetch Henry Holston, the man who had given the missionaries shelter the previous night. Shocked at the turn of events, Holston rushed to the site of the shooting and built a shade over Standing, who was still not yet dead but clearly beyond any chance of recovery, and then returned home, reporting later that he spied some of the posse lurking in the woods nearby. Clawson borrowed a horse and rode five miles to Catoosa Springs to summon the coroner. As he rode, the missionary ran into six or seven members of the gang, who were apparently fleeing the scene of the crime. They stopped him and demanded to know where he was going. When he pointed west, they let him go, thinking he intended to ride, for fear of his life, all the way back to Utah. Upon arriving in town, Clawson soon found the coroner and then quickly telegraphed the governor, the prosecuting attorney of Whitfield County, and Southern States mission president John Morgan to tell them what had transpired.[16]

When Clawson returned with the coroner, Holston and a few other onlookers joined them as they went to the spot where Standing's now-dead body lay. Immediately they noticed that the body had been "frightfully mutilated" with multiple gunshot and possibly knife wounds since they had last seen it, leaving "ugly wounds" all over his face and neck. Clawson surmised that at least some of the mob had returned after he and Holston had left the body and had emptied their guns into Standing while he was "presumably" still alive. The only explanation, it seemed, was that the one man who had initially shot the missionary convinced his comrades to return and become "accessories to the crime and thus share with him in the guilt by shooting into the dead man's body." This strategic spreading of guilt, which ex post facto implicated all the members of the gang in the murder, would become particularly important in the later trial as a means of preventing blame from being squarely placed on any single individual. A coroner's jury was quickly assembled, which determined that Standing had been killed by "20 shots or more from guns and pistols," inflicted on the head and neck. After interviewing witnesses from the gathering crowd, the jury released the names of the twelve men in the mob, and recommended that a warrant be issued for their arrest. Standing's mutilated body was taken back to Holston's, where Clawson stayed up far into the night cleaning and dressing it by candlelight.[17]

In the aftermath of the murder, Mormons reacted with a mixture of fear and anger. One elder in Kentucky wrote to a fellow missionary in England expressing his concern that if the "perpetrators of that black deed" went unpunished, as they almost surely would, "it will renew the energy of the ministers and the lawless to do acts of violence against the Saints."[18] Sensing this general apprehension, mission president John Morgan, who was in Salt Lake City at the time, immediately sent a letter to all Latter-day Saints in the Southern States Mission. In general, it was an epistle of counsel and encouragement, calling on the missionaries to "continue to perform their duties," and for members of the church to remain faithful and undaunted. He also pleaded that there should be "no act of recrimination, on the part of any one, either by word or deed." While such long-suffering would be good for public relations, the suggestion actually came from a position of weakness. Latter-day Saints would undoubtedly be overwhelmed in any kind of open conflict, so Morgan smartly realized that the best—and only viable—strategy would be to take the moral high ground by not retaliating. Morgan's closing paragraph was especially telling. Whereas the bulk of the letter encouraged Latter-day Saints in the South to stand their ground and maintain "the hitherto bright record that the saints have made in the mission," Morgan concluded by suggesting, almost whispering, that "Those who are in a situation to do so would do well to prepare to emigrate and gather where they can be protected."[19]

This pro-emigration statement is conspicuous given its seeming inconsistence with the letter's predominant counsel for the southern Saints to stay put. It makes more sense in light of early Mormon doctrine and practice. Throughout the nineteenth century, LDS scriptures and church leaders encouraged the faithful to "gather" with the Saints. The notion of gathering was the root of Mormon communalism in Ohio, Missouri, and Illinois, and provided the glue which held the majority of believers together in the aftermath of Joseph Smith's assassination in 1844 and the subsequent exodus to and colonization of Utah. For Mormons, gathering to the prophetically proclaimed "Zion" would, in a very real sense, "be for a defense, and for a refuge from the storm, and from wrath when it shall be poured out."[20] This notion of divine protection and strength in numbers rang true for Latter-day Saints who had been assailed by mobs on the Jacksonian frontier and besieged by the federal army during the so-called Utah War of 1857–58, and were now assaulted by violent mobs in the postbellum South. Not only was gathering a defensive strategy, but as fervent premillennialists early Mormons were convinced that their task was to prepare the kingdom of God and to call out the righteous from Babylon to gather to Zion in anticipation of the return of Jesus Christ to the earth.[21] Church leaders encouraged new converts to the faith, whether in the South or around the world in the church's various international missions, to move, as soon as possible, to the Saints' gathering place in the intermountain West. The doctrine of gathering therefore had profound social, cultural, and spiritual implications for nineteenth-century Mormonism: it was the impulse that inspired Mormons to build cohesive communities and then rationalize and maintain a high degree of separation between themselves and the outside world.[22]

If the general advice to all converts was to gather to Zion, and considering the dangerous antipathy toward Mormons throughout the region, why was the primary message of John Morgan's letter for southern Mormons to remain where they were? It seems that Morgan sought to keep a lid on the inevitable panic that may well have arisen among southern Mormons in the wake of Standing's murder. An open call from Salt Lake City for Latter-day Saints to flee the region would have only exacerbated an already tense situation, so while Morgan quietly encouraged emigration for those who could arrange it, he did not want to make the option sound like an imperative. In circumstances already pregnant with hostility and suspicion, Morgan wisely downplayed the Mormon doctrine of gathering in this particular case, making it seem an afterthought in his public advice to the southern Saints.

While the initial reaction to Standing's death among many southern Mormons was fear and uncertainty, for those in the protected mountain valleys of the West it was anger. Given the nature of the tragedy, this sentiment is not particularly surprising; what is telling is where Mormons focused their resentments. The LDS press in Utah emphasized that southerners as a whole were not to blame, asserting that "the general sentiment of all good citizens . . . is one of abhorrence for the murderers and sympathy for the deceased."[23] Mormons portrayed government and law enforcement officials as morally paralyzed and ineffective, either through their own indifference or because of political expediency. While not held blameless, these officials were generally treated as though no other response could be expected—the Latter-day Saints' experiences with state governments in Missouri and Illinois and the federal government in Utah had taught them to have little confidence in non-Mormon public authorities. The most natural and obvious targets of Mormon resentment were of course the members of the mob that actually killed Standing. However, while the "mobocrats" were impugned for carrying out the murder, they came across as secondary actors in the drama.

The root cause of the problem, Mormons asserted, was not in political machinations or mobocracy but rather in scheming religious figures. In its very first article reporting Standing's murder, the church-owned *Deseret Evening News* immediately drew conclusions about where "the real responsibility of this terrible crime" lay: "In the eyes of Heaven the greatest culprits are those who under the guise of religion instigated the attack, who circulated falsehoods to stir up the unthinking, who planted the seeds of prejudice and hatred which have brought forth this crop of violence."[24] A later report reinforced this opinion even more specifically, asserting that "the horrid act was instigated by the preaching of three 'Christian' ministers, two Methodist and one Baptist, who, jealous of the increasing success attending the labors of the Mormon missionaries in that region, had in the heat of their holy passion let fall remarks which were seized upon by the ignorant perpetrators of the act as an incitement to their wicked deed." This indictment against the local Protestant establishment was supported with "corroborative evidence" that "one of the band of assassins," Benjamin Clark, "was a Baptist deacon."[25]

Further proof came when the defense attorneys at the trial of three of the mob members regularly consulted a "leading minister, and the deacons of two Baptist churches." According to John Morgan and Rudger Clawson, who were both present at the trial, these three churchmen were "openly and shamelessly seeking to protect the murderers from their just dues."[26] All of this combined to convince Mormons that Protestant clergy were responsible for the murder and that the conniving of corrupt religious leaders provided the primary fuel for the nationwide anti-Mormon campaign.

In subsequent weeks, Mormons expanded the circle of blame by implicating the anti-Mormon faction in Utah. The first intimation of this indictment came five days after the murder in "Resolutions of Respect and Condolence" adopted by the Young Men's Mutual Improvement Association, the LDS organization for teenage boys. The resolution strongly condemned the mob, but insisted that the masterminds behind the crime were non-Mormons in Utah who sent "false reports to the world, slandering the Saints under a cloak of religion." This provocation "incited lawless men to murder," thus making the Mormons' religious and political opponents in Utah accomplices in Standing's death.[27] Other LDS editorials repeated this opinion, berating the "fiendish and corrupt persons, male and female, in this city [Salt Lake City], who have sent forth their hellish falsehoods to poison the minds of the people in the North and in the South." The *Deseret News* consistently reminded its readers to let God be the final arbiter of justice, but it felt comfortable inferring what His final verdict would be: "Before God and Eternal Justice, the souls of [the anti-Mormons] are stained with the innocent blood of Joseph Standing."[28]

Although the Saints' claims about a nationwide conspiracy spurred on by anti-Mormons in Salt Lake City was not entirely without foundation, directly connecting preachers, politicians, and the Utah press to a murderous mob in rural Georgia is complicated. True, the Standing case was a kind of extreme symptom of the nationwide hostility toward Mormons, much of which was fed by salacious accounts of Mormon debauchery in letters, tracts, and books by non-Mormon residents in and visitors to Utah.[29] In the end, however, Standing's death was, as the *New York Times* suggested, "a local affair—a Southern way of disposing a knotty case," a spontaneous and unplanned result of local antagonisms.[30] Nevertheless, the Standing murder was also a flashpoint in Mormon-Gentile relations, and it provided Latter-day Saints with an opportunity to vent their frustration with the steady stream of reports coming from Utah impugning their character to a national audience all too willing to believe any ill spoken of the Saints.

Even as the Mormons portrayed themselves as innocent victims of religious bigotry, martyrs for the truth, native Georgians painted a different picture. Virtually every newspaper across the state carried news of Standing's murder, but they took noticeably disparate tones. Those in urban areas, particularly Atlanta, the so-called capital of the New South, adopted a law-and-order stance that condemned mob violence as an unjustified response to Mormon proselytism. The *Atlanta Constitution*, the most significant newspaper in the post-bellum South, was also among the most temperate of the state's news organs in its initial coverage of the murder. Although the editors of the *Constitution* were hardly advocates of Mormonism and its doctrine of plural marriage, they did not see violence as an appropriate response. Rather, they condemned Standing's death as being "almost without excuse" and "entirely unwarranted," and emphasized that mob law in general was not "prudent, wise or lawful." The "one remedy for Mormonism," according to the *Constitution*, was not extralegal vigilantism but instead "a rigid and impartial enforcement of the law."[31] Another influential Atlanta newspaper, *The Christian Index*, echoed this call for law and order. Its editor hoped that "justice will be meted out" to all the members of the mob, regardless of who initially pulled the trigger. Even if the mob did not "intend homicide in the first instance," the *Index* argued, they "intended it in the last instance and that is enough." That Standing pulled a gun on his guards did not alter their collective guilt, since they had captured him in the first place and he was acting in self-defense, just as "any other brave man would have done." When the mob discharged their weapons into Standing's body as it laid on the ground, the twelve men unquestionably became "*all* guilty and *equally* guilty."[32]

The local press, however, reacted much more sympathetically toward the mob. Rural and small-town newspapers closer to the scene of the crime placed the mob's action in the vaunted vigilante tradition in which members of a community banded together to defend themselves against unwanted and dangerous intruders. In this light, it could be argued that the twelve men responded with appropriate force to the moral bankruptcy of the itinerant Mormon elders and the threat they posed to the Christian morality of southern communities. Northern Georgia's *Catoosa Courier*, for instance, thought the killing was justified because "the good citizens" of the region "could not stand any longer the bad influence that [Standing's] preaching had upon the female portion of the neighborhood."[33] The *Sparta Ishmaelite* was even more belligerent, referring to all Mormons as "lawless and licentious fanatics," "scoundrels," and "moral lepers." It called on state authorities to "wage war" on the Mormons before they became too "strongly entrenched" and their "lawless and shameless teachings" irrevocably polluted all that was "pure in society."[34] The common denominator in these accounts was the moral danger that many southerners perceived that Mormonism, and especially Mormon elders, posed to their communities because of the threat of polygamy. By the late 1870s, Mormon polygamy had come to represent something much more than what a few half-cracked or deluded religious zealots were doing in the privacy of their desert homes. Even non-polygamist Mormons were presumed guilty of moral degeneracy. Mormon women and especially girls often passed as objects of pity, but Mormon men were "monstrous fanatics" who preyed upon unsuspecting females to fulfill their insatiable sexual appetites.[35]

This pattern of prejudice helps explain the social and religious dynamics that culminated in Joseph Standing's death. A month after his killing the *Atlanta Constitution*, which hitherto had been one of the most moderate voices in Georgia concerning the murder, ran a sensational profile of the young missionary entitled "A Lustful Lout." Up to this point, most newspaper stories had described a vague unhappiness among local residents about the intrusions of the Mormon elders, who had enjoyed some success in Whitfield and surrounding counties. These accounts often included insinuations of the inherently immoral Mormon character, but such vague references simply perpetuated a general discourse about Mormon depravity without advancing any particular details. A few articles made the point that polygamy was neither preached by Standing and Clawson nor practiced by local Mormon converts, but this fact quickly became overlooked when the press began to paint a more lurid picture of the missionaries and their debauched exploits throughout the South.[36]

"A Lustful Lout" exemplifies this style of nineteenth-century journalism. Its salacious claims are significant less as historical fact—no substantiating evidence exists for any of its accusations—but rather as part of the broader milieu of late-nineteenth-century anti-Mormon literature that contributed to a culture of violence against Mormons. The article, purporting to provide readers with information about Joseph Standing's "character and the circumstances leading to his murder," described a series of sexual conquests by Standing throughout the counties of northern Georgia. He allegedly began by "accomplishing the ruin" of two young daughters of a widow (all unidentified) in Walker County, then went to Catoosa County where he converted the Elledge family and fathered a child with one of the daughters, "which mysteriously disappeared immediately after its birth." The elder then impregnated the girl a second time, after which the Elledges moved west "to the Mormon country." His lust unsatisfied, Standing became "too intimate" with some of the married women in the area, which "caused one husband and wife to separate." In the end, three or four—"if not more"—young women in the area "met with their ruin by this man"; tellingly, the article identified one of the victims as "the daughter of one of the murderers."[37]

As mentioned, no independent facts verify any of these stories of Standing's ostensible sexual escapades throughout the counties of northern Georgia. To the contrary, less than three weeks earlier, the *Constitution* had remarked that "there has been a great deal of general scandal about the morality of these elders, but we could find no man who believed it."[38] Similarly, William Kaneaster, a local resident whose mother, grandmother, and aunt were baptized by Joseph Standing on New Year's Day, 1879, but who personally remained unbaptized as a Mormon until 1891, witnessed the workings of Mormon missionaries in the area, including Standing, and found them faultless.[39] The particulars outlined in "The Lustful Lout" can therefore be dismissed as a sensational attempt to reduce the real person of the murdered Joseph Standing to a caricature of the lecherous Mormon polygamist.

The one possible connection between "A Lustful Lout" and actual events may be in the story of the aforementioned Elledge family. According to historian Ken Driggs, Elizabeth Jane Elledge, the one woman identified by name in the article, was probably a cousin of William, Joseph, and David Nations, three of the indicted mob members who never came to trial. Standing had in fact baptized Jane in March 1879, and her mother a few months earlier. The entire Elledge family—including Jane's brother and father (a former captain in the Confederate army), who were baptized by John Morgan in August 1879, shortly after Standing's death—emigrated to a Mormon colony in Colorado in late 1879, where Jane later married a Mormon. Driggs posits that it is "very likely that the mob's abduction and murder of Standing was motivated by resentment over his part in converting the Elledge family to the LDS faith."[40] While this does not substantiate the claims of "A Lustful Lout"—to the contrary, it undermines the more sensational claims about Standing's sexual conquests—it does attest to the volatile milieu surrounding Mormon conversions, which were perceived to upset kinship networks. The fictional Standing destroyed family bonds with sex; the real Standing disrupted them with baptism.

Emotions ran high in the days and weeks following Standing's murder. When the case eventually came to trial, curious onlookers poured in from around the region to witness the spectacle. One reporter covering the proceedings for the *Constitution* observed, "Never has a case in the annals of the criminal courts of this county excited the interest which has invested this trial."[41] That a trial would be held at all was in doubt, given the widespread local hostility manifested toward the Mormons and the sudden "disappearance" of the twelve men connected with the murder. However, three of the men identified by coroner's jury—Jasper Nations, Andrew Bradley, and Hugh Blair—were captured and brought to trial, facing charges of murder, assault and battery, and riot. Governor Colquitt had, at the urging of the Catoosa County sheriff, offered a "nominal reward, conditioned upon conviction"— which, the *Deseret News* sarcastically commented, "did not in the least endanger the treasury of the State"—but the three men's capture was actually secured through "the instrumentality of some of Elder Standing's friends."[42] The fervor among most native Georgians for bringing local men to justice for the death of an agent of polygamy was tepid at best.

The trial itself was, as John Morgan recorded in his journal, "a farce."[43] Even the state attorney, arguing on behalf of the Mormons, admitted before the proceedings began that "it will be impossible to reach conviction on account of the prejudice of the people"; indeed, 130 men were dismissed out of hand before the resemblance of an impartial jury was assembled.[44] The court had subpoenaed Rudger Clawson as a key witness, so he and Morgan traveled from Salt Lake City to attend the trial, testify against the defendants, and report back to the interested Saints in Utah. When Clawson was called to the stand, the otherwise boisterous crowd came to a complete hush as he related the events surrounding the murder. The defense sought to discredit his testimony not by any appeal to facts but rather through sensationalism, pointedly asking Clawson, "Are your parents living in the practice of polygamy and are you a polygamous child?" When it came to presenting their own case, the defense's only witnesses were the three defendants themselves, who never denied killing Standing. Nevertheless, the jury found the men not guilty on all charges.[45]

Figure 2.2 Photograph of monument to Joseph Standing in Salt Lake City Cemetery, ca. 1880. Courtesy of the Church History Library, The Church of Jesus Christ of Latter-day Saints, Salt Lake City, Utah.

The various reactions to the jury's ruling were predictably mixed. Mormons greeted the verdict as expected but detestable nonetheless. In their report to the *Deseret News*, Morgan and Clawson identified the entire affair as yet another chapter in the long history of religious persecution, comparing the Georgia crowd with those who called for Jesus's crucifixion, or the martyrdom of the early Christians, or the extermination of the Latter-day Saints in frontier Missouri. They reached the lamentable conclusions that "religious bigotry stood at the head of this murderous array and guided the current of popular opinion and prejudice," and that, at least momentarily, "public prejudice was stronger than truth, and bigotry outweighed logic and reason."[46] The *Atlanta Constitution* provided a fairly objective account of the trial, and did not editorialize extensively on the outcome, other than a brief notice that the acquittal was met with the "intensest wrath" in Salt Lake City.[47] The local newspaper, the *Catoosa Courier*, consistent with its earlier diatribes against the Mormons, vigorously applauded the not guilty verdicts, a stance which was roundly denounced by other southern newspapers.[48] As a general rule, newspapers in urban centers such as Atlanta, Chattanooga, and New York took a measured stand, denouncing mob violence as dangerous to public order while taking care not to seem overly sympathetic to the unpopular Mormons.

Joseph Standing's body was taken back to Utah and buried in the Salt Lake City Cemetery. A little over a year after his interment, a fifteen-foot tall marble monument was erected over his grave. Carved on the sides of the memorial are the names of the twelve members of the mob that killed the missionary. The inscription that follows refers to the acquittal of the murderers "through bigotry and prejudice" and closes with the refrain, "There is no law in Georgia for the Mormons."[49]

3

Rumors, Religious Competition, and Community Violence

The Cane Creek Massacre

On Sunday morning, May 4, 1884, John Gibbs, a Welsh convert to Mormonism, immigrant to Utah, successful missionary, and newly appointed president of the LDS Church's North West Tennessee Conference, traveled to Cane Creek to hold services with the small church branch there.[1] Upon arriving, rather than finding the recently constructed log meetinghouse brimming with worshippers inside, he discovered a pile of ashes and a note. The anonymous author, presumably also the arsonist, ominously scribbled:

> This is the last time that we will notify you that we will not have any more Mormans preaching in hickman perry and lewis [counties] we are the shilow men and we are going to have it stopped as we will take some or all of your lives . . . if you dont leave at this order we will use there hickory switches freely . . . the book speeks of faulty teaching and you are them you are low down scrapings of the devil and we are going to stop it if we will have to cause wore[2]

Gibbs, whom local church members had warned the night before about possible mob activity, was unfazed by both the smoldering meetinghouse and the death threat. Ignoring the pistols and shotguns brandished by a few of his enemies in the small crowd gathered around the rubble, he began preaching. When several people responded to his sermon by immediately demanding baptism, members of the "Shiloh band" watched from the banks of the creek as Gibbs honored the new converts' request. In letters he wrote to family members concerning the episode, Gibbs rejoiced that God had transformed the work of the mob into an opportunity to save eight souls. But he was not naïve about the precarious situation, acknowledging that "it may be that this will only tend to incite them to persist in their bold plans. . . . Threats and notices of leave are now the order of the day."[3]

Three months after the church burning, Gibbs and his missionary companion William Jones returned to Cane Creek following a speaking tour through Tennessee and Mississippi, where church leaders had sent them to

Figure 3.1 Photograph of William Jones and John Gibbs (seated), taken during their speaking tour of southern cities in early summer 1884. Courtesy of the Church History Library, The Church of Jesus Christ of Latter-day Saints, Salt Lake City, Utah.

give a series of public lectures on "the political, historical, moral & social phases of the Mormon Question."[4] The purpose of the tour had been for Gibbs—who from all accounts was a gifted public speaker—to plead the case of Mormonism to a misinformed southern populace.[5] Although Mormon elders in the South typically avoided large towns and cities, preferring to share their message with the humbler folk of the backwoods, Gibbs' specific target audience on his lecture circuit were the "refined, educated people" of the urban South.[6] The tour was part of a larger public relations campaign by Latter-day Saints in the mid-1880s to counter the swelling chorus of disparaging voices calling for increasingly strict legislative and judicial measures to stamp out Mormonism and particularly its institution of plural marriage.[7]

While the idea of the speaking tour was sound, and Gibbs was almost certainly the right man for the job, in retrospect the enterprise must be judged as a qualified failure—qualified, because the Mormons generally shared P. T. Barnum's philosophy that any publicity was good publicity, but nevertheless a failure on every other count. Rather than dispelling fears about polygamy, the lecture series actually stoked the embers of southerners'

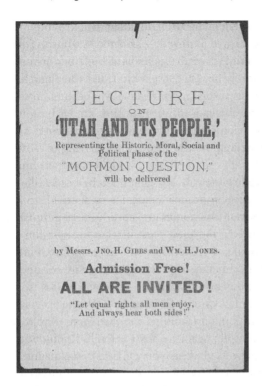

Figure 3.2 Broadside used by Elders John Gibbs and William Jones to advertise their public lectures during their speaking tour of southern cities in early summer 1884. John H. Gibbs Collection. Courtesy of L. Tom Perry Special Collections, Harold B. Lee Library, Brigham Young University, Provo, Utah.

anxieties, as the missionaries' presence gave urban dwellers in Tennessee and Mississippi a unique opportunity to engage in "hot debate" on the topic. Gibbs's letters home revealed that the one issue his audiences constantly wanted to speak about was polygamy. On June 24 he wrote, "the ladies were becoming very attentive while the subject of Polygamy came up"; on July 3 he noted that he needed to study law, because "it all comes up in the Mormon Question. Polygamy especially"; on July 31 he commented that in regards to "Polygamy they do go down on that subject most decidedly"; and in early August he complained that he had "to answer a thousand and one questions on Polygamy from the women."[8] Rather than welcoming Elders Gibbs and Jones as distinguished traveling ministers of the gospel, local newspapers vilified the pair.[9] The missionaries, and the leaders of the church who sent them on the tour, had imagined taming anti-Mormon sentiment by cool, logical reasoning, but they found instead that they had walked straight into the lion's den, facing hostile crowds who attended the lectures not to be persuaded by the elders but to see them eaten alive. When the elders cut their trip short because of depleted funds, Gibbs was not overly disappointed, confiding to his wife that after the unspectacular results of the tour he was "anxious to get back" to his normal field of labor in rural northwest Tennessee.[10]

Part of the reason Gibbs was anxious to return was that the situation in northwest Tennessee had degenerated during his absence. The Mormon elders assigned to the region had encountered fierce antagonism in the months following the church burning in May 1884. While Gibbs was away, he received periodic updates from his fellow missionaries, all reporting heavy opposition. In June, he read a letter from four elders in Humphreys County that complained of dwindling success and a climate of general hostility, including multiple threats demanding that they leave the area. Elder Willis Robison glumly spoke for the group when he wrote, "I neaver [sic] saw the day seem so dark as it does now with us."[11] Gibbs was concerned as a fellow missionary and friend and as the church leader who had ecclesiastical stewardship over the region. He relayed his worries about the situation to his wife: "The Elders under my charge in the N. W. Tenn. Con[ference] are in a bad fix. They have been driven and persecuted very much lately. They have not baptized any since I left." He concluded by trying to reassure her that things would work out, but even his encouragement sounded fatalistically flat: "We cannot tell what lies in the future, so all I can say is let the morrow take care of it self, and we will await the final decision of the future developments."[12] It seemed that even the indefatigable Gibbs, who just a few months earlier had confidently declared that God would prevent his opponents from doing him any harm, felt a heavy black cloud hovering over the work of the Latter-day Saint elders as he returned to Lewis County in early August.[13] Indeed, Gibbs's report to his wife of the gathering persecution in the area, followed by his hollow words of reassurance to her, would be among the last messages she ever received from him.

MASSACRE AND EXPULSION

Elders William Berry and Henry Thompson, both hailing from Utah, had arrived in Cane Creek on August 5. After a few days of normal activities, with no particular hints of hostility from the local residents, the missionaries scheduled to hold Sunday worship services at the home of James Conder on August 10.[14] The night before, they stayed at the home of Thomas Garrett, a non-Mormon who was one of the elders' closest friends and allies in the area. Berry and Thompson were unexpectedly joined by Elders Gibbs and Jones, recently returned from their speaking tour and eager to see if they could reenergize the work in Lewis County. On Sunday morning Elders Gibbs, Berry, and Thompson headed to the Conder home, about a mile away, while Jones lingered behind to finish reading some sermons sent from Salt Lake City. About an hour before services were to begin, Jones started down the road but was soon confronted and seized by a band of masked men armed with pistols and shotguns. They forced the missionary over a fence into a nearby cornfield, where they kicked and punched him with their guns before questioning him about the whereabouts of Gibbs. Upon finishing their interrogation, the mob hurried off, leaving one member (and his double-barreled pistol) to guard Jones, with orders to shoot if the missionary tried to escape.[15]

Jones' captor swore that he would shoot the elder if he tried "anything unfair," but that if he cooperated he would be treated "like a brother." The two men walked over a hill, where the guard confessed that he intended to release Jones, and revealed that "these mobbers intended murder, they were the meanest men in the county, and were old guerillas who had 'killed their dozen men.'" As the two conversed, they heard a gunshot in the distance, then two or three, then up to twenty more rounds. At that point the guard exclaimed, "It's as I told you, they have shot among the women and children. Run! they will come back and take revenge on you." As Jones began to flee, the guard followed until he surmised that the missionary was safely away. When Jones asked why he was so generous with his charge, the man said that "he was pressed into [the gang], and wanted to see that we were not harmed, for he had always been a friend to the Mormons and had never seen anything wrong in them." Jones knew full well that the man's involuntary infiltration of the mob most likely had saved his life.[16]

The shots they heard had indeed come from the Conder house. The elders were singing hymns as people milled about the home, and Gibbs had just picked up his Bible to look up references for a sermon. All of a sudden, the group of approximately a dozen masked men burst from the surrounding woods into the yard and assaulted James Conder, the patriarch of the family and owner of the farm. He shouted to his son Martin Conder and stepson J. R. Hutson, who were in the orchard, to get their guns and protect the elders. The two young men ran to the house, Martin arriving at the back door just as the leader of the mob, David Hinson, barreled through the front door. They both headed for the shotgun resting on deer horns above the fireplace and grabbed it simultaneously, struggling for possession of the weapon. Hinson pulled out a pistol and snapped it at Conder. The gun failed to discharge, but Conder drew back, and Hinson wrestled the shotgun out of his hands. He immediately turned and fired the gun at Gibbs, who was standing nearby. The shot entered Gibbs's body just under the arm, and the missionary slumped to the floor, instantly killed.

At the same moment, one of the masked men pointed a gun at Elder Thompson, but Elder Berry grabbed it with both hands, which allowed Thompson the opportunity to escape through the back door and into the nearby woods. Just as he left the house, he saw two guns being leveled at Berry, who was shot in the waist and fell without a sound. Martin Conder was still tangling with Hinson when one of the gang shot him dead. Hinson ran

to the door to leave, apparently satisfied with the shootings of Gibbs and
Berry. Unexpectedly, Hutson descended from the loft where his gun was
stashed. Two attackers grabbed him, but he twisted free long enough to shoot
Hinson just as he was bolting out the front door. As Hinson dropped in the
doorway, someone shouted, "I'll have revenge," and another shot rang out
and hit Hutson, who died an hour later. Before retreating, a few members of
the mob came to the window and fired into Elder Berry's body again, making
sure he was dead. Some of the buckshot lodged in the hip of Malinda Conder,
the wife of James Conder and the mother of Martin and J. R.; she recovered
after some initial doubt, but for the rest of her life walked with pain and a
serious limp. With that, the mob grabbed the body of their fallen leader
Hinson and retreated, the entire melee finished in a matter of minutes.
When all was accounted for, four Mormons—Elders John Gibbs and William
Berry, and the two half-brothers, Martin Conder and J. R. Hutson—as well as
the leader of the attacking party, David Hinson, lay dead.

For the next several days, frantic rumors flew around the countryside,
and conflicting accounts swirled as to the details of what came to be known
alternately as the Mormon Massacre, the Tennessee Massacre, or the Cane
Creek Massacre. The earliest newspaper stories not only had varying details
but also different names and numbers of those killed and wounded.[17] Church
leaders in Salt Lake City sent excited telegrams to their counterparts in Tennessee trying to gather correct information.[18] Their first priority was to
discover precisely who was alive, dead, or wounded. The most trusted reports
came from the two missionaries, Jones and Thompson, who had managed to
escape the shooting spree. Additional news came shortly thereafter from
Elder Willis Robison, who made a daring scouting mission in and out of the
county, which by that point was heavily patrolled by vigilantes on the look-
out for Mormons.[19]

The Mormons' second priority, once they more or less ascertained what
had occurred, was to retrieve the bodies of the fallen elders so they could be
shipped back to Utah for proper burial, away from their enemies. The task of
recovering Gibbs's and Berry's remains fell upon Brigham (B. H.) Roberts,
the acting president of the mission and future chronicler of the episode (and
the first century of Mormon history more generally). With the help of church
members and other local sympathizers, Roberts fitted two wagon teams and
recruited three other men to accompany him on the dangerous journey to
Cane Creek.[20] Roberts—who was known to some of the anti-Mormons in the
area and would have been a prize catch for the mob—took care to conceal his
true identity, shaving off his beard and mustache, donning an old set of
clothes, and smearing dirt on his face. With the help and armed protection
of Thomas Garrett, the non-Mormon who had housed the missionaries the
night before the massacre, the disguised Roberts and his small company

Figure 3.3 Photograph of Brigham
H. Roberts in "hobo" dress, taken
while en route to recover the
bodies of John Gibbs and William
Berry from Cane Creek, Tennessee,
August 1884. Courtesy of the
Church History Library, The Church
of Jesus Christ of Latter-day Saints,
Salt Lake City, Utah.

traveled to the Conder farm. They placed the bodies of the fallen missionaries in metal caskets, which they drove to Mount Pleasant before sending
them on the railroad back to Salt Lake City. Roberts, who remained incog-
nito, had an overwhelming urge to reveal himself and render some words of
comfort to the brokenhearted people at the scene of the massacre, especially
the "grief stricken father" and "bereaved mother" of the fallen boys. He sadly
concluded, however, that "it was not wisdom to take such a course," as "the
enemy was still on the alert."[21] Martin Conder and J. R. Hutson were promptly
buried in a family graveyard on the corner of the farm, where their graves
were later memorialized with a headstone reading, "Noble Defenders of the
Truth. Greater love hath no man than this, that a man lay down his life for a
friend. St. John 15:13."

Unlike the Joseph Standing case, in which the wheels of justice rolled
slowly before coming to a complete stop, following the Cane Creek killings
there was not even a halfhearted effort to bring the mob to trial. The Mormons, who by 1884 were even more pessimistic than they were five years
earlier about their chances for a fair hearing anywhere in the United States,
immediately presumed that the murders would go unpunished, and probably even uninvestigated. One of the earliest editorials in the *Deseret News*,

appearing even before all the details of the massacre got to Salt Lake City, set the general tone: "'No arrests have been made.' So says the dispatch [from Tennessee]. It is quite likely that none will be made, or at any rate, that the cowardly murderers will escape punishment at the hands of the law."[22] There were some early encouraging signs that the people of Tennessee might demand that authorities bring the guilty parties to trial, as evidenced in a strongly worded editorial in Nashville's *Daily American*, one of the state's leading papers. Three days after the massacre, it argued that "no matter" the prejudices held against Mormons, the county and state authorities could not afford to "ignore the crime of murder. . . . Butchery of this savage character for any cause cannot be tolerated in a civilized country."[23] Such pleading ultimately had no effect, validating the Mormons' cynicism. In the first week after the incident, the *New York Times* reported that "There is no clue to the slayers of the Elders, and as yet the authorities have taken no steps in the matter." Two reasons were given: first, the mobs wore masks, and thus the only clearly identified member of their party was David Hinson, who was killed; and second, especially because of the gravity of what happened, the "rioters" would "keep their own counsel" and take all necessary steps to guard their identities, thus requiring "extraordinary efforts to successfully track them."[24]

Partly in response to continuing criticism from "those who believe that the guilty persons should be ferreted out and punished," Governor William Bate offered a $1,000 reward "for the apprehension and conviction of the parties who murdered the Mormon elders in Lewis county." The gesture seemed more magnanimous than it actually was. Not only did it come nearly two weeks after the incident, but in requiring both the capture and the conviction of the perpetrators, chances were slim that the reward would ever be claimed. Furthermore, Tennessee state authorities would hardly have been enthusiastic to pursue the mob after Governor Bate received a telegram from Eli Murray, territorial governor of Utah and noted enemy of the Latter-day Saints. Murray began by condemning "lawlessness" as "reprehensible," but then suggested that the real criminals in the case were actually the "murdered Mormon agents." These men, Murray claimed, were not so much missionaries as "emigration agents" and "representatives of organized crime" whose actual mission was to induce unwitting Tennesseans into immigrating to Utah; that the converts would then be added to the ranks of the polygamous did not need to be spoken. Considering all of these developments militating against an active pursuit of justice, the *New York Times* concluded, "Whether any attempt will be made to discover the perpetrators of this crime is a question concerning which there is much doubt. The general impression is that there will not be."[25]

Even had the civil authorities made a genuine effort to apprehend the guilty parties, their task would have been extremely onerous, as Lewis and

Hickman counties essentially degenerated into mob law following the massacre. Outsiders were uniformly suspect, and the vigilantes were not afraid to use violence to protect their claimed territory. An unnamed eyewitness who returned to Nashville from Hickman County asserted that "it would be unsafe for any one to go to Lewis county for the purpose of arresting any of them." He testified that they "would have no hesitancy in killing anyone who attempted to obtain the names of any of the band."[26] Even non-Mormons were unsafe, especially if they started asking questions. An Evansville, Indiana, detective was lured to the area by the governor's offer of reward money, but patrolling vigilantes apprehended and very nearly lynched him. They only released the frightened detective on the condition that he would immediately leave the state and stop his investigation.[27] Short of utilizing overwhelming force and perhaps imposing martial law to counter the vigilantes' strength, outside authorities would have found it extremely difficult to identify, arrest, and prosecute the murderers.

The massacre, and the ensuing paralysis of effective law enforcement, only encouraged and emboldened the vigilantes. In early September, a month after the killings, the *Deseret News* reported that "the murderous mobocrats in Lewis County are becoming bold in their immunity from punishment for their crimes. They are ordering members of our Church to leave the neighborhood."[28] Written notices, ornamented with the drawing of a coffin, appeared throughout the county warning all Mormons to flee: "Mormons, leave! Members of the Latter Day Saints are notified to leave this county, and 30 days are given for you all to go. An indignant and outraged people have said it, and go you shall. If any are found in this county after 30 days, you will go like the others. Go peaceably if you will, but you must."[29] Similar warnings were posted in Maury, Hickman, and Wilson counties, and local residents watched nervously as the deadline approached, fearing another outbreak of violence. Lest anyone think the notices were empty threats, "masked men, armed with revolvers and wearing robes decorated with a red cross, skull and cross-bones were seen riding near the Mormon settlement" in Wilson County.[30] It became evident that the same vigilantes were mounting a concerted anti-Mormon campaign throughout the region, suggested by a similar white banner with a red cross in a circle placed near the site of the massacre at Cane Creek. The masked men reportedly constituted an "organization formed to preserve order and protect citizens from evil-doers," thus framing their opposition to Mormonism within the classic conservative social control rhetoric of American vigilantism.[31]

Naturally, Latter-day Saints in the area were greatly alarmed. Although some were determined to stay the course, most decided not to test the mob's determination and quickly made arrangements to vacate their homes and farms. As the end of September approached, newspapers reported that in the wake of a second notice warning all Mormons to leave by October 1, many were closing their businesses, selling their farms—usually far below their actual value—and otherwise preparing to relocate; some had even allegedly "renounced their faith in order to save themselves trouble."[32] The vigilantes not only drove out local Mormons (including the surviving Conders), but also Mormon sympathizers and other "people who had been friendly" to the missionaries, such as Thomas Garrett. Far from being a haphazard undertaking, the expulsion was a coordinated, systematic effort, a minor pogrom. Expelled families could apply for a "safe conduct patrol pass," which they would show to any vigilantes they might encounter on the road, proving that they were indeed making their way out of the area. Some twenty to twenty-five people left Lewis County alone, representing the greater part of the Mormon population there.[33] The entire scene, with bedraggled Latter-day Saint families uprooted, piling their possessions in wagons and leaving their homes for an unknown future, was reminiscent of the Mormons' earlier troubles in Missouri and Illinois. The pattern was depressingly familiar: the arrival of Mormons followed by a gradual rise in community conflict, culminating in extralegal violence, and finally concluding with forced expulsion.

JUSTIFYING VIOLENCE

In the weeks and months that followed the Cane Creek episode, Mormons and non-Mormons alike spilled a good deal of ink explaining and, ultimately, assigning blame for the murders. The non-Mormon refrain was familiar—so familiar, in fact, that the newspapers were able to explain *why* the massacre occurred even before they knew the details about *what* had occurred. The earliest reports talk about the "very bitter feeling" that had been growing against the Latter-day Saints. This hostility had steadily intensified because the missionaries had "succeeded in inducing several persons to embrace their doctrines," which led to the separation of families, most notoriously the breakup of husbands and wives and the emigration of young women to the West.[34] Increasingly upset about the presence of the elders, community members reportedly warned them several times to "quit the neighborhood," then considered more serious methods of persuasion when the missionaries refused to go.[35] The triple combination of the Mormon elders' success, stubbornness, and alleged licentiousness incited the citizens of rural northwest Tennessee to rise up in defense of their homes and honor.[36]

The first two charges—of the elders' proselytizing success and their stubborn refusal to leave the area when asked (or told)—were unquestionably true. The missionaries, and most notably John Gibbs, had indeed enjoyed considerable success in the area, especially in Lewis and Hickman counties, which had sparked quite a sensation among the local population. According to Gibbs's record, there were forty-four baptisms in northwestern Tennessee from September 1883 through May 1884, with all but eight occurring from February through May. Growth in the region was substantial enough that in April 1884 the church's West Tennessee Conference was divided in two, with the northwestern division consisting of seven branches and seventy members.[37] William Jones, the missionary who had been released by his captor on the day of the massacre, later testified that the success enjoyed by the elders was "one of the chief causes of the bitter enmity against us." Specifically, he cited the baptism of "an intelligent young lady" (otherwise unidentified) in the late spring of 1884. Some two hundred people gathered on the day of the baptism "to see if it could really be true that she was about to espouse so despised a cause as 'Mormonism.'"[38] Gibbs was particularly effective in persuading Tennesseans to accept the faith, personally baptizing twenty-six people in the Cane Creek area in April and May 1884 (see Figure 3.4).[39] By August 1884, the majority of members of the Cane Creek branch had come into the church under Elder Gibbs's auspices, including four members of the Conder family.[40] Had Gibbs, who seemed to be the catalyst of the explosive growth in Lewis and Hickman counties, remained for the summer rather than going on his lecture tour, Mormonism may have enjoyed even more remarkable growth in the area.

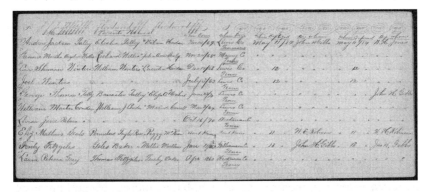

Figure 3.4 Page from John Gibbs's ledger book recording baptisms in the area of Cane Creek, Tennessee, May 1884. Gibbs's success in baptizing converts to the LDS Church was a significant factor precipitating hostility against Mormons in the area. Among those whose names are recorded here is William Martin Conder, who was killed along with Gibbs during the attack on the Conder farm in August 1884. "Account of Baptisms Etc. in the North West Tennessee Conference and scattered branches South – Recorded by Elder John H. Gibbs," John H. Gibbs Collection. Courtesy of L. Tom Perry Special Collections, Harold B. Lee Library, Brigham Young University, Provo, Utah.

However, while the church's rapid progress delighted the missionaries and converts, it engendered considerable resentment among the segment of the population who felt threatened by the local expansion of Mormonism. As Gibbs's ministry in the region enjoyed increased success, the incidence of threats and minor violence against the Mormons began to rise dramatically. In January 1884, Gibbs received a written threat that was unsigned, but apparently came from a man named F. T. Smith, who had publicly boasted that "he could shoot down a Mormon Elder as quick as he would a squirrel." The barely decipherable note threatened that if Gibbs did not leave, he could expect to be either hung or shot and then left to the buzzards, as it was the author's "intention to kill." Then in early May there was the warning from the Shiloh band, left with the ashes of the burned log meetinghouse. Shortly thereafter Gibbs received another notice from the postmaster of McEwen announcing that there was a mob already assembled and prepared to drive all the Mormons out of Hickman, Dickson, Humphreys, and Perry counties by the first of June. If any missionaries remained after the appointed date, they would be tarred and feathered and then killed. Other elders in the region received similar notices and reported that missionaries in other states were experiencing much of the same. Gibbs confided in his journal, "I have never seen a hotter time since I have been out. We have been threatened on every hand. . . . The Devil . . . is doing his utmost."[41]

LDS church leadership recognized the rising level of violence (both actual and threatened) against missionaries in the South, and encouraged the elders to exercise great caution. In a letter circulated to all conference presidents and traveling elders in the Southern States Mission, John Morgan and B. H. Roberts warned that "it may be that the ignorant and ungodly will take license to commit acts of violence against you; we therefore caution you in regard to this matter as we do not wish the Elders to expose themselves to danger if it [may] possibly be avoided." If a spirit of violence arose in any of the districts they labored in, missionaries were "to leave those localities and not expose your persons to their wrath."[42]

Even with official permission to move on whenever antagonism arose, most elders stayed the course, giving little or no heed to menacing threats. The prevailing attitude among many missionaries was reflected by Gibbs, who frequently expressed his confidence that all the anti-Mormon persecution would eventually come to naught, and that he and his fellow laborers would be shielded by God in the meantime.[43] After his death the *Nashville Banner* said of Gibbs, in a eulogy he certainly would have appreciated, "the more he was threatened the harder he would work."[44] Not all missionaries were as zealously committed as Gibbs, and in a few cases some returned home, unable or unwilling to handle the stress of the increasing hostility manifested toward them.[45] For the most part, however, intimidation tactics did not work against the missionaries, whose enthusiasm and sense of divine protection typically overrode concern for personal safety. The obstinate refusal of Gibbs and many of his fellow missionaries to pay attention to intimidation only served to further frustrate and infuriate their opponents, which consequently drove them to apply increasingly extreme measures.

As important as the missionaries' success and stubbornness were in sparking violence, they were not in themselves sufficient or primary causes. What separated Mormon elders from the itinerant preachers of other faiths commonly found throughout the South were the rumors and accusations of their debauchery, all stemming from the Mormon doctrine and practice of plural marriage. The missionaries' alleged corruptions were well documented by contemporary sources, which charged the elders with a litany of abuses. Any one of them may well have sparked a community's outrage, but when added together the cumulative effect of the missionaries' presumed offenses made them appear truly profligate. A group of Mormon elders conveniently summarized the most prevalent—and serious—charges in a petition sent to Governor Bate ten days after the massacre. Their statement recapped some of the prevailing myths used to justify anti-Mormon violence: that missionaries baptized women in the nude; that they had a "special mission" to break up families; that they sought to establish polygamy in the South; that female converts were "initiated by degrees into prostitution"; and that the elders were "commonly licentious and corrupt." The petition dealt with each of the accusations in turn, categorically denying that Mormons ever practiced nude baptisms or prostitution, or that families were broken up as a result of the elders' teaching. While plural marriage was defended as a true religious principle and an appropriate practice in Utah, the petitioners swore that no effort was being made to introduce polygamy into any of the southern states, including Tennessee.[46] In personal interviews, acting mission president B. H. Roberts consistently maintained the same positions, adamantly defending the upright conduct of the elders in the mission and dismissing all accusations of Mormon immorality as scurrilous rumors.[47]

The Mormons' attempts to defuse allegations of their wickedness had almost no effect. Not only the press but also the other churches were happy to fan the flames of anti-Mormon sentiment. For example, in a lecture delivered just two weeks after the massacre to an overflow crowd at Edgefield Baptist Church in Nashville, Reverend William H. Strickland, who the following year was made an officer in the Tennessee Baptist Convention, endorsed the accusations brought about by "law abiding citizens" against "these Mormon missionaries, so called." Specifically, he charged "that under the guise of religion, they were attempting to seduce their wives and daughters from the paths of virtue." Strickland asserted that monogamous Christian marriage was the "corner stone of our republic" upon which the nation's greatness was founded. "If our homes are to be polluted, if the marriage altar loses its sanctity," he warned, "then our great republic will totter and fall. . . . Let Mormonism prevail and we sap the very foundation of society and wipe out the Christian home." The feared expansion of polygamy, whether in Utah or in Tennessee, was therefore not only a moral tragedy, but it also had dire social and political consequences. The Mormon missionaries, or "emissaries of their rotten Gomorrah at Salt Lake City," were guilty of "perpetrating the greatest crime known to humanity"—not murder, but seducing the wives and daughters of the South "into shame and everlasting disgrace." Accordingly, the dishonored "fathers, husbands, [and] brothers" of Lewis County had demanded that the missionaries leave the country, and when they did not, more drastic measures were taken.

At this point Reverend Strickland paused to consider whether the men of Lewis County were justified in killing the Mormon elders in order to defend their "peaceable, virtuous homes." His initial thought was that they were not, and that men taking the law into their own hands led to anarchy and subverted the law. But, he reasoned, "justice moves so slowly," and "the delays of the law are so many." Furthermore, a jury conviction was often difficult to achieve, meaning that "so many bad men escape justice that at times men become so outraged that they rise up in their righteous indignation and execute justice for themselves." In the case of some extreme crimes—and he had already argued that the missionaries were guilty of the worst possible offense—"a strong rope or the deadly bullet relieves the tedious, uncertain processes of criminal courts."[48]

In the space of a few sentences, Reverend Strickland perfectly captured the fundamental tension behind the American vigilante impulse, which remained strong in the postbellum South even as it died out in other regions of the country. The whole point of organized government and duly appointed law enforcement officials was to administer justice, absolving ordinary citizens of both the right and duty of doing so. But in settings where law enforcement was weak or ineffectual—or "tedious" and "uncertain"—many nineteenth-century citizens, acting under the time-honored notion of popular sovereignty, believed they retained the wisdom to determine guilt and the power to mete out punishments when regularly constituted authorities would or could not. In the cases of Parley Pratt, Joseph Standing, and the victims at Cane Creek, the threat posed by the Mormons was considered to be so dangerous to community morals that vigilant citizens were virtually forced to act; to do nothing would essentially make them complicit in the crime.

Extralegal violence could only be legitimated if its victims posed a serious enough threat to the morals or members of the community. Rumors of Mormon depravity were thus essential not only before the incidence of violence in order to spark public outrage, but they also served as an ex post facto validation of mob action. John Gibbs was a special target of the post-massacre rumor mill in Tennessee, and was made out to be among the worst class of sexual predators. The *Nashville Daily American* reported that he told a young female convert "that as a prerequisite to baptism God had revealed it to him to sleep with her, which he did." He allegedly attempted to seduce another young woman, who barely escaped from his clutches as he tore the clothing from her body, then was caught in yet another compromising situation with a young female convert, this time on the public roadside "with one arm around her waist and the other in her bosom."[49] Speculations such as these led one newspaper to conclude, "It is the business of the proselyting Mormons to break up families and destroy womanly purity, and they propose no church in Tennessee, but proselyte that they may swell the number of law breaking bigamists in Utah. . . . The Mormon is a libertine and his profession is bigamy."[50] The Christian society of the South could not tolerate such an open and unabashed peril within its midst.

When reporters traveled to the area twenty-five years after the massacre, they discovered that local people still held strong prejudices against the Mormons and defended the violence against them as legitimate. Rumors persisted that the missionaries had come to the area teaching male converts "that it was alright to have a dozen or so wives and many other things too repulsive to mention," and telling female converts, "Sister, you are now as much my wife as your husband's." While men were ritually given the gift of the Holy Ghost on the banks of the creek after their baptism, missionaries supposedly took female converts to a private house for another variety of "laying on of hands." Under the bedeviling influence of the Mormon elders, local girls were "ensnared and captivated, dethroned of all reason, excited and entranced and lured off" by agents of a religion that taught them "to commit fornication and where adultery is no longer a sin." Justifying the actions of their forebears, local residents a generation later asserted that responsible citizens had no choice but to fight in self-defense against the missionaries "with a determination to put an end to the corruption that was then becoming so notorious among certain families in the neighborhood."[51]

What is somewhat surprising, especially given the hysteria over Mormon depravity, is that the public did not discover the one verifiable instance of sexual impropriety by a Mormon elder in the South. The fact that it was not widely publicized suggests that LDS Church authorities, other missionaries, and those involved effectively kept the incident quiet. The details are somewhat sketchy, and appear only in John Gibbs's private correspondence to his wife and another missionary, although he suggests that it had become common knowledge among the other elders in the mission. According to Gibbs, a missionary in Kentucky first attempted then later succeeded in raping a young female member of the church, probably sometime in late December 1883 or early January 1884.[52] In another letter, Gibbs suggested that the missionary's terrible misdeed might not have come as a total surprise, saying that "I know his weakness, and also know what and how many temptations are strewn in the path of an Elder of Israel." As much as anything, Gibbs felt the incident would be a significant hindrance to the reputation of the remaining elders in the mission: "We allways [sic] have told the people that we could testify to what President Morgan wrote to the Nashville paper some time ago, that there never was an Elder ever caught in lewdness or with bad women in the Southern States. But now we have to rein up on that point, which makes an Elder mourn for it was a fine subject to talk upon."[53] In a somber letter to a fellow missionary, Gibbs briefly addressed the scandal, mentioning that he had received word that the perpetrator's wife back in Utah was leaving him.[54] Even though the matter seems not to have become public knowledge, it was a sobering and painful experience for Gibbs to deal with, and a black mark on the reputation and performance of the Mormon elders in the South. By all indications, the rape was an exception to the decency typical of Mormon elders' comportment in the South. Nevertheless, given the scrutiny with which southerners subjected the Mormon missionary effort, it is remarkable that the episode was never discovered and used as damning evidence that the elders were in fact the "low-down lot of scoundrels and blacklegs" they were accused of being.[55]

MORMON EXPLANATIONS

Although Mormons typically ignored the fantastic rumors that swirled about them, the violence in Tennessee prompted them to publicly defend themselves from false charges and to explain what they believed to be the causes of the massacre. Four days after the massacre, B. H. Roberts responded to the barrage of accusations about Mormon polygamy. Although he unashamedly acknowledged that plural marriage was a true doctrine of the church and an accepted practice in Utah, he was unequivocal in asserting that the missionaries in the South "had never taught any one to practice polygamy nor to violate in any way the laws of the land."[56] Roberts was less clear on whether or not the missionaries were themselves polygamists; as one newspaper reporter related after an interview with him, "he was not aware that any of the elders engaged in proselyting in the South had more than one wife, though he might have for all he knew."[57]

Roberts's statements were true for the most part, though it seems unlikely that he would not have known that William Berry, one of the victims of the Tennessee shootings, was a polygamist, with two wives and thirteen children at home in Utah.[58] Being constantly on the defensive about plural marriage made most missionaries increasingly convinced of the principle.

They sometimes expressed intentions to take plural wives upon returning home, but most were either single or monogamous at the time of their missionary service.[59] Missionary journals and correspondence do contain numerous accounts of the elders talking with southerners about plural marriage and vigorously defending both the principle and practice, but in almost every case the topic was brought up by hostile locals. For most elders in most circumstances, caution was the watchword. The 1884 circular letter from mission presidents Morgan and Roberts to all the elders in the South clearly suggested, without specifically mentioning polygamy by name, that the subject should be handled delicately, if at all. They admonished the elders to "preach the First Principles of the Gospel . . . leaving the more advanced doctrines to be taught after the First Principles are thoroughly understood."[60] Had southerners been privy to this statement, they surely would have interpreted it as part of a cunning stratagem used by the missionaries to deceive their listeners before revealing their true designs.

Mormon elders were correct in asserting that their southern converts did not, in fact, practice polygamy—either in the South or even when they migrated to the West. LDS converts from the South were generally encouraged to gather not to Utah but rather to the San Luis Valley in south-central Colorado. One rationale for this directive was that southern converts were typically poor, and they could acquire government land in the San Luis Valley at much lower prices than they could purchase a home in rapidly developing Utah. Church leaders also asserted that in Colorado southern converts would be living among like-minded people, rather than alongside the Yankees and northern Europeans that settled the Mormon heartland. Finally, plural marriage was not practiced in the Mormon settlements in Colorado, so there would be no pressure or expectation for the converts, many of whom were not necessarily enthusiastic about polygamy, to adopt the institution. Just how significant a factor this was in the church's original decision to steer southerners away from Utah is unclear, but after the fact it allowed the church to argue that the Colorado solution "effectually disposes of the charge that the object of our missionary work there [in the South] is to 'obtain supplies for harems.'"[61] While never backpedaling on their stance that plural marriage was a spiritual truth that they had every right to implement, for the sake of public relations Mormons were quite willing to advertise that it was not practiced universally within the church, and that it was not forced on southern converts even following their removal to the West.

Like their arguments about polygamy, the Latter-day Saints' explanations for the massacre were more effective at convincing themselves of the rightness of their cause than persuading others to agree. In the days and weeks following the tragedy at Cane Creek, the Mormon press was hot with indignation. The Latter-day Saints, both on the scene in Tennessee and back in Salt Lake, placed blame on the hostile religious establishment and the anti-Mormon faction in Utah, just as they had following Joseph Standing's murder four years earlier. Three days after the massacre the *Deseret News* issued a piercing judgment against the "orthodox preachers and writers for a licentious press in this city," who had "stirred up the basest passions of lawless men" and thus "inflamed the blood of the mobocrats by their murderous suggestions."[62] Multiple articles and editorials followed, all with the same basic message: that guilt for the murders of Gibbs, Berry, Conder, and Hutson laid not only with the mob, but also with the evangelical Protestant ministers in both Salt Lake and Tennessee and with the anti-Mormon press in Utah. Indeed, the mob was portrayed as the inevitable result of the machinations of the churches and the press, the unthinking puppet manipulated by a much larger and more diabolical master. While Mormons were not afraid to level blame at the highest levels—they considered "Cabinet officers, Members of Congress, Governors, Judges and other State, Territorial and county officers" accessories to the crime, through negligence if not open hostility—it was the "preachers and editors" who were the targets of the Saints' fiercest ire.[63]

Mormon anger about the massacre and its causes climaxed in an address delivered by John Nicholson in Salt Lake City on September 22, 1884. Nicholson was an associate editor of the *Deseret News* and a favorite among the Latter-day Saints in Utah for his writing and public speaking abilities, particularly in his diatribes outlining government abuses against the Mormons. His lecture, later sold in booklet form and titled *The Tennessee Massacre & Its Causes; or, The Utah Conspiracy*, drew what was described as "probably the most densely packed audience ever within the walls of the Salt Lake Theatre." Nicholson argued that the Tennessee massacre was only the latest and most violent manifestation of a conspiracy against the political and religious freedom of the Mormons. Although it had tentacles reaching into the national press and the federal government, the nerve center of the conspiracy was in Salt Lake City, among a "small minority" who sought to "seize the reins of government, and despoil, and crush, and injure an innocent community." Nicholson asserted that the persecution the Saints were facing in the early 1880s was far more sinister than general prejudice; rather, they were fighting against a "systematic, determined" conspiracy comprised of both political and religious elements. He located the roots of this plot in a May 1882 gathering in Salt Lake City, specifically convened "for the purpose of working up a prejudice against the 'Mormon' community." The attendees and agenda, according to Nicholson, represented a clear "amalgamation of church and state"—a combination, he slyly noted, that was "very objectionable to them, except, of course, when they engage in it themselves." Some of the most prominent non-Mormon politicians and preachers in the territory, including Governor Eli Murray, attended this meeting. The Methodists took particular pride in leading the proceedings, as they "had always occupied the front rank in opposing 'Mormonism,'" including lobbying Congress for more stringent antipolygamy legislation.[64] Nicholson identified this group of political and religious leaders, still very much active in 1884, as the heart and soul of the vast anti-Mormon crusade.

Although "conspiracy" is a loaded term, it is true that the national anti-Mormon movement fed upon the reports they received from their faction in Utah, and the people Nicholson mentioned would hardly have been embarrassed to be identified with organized anti-Mormonism. But Nicholson was not satisfied with generalities, arguing more specifically, and damningly, that the "Utah conspiracy" had a direct association to the Tennessee killings. In the case of Joseph Standing, it was almost impossible to make a strong link between the murder and the national anti-Mormon movement. In connection with Cane Creek, however, Nicholson claimed to have found the smoking gun. On March 15, 1884, the non-Mormon *Salt Lake Tribune*—"the organ of the conspirators"—published what it called "A Red Hot Address." It purported to be a stenographical report of a sermon delivered the previous Sunday by a "Bishop West" in remote Juab, Utah. The address advocated an all-out war against the "Gentiles," who were "eyesores in the sight of the Lord." Bishop West explicitly called for the assassination of Governor Murray, whom he dubbed the "high priest of the devil" and "the Cain of our generation."[65]

The *Tribune*'s explosive "Red Hot Address," it turns out, was a forgery. There was in fact no "Bishop West" in the entire church in 1884. Furthermore, there was not even a church meeting held in Juab on the date on which the address was said to have been delivered, as a washout that day had occupied the labor of all available local church members.[66] Nevertheless, that it was entirely fabricated did not prevent the "Red Hot Address" from being reprinted and circulated around the nation. What made this particular piece of anti-Mormon literature distinctive was that it surfaced in Lewis County, Tennessee, where a Baptist preacher named Vandever apparently used it to stir up hostility against John Gibbs and the other Mormon elders laboring in the region.[67] Elder William Jones said the address was "thrust at me wherever I went," and that "quite a feeling of enmity was created owing to the false newspaper stories so industriously circulated."[68] In another letter Jones made particular mention of Vandever, who "worked up prejudice against us in that section by giving it [the 'Red Hot Address'] wide publicity, and by his pretended credence to the falsehood, causing great excitement." Although Elders Jones and Gibbs reportedly sent Vandever a refutation of the address, their protests had no effect.[69] Vandever's circumstantial connection to the massacre is augmented by intriguing, though unsubstantiated, evidence suggesting he may have worked with David Hinson—the leader of the mob at

Cane Creek and according to Mormon accounts a local Methodist preacher who lived only a few miles from the Conder farm—in stirring up anti-Mormon sentiment in the area.[70]

Although none of this evidence is corroborated by non-Mormon sources, pieced together it suggests a possible explanation for the local anti-Mormon fervor preceding the massacre. Vandever and Hinson may have been part of, and possibly led, an interdenominational alliance against Mormon intrusion in Lewis County. Local resistance to LDS proselytizing was fanned by, and included the distribution of, anti-Mormon literature that emanated from Salt Lake City. Latter-day Saint missionaries and Protestant ministers in Lewis County apparently knew each other personally, and even chance meetings were marked by tension and hostility. Furthermore, Hinson must have been well aware of Mormon activity at the Conder farm, since in rural Lewis County he would have been considered a not-too-distant neighbor. It is even conceivable that Vandever knew of or perhaps participated in the mob that attacked the Conder farm in August 1884. These tentative relationships between the national and local anti-Mormon movements and between local Mormons and non-Mormons help sketch out some of the interactions that may have led up to the Cane Creek massacre and suggest ways that anti-Mormonism was transformed on the ground from rumors and abstract rhetoric to vigilante violence.

AFTERMATH

While non-Mormons blamed Mormon debauchery and Mormons blamed the anti-Mormon conspiracy for the massacre, another significant difference in the two sides' respective reactions to the tragedy was a debate over the original intentions of the mob. Before releasing him, Elder Jones's guard had clearly intimated that the objective of the mob was the death of at least John Gibbs, specifically stating (at least in Jones's recollection of the episode) that "these mobbers intended murder."[71] However, this later became hotly disputed, with positions taken along predictably partisan lines. B. H. Roberts summed up the Mormons' argument that the mob was planning murder from the beginning: "It seems strange that anyone should say the mob did not intend to commit murder, going in disguise as they did, armed with shot guns. Every indication is that they meant the mischief they performed."[72] Although the *Deseret News* conceded that there was no evidence that the mob designed to kill the Conder boys, Mormons were convinced that the missionaries' deaths were no accident.[73] On the other side, non-Mormons claimed that the mob simply aimed to drive the Mormons from the area and that the situation spiraled out of control. The *New York Times* reported that the mob was "bent on chastising the Elders and forcing them to leave the county," a position reinforced by Nashville's *Daily American.*[74] Other Tennessee papers did credit the mob with wanting to inflict some violence on the elders, but only in the limited sense of a whipping or "thrashing," before sending them out of the county.[75] A moot point after the fact, this dispute over original intent had important ramifications for each side's larger claims about anti-Mormon vigilantism. Whereas Mormons wished to construct the massacre, and by extension all anti-Mormon violence, as premeditated murderous bigotry, non-Mormon southerners wanted to construe the incident as a justifiable case of community defense gone awry.

This debate over the attackers' intentions may have assumed greater significance if the alleged perpetrators had ever been brought to trial. However, given the strong-arm tactics of the vigilantes after the massacre and the intense anti-Mormon sentiments in the area, it was doubtful that anyone would be arrested and tried.[76] A grand jury finally assembled, more than two months after the killings, in the circuit court in neighboring Hickman County. Judge Thomas P. Bateman gave a strong charge to the jury, reminding them that both the federal and state constitutions guaranteed freedom of worship, "whether the worshiper be a Christian, a Jew, a Mohammedan, a Mormon, a Buddhist, or any other sect." Bateman also spoke boldly against mob violence, but admitted that the court's proceedings were largely "futile" since "a part of the clergy, a portion of the press and a large number of the people" supported vigilantism, particularly in this case, and most likely would not support legal proceedings.[77] The judge's assessment proved correct—no arrests were made, and no trial was ever held for the murders of Gibbs, Berry, Conder, and Hutson. The Mormons, now jaded by the repeated failure of justice on their behalf, were unfazed.

Violent persecution was not southerners' only weapon to suppress polygamy in particular and the spread of Mormonism in general. Increasingly in the 1880s, they followed the example of the federal government by turning to legislative and legal proceedings to root out Mormonism when all other tactics—from polemics to murder—could not. Tennesseans such as Reverend William Strickland complained in the aftermath of Cane Creek that "for fifty years this ulcer has sent forth its foul odors to defile the atmosphere of our Christian homes," and it was time that the government acted to "administer heroic treatment and amputate it."[78] Statements like this represented a surging tide of anti-Mormon sentiment within the state. In response, legislators rushed to catch up to their increasingly boisterous constituents and do their part in the campaign against polygamy. In the 1885 session of the Tennessee General Assembly, a bill "To define and suppress the teaching of polygamy" went virtually unchallenged, passing 25–2 in the state senate, and 69–2 in the House. The law made it illegal for anyone to "teach others the doctrine or principles of polygamy" in the state, or to "induce" others to "embrace or adopt polygamy" in any way. Furthermore, the statute proscribed encouraging anyone to "emigrate to another State or territory of the United States for the purpose of embracing, adopting or practicing" polygamy. Violators could face up to two years of hard labor in the state prison and a $500 fine.[79] An even stricter bill was introduced two years later, which would have increased the punishment to up to eight years' hard labor and also made it illegal to bring any printed literature into the state that advocated "the doctrine of polygamous marriages." Although this bill quickly passed its first and second reading and was referred to the Judiciary Committee, it never came to the floor for a final vote, perhaps because it seemingly violated the First Amendment freedom of the press.[80] Neither bill mentioned Mormons by name, but there was no question whom the legislation targeted. Tennesseans thus delivered Latter-day Saints, and especially missionaries, a strong message, at gunpoint and in the halls of the state legislature, that they were not welcome in the state.

When two Mormon elders were arrested and jailed under the provisions of the 1885 Tennessee law, the prosecuting attorney in the case was John Simmerly, the sponsor of the harsher 1887 bill. John Morgan suggested that Simmerly harbored personal resentment toward the missionaries "on the grounds that his Father was about to become a convert to Mormonism." The elders languished in a county jail for six days before being released on bail. In their trial, the judge argued that the state antipolygamy law was "unconstitutional in part," and the remainder was "of doubtful propriety" because of its limits on free speech. Charges were dropped against one elder, and while the second missionary was found guilty, due to a clerical error he was liable only for paying a $5 fine, rather than the $500 stipulated by the law.[81]

After Latter-day Saints officially abandoned the practice of plural marriage in 1890, Tennessee's antipolygamy legislation quickly faded to obscurity before being repealed a century later. However, the passing generations in Lewis County did not quickly forget their contribution to the anti-Mormon crusade of the 1880s. In 1931, a Nashville newspaper sent a reporter to the county to discover how residents nearly fifty years later felt about the incident at Cane Creek. The reporter discovered that local citizens still retained "deep bitterness" toward Mormons for leaving the "scars of their faith" on the community, and that "old men and women" still "told and retold the story" of the massacre. As they did, the younger generation would "listen with bated breath to the tale of the death blow which their ancestors dealt to polygamy on Cane Creek."[82] As the following chapters will show, the mob in Cane Creek was not alone in their efforts to deal polygamy a "death blow."

4

This Congregation of Sensualists

Polygamy in the Southern Mind

In 1889, a report emerged about a secret organization of young men in northeast Alabama being "rapidly though cautiously formed to fight Mormonism" in the South. The group, called "The Friends of Right," was so secretive—or perhaps so small—that "in several towns not a soul outside its membership is aware that there is such an organization." Whenever LDS missionaries would begin proselytizing in an area, the Friends of Right would flood the community with information about the "poisonous nature" of Mormonism, "physically, morally, and socially." They would resort to overt violence only "in case of great need," but if a Mormon missionary would not willingly leave a town after being warned, he would be "assisted to depart."

The group purportedly originated in a series of events that began two years earlier, when an unnamed Mormon elder began preaching in the region and converted Myra Hutton, a farmer's daughter described as being "rather pretty, unusually intelligent, and a great favorite." When she first met the missionary, she was engaged to a local man named Huston. Upon converting to Mormonism, however, she emigrated to Utah at the behest of the missionary, leaving behind her family and her betrothed. As if taken from the pages of a Shakespearean tragedy, the girl soon grew "disgusted" with Mormonism in Utah and fled back to her native Alabama, only to discover that her former fiancé had committed suicide upon hearing reports that his beloved had married a Mormon, assumedly in a polygamous union. This tragic revelation in turn drove her to insanity. Out of a sense of duty and revenge, the brothers of the star-crossed lovers joined together to fight the further invasion of Mormonism in Dixie, and out of their determination sprang the Friends of Right.[1]

Corroborating evidence for the alleged Friends of Right is scarce. Whether the covert group actually existed, or whether the story was simply a fallacious tale concocted to sell newspapers, it highlights some of the prevailing myths and fears that dominated southerners' thinking about Mormonism and suggests how deeply determined they were to expel Mormon elders from their midst. Southerners widely regarded Latter-day Saint missionaries as transient outsiders who imported heterodox religious beliefs and disrupted family ties and communities. Most seriously, however, southerners saw missionaries as recruiting agents for the LDS Church's most infamous practice—polygamy—and thus perceived them as sexual predators who seduced young women and lured them away to their polygamous harems in the West. Although of a different type than the "black beast rapist" who supposedly forced himself on unwilling white women, the image of the Mormon seducer tapped into many of the same fears that captivated southern white men in the late nineteenth century and provided the rationale for hundreds of lynchings. The violence that targeted Mormon elders in the South was therefore not only a socially conservative defense of community from the intrusion of outsiders but also a reflection of late nineteenth-century cultural ideals in which the protection of innocent and helpless white women represented a defining point of southern manhood.

The "Mormon Question"—which, as the *St. Louis Christian Advocate* noted, was "one and the same thing" with the polygamy question[2]—thus confronted late nineteenth-century white southerners with the dilemma of how to defend themselves, their homes, and their wives and daughters from the intrusion of lust-driven Mormon missionaries and their depraved system of plural marriage. The threat of Mormon polygamy was felt throughout the United States, and politicians, preachers, and newspaper editors regularly discussed how to effectively stamp out the practice. Southerners paid close attention to statements by Presidents Hayes, Arthur, and Garfield on the subject, and their approval of the chief executives' strong stance against polygamy increased their bonds of sympathy to a federal government that they had vilified during the Reconstruction era. Southern ministers from all denominations preached and wrote frequently on the Mormon menace, and used their significant influence to direct public policy without transgressing, in their own formulations, the delicate separation of church and state. Methodists, Baptists, and Presbyterians came together in interdenominational efforts to solve the Mormon problem, with the churches claiming their prerogative as guardians of moral virtue to assert a vigorous public role in denouncing and abolishing "the great sin of polygamy."[3]

This chapter begins by sketching out the broad contours of the late nineteenth-century antipolygamy movement on a national level, focusing particularly on the actions of the federal government. It then outlines southerners' attitudes toward Mormon plural marriage, first in general terms and then more specifically through the lens of southern Protestantism, exploring why polygamy constituted such a threat to southerners' conception of the good society. The following chapter then discusses the various concrete approaches southerners took in seeking to eliminate polygamy. Antipolygamy helped many southerners find common cause with northern reformers, religious leaders, and politicians. It represented one of the early developments in the broader narrative of national reunion, and advanced the South's limited embrace of the expansion of federal authority in the postbellum period.

FEDERAL ANTIPOLYGAMY

Anti-Mormonism had been a feature of federal policy dating back to at least the late 1850s, when President James Buchanan sent the federal army to quell a supposed Mormon rebellion in Utah Territory, and the Republican Party platform listed polygamy alongside slavery as the "twin relics of barbarism" targeted for eradication. The Civil War intervened, and the Lincoln administration took only a token stance on the issue, passing the unfunded and ineffectual Morrill Anti-Bigamy Act of 1862. The Poland Act of 1874 sought to enhance enforcement of the Morrill legislation by limiting LDS power over courts in Utah. The rate and success of bigamy prosecutions rose, but increased enforcement also heightened resistance from the Mormons, who asserted their constitutional right to practice their religion freely. The Supreme Court denied that claim when it ruled against the LDS Church in *Reynolds v. U.S.* (1879), establishing the principle that the First Amendment guarantee of freedom of belief did not protect religious practices that directly countered federal law.[4]

The anti-Mormon movement not only took new initiative with the *Reynolds* decision but assumed a decidedly bipartisan and national character in the late 1870s. Indeed, the end of Reconstruction in the South in 1877 meant the federal government could afford to turn its gaze—and direct its increased regulatory powers—toward problems in the West, including Indians and Mormons. The executive branch of the federal government played a prominent role in the fight against polygamy throughout the late 1870s and 1880s, beginning with the administration of Rutherford Hayes. The Republican president did all he could to lead the charge—partly out of personal conviction, partly because of the political popularity of the cause, and partly due to his wife, Lucy, who was the chairwoman of a Protestant missionary organization dedicated in part to eradicating polygamy. Hayes attached such significance to the *Reynolds* case that he assigned his attorney general to make the government's argument before the Supreme Court. Later that year, following the Court's decision in favor of the government, the president implored Congress to amend the existing antipolygamy acts, which were largely ineffectual in stemming the practice. Hayes recommended "more comprehensive and more searching methods for preventing as well as punishing" polygamy, and if necessary, stripping its Mormon practitioners of "the enjoyment and exercise of rights and privileges of citizenship" in order to cajole them into abiding by the law.[5] The following year Hayes extended his call for stringent measures against Mormon polygamy, declaring before Congress that "the sanctity of marriage and the family relation are the corner stone of our American society and civilization."[6]

Hayes's pleading helped set the table for the passage of the 1882 Edmunds Act, which, along with the *Reynolds* case, marked the real beginning of the end for Mormon plural marriage by declaring it a felony, disenfranchising convicted polygamists, and pronouncing them ineligible for jury duty or public office.[7] Beyond working with Congress to pass antipolygamy legislation, in August 1879 the Hayes administration sent a letter to the governments of Great Britain, Germany, Norway, Sweden, and Denmark, asking them to prevent Mormon converts from immigrating to the United States. The stated grounds were that "all who come to this country for the purpose of affiliating with the Mormon Church do so with the avowed intention of becoming criminals" by engaging in polygamous marriages once settled in Utah. The European governments respectfully declined the request; London cited the "difficulties" of prosecuting people for supposed criminal intent, short of any actual illegal action.[8] Its failure to convince foreign powers notwithstanding, the Hayes administration's proposal demonstrates that anti-Mormonism decisively affected the highest levels of domestic and even foreign policy making in Washington. In the late nineteenth-century mind, Mormonism had gone beyond heresy or falsehood and entered the realm of the criminal, with an explicit suggestion from the elected head of state that citizenship rights be revoked for members of the LDS Church.

Subsequent presidents maintained the basic position that Hayes had laid out. In his March 1881 inaugural address, Republican James Garfield stated that Mormonism "offends the moral sense of manhood," and called on Congress to legislate accordingly.[9] Following Garfield's assassination, Chester Arthur picked up the gauntlet and delivered multiple speeches against polygamy and Mormon political power. In December 1881, Arthur proclaimed that the government should fight "this odious crime, so revolting to the moral and religious sense of Christendom," and two years later vowed he would do so with "the stoutest weapons which constitutional legislation can fashion."[10] Arthur backed up his forceful rhetoric by signing the aforementioned Edmunds Act, the strongest federal antipolygamy legislation to date.

Antipolygamy sentiment was not just limited to Republican administrations. Democrat Grover Cleveland spoke strongly against polygamy in 1885 and reported glowingly about the effects of the 1887 Edmunds-Tucker Act, which disincorporated the Church of Jesus Christ of Latter-day Saints, seized church property in excess of $50,000, and established even harsher methods and punishments designed to eliminate Mormon plural marriage. President

Cleveland contrasted the miserable "homes of polygamy" with "our homes, established by the law of God, guarded by parental care, regulated by parental authority, and sanctified by parental love." Christian mothers delighted in "the warm light of womanhood, unperverted and unpolluted," as opposed to "the cheerless, crushed, and unwomanly mothers of polygamy." In short, Cleveland maintained, "There is no feature of this practice or the system which sanctions it which is not opposed to all that is of value in our institutions." He renewed Hayes's old proposition of sealing the borders by recommending that Congress pass a law "to prevent the importation of Mormons into the country."[11] Though nothing came of this proposed measure, its timing, coming in the same decade that the government closed the nation's borders to Chinese immigrants, suggested the wide degree of contempt held by Republicans and Democrats alike not only for the institution of plural marriage but also for Mormons and their religion. By the 1880s, hostility to Mormonism had motivated heated discourse and concrete action in all three branches of the federal government.

Throughout the 1870s and 1880s, southerners became increasingly convinced of the severity of the Mormon threat and endorsed federal action to address the issue. Apparently ranking slavery, secession, and Reconstruction as minor nuisances, in 1882, the *Christian Index*, a highly respected and widely read Baptist organ based in Atlanta, proclaimed that "the battle with Mormonism is the most important that has ever engaged the attention of our National Government."[12] Many African American southerners agreed. Reverend L. M. Hagood, a black Methodist, explained that Mormonism would be particularly "troublesome" for the government to deal with, even considering its experience with the evils of "Human Slavery, Kukluxism, and Intemperance." Precisely because the task of extirpating Mormonism was so daunting, Hagood insisted that the government act immediately, "for to-morrow we may find its fangs fastened inextricably in the very vitals of our happy homes, impeding the progress of our system of education and destroying our darling ones."[13] If polygamy was not eliminated soon, it had the power to destroy America's children, its homes, and ultimately the nation itself.

Southerners actively joined the nationwide fight against polygamy because they saw it as a danger to Christian civilization as well as to the American nation. While Christian marriage was of inestimable spiritual value and merited protection simply for that reason, Protestants in the South also emphasized its central role for the health of society and the strength of the state. Not just any form of marriage would do—only monogamous (and needless to say, intraracial and heterosexual) unions were acceptable. Polygamy, southern Protestants argued, threatened sexual purity, monogamous marriage, Christianity, the state, and civilization itself. According to the *Alabama Christian Advocate*, Mormon polygamy was a clear "violation of the sacredness of marriage . . . and of the purity of sexual morality," and was therefore "subversive of social and political integrity."[14] Morality and politics worked in a reciprocal relationship: the state proactively preserved Christian marriage, which in turn provided the moral and social foundation for a healthy state. Southern anti-Mormon literature recognized this intricate connection, as well as the danger posed to it by the Latter-day Saints and their marriage practices: "Mormonism is an organized, systematic attack on the permanence and purity of the Christian home. . . . The law must guard the Christian home as the main pillar of the State."[15] Or, as Reverend William Strickland of Tennessee simply but forcibly warned, "Let Mormonism prevail and we sap the very foundation of society and wipe out the Christian home."[16]

Based on this set of beliefs, the spread of Mormonism in the 1870s and 1880s represented an aggressive assault on the very foundations of Christian society and the nation. Numerous southern authors surmised that Mormonism posed one of the greatest dangers in the history of the republic, and that a veritable clash of civilizations was underfoot. Southerners joined the national chorus in tracking and combating the growing Mormon menace. In their newspapers and other publications, both secular and religious, southerners followed the Mormons' proselytizing efforts, their gathering strength in the West, the centrality of polygamy to the Mormon belief system, and the degrading effect of polygamy, particularly on women and children.

THE MORMON MISSIONARY AS "HOME WRECKER"

Most late nineteenth-century observers equated Mormonism and polygamy as if the religion could be entirely reduced to its peculiar marriage system. In explaining the dogged persistence of both polygamy and Mormonism, a prominent Methodist newspaper pointed out that because Mormonism's "vilest element" was connected with its doctrine of salvation, polygamy had "a theological as well as a social significance" to Latter-day Saints.[17] A Georgia newspaper reprinted a correspondent's report that at a recent conference of the LDS Church held in the Salt Lake Tabernacle, "the vast Mormon audience cried out 'Amen' every time that the polygamy doctrine was proclaimed as coming from God." The correspondent further noted that the Mormon people expressed their willingness to "leave this city and the whole Territory in ashes" if forced to give up "the doctrine of 'spiritual wives,' as they politely call it."[18] Such assessments of the central role of polygamy in late nineteenth-century Mormon theology and identity were in many ways correct, but they left readers with the impression that polygamy was "the taproot of Mormonism," the sine qua non of the entire religious system.[19] Even after LDS president Wilford Woodruff formally announced the end of plural marriage in 1890, many writers from Protestant churches continued to place polygamy at the heart of the religion. For instance, in his early twentieth-century pamphlet *What the Mormons Teach*, Reverend Wildman Murphy contended (correctly) that Woodruff's "Manifesto" did not repudiate the doctrine but only suspended the practice, and that because polygamy was "a sacred and fundamental doctrine of the Mormon Church . . . all Mormons believe in the principle now, just as much as they ever did."[20]

With polygamy thus ensconced at the heart of Mormonism, southerners became convinced that everything that Mormons said or did ultimately purposed to expand or strengthen the institution. Due to its high visibility, the extensive Mormon missionary enterprise drew special attention. Atlanta's *Christian Index* observed in 1887 that Mormon "emissaries" had been busily working for years throughout Europe and America, and that the growth of the religion was highly dependent on this missionary activity.[21] In her 1906 exposé of Mormonism, Jennie Fowler Willing—who remembered the first Mormon elder she ever met as "a smooth-faced, oily-tongued man, with dark, magnetic eyes, and insinuating address"—warned that "the system has become strong enough to send missionaries swarming over the country like the frogs of Egypt."[22] While many Christian churches in America established both foreign and domestic missions during the late nineteenth century, southerners saw the Mormon missionary enterprise in an entirely different light. The problem with Mormon missionaries was that they went "among the people more as emigration agents than as emissaries of the new religion."[23] And this emigration had a particular, and nefarious, purpose. In July 1883 the New Orleans-based *Southwestern Christian Advocate* reported that some five thousand Mormon converts were due to arrive in Utah that month alone, and that they came not as genuine truth-seekers or religious pilgrims but as "recruits for the harems, and open violators of all the laws of God and men."[24] As evidence for this claim, the *Christian Index* gave notice of a party of about a hundred converts from north Georgia and east Tennessee that emigrated to Utah under the direction of a Mormon elder who allegedly boasted that it was "an easy matter to induce people to leave this section and become proselytes of polygamy."[25] Another newspaper described how Mormon missionaries made a special effort "to pervert young women and girls," promising relief to the poor, free education for the young girls, and passage to Utah. With this package of assurances, missionaries were able to "dupe many," and "export to Utah hundreds of innocent victims for polygamy."[26] For their part in this scheme, it was said, faithful elders were rewarded upon their return with the opportunity to "pick out some 'sister' whom they converted during their absence" and add her to their polygamous household.[27]

Southerners were most alarmed with the immediate presence of Mormon missionaries in their homeland and the attendant threat of southern women being lured away to Utah. Newspapers tracked the comings and goings of the elders, warning residents of the lurking menace. "Mormon evangelists, so-called, are traversing the mountain regions of Alabama and making numerous converts to the faith of the Polygamists," the *Alabama Christian Advocate* informed its readers.[28] North Carolinians were similarly told that three Mormon elders "have been laboring in the lower edge of Edgecombe and the Bethel section of Pitt with some success, and that their meetings are well attended and the arguments closely followed."[29] The Memphis *Commercial Appeal* reported the arrival of twenty-two new missionaries to the Southern States Mission in October 1897, and documented where each of them was assigned to labor, noting a particular concentration in Kentucky, Tennessee, and Alabama.[30] Over the course of several months in 1900 the *Atlanta Constitution* steadily traced the activity of Mormon elders in the state, following them as they expanded their fields of labor to Columbus, Fairplay, Dahlonega, and finally Atlanta.[31] Even when the reports were straightforward and unbiased, the message was implicit: the enemy is at the gates, and all good citizens should be wary.

Figure 4.1 Photograph of a group of twenty LDS missionaries recently arrived in Chattanooga, Tennessee, to begin labor in the Southern States Mission, November 1896. Courtesy of the Church History Library, The Church of Jesus Christ of Latter-day Saints, Salt Lake City, Utah.

It was one thing to have strange men traipsing around the southern countryside seeking converts to an exotic faith, but it was quite another to have these men entering Christian homes and corrupting Christian women. A few accounts, usually originating from outside the South, defended the integrity of the Mormon elders canvassing the southern states, saying they were "models of morality," "honest to a penny in all their financial dealings," "upright, honest, and clean," and "so gentlemanly and so amiable that . . . no fault can be found with them"—except, of course, for their association with the "pernicious dogma" of Mormonism.[32] Native southern reports were not so effusive in praise. The southern press commonly lambasted Mormon missionaries as "bad, low men," "hyenas of society," "emissaries of hell," and "false teachers" who brought their "lustful doctrine of polygamy" into southern homes with designs of leading "silly women" into "social bondage."[33] Reverend W. C. Hale railed against Elder Clarence Cowley after he and his companion attended the Baptist preacher's sermon. Hale denounced Cowley, and implicitly all LDS missionaries, as "an impious fraud, a fit subject for the lowest depth of hell, a miserable, meddlesome fool, a representative of the most degraded, ignorant, selfish, vice-stricken people on the face of the

Figure 4.2 Photograph of Elders Farmer and Bills of the Southern States Mission. Missionaries dressed well in order to enhance their image of respectability. Courtesy of the Church History Library, The Church of Jesus Christ of Latter-day Saints, Salt Lake City, Utah.

earth."[34] According to Reverend Martin Luther Oswalt, a former convert to Mormonism who became disenchanted with the faith and then returned to his home in Mississippi to sway others from following the same path, the very presence of LDS missionaries could create a "tumult" in an otherwise peaceful community and "destroy the unity and happiness of families and communities."[35] As the *Atlanta Constitution* observed, Mormon missionaries were, in short, "home wreckers."[36]

The elders' allegedly deceptive tactics provided proof of their nefarious purposes. Several publications chronicled—often with conflicting details—the stealthy strategies employed by missionaries to avoid causing a stir and maximize their chances of ensnaring unsuspecting victims. Upon entering a community, they would go from house to house simply asking for a drink of water or a meal, in the process assessing which women would make likely victims. They held meetings at night or in lonely places where their indoctrination of potential converts could proceed without disruption.[37] A distraught Tennessean, anticipating the kind of language that Thomas Dixon would later use in describing African Americans' rapacious instincts, likened their methods to those of a nocturnal predator: "Lion-like they den themselves during the day, and at the approach of night go forth in search of prey until the dawn of day, then sneak off to their hold and plan and set snares for others."[38] Another author speculated that the elders employed hypnotism to brainwash unsuspecting and weak-minded individuals.[39]

Most southerners were not necessarily afraid that Latter-day Saints would institute polygamy in the South in any kind of substantial way, although stories to that effect occasionally circulated.[40] Rumors of the elders' impropriety notwithstanding, the real concern was less the Mormons' treatment of women in the South and more their supposedly salacious behavior once they had seduced them from their native land. Every baptism of a southern woman thus led the daughters of the South down the path of degradation to the ultimate end of "a life of misery and shame."[41] Southerners rallied not to protect religious orthodoxy but rather the chastity of their women and the sanctity of their homes, the cornerstones of society that southern men had charged themselves to protect at all costs.

White womanhood held an exalted place in the southern mind, and its protection was central to southern men's conceptions about honor and manliness. Since the antebellum era, southern men had defined their roles as men to a substantial degree by the protection they provided for virtuous white women. These relationships were not only deeply gendered but also racialized; the cultural place of white women and men was almost always framed in contrast with the degraded nature of black women and men. Southern white men's self-appointed role as protectors of pure womanhood assumed even greater importance in the postbellum period. One result of emancipation was that blacks were free to wander the countryside at will, a fearful image for many white men, who projected their own longtime sexual abuses of black women onto their black counterparts. This translated into largely irrational fears that political liberty for blacks would also lead to unrestrained sexual liberty, which meant that attacks on white women were imminent and must be stopped at all costs.[42] Whites characterized blacks in various ways, but one of the common tropes was that they were uncivilized, savage brutes who would, without proper controls, descend into orgies of rape and murder, targeting in particular the innocent white women they lusted after.

Especially in the late 1880s and 1890s lynching became a primary means of controlling this "black beast rapist" and preventing him from carrying out his malevolent designs. Violence was always seen as justifiable in defense of home and hearth, and according to the "rape complex" that pervaded the late nineteenth-century South, white men had no more important function than to protect their wives and daughters from the beasts that stalked them. The fact that this myth of the black rapist was indeed largely an illusion, and was proven to be so by contemporaries such as Ida B. Wells and many other black intellectuals, did not alter the fact that white men were quite willing to exercise the full force of the law—and failing that, extralegal violence—to fulfill their manly duty. Historian Jacquelyn Dowd Hall described this entire complex of beliefs and practices as a "southern obsession with rape," which spun the myth of the black rapist into "pathological proportions," thus engendering a "hysterical counterattack from the spokesmen of sexual orthodoxy." The assault on white womanhood became the principal justification for both violent and legislative restrictions on African American freedom.[43]

Although no one at the time seems to have made explicit the connection between Mormon polygamy and black rape, in retrospect the rhetoric and fears about the lecherous Mormon elders on the hunt for sexual prey bore remarkable resemblances to the images and language commonly used to describe the predations of African American men. Ben Tillman of South Carolina fumed on the Senate floor about how white women in the South were constantly imperiled by the black beasts roaming the countryside seeking their next victim, their "breasts pulsating with the desire to sate their passions upon white maidens and wives."[44] In parallel fashion, the *Alabama Baptist* declared that the "great and ultimate object" of Mormon men was "Polygamy and a Harem with the faithful," and that they were "bent upon gratifying their unbridled lust to their hearts' content."[45] Baptist minister William Strickland, in the wake of the Cane Creek Massacre, asserted that "the queen of our Christian home is the wife and mother," but that Mormonism, driven by "lust and brutality," sought only to degrade her into becoming nothing more than "the tool and convenience of man."[46] The *Chattanooga Times* did note the simultaneity of mob violence against blacks and Mormons

in Georgia.[47] But the closest parallel between the supposed transgressions of
each group appeared, briefly, in the *Atlanta Constitution* after a particularly
distasteful episode in which a Georgia woman trying to protect missionaries
from a mob had half her face blown off by a vigilante's shotgun blast. The
Constitution noted that the mob, which apprehended the three elders and
marched them to the county line, operated under "the plea of the protection
of home." Their charge was not as strong as that which compelled "the lynching of the ravisher," but the expelled Mormon seducer and the lynched black
rapist were essentially considered by local citizens to be "on the same line,"
different in degree but not necessarily in kind.[48] Certainly there was a distinction in that the black rapist forced himself on unwilling white women
while the Mormon seducer charmed them with his wiles, but southerners'
emotionally charged rhetoric often blurred the distinctions between these
dual threats to southern womanhood.

   The disparate levels of violence and repression inflicted upon against the two
groups renders the Mormon and the African American experience in the postbellum South incomparable. However, the language and imagery used to describe
each group, and the violent passion employed to keep them out of southern
homes and away from southern white women, were parallel if not entirely similar. The Mormon case provides another example of the centrality of the home
and the virtue of womanhood in white southerners' self-conceptions. The fact
that actual instances of blacks raping white women were relatively rare does not
outweigh the profound fear that such an image generated in the southern white
mind and the ways that fear precipitated violence and legislation. Similarly, the
fact that LDS missionaries never attempted to institute polygamy in the South,
and that their conduct toward southern women was almost without exception
honorable, failed to effectively counter the dominant myth of the lustful Mormon elder come to steal away the daughters of the South. In a qualified sense, we
can view Mormon missionaries as the white counterparts to the mythical black
rapist. Their small numbers, white skins, and the subtle but key distinction
between a seducer and rapist help explain why Mormon elders were not killed
more often or subjected to the grisly and highly sexualized torture common in
spectacle lynchings and associated with the southern defense of womanhood.[49]
Nevertheless, the widespread fear of and organized campaign against the Mormon presence in the South demonstrated that many southerners simply would
not tolerate such a threat in their communities or in their homes.

THE SAINTS' "MONSTER VICE"

One dilemma that southern writers faced when identifying the polygamous
threat that Mormon missionaries posed was that, in fact, the missionaries

rarely talked about plural marriage in their preaching. John Morgan, who presided over the Southern States Mission from 1878 to 1888, told a reporter from the *Chattanooga Times* that the elders "preach faith, repentance, baptism for remission of sins, and the laying on of hands for the reception of the Holy Ghost. They very rarely refer to polygamy, and then only in response to inquiries."[50] Various non-Mormon sources verified Morgan's statement. In reporting the spread of Mormonism in the South, the *New York Times* stated that "never a word is said of polygamy except to denounce Gentile misrepresentations," and "of polygamy they [the elders] say little."[51] The *Atlanta Constitution* pronounced that missionaries in the South, as far as it knew, "have not preached licentious doctrines at all, but have kept the polygamic feature of their religion in the background."[52] Another Atlanta paper, the *Enquirer*, confirmed that "the elders have very little to say about polygamy and tell their converts that only the Church officials or any pious members are allowed to have more than one wife."[53]

Rather than assuaging southern apprehension, however, the Mormons' relative silence on the topic of polygamy only fueled local fears. Because southerners were convinced that the entire Latter-day Saint religion revolved around polygamous lust, and that any purveyors of such vice could not be trusted at their word, the elders' reticence to discuss polygamy in public signaled not innocence but the depths of their characteristic deviousness. "True," South Carolina's staunchly anti-Mormon *Yorkville Enquirer* conceded, "the elders operating in York county may not preach this doctrine, but the fact remains that it is a cardinal principal of the Mormon faith."[54] A minister writing to the *Alabama Baptist* documented how the missionaries preached only out of the Bible, and "carefully concealed their polygamous views in their sermons as well as their conversations." This, however, was merely a shell game, a ruse "carefully laid to entrap the unthinking."[55] As late as 1900, ten years after Wilford Woodruff's Manifesto had purportedly put an end to polygamy, Governor A. J. McLaurin of Mississippi was convinced it was just another Mormon deception. In his closing address to the state legislature in 1900, he cautioned, "There is no threatened danger to the state more baneful than the lecherous teachings of the Mormon apostles of polygamy. It is more dangerous because it is taught under the guise of ministry of gospel. The Mormons disclaim the open teachings of polygamy in the pulpit, but they teach it in the corner."[56] Missionaries in the South were occasionally arrested for openly preaching polygamy, but for the most part it was acknowledged that they plied their trade in secret, and that made them all the more dangerous.[57]

Late nineteenth-century southerners learned about Mormon polygamy via newspapers, public lectures, and sermons. Some of these presentations were little more than caricatures, with critics telling stories that ridiculed the

Latter-day Saints and their marriage system. In a lecture based on observations from his recent trip to Utah, Reverend John Philip Newman, Senate chaplain and close personal advisor to President Ulysses S. Grant, joked that "unlike the Monogamist, the Polygamist has no home. If he would retire at night to the bosom of his family, the question is, which family shall he go to?" Referring to Brigham Young's thirty-or-so wives, Newman remarked that his personal motto must be "variety is the spice of life."[58] The much-married Mormon prophet was the frequent butt of jokes. In one tale a woman called upon the prophet asking for a favor, and when Young declared that he did not recall ever seeing her before, she answered to his astonishment that she was one of his wives.[59] Other stories, though still caricatures, were infused with a darker pathos suggesting that polygamy was a fundamentally coercive and abusive system. One narrative told of an old Mormon man who married a woman before forcing her two teenage daughters to also marry him and bear his children.[60]

As narrated through these anecdotes, southerners regarded polygamy as acutely evil precisely because it victimized women and children, the groups idealized as innocent and virtuous—and considered especially vulnerable—in southern Victorian culture. Southern periodicals detailed the status of women and children inside polygamous Utah, their reports often written by Protestant ministers and churchwomen who visited the territory. Some observers returned with surprisingly upbeat reports about what they saw. One woman who visited the territory declared that Mormons adopted polygamy with gusto because they sought to increase their numbers as fast as possible. As a result, she said, Mormon children, "instead of being dreaded and provided against, as in some other circumstances, are desired and welcomed." Furthermore, she reported that "the children of polygamous parents are unusually strong and healthy."[61] This glowing report was the exception to the rule. More typical were the findings of another correspondent who related the atrocious conditions facing children in a polygamous household in Utah:

> The boys and girls slept together indiscriminately. . . . In no case did they ever get any but the coarsest kind of food, and frequently not enough of that, though forced to work constantly and always very hard; the girls being obliged to labor out of doors, hoeing potatoes, chopping wood, and doing other work generally elsewhere assigned to men. . . . These girls had received but little schooling, being barely able to read and to scrawl their names in a scarcely intelligible manner. . . . Without being lewd, their thoughts seemed to have been trained mainly to the contemplation of such subjects as courtship and marriage, the relation of the sexes, theatres, and other frivolous amusements.

The report claimed that Mormon girls were not only subjected to deplorable living conditions, but were the victims of parental and ecclesiastical abuse. Knowing that their parents and the church hierarchs would force them into polygamy, many girls allegedly began early in life to plot their escape, some leaving home by the age of sixteen to avoid being placed in a polygamous marriage against their will.[62] For southerners, who clung tightly to the cult of true womanhood and the corresponding priority of sheltering girls from the evils of the world, such depictions of young girls simultaneously being de-sexed so as to perform manual labor and being schooled only in the base passions that drove the polygamous system proved shocking to their sensibilities. Whereas the traditional Victorian model had the home as the site of Christian nurture and education, the polygamous Mormon household inverted and perverted the ideal by becoming the place where children learned vice rather than virtue, sensuality rather than morality, lustful abandon rather than chaste discipline. The only hope for such unfortunate children, subject to Dickensian squalor and oppression, was the complete and utter destruction of polygamy.

As distressing as the perils facing children under polygamy were, southerners denounced even more strenuously the subjugated status of women in Utah. Here, in Christian America, existed a system that "debases women to the Turkish level," reducing women to absolute dependence on and subservience to their husbands.[63] Outside observers noted the burdens that polygamous wives endured in maintaining themselves and their household, compared to the "care-free" life of their husbands, especially those among the church leadership; one Mormon woman supposedly confided to a visitor that "it is a good religion for the men, but hard on the poor women."[64] Many critics, perhaps drawing on the Republican Party's identification of slavery and polygamy as the "twin relics of barbarism," described the existence of Mormon women in terms that vividly recollected chattel bondage, with claims that Mormon elders kidnapped southern women and took them to Utah "to make worse than slaves of them."[65] Once in the (figurative and literal) clutches of the Mormon elders, these women were subjected to "a condition of life far worse than slavery ever developed," a statement that had special resonance for southerners in the immediate aftermath of emancipation.[66] Jennie Fowler Willing wrote of seeing young convert girls coming to America on a boat from Europe, supervised by a Mormon missionary. "I knew the plunge into the awful sea of sensuality that awaited them," she lamented. "They would be taken to Utah, and at each station, the men would flock about the train, picking out the girls that suited their fancy, paying the missionary for them, each loading his purchases into a wagon, and driving off to the farm where the poor thing would be set to raising pigs, poultry, and babies for her master's enrichment and aggrandizement." Willing made the slavery comparison explicit when she referred to polygamous wives as "chattels," "slaves in every sense," and "white slaves."[67]

When outsiders wondered why Mormon women accepted such inhuman treatment, the common answer was that domineering patriarchs kept them against their will, or that they had bought into a bogus religious system that tied their salvation to polygamy and subjugation to their husbands. It was inconceivable that a woman would voluntarily surrender to "one of the vilest humiliations of her sex," so reformers and anti-Mormons insisted that the system relied on male religious coercion.[68] One of the loudest voices blaming the Mormon religion for the subjection of its women was Fanny Stenhouse, an English convert to Mormonism who became disaffected after relocating to Utah and in 1872 published her influential *Exposé of Polygamy: A Lady's Life among the Mormons* (a new edition titled *Tell It All* came out two years later). Stenhouse insisted that Mormon women did not accept polygamy on their own volition, but "were betrayed into obeying a revelation which was said to come from God, which made it necessary to their salvation and exaltation in heaven that they should give to their husbands other wives." She corrected the misconception that polygamy was enforced exclusively by lecherous patriarchs. The arrangement was also propped up, she argued, by "a class of women in Utah professionally devoted to polygamy . . . who act as drill-sergeants to the other women."[69] These women betrayed their sisters in exchange for a few token privileges, and illustrated the depths to which society had descended in "that valley of moral midnight." After all, if Mormonism had corrupted its women so thoroughly that they actually supported a system as vile as polygamy, then nothing of morality or virtue remained in the community. Protestants who sought to rescue women from polygamous bondage told themselves that "many" Mormon women "would gladly escape from that life if an opportunity was presented to them."[70] That more LDS women did not in fact flee to the rescuing arms of the Gentiles only substantiated in the anti-Mormon mind the depths of female captivity and Mormon depravity.

The mounting evidence convinced southerners that the Saints were anything but holy, and that their entire religious and social system was based on immorality, sensuality, and lust. The *Alabama Christian Advocate* stipulated that "there is not a form of idolatry in China, dark and benighted as it is, more gross, sensual, earthly, and devilish, than is Mormon idolatry in the United States. . . . It maintains itself by fraudulent appeals to an illiterate peasantry abroad, and by perjury, theft, and murder at home."[71] The *Raleigh News and Observer* cautioned its readers not to be entrapped by "this congregation of sensualists."[72] "Venus is the goddess of Mormonism," a Methodist newspaper asserted, and the LDS belief in the eternal nature of marriage and procreation meant that "a Mohammedan Paradise is not a whit more sensual than a Mormon one."[73] In his lengthy tome *Mormonism Exposed and Refuted*, William Kirby characterized the religion as "strictly carnal and

Satanic" in nature. Mormonism's inherent immorality began with its founder, Joseph Smith, whose life Kirby depicted as being one of fraud, cowardice, treason, bribery, and lechery.[74]

Such inauspicious beginnings resulted in a degenerate creed that culminated in the decadent Mormon household. A visitor to Salt Lake Valley was impressed by the beautiful homes throughout the Mormon capital but quickly became disenchanted after realizing that "three-fourths of those elegant private residences are but *harems*—houses of prostitution,—rather than Christian homes and pure springs of morality. In this sense Salt Lake City is a very Sodom."[75] Without proper Christian nurture and discipline in the home, it was no wonder that Mormondom became the very picture of moral looseness. Several Protestant writers commented on the prominent place that dances and the theater played in Salt Lake society, and speculated that such "worldly" and "frivolous amusements" naturally led to sexual abominations including polygamy.[76] Jennie Fowler Willing summarized much of the southern attitude toward Mormon wickedness when she concluded that "Mormonism is an organized, systematic attack on the permanence and purity of the Christian home. It is licentiousness by rule. . . . The vices that in Christian lands hide from the day, and from the eyes of decent people, are preached and practiced among Mormons, openly, boastfully, and as part of their religion."[77]

Assertions of Mormon depravity filtered into the general southern populace and contributed to mobilization against LDS missionaries proselytizing in the region. For instance, in the summer of 1879, shortly after the Joseph Standing murder, Elder Francis McDonald was preaching in a Johnson County, Kentucky, schoolhouse when he was surrounded by a hostile group of fifty to sixty men. They handed him a note demanding that he leave the area immediately, since his doctrines were "a cuss and a Slander to our people." The note warned McDonald that his "punishment Shall be great" if he returned, as the community refused to allow a member of "An adulterous Set" to preach among them.[78] In 1881, residents of Habersham County, Georgia, passed a series of resolutions calling on "all good citizens and orthodox religious denominations . . . to unite to put down and suppress Mormonism with all its doctrines." They reasoned that based on its embrace of polygamy, "Mormonism is calculated to corrupt the morals of the rising generation," and as such the people must come together to "drive the monster vice from our midst."[79] In another example, a number of "well known citizens" assembled in Warren County, West Virginia, concerned that Mormon elders were "able to deceive the women" through their denials of any allegiance to polygamy. The self-appointed regulators seized a pair of missionaries as they left a house, escorted them to a swamp where the elders were "disciplined with a buggy trace," then ordered them to leave the county and not return.[80]

These missionaries, and hundreds of others, learned firsthand how fiercely southerners opposed them and their peculiar institution.

POLYGAMY AND SOUTHERN PROTESTANTISM

The national and regional antipolygamy campaigns proceeded with the wholehearted support of the Protestant clergy, who saw the growth of Mormonism as a spiritual as well as social crisis and the fight against it a moral crusade. For many, their assault on plural marriage constituted a defense of true Christian marriage. "The family is the oldest institution in the world, and the most sacred," declared Reverend A. J. Frost in a series of articles on marriage and divorce he authored for the *Tennessee Baptist* in 1884. Marriage was sacred because it was ordained by God and typified the "union of Christ and the church." Any desecration of "this holy ordinance" was therefore commensurate with "profaning the very 'holy of holies,'" one of the great blasphemies condemned in scripture.[81] Among the greatest contemporary threats to the sacred institution, including false notions perpetuated by "infidelity" and "Romanism," was Mormon polygamy, which perverted holy Christian marriage simply "for the gratification of lust" and thus constituted an affront to Christ himself.[82]

The ministers and members of the various Protestant denominations agreed that the modern practice of polygamy, despite the Mormons' protests and appeals to Old Testament precedents to the contrary, was not countenanced by the Bible. Southerners had to admit that polygamy did exist in ancient Israel and even seemed to have been endorsed by God in the cases of biblical luminaries such as Abraham, Jacob, Moses, David, and Solomon. Their counterargument was that the New Testament teachings of Jesus, particularly those condemning divorce and enjoining a single man and woman to come together in holy matrimony, superseded any practice of the Israelites under the Mosaic law.[83] Based on this reading of the Bible, southern Protestants insisted that a man could not marry a second woman unless a proper divorce had been obtained based on "scriptural cause," namely adultery. No matter what they called themselves, or what society thought of their union, Reverend Frost asserted, Mormon polygamists were adulterers, and Mormon unions beyond the first were illegitimate: "Brigham Young had but one wife, all the rest were concubines. It is absolutely impossible for a man to be married to two women at the same time. For if he puts away his wife and marries another, he commits adultery."[84] J. W. Hinton, also a southern Methodist, made a more careful distinction. He compared polygamy to slavery, another Old Testament institution, and argued that both practices were *malum prohibitum* rather than *malum in se*—in other words, evil because prohibited rather than evil in themselves. "Had polygamy been a *malum in se*," Hinton reasoned, "God could never have tolerated it at any period." However, in the modern period and under the law of Christ, polygamy was prohibited and deserved universal condemnation as "a source of innumerable evils to the body politic," and particularly "as a fruitful source of social evils and a dreadful degradation of woman."[85] Regardless of how southern Protestants formulated their arguments, they arrived at the same conclusions: polygamy was a moral evil unsanctioned by a responsible reading of the Bible, and the Mormon claim of plural marriage as an authentic religious practice for Christians was thoroughly spurious. In so doing, they essentially contended that not only was polygamy un-Christian, but that Mormonism itself fell outside "the pale of Christian society."[86]

Anti-Mormonism occupied the labors of ministers both great and small. In 1884, two Mormon elders laboring in Hickman County, Tennessee, attended a college commencement address by the renowned Reverend James D. Barbee. The scion of a distinguished family that descended from the original settlers of Virginia and whose members had served in the American Revolution and War of 1812, Barbee had spent over three decades preaching in Alabama and Tennessee. In 1883 he was appointed pastor of Nashville's McKendree Church, the largest and most prominent Methodist congregation in the state. During his ministry at McKendree, Barbee was elected to the chaplaincy of the Tennessee state senate, where he exerted considerable influence on state politics. Enormously well respected, he was remembered upon his death for his friendship with members of other faiths (including Jews and Catholics) and his principled avoidance of "sensational preaching."[87] Given this reputation, the two Mormon missionaries were somewhat surprised when Barbee began his commencement address with what they called "the most abusive and slanderous attack upon our people that we ever heard fall from the lips of mortal man." They reported that Barbee concluded his remarks by asserting that the "strong arm of government should be employed to wipe from the face of civilization every Latter-day Saint in Utah, men, women, and children."[88] If the missionaries' account of Barbee's sermon can be trusted, then even the most ecumenical ministers of the South could be counted as staunch opponents of polygamy and its parent system of Mormonism.

In addition to its embrace by the "big" pastors of the South, anti-Mormonism was also a cause célèbre among local congregations and ministers. Indeed, Mormons placed primary blame for the bitter spirit aroused against them in the South and around the nation on the evangelical Protestant clergy. LDS missionaries observed that the "antipolygamy furor" in the South was "agitated chiefly by sectarian priests" (a phrase they directed toward all non-Mormon clergymen, Catholic or Protestant). An elder returning from his labors in the South in September 1881 reported that "preachers stir up most of the persecution, Methodists and Hardshell Baptists being the most actively malicious."[89] Examples of southern ministerial anti-Mormonism abound. For instance, a set of elders was prepared to preach in Benton County, Tennessee, in September 1880 when a "learned divine" endeavored to break up their meeting. He stood outside the home where the missionaries were scheduled, denouncing the elders as "a set of outlaws and infidels" and railing against Mormonism as a "hideous, infernal" lie.[90] John Morgan recorded in his journal the opposition of a Baptist preacher in rural Alabama who "preached a long tirade against us . . . misrepresenting everything," then instigated a "crowd of drunken roughs" against the elders. In a letter he wrote shortly thereafter to LDS church president John Taylor, Morgan described how ministers led "a crowd of drunken and infuriated 'christians,'" brandishing knives and pistols, against him and the other elders. The missionaries managed to escape without harm, but the next day the same local preachers "were busy riding from place to place securing a mob to force us to leave."[91] Latter-day Saints had an ideological ax to grind against Protestants, and in their persecution narratives, newspaper articles, and personal correspondence, they certainly overemphasized the complicity of ministers in anti-Mormon violence. Nevertheless, the mobilization of the evangelical establishment, local and national, against Mormonism in the late nineteenth century suggests that elders laboring in the South were not entirely fabricating their claims, even if they delighted in revealing the un-Christian behavior of the "insidious and adulterous priests" who made up the Protestant ministerial class.[92]

One of the hallmarks of the Protestant response to polygamy was its interdenominational character. In an era when denominational newspapers promulgated the minutia of doctrinal and ecclesiastical debates designed to differentiate one Christian group from another, the ecumenical spirit of the anti-Mormon crusade stands out in sharp relief. Methodists lauded the work of Presbyterians, who spearheaded several missions to the Mormons in Utah, and adopted much of the same platform in their dealings with Mormonism.[93] A correspondent to the *Alabama Baptist* similarly recommended a "timely lecture by a Cumberland Presbyterian minister" that, the writer hoped, would "have the desired effect" of squelching Mormonism in the region.[94] An antipolygamy meeting in Washington, D.C., brought together the pastors of all the Protestant churches, "for the purpose of giving expression to the sentiment of the Christian public on the question of polygamy."[95] In early 1882, ministers from the various Protestant denominations in Alabama met to discuss the Mormon question. Together they drafted a petition to Congress calling for the "immediate suppression" of Mormonism, then resolved to publish the petition in the newspaper of every church and to circulate it throughout the state.[96] This ecumenical spirit transcended not only denominational but also sectional lines, with southern Methodists sanctioning and reprinting an antipolygamy petition to Congress drafted by their northern counterparts of the Methodist Episcopal Church. In defending their move to "heartily endorse the memorial of our brethren" across the Mason-Dixon Line, they opined, "It is time the churches were moving solidly against this moral and social monstrosity in the land."[97]

For many southern Christians, the most troubling aspect of the Mormon "monstrosity" was not its existence—heresies had come and gone over the centuries—but its persistence and growth. Particularly in the early 1880s, southern presses were filled with lamentations over the apparent ineffectiveness of virtually all efforts to stem the tide of expansive Mormonism. Following the death of Brigham Young, the *Alabama Baptist* expressed surprise at "how slowly an error dies," even after the death of its prophet, but the newspaper still maintained confidence that Mormonism would in fact waste away, even if was a slow process that took generations.[98] The Methodist *Alabama Christian Advocate* disagreed, musing in 1881 that it was a "vain hope" that Mormonism would "die of itself." The newspaper pointed to the continued growth of the church, both in terms of converts and territorial control, and expressed fears that without "a strong and effectual check, no one can tell to what proportions it may grow."[99] About the time the Edmunds bill was being debated in Congress in early 1882, New Orleans' *Southwestern Christian Advocate* complained that "Mormon ranks are being steadily replenished, and Mormonism is stronger than ever before."[100] Southerners, like others in the antipolygamy movement, believed that the Edmunds Act, once passed, would sound the death knell for Mormonism, but a few months after its enactment they began to express disappointment at the inefficacy of the bill and astonishment at the resilience of Mormonism. Unfortunately, they said, Mormons "have sagacity enough to adapt themselves to the new conditions, that they would compromise at some points, elude others," and use backroom politics and influence-peddling to secure "immunity" from the worst of federal prosecution.[101]

Fundamentally, southerners saw polygamy as a direct affront to their most cherished values and traditions. The prospect that polygamy would infiltrate their homes and communities precipitated widespread fear that compounded with every new report of missionary activity, baptisms, and southern converts' immigration to the West. Southerners felt besieged by the Mormon missionary effort, and the only defense was to sound the alarm and work proactively to stave off the invasion. It was an epic contest between competing civilizations, one monogamous and the other polygamous, one Christian and the other idolatrous, one dedicated to defending the purity and virtue of southern womanhood and the other intent on debasing it.

Nothing short of complete victory, meaning the eradication of polygamy—
and the entire Mormon religion if need be—would be sufficient in defending
southern homes from "the fiend of lust and crime set up under the garb of
religion."[102] The following chapter illustrates the different approaches
adopted by southerners in their campaign to save themselves and the nation
from polygamy, and how the debate over these varying tactics helped shape
southerners' attitudes toward the interplay of morality and the public
sphere, the proper relationship between church and state, and the limits of
religious freedom.

5

The Second Reconstruction

Southern Anti-Polygamy and the Limits of Religious Freedom

The slew of anti-Mormon sermons, editorials, laws, prosecutions, court decisions, presidential speeches, and vigilante actions throughout the 1870s and 1880s did little to quell the Latter-day Saints' commitment to plural marriage. If anything, open resistance characterized the prevailing LDS attitude toward the federal government, law enforcement, and national antipolygamy campaign during this period. The continuation of plural marriages and public denunciations of the Supreme Court's 1879 *Reynolds* decision typified the Mormons' confrontational posture. The Richmond *Christian Advocate* observed that the court's ruling was being "openly treated with contempt," and that "the Mormons are defiant as ever."[1] Mormon defiance of the law frustrated southerners and in turn galvanized anti-Mormon sentiment in the South. Setting aside the glorification of their own legacy of conflict with intrusive federal authority, southerners decried the Mormons' staunch—and very public—resistance.

The death of Brigham Young in 1877, like the death of Joseph Smith over thirty years earlier, gave temporary hope to Mormonism's enemies that the church would fall apart without his charismatic and authoritarian leadership. Southerners were disappointed when they learned that Young's successor in the presidency of the LDS Church was John Taylor, "a pronounced polygamist" who would "do everything to defend and preserve this barbarous relic of the olden time."[2] Taylor lived up to anti-Mormon expectations, presiding over a period of pronounced Mormon noncooperation with civil authority. If anything, Taylor took an even harder line than did his predecessor, zealously fighting for plural marriage and against federal authority in Utah, and taking the church government (including himself) underground for the better part of his administration in order to avoid prosecution and imprisonment. When Taylor did surface, it was to rally the troops and profess his—and by extension the church's—undying devotion to plural marriage as the central social and theological fact of Mormonism. A southern newspaper correspondent who attended an 1882 meeting in the Salt Lake Tabernacle, filled to capacity with some twelve thousand Mormons, adeptly captured the attitude of the church under President Taylor: "They declared they had nothing to yield, no compromise to make; that they would go on in their course, and that all the powers of earth and hell could not prevent it."[3]

The Mormon mantra of no retreat, no surrender echoed throughout the southern press and left a strong impression that only a proactive program bringing substantial pressure to bear on the Saints would succeed in ridding the nation of polygamy. The question was what kind of program, and how much pressure should be exerted. It was evident by the early 1880s that virtually every segment of society—from the White House to the statehouse to the church meetinghouse—could be counted on to join the battle in defending southern homes and southern women from the Mormon menace, but southerners disagreed among themselves regarding the best way to cleanse the nation of so great an evil. In debates over whether a law-and-order approach (including federal legislation, punitive law enforcement, and perhaps a constitutional amendment), Christian missions and education, or more aggressive tactics (including violence) would represent the best solution to the Mormon problem, southerners revealed much about not only their assessment of the particular threat but also their broader views of the nature of society and the state. In a region sometimes portrayed as monolithic, the discussion over which tactics would be most efficacious in defeating Mormonism demonstrated genuine diversity of opinion regarding the role of religion in the public sphere and the relationship of public morality and private belief.

The debate over how best to extirpate Mormonism, or at least polygamy, led to a second dilemma: how to do so without violating the principles of religious liberty and localism, two of the primary pillars of the dominant southern worldview. Whereas some southerners enthusiastically embraced a vigorous federal program to suppress Mormon immorality and recalcitrance, others worried that such a path of action would amount to a second wave of Reconstruction that would enlarge the authority and powers of the national government, thus threatening local freedoms and leading to the erosion of state and individual sovereignty. Virtually all southerners agreed that polygamy needed to be eliminated in order to preserve Christian civilization, but their disagreements on how to proceed spoke to weighty concerns that went beyond the Mormon question to larger dilemmas of how to structure a modern social, political, and legal order that could accommodate genuine pluralism, balancing community values on the one hand and minority rights and freedom of conscience on the other.

Historian David Blight has shown that in the decades after the country was ripped apart during the Civil War and Reconstruction, whites ironically, and purposefully, used race as a healing balm to repair the sectional divide and reconcile former enemies. White southerners willfully manipulated their postbellum narratives about the war, arguing that the conflict had been about any number of things (such as states' rights), but not race. White northerners, most of whom had tired with the work of Reconstruction by the mid-1870s and who were never particularly enthusiastic about the prospect of racial equality, gladly obliged their southern brethren's (mis-)interpretation of events. Together they sacrificed the rights of the freedmen on the altar of sectional harmony and white national unity.[4] Though generally neglected in historians' narratives of sectional reconciliation and certainly not as pervasive a harmonizing discourse as was race, the antipolygamy movement of the 1870s and 1880s also provided a substantial vehicle for southerners to join in a common cause with their erstwhile antagonists, especially with northern Protestant moral reformers and Republican presidents and legislators. Those southerners who opted for either Christian missions or coercive legislation echoed the tactics of their northern counterparts in the antipolygamy campaign. Many individuals and groups worked together across denominational, sectional, and partisan lines, making the fight against Mormon polygamy a powerful regional and national unifier, particularly among white Protestants. Many southern Democrats, who had previously sided with Mormons in mid-nineteenth-century debates over popular sovereignty, flipped their position in the 1880s, with moral concerns trumping a political ideology of limited federal power. The threat of polygamy thus induced southern champions of local rights to lend their active support to legislation authorizing the federal government to employ its punitive authority in reconstructing a people condemned originally by northern Republicans for clinging on to one of the "twin relics of barbarism."

"THE GEORGIA METHOD IS BEST": VIGILANTISM

White southerners generally adopted one of three approaches to purge the nation of polygamy, and in so doing protect their own homes and communities. These methods were not mutually exclusive, as some individuals and publications embraced a multipronged strategy or changed their position according to circumstance. Rather, the three approaches—vigilantism, Christian missions, and legislation—should be seen as three points that southerners generally clustered around on a broader continuum of possible responses to Mormonism, and social ills in general.

The most aggressive option called for a no-holds-barred approach allowing for—and even encouraging—violence. Many southerners, white and black, and particularly in rural areas, retained extralegal violence as a cherished tradition of community defense well into the twentieth century. This increasingly separated the South from the North, where vigilantism was for the most part curbed by the late nineteenth century and where violence was rarely used against Mormons after the Civil War—a sharp contrast to the Mormons' rough treatment in 1830s Missouri and 1840s Illinois. Southern apologists for extralegal violence contended that words—whether in the form of speeches, sermons, or laws—were too weak to counter imminent dangers such as Mormon polygamy and black rape. To guarantee the safety of their communities and families, citizens needed to take matters into their own hands. Nobody liked violence, the rationale for vigilantism went, but it was sometimes necessary to keep social evil in check.

For instance, the *Alabama Baptist* did not recommend tarring and feathering Mormons in usual circumstances, preferring instead to "let a committee of prudent citizens notify them that their presence is odious to the community and that they must leave at once." If missionaries refused such a polite invitation, however, then "every neighborhood understands its own business," and more desperate measures might be attempted.[5] South Carolina's *Yorkville Enquirer*, whose pages featured a particularly vitriolic brand of anti-Mormonism, maintained that "we deprecate violence," but at the same time warned Mormons that "they should remember that in their advocacy of sentiments at variance with the laws of the land, they and their followers place themselves outside the pale of martyrdom."[6] Arguing that Latter-day Saints' immoral pursuits left them beyond the protection of the law, the *Enquirer* tried to whip up its readers to resort to any means necessary to defeat Mormonism: "All efforts should be exerted by honest, virtuous citizens to stop it. . . . Every patriotic citizen will strive to secure the day when it shall be wiped from the face of the earth."[7] Another South Carolina newspaper, the *Greenville Weekly News*, approved of citizens who had run Mormon elders out of the county. It warned, "The Mormon Elder must go from this region; he must go in a hurry. If he insists on staying his visit will be made very permanent, excessively quiet, and satisfactory to everybody except the Elder."[8] The *Lauderdale News* encouraged Alabamans to "decorate them with tar and feathers, ornament a tree with seven Latter-day Saints. This 'Mormon' business should, can, and must be stopped." Its recommendations concluded with an ominous reference to Joseph Standing's murder: "The Georgia method is best."[9] The belief that vigilantism offered a cure for Mormon vice thus pervaded broad sections of the southern populace and contributed to violence against LDS missionaries in the region. The Joseph Standing and Cane Creek cases were among the most dramatic examples, but similar (though less lethal) scenes played out across the South in the late nineteenth century, as detailed in chapter 7.

Not all southerners agreed with such iron-fisted tactics. Southern States Mission president John Morgan commended a number of "right-thinking, honorable men and women" who, despite their hostility toward Mormonism, nevertheless argued that "mob-violence, persecution, and unauthorized, illegal prosecution" were improper tactics in addressing the problem.[10] One such outspoken critic of the brutality of anti-Mormon violence was Rabbi Louis Weiss of Chattanooga. Without expressing any particular sympathy for the Mormon religion itself, Weiss nevertheless protested the "brutal assaults" that had been perpetrated against the Latter-day Saints in the South. Such violence was a stain on "this land, where religious liberty marks the color of our banner with the sweetest hue of freedom." The rabbi's message was certainly tinctured with a shade of self-preservation when he lamented that violent treatment of any religious minority group existed "in our days and in America." He concluded by appealing to universal sentiments: "I am always at the side of perfect justice, regardless upon whom the injustice is perpetrated, and mob violence is always brutal."[11]

By the late nineteenth century, many other southerners, particularly of the middle and upper classes, also found mob violence to be a rather blunt instrument that, while not entirely useless, should be resorted to only in the most extreme circumstances. Without condoning what they saw as the immoral behavior of the targeted groups, they nevertheless believed extralegal violence to be a counterproductive measure in addressing the threats posed by groups such as blacks and Mormons. In July 1899, less than a week after a mob of thirty masked men apprehended three Mormon elders from the home of William and Emily Cunnard in Jasper County, Georgia, and, in the altercation that ensued, shot off the left half of Emily's face, Governor Allen Candler gave a speech appealing to the citizens of the state to end mob violence. The governor specifically addressed the issue of black lynching, but given the timing of the speech and the publicity of the recent anti-Mormon incident, which appeared prominently in all the regional newspapers, surely he was also alluding to the Mormon case when he said the mob "never knows where to stop, but after punishing the guilty, drunk with the blood of one victim, it thirsts for the blood of another, and often sacrifices on the altar of vengeance those who are guiltless of any crime." He continued, "We must do away with [the] mob. We must re-enthrone the law. . . . This requires the strong power of the statute law, sustained by . . . vigorous public sentiment."[12] Two days before the governor's speech, the *Atlanta Constitution* editorialized that unchecked violence against Mormons, admittedly a "despised sect," would lead to later abuses against other groups, the end of which would be "a condition of anarchy, one in which there would be no legal arbiter, and of which the mob would be the sole judge."[13]

Such law-and-order sentiments also appeared in the 1880s at the height of the antipolygamy crusade. In a speech on the House floor in debates leading up to the 1887 Edmunds-Tucker Act, Democratic Congressman Risden Bennett of North Carolina queried, "Are you called upon to resort to the cruel surgery of the sword to cure every ill?"[14] Representative Bennett meant to chastise what he saw as an overzealous federal government that was increasingly willing to use all its brute force to crush not only polygamy but also the institution of the LDS Church, but the same line of reasoning existed within the South as well. The chief organ of the progress-oriented New South, the *Atlanta Constitution*, acknowledged that "the shotgun, of course, is a remedy," but then countered that "it is a very brutal one—not less brutal certainly than Mormonism, but too brutal to be employed by those who claim to be civilized."[15] The response of the *Alabama Baptist* to the 1884 Cane Creek Massacre followed a similar logic: "The murder of the Mormon elders in Tennessee is a shame to our civilization. Mormonism itself is a shame and should be wiped out, indeed it should have been throttled long ago; but such acts of violence as those perpetrated in Tennessee will not effect this end." Not only was vigilantism uncivilized, the *Alabama Baptist* reasoned, but it was counterproductive: "Persecution arouses sympathy, always, and such deeds of violence will only add fuel to the increasing flame of Mormonism."[16]

Unlike Rabbi Weiss's appeal to the ideals of religious liberty and tolerance, many southern denunciations of violent force against Mormonism were tactical rather than principled, more concerned with the corrosive effect of violence on the perpetrators rather than victims. It was not that Mormonism did not deserve an ignominious death—it did—but a civilized, Christian people should find a better way than vigilantism. While violence might solve the proximate problem, it would contribute to the breakdown of law and order and might, even worse, lead ultimately to the growth of Mormonism, which displayed a remarkable capacity to absorb persecution and transform it into greater missionary activity and additional converts.

"THE SWORD OF THE SPIRIT:" CHRISTIAN MISSIONS AND EDUCATION

A number of southern clergy and church members became principal advocates of a second, nonviolent solution to the problem of polygamy. Viewing polygamy as a sinful symptom of false theology, these southern Protestants believed that they could resolve the Mormon problem through an active program of Christian missions and education. This perspective was not limited to a particular denomination, although it did reflect a certain theological conservatism—common in the South—that was suspicious of any efforts, regardless of origin or sponsorship, to build a godly society that did not begin and end with the preaching of the gospel and the salvation of souls. Mississippi Baptist preacher (and former Mormon) Martin Luther Oswalt criticized the vigilante approach, asserting that "the shot gun and tar and feathers" would not "rid the country of Mormonism," but that the religion could only be fought effectively with "the sword of the Spirit, which is the word of God."[17] The *Alabama Baptist* similarly suggested that "preaching the Gospel in Utah" was the lone means of stopping Mormonism.[18] In mid-1882, following the enactment of the Edmunds Act, the major Methodist publication in the state, the *Alabama Christian Advocate*, tended to agree with its Baptist counterpart. It published articles arguing that secular means would be "powerless" in altering the "hideous structure" of Mormonism. Only the "pure light of the Gospel," spread via Christian missionaries and schools, could dispel the darkness that enveloped "the debauched thousands of Utah."[19]

An evangelical approach helped form and shape the political decisions of many religious southern lawmakers. In a pair of speeches in 1884, Senator Joseph Brown of Georgia, who had loudly opposed the 1882 Edmunds Act, championed missionary work among the Mormons instead of more coercive measures. "It may be easier to cry 'Crucify them' than it is to try and help convert them," Brown argued, but sending "missionaries from Christian churches to teach the people of [Utah] Territory the truths of the Gospel [represented]

Figure 5.1 Photograph of riverside baptism in Southern States Mission, ca. 1912. Southerners debated about the most effective way to stop Mormons from gaining additional converts and influence in the region. Courtesy of the Church History Library, The Church of Jesus Christ of Latter-day Saints, Salt Lake City, Utah.

an infinitely better remedy than unconstitutional, arbitrary, and oppressive enactments by Congress."[20] Senator Brown approvingly cited the famous preacher Henry Ward Beecher, who spoke against a heavy-handed military or legislative approach to eradicating polygamy. Brown encouraged instead a softer "moral" solution, including receiving Utah into the Union, replacing the army with Christian preachers and teachers, and in general substituting harshness with kindness and persuasion.[21] This approach recalled the federal government's earlier "peace policy" toward Native Americans, which in the early 1870s had employed various Christian churches to provide food, clothing, and schooling to the tribes in the hope that the Indians could be assimilated into the nation through softer means than brute military force.

If southern churchmen believed that preaching the gospel could save the nation from the menace of Mormonism, they were even more certain that such a tactic would save the South from polygamy's agents. Preaching against Mormonism and Mormon missionaries became a staple of the southern pulpit, becoming at once an ecumenical movement and a device to strengthen individual denominations. "A Lover of Truth" writing to a Baptist newspaper praised Presbyterian ministers for their lectures exposing the evils of Mormonism and hoped that as a result all southern Christians would say "Get thee behind me Satan" to the "followers of Old Joe Smith."[22] Alabama Baptists believed that preachers of the true Christian gospel could do much to halt the progress of Mormon missionaries in the region, and that if the denomination sent educated ministers throughout the state, "in a few years a Mormon could not find a hearing."[23] The Tennessee Baptist Convention became greatly alarmed at the level of Mormon missionary activity in the state in the 1890s and passed a resolution encouraging a stronger denominational response as a bastion against the Mormon onslaught.[24] Accordingly, the convention's board published a leaflet, *Catechism on Mormonism*, which provided its readers with "a brief statement of this most corrupting doctrine and its founders" and was to be distributed to Baptists throughout the state.[25] Mormonism thus provided an opportunity for many southern churches to act on their imperative to fight evil in the world, and in their midst. While some southern churchgoers and even ministers participated in anti-Mormon mobs, others saw Christian evangelization to be the only effective cure, both within the South (to preserve innocent souls) and in the Mormon heartland (to reclaim errant souls).

"WISE AND STRINGENT LAWS": LEGISLATION

Another group of middle-class and elite southerners advocated a third tactic in addressing the Mormon problem. They emphasized a law-and-order approach, with "wise and stringent laws, faithfully executed," over vigilantism or an exclusive reliance on missions.[26] While white southerners almost universally preferred local solutions to externally imposed mandates, many, including a number of Christian leaders and publications, recognized that Mormonism had become so entrenched and powerful, especially in the West, that only the strong arm of government had sufficient power to take on polygamy. For instance, in 1879, the Atlanta-based *Christian Index* approved of the abandonment of "complex marriage" by the residents of the Oneida community in New York, and added that it would "be glad to see Mormonism follow suit." It admitted, however, that Mormon polygamy would not go away so easily or quietly, as "that iniquity is on a much larger scale and will probably make a harder struggle for life." The lone solution to the "horror" of Mormon polygamy was therefore "prohibitory laws" that would be "rigidly enforced."[27] To counter the spread of Mormonism in the South, the *Raleigh News and Observer* recommended that state legislatures make it illegal "to persuade or to attempt to persuade a young woman to forsake her home and go to Utah." Such statutes would be in line with the duty of governments to preserve "good morals" and would effectively stem the tide of "female accessions" to Mormonism.[28]

Some southern state legislatures did take up the cause, most notably Tennessee's in the wake of the Cane Creek Massacre. The pressure mounted in other states as well. Mormons reported feeling threatened by the antibigamy laws in Georgia and feared restrictions against the preaching of Mormonism itself.[29] A North Carolina newspaper lauded the law in Mississippi, which provided for up to ten years in prison for convicted polygamists, as a model for stopping the spread of Mormonism.[30] Because Mormon missionaries and converts did not in fact contract plural marriages in the South, the bark of state antipolygamy laws was worse than their bite. For instance, when a local officer arrested two missionaries in Mississippi for preaching polygamy, the judge reduced the charge to vagrancy and simply threw the elders in jail for two days and nights.[31] Even without stringent enforcement, however, state antipolygamy provisions simultaneously revealed and reinforced a deep-seated southern antipathy toward Mormonism, with polygamy at the core of the conflict. They put the power of the state squarely behind the broad anti-Mormon sentiment of the people. Similar to the racial disfranchisement laws that would be written into southern state constitutions beginning in the 1890s, antipolygamy legislation targeted a particular minority group by employing language that marginalized them as being outside the bounds of acceptable citizenship. State lawmakers structured such discriminatory statutes so that they abridged minority rights without explicitly violating the Constitution. Although in the end the function of state-level antipolygamy legislation was more symbolic than punitive, the message was not lost on the Mormons, who felt the weight of not only the federal but also state governments acting against them.

Even if state legislatures had the power to impede polygamy's fortunes in the South, however, they could have little or no effect on the nerve center of Mormon power in Utah Territory, which the federal government administered. Acknowledging this political reality, many southerners agreed that the only answer to the Mormon question could and should come from lawmakers in Washington. The *Alabama Christian Advocate*, for instance, unabashedly proclaimed "the urgent duty of the general government to apply at once adequate remedies for the extirpation of Mormon polygamy."[32] Thousands of southerners signed petitions urging Congress to enact legislation that would result in the "immediate suppression" of polygamy.[33] None of these proposals acknowledged the clear irony of white southerners calling on the federal government to exercise its coercive power to dictate domestic arrangements contrary to prevailing local beliefs. Indeed, in 1877, the year commonly marked as the end of Reconstruction, a rural Mississippi newspaper expressed its hope that through federal intervention, "Utah will be Americanized, and politically and socially redeemed."[34] In speaking of the Mormon question in the West, some southerners thus inverted the political rhetoric of "redemption," which they typically applied to casting off the yoke of federal power and reinstituting local sovereignty.

The call for an active federal intervention against polygamy marked a significant departure from the earlier position of southern Democrats in particular. The logic of popular sovereignty had in antebellum times made common bedfellows of Mormons and southerners, who allied to oppose antipolygamy bills proposed by Republicans. Any expansion of federal power over domestic relations provided "an opening wedge into interference with slavery," as historian Sarah Gordon has observed. To southern Democrats, granting additional (and arguably unconstitutional) powers to the federal government "was far more dangerous than the practice of polygamy by Mormons in Utah."[35] Southern fears that the Republicans' "twin relics" rhetoric would result in concrete federal action against both polygamy and slavery proved to be well founded: only three months after the Morrill Anti-Bigamy Act passed in July 1862, Abraham Lincoln issued the preliminary emancipation proclamation.[36]

White southerners' commitment to states' rights survived at least a century beyond Appomattox, but their alliance with Mormons waned in the decade following the end of Reconstruction. Once the slavery question had been settled and the federal government's interference in southern race relations had been more or less neutralized, it became less advantageous for southerners to defend Mormon rights. Some, still smarting that the first of the twin relics had been "wiped out" by the Republicans, refused to join with the "Yankees" in their postbellum quest to complete the task.[37] By the early 1880s, however, many southerners not only went along with but also actively called for the political, social, cultural, and religious reconstruction of Utah, with local control sacrificed to a moral agenda imposed by outsiders and enforced by federal legislative and military authority.[38] The debate over the 1882 Edmunds Bill revealed a split opinion among southern representatives in Congress. The majority of southern Democrats voted against the bill, representing a large share of the minority opposition on the matter, but eighteen ultimately cast their lot with northern Republicans against polygamy.[39] Many southerners committed to a legislative solution of the Mormon problem celebrated the Edmunds Act, hoping that it would be "carried into effect with all possible energy." Optimistic, they were not naïve: they knew Mormons would resist and anticipated that "additional and prompt legislation" might be necessary to close any loopholes the polygamists inevitably found.[40] In some ways, this reliance on federal authority was an easy out. Because Mormonism was headquartered in a territory rather than a state, southerners could call on someone else to do the dirty work of disposing with Mormonism while still maintaining their commitment to states' rights. Nevertheless, southerners' call for an expanded federal role in local and domestic affairs marked a striking departure from the recent past.

Faced with the proposed antipolygamy legislation of the 1880s, many southern Democratic congressmen and senators struggled to reconcile the seemingly incompatible principles of fidelity to local rule and limited government on the one hand and opposition to polygamy on the other. A prominent example was Joseph Brown, a Democrat whose tenure as governor of Georgia from 1857 to 1865, chief justice of the state supreme court from 1865 to 1870, and U.S. senator from 1880 to 1891, established him as one of the most dominant figures in late nineteenth-century Georgia politics. Brown thundered against polygamy in a May 1884 speech to his colleagues in the Senate, denouncing it as "grossly immoral—in violation of the laws of God and man."[41] In so doing, he joined the cavalcade of leaders from around the country that decried the practice and called for its extinction. At the same time, however, Brown declared the Edmunds Act of 1882 "a palpable violation of the Constitution of the United States" that he considered "null and void." He specifically railed against the powers given by the act to military officers and appointed commissioners to prosecute suspected polygamists and deny them of the rights to vote and hold office. He considered these provisions a clear violation of the Fifth Amendment, especially its guarantees of due process and trial by jury. Drawing a clear parallel with the detested period of Congressional (or Radical) Reconstruction, he worried that the Republican-controlled Congress was governing the territories "by commissions of military men, or civilians, or satraps, or provisional governors in an arbitrary, tyrannical, or unconstitutional manner, violative of the very first principles of republican government."[42]

A proud southerner and only slightly reconstructed Confederate, Senator Brown opposed the draconian federal antipolygamy legislation of the 1880s from a distinctively sectional perspective. He claimed that polygamy was simply a subset of the broader national sin of adultery, which included prostitution, abortion ("foeticide"), and birth control ("the prevention of conception"). Although admitting that the southern states were not entirely chaste, he claimed the prevalence of adultery in all its forms was "five times as great in New England as it is in Utah."[43] Furthermore, Brown framed the increasingly harsh tactics approved by Congress to destroy plural marriage and punish Mormon offenders as a second Reconstruction initiated by New Englanders in a reprisal of their recurrent role as moral and political meddlers. To Brown, the timing of the anti-Mormon crusade was anything but coincidental. After federal troops marched out of the South following the Compromise of 1877, suddenly New England Republicans found themselves "out of a job, or unemployed in the regulation of other people's affairs." Imbued with a self-inflated sense of "mission" and "inspired calling," restive New Englanders looked around the country "for a proper subject for the exercise of their peculiar prerogative." When their eyes rested upon Mormonism, "they determined to regulate it" just as they had the affairs of the South. Convinced of the conspiracy he had uncovered, Brown took a stand, declaring, "I, for one, shall not be a party to the enactment or enforcement of unconstitutional, tyrannical, and oppressive legislation for the purpose of crushing the Mormons or any other sect for the gratification of New England or any other section." He urged his fellow southerners to remember their suffering at the hands of Thaddeus Stevens and his band of "restless regulators" and to resist becoming party to this new form of "fanaticism" born of New England Republicanism. It may be that the nation would go forward with its scheme to "regulate Mormonism outside of the Constitution," Brown conceded, "but why should Southern men become camp-followers in this crusade?"[44]

Another southern Democratic legislator, Representative John Randolph Tucker of Virginia, ultimately came to a different resolution of the tension between political and moral principle and the appropriateness of federal legislation to combat polygamy. Originally, Congressman Tucker echoed many of Brown's arguments from the Senate. During the debates preceding passage of the 1882 Edmunds Act, Tucker was one of the leading House Democrats who denounced polygamy but refused to support the proposed legislation. Tucker said he shared the legislation's broader goals, stating that society could only be "virtuous, prosperous, and happy" if built on the foundation of Christian monogamous marriage. He worried, however, that the Edmunds Bill's stringent antipolygamy mechanisms were unconstitutional on multiple grounds, watering down the right to a jury of one's peers, depriving citizens' civil and political rights without a fair trial, and regulating belief, not just action. Despite concurring with the spirit of the proposed law, he felt obliged to vote against a bill that he believed "makes a precedent of evil omen to the liberties of the people." Although as a southerner he could not in good conscience support the Edmunds Act, which sought "to eradicate one vice by an act of usurpation of power," Tucker publicly expressed his hope that "this great evil of Mormonism may be extirpated by some new measure without a violation of the Constitution or detriment to the Republic."[45] Tucker's speech represented sentiments shared by fellow southern Democrats who similarly opposed the 1882 bill and paralleled the arguments made by a number of Senate Democrats.[46] As historian Gaines Foster has shown, southern Democratic opposition to Senator Edmunds's antipolygamy bill represented a combination of traditional southern views on liberty and freedom, a commitment to constitutional guarantees of religious freedom, and a devotion to the philosophy of local control, which paralleled a concern that the electoral commission in Utah established by the law "might have served as precedent for intervention in southern elections to enforce black suffrage."[47]

Within a few years, though, Tucker reversed his position. In doing so, he was one of a substantial group of southerners who protested the coerciveness of federal legislation early in the 1880s but later in the decade came to concede the necessity of a strong national response to the Mormon threat. The Mormons' stubborn refusal to abandon plural marriage, and the pressing likelihood that Utah would become a state, prompted Congressman Tucker not only to change his vote but also to help lead the charge against polygamy. With Democrats controlling both Congress and the White House, 1887 seemed an unlikely moment for major antipolygamy legislation to pass. But Tucker, a staunch Presbyterian who asserted the centrality of Christian marriage to the health of the state, saw polygamy as a serious moral offense and thus a genuine danger to the union. As chairman of the House Judiciary Committee, he shepherded through a new bill which, when combined with Edmunds's latest bill in the Senate, resulted in the harshest, but most effective, antipolygamy (and anti-Mormon) legislation on record. In his January 12, 1887 speech immediately preceding a House vote on the bill—which Mormons claimed "the oily Tucker" railroaded through the Judiciary Committee without sufficient time or discussion—the Virginia senator animatedly based his legislative position on a biblical foundation, exclaiming, "They twain, they twain, they twain shall be one flesh . . . not they bundle." Tucker argued that the "rising generation" of Mormons increasingly distanced themselves from the doctrine of plural marriage, and that in fact his bill was in the best interest of the Mormons, as it would allow Utah to finally become a state.[48]

The Edmunds-Tucker Act, as it came to be known, finally gave federal courts and law enforcement officers sufficient power to induce the LDS Church to abandon polygamy, which it did three years after the law passed. The act required plural wives to testify against their husbands, finalized the disincorporation of the LDS Church (which was initiated with the 1862 Morrill Act), raised the penalties for polygamy to a fine of between $500 and $800 and imprisonment for up to five years, and confiscated all church properties valued at more than $50,000. Whereas the majority of southern Democrats had voted against the Edmunds Bill in 1882, five years later they solidly, though by no means unanimously, backed the legislation that gave more power and authority to the federal government than any previous marriage statute.[49] As the culmination of the national antipolygamy crusade, the Edmunds-Tucker Act illustrated how far southerners like John Randolph Tucker had come in joining their northern and Republican counterparts in supporting strong federal legislation regulating domestic affairs in Utah.

Some southerners believed that even federal statutory law was not enough to stamp out polygamy and that a constitutional amendment was necessary. Although the idea had been floated previously by southerners including Representative Tucker, the movement gained energy especially in reaction to three separate but related events around the turn of the century: Utah's admission into the Union as a state in 1896, which released it from direct federal supervision; the controversy over Utahans' election of Brigham H. Roberts, a practicing polygamist, to the U.S. House of Representatives in 1898; and the national debate over the seating of Reed Smoot, a monogamous Mormon apostle from Utah, elected to the U.S. Senate in 1902. The Smoot case was particularly alarming. Senate hearings on the question of his seating revealed that the LDS Church continued to countenance some plural marriages even after the church's 1890 declaration that supposedly had ended the practice.[50] Reviewing their efforts in the antipolygamy crusade over the past decades, many southerners became disenchanted with the string of federal laws dating back to the 1860s that apparently curtailed polygamy in only superficial fashion. Along with other reformers around the country, they began to call for an amendment to the Constitution that would bring marriage and divorce law under federal jurisdiction. A number of southern religious writers took up the cause, as did a formal resolution by the General Conference of the Methodist Episcopal Church in 1912.[51] While the movement never gained the kind of momentum that Prohibition did at the same time, it reflected a Progressive tendency among certain southerners, most often churchgoers, which militated against the traditional states' rights standpoint. The proposed antipolygamy amendment demonstrated their willingness to extend the regulatory power of the national government over an area that traditionally had been the exclusive purview of the states, all in the name of guaranteeing a moral social order.

THREE APPROACHES

The debate among southerners about the best way to handle the Mormon menace reflected more than just tactical disagreements. In some ways, it represented fundamentally different outlooks on society and the acceptable roles and practical limits of government. Those who advocated violent mob action against Mormon missionaries typically were not sociopaths acting out of irrational rage. Instead, extralegal violence provided an effective means of protecting communities in circumstances when citizens perceived that government was either unable or unwilling to handle the imminent danger. This orientation was not necessarily anti-government but emphasized government's limitations, whether at a local, state, or national level, and maintained that individual citizens should assume primary responsibility for the preservation of their communities. Applied to the Mormon question, violent assaults on Mormon missionaries became an increasingly distinctive southern practice in the years after the Civil War, whereas anti-Mormon violence had been characteristic of virtually every northern locale of Mormon settlement during the antebellum period.

Theological conservatives offered a nonviolent alternative. They remained deeply skeptical about the ability of human beings to improve their society or create a just social order without the basic foundations of true religion—which in the late nineteenth-century South meant evangelical Protestantism. They were equally, if not more, dubious than vigilantes about the ability of the state to effect genuine reform for righteousness' sake. Virtually all social evils had spiritual roots, so spiritual remedies provided the most effective solutions. Violence was counterproductive and (usually) un-Christian; legislating was an insufficient and often misguided approach. Only the divine power of the pure gospel could save individuals and redeem society from evils as base as polygamy.

Alternatively, the law-and-order advocates who emphasized a legislative solution to polygamy were part of the vanguard of the modern American state. Churches had been the primary arbiters of community morality in the antebellum South, but many southerners recognized that model as insufficient in a modernizing society. They reflected a Progressive-era mentality that diagnosed social ills on a structural and not simply an individual level, and therefore recommended solutions that inevitably involved action by the government and not simply private citizens or churches. They argued that the complexities of modern life required a more expansive modern state with increased powers that would have been unthinkable to previous generations. Naturally, supporters of an expanded civil administration had sharp arguments among themselves about the proper nature and extent of government involvement and regulation, but they agreed that the government had an important role in the social sphere and believed that it could be a positive force for change. Many of these people, like Congressman Tucker, were personally religious and even theologically conservative, but they believed that some social problems, such as Mormon polygamy, were too deeply entrenched for the churches alone to address.[52]

These distinctive approaches illustrated the intricate dance between religion and politics in the postbellum South. Antebellum southern Protestants had resisted any explicit fusion of church and state, particularly in reaction to what they saw as the offensive moral crusading of abolitionists and the emergent Republican Party; most southern white churches, for instance, considered slavery a civil and not a religious issue. During Reconstruction, northern evangelicals again took the lead in working through federal and state governments to pass a wide range of societal reforms, many of which targeted the vanquished South. White southern Protestants often railed against this unholy mixture of politics and religion, but the Civil War and the creation of Confederate nationalism blurred many of the distinctions between the causes of God and country. Postbellum southern evangelicals increasingly leaned on religion to justify their political commitments, and depended on the power of the state to legislate on "moral" issues that were mediated in the public sphere, such as Sabbath observance, gambling, temperance, and of course polygamy. This subtle but important shift occurred gradually, with many southern congregations remaining apolitical well into the twentieth century, but white southern Protestants had certainly begun to re-conceptualize the dynamic between religion and the public sphere.[53]

An example of the vague and often shifting boundary between religion and politics in the late nineteenth century South came from the front page of an issue of Atlanta's *Christian Index*, the most prominent Baptist newspaper in the postbellum South. An article entitled "Political Preaching" decried those ministers who "seem to have an ungovernable hankering to mix a strong decoction of politics with their pulpit effusions." Northern Methodists, the author claimed, "are proverbially addicted to this questionable amusement," but it must be admitted that even southern preachers can engage in "this politico-moral mosaic work." The article asserted that "the right or wrong of political parties has nothing in the world to do with religion," and that "the preacher's duty is to minister to the spiritual wants of his flock," nothing more nor less. Perhaps the editor did not see the irony, but his vehement condemnation of combining religion with politics was situated next to an editorial denouncing the role of whiskey in politics and a large picture of a newly dedicated Confederate monument in Augusta,

Georgia.[54] Just a few months later, the same newspaper proclaimed, "The Index takes no part in politics. . . . Whatever our opinions may be on political subjects, they shall never appear in the columns of this journal." Only a few paragraphs passed, however, before the editor asserted that "the time has come, when the Christian people of this country ought to make themselves felt *as such*, in all our elections."[55]

From a staunchly secularist perspective, the *Christian Index*'s position seems highly contradictory, proclaiming its principled independence from politics while editorializing on whiskey, celebrating Confederate nationalism, and encouraging Christians not just to vote but to take their religion to the polls. But the *Christian Index* was not operating in a staunchly secularist context. It operated under the assumption of an avowedly Christian society with Christian values, in which the churches had a public role as guardians of morality, just as mothers operated as moral guardians within the private sphere. The *Richmond Christian Advocate* approvingly reported that Georgia, as just one example, was "a Methodist Commonwealth," and that the "Methodist Church is a great social and moral factor in that State."[56] Even more tellingly, the *Raleigh News and Observer*, a putatively secular paper, unabashedly proclaimed, "This is a Christian community and a Christian country." The South was no theocracy, the paper qualified, but its laws were substantially Christian, and "probably they in no instance conflict with the teachings of the Saviour." A Christian society had particular responsibilities in enforcing Christian morality, and therefore, the paper argued, "We should tolerate no practice at variance with the universal custom of the Christian church or repugnant to the enlightened sentiment of Christianity."[57]

Few practices were more at variance with Christian tradition, or more repugnant to Christian sentiment, than polygamy. Because southern Protestants saw polygamy as fundamentally anti-Christian, and because southern society was fundamentally Christian, southerners had a compelling interest in eliminating polygamy along with those who actively promoted it. Like a cancer, polygamy had to be removed or it would overtake the entire social organism. Southerners might agree on the end—a society built upon the lasting foundation of the Christian home and in which Christian men protected the innocent virtue of their women and children—but not on the means, thus precipitating the debate between the relative merits of violence, evangelization, and legislation. It might be by force, by the gospel, or by law, but ultimately, southerners believed, polygamy must be rooted out and Mormonism vanquished.

THE LIMITS OF RELIGIOUS FREEDOM

For many southerners, the Mormon question raised the vexing dilemma of how to stamp out polygamy without violating the Constitution. Senator Brown and Representative Tucker each expressed reservations over the Edmunds Act's enforcement mechanisms that they believed violated the Fifth Amendment. Equally at stake was the First Amendment's protection of religious freedom, which was among the most hallowed articles of faith for virtually all Americans. All three approaches to eliminating polygamy had the potential to infringe on religious freedom, but southerners committed to a legislative approach were among the most self-reflective about the quandary. Brown reminded his Senate colleagues that the Constitution "guarantees to every citizen of the United States the free exercise of his religion, whether he be a Christian, Turk, Hindoo, or Mormon." Because the First Amendment ensured that the government could not punish any citizen for their religious belief, Brown asserted, it was unconstitutional to confiscate the property or restrict the political liberties of any Mormon who professed belief in polygamy but did not practice it, as he believed the 1880s legislation did. To prosecute unpopular beliefs set a dangerous precedent in which any minority religious group, "whether the Baptists, or the Catholics, or the Quakers," could be "selected for the next victim." Nevertheless, Brown supported the distinction between belief and practice as outlined by the Supreme Court in the *Reynolds* case, and asserted that constitutional free exercise "does not authorize the practice of gross immorality under the cloak or in the name of religion."[58]

Some southerners interpreted Senator Brown's speeches as being too soft on Mormonism.[59] There were a few whose application of the First Amendment was not so capacious as to include Mormons at all, such as those in a North Carolina mob who whipped Elder Joseph Parry while saying they "did not care for the law or constitutional liberty."[60] Most southerners, however, found themselves in agreement with the basic belief-action distinction outlined by Brown and established by the Supreme Court, which outlawed polygamy in practice but protected Mormons' right to hold it as a theological (and purely theoretical) doctrine. The *Chattanooga Times* argued that so long as Mormon elders broke no law, respected other citizens' rights, and did not promote polygamy, they should be free to teach their doctrine without the interference of "ignorant bigots," and that attacks against them were "un-American and cowardly."[61] The *Raleigh News and Observer* used its defense of religious liberty to repudiate the standard Mormon argument that to prohibit polygamy was to abridge liberty of conscience:

> A Mormon has a right to believe what he will. His thought may be as free as the unconfined air, and his conscience should by no means be restrained by legal enactments. But his acts are quite a different thing. He may believe, but he must not act. A Guiteau may believe it his religious duty to murder a President; he may think about it, if he will. But the first time he does an act in that direction he makes himself amenable to the law. The law can deal with acts, and not with thoughts, beliefs or matters of conscience.[62]

Law was thus concerned with outward acts so as to maintain social order, but the First Amendment, as interpreted by the Supreme Court in the *Reynolds* case, guaranteed that in America all citizens would have the right to fill their heads with whatever ideas they pleased, no matter how scandalous. Most southerners agreed that even the doctrine of plural marriage, however reprehensible, was protected by the Constitution, so long as it remained an abstract ideal.

Difficulties arose, however, when heterodox beliefs transformed into transgressive practices. As the *St. Louis Christian Advocate* noted, in a nation dedicated to religious liberty, "the diseased conscience is equally free with the healthy one." In a market of beliefs, with individuals exercising their unimpeded freedom, "it is reasonable to suppose that many will choose the wrong," which meant that "the disease in the conscience" became embodied in social "evil."[63] In such a case, when offending religious practices clearly opposed the laws that guaranteed order and general morality, government was authorized—indeed, mandated—to step in and restrict unacceptable behavior. This is why polygamy, which southerners readily admitted was a central tenet of the Mormon faith, could still be prohibited and suppressed by the government. As the *Yorkville Enquirer* stated, "It is true the Constitution permits the greatest religious tolerance; but it must be remembered that certain rites of the Mormon faith are repugnant to the Constitution and laws of the land."[64] Or as the *Alabama Baptist* reasoned, "Liberty, whether civil or religious, is not lawlessness; and on the other hand, checks against license and penalties against evil doing are not tyranny."[65]

Implicit in this argument separating freedom from license were two assumptions: first, that societies (whether local communities or nations) were built upon a shared sense of moral values that provided the common foundation for their law and ethics; and second, that those values were tacitly determined and agreed upon by the majority of the citizens in a kind of social contract. Added to these republican sensibilities in the late nineteenth-century South was a reliance on natural law that qualified the autonomy of popular will with the belief that God had decreed certain acts right or wrong. Humans were not justified in violating God's law even if they unanimously consented to do so; the fact that Mormons and Muslims believed in polygamy did not make it a morally acceptable practice even in Utah or the Ottoman Empire. Southerners' strong preference for localism over federal control should not be mistaken for radical individualism or libertarianism. Rather than seeking to be free of communal norms, they asserted their right to live according to their own shared values as opposed to outsiders imposing foreign values onto their righteous society. Freedom was to be exercised within communally approved boundaries—to go outside those boundaries threatened social order, and to maintain the boundaries maximized freedom for the whole. Allowing an individual or a group to follow their own con-science in transgressing established boundaries made every person a law unto themselves and destroyed the moral and political bonds that held society together.

Southerners disagreed over whether or not Mormon missionaries could legally preach the doctrine of plural marriage in their proselytizing throughout the South. Some defended the elders' right to teach any prin-ciple they wished in accordance with constitutional guarantees of free exercise and free expression. As a Meridian, Mississippi, newspaper argued, "This is a country of religious liberty. . . . As long as the Mormons go forth to preach their peculiar religious tenets and obey the local law they have full right to teach their tenets, even their abhorrent doctrine of duality or plurality of wives."[66] Others sought to restrict that right, essentially arguing that when Mormon elders preached polygamy, they did so with the intent of seeking new recruits for the illegal practice, which amounted to incite-ment to commit crime. This logic led the Tennessee General Assembly to pass its 1885 bill designed "to suppress the teaching," and not just practice, of polygamy.[67]

For many southerners, the decision to limit the Latter-day Saints' free-doms originated in their belief that Mormonism was not, in fact, a legitimate religion. The basis of perceived Mormon illegitimacy fell into two categories: Mormonism as a false religion, and Mormonism as no religion at all. Those Christians who believed Mormonism was simply a passing superstition were often content to let it go the way of other historical heresies. As the editor of the *Christian Index* confidently affirmed, "It is a fair contest between truth and error, and we are not uneasy as to the final result."[68] Many other south-erners were not so patient, perceiving Mormonism as a wolf in sheep's clothing that must be exposed and exterminated immediately. The *Alabama Baptist*, which characterized Mormonism as "the most repulsive of false reli-gions," typically took this more alarmist position, exclaiming, "It is lamen-table to know that these poisonous, God-defying, self-assumed Saints, imposters and blasphemers, are tolerated in this community!"[69] A few years later, the periodical was even more direct, decreeing, "It is Mormonism itself that is to be hated, to be feared, to be crushed."[70]

Yet, at other points the writers at the *Alabama Baptist* denied Mormonism the dignity even of being labeled a false or corrupt religion, and they casti-gated it as a lustful and criminal enterprise simply "set up under the garb of religion."[71] One writer for the *Atlanta Constitution* wrote that Mormonism "sprung up as the invention of a crafty worker in the credulity of the human race," and existed solely to give the "cloak" of legitimacy to vice.[72] Nineteenth-century writers often employed scare quotes to set off Mormonism as some-thing other than legitimate worship, as in references to "the vileness and villainies of Brigham Young's 'religion'" or a complaint "that the Mormon body should be called a 'Church' is revolting, in view of its leading characteristics."[73] The ever-hostile *Yorkville Enquirer* put the matter most bluntly, proclaiming that Mormonism "cannot properly be denominated a religion."[74] A Butler County, Tennessee, judge translated this logic into his application of the tax code. When missionaries protested court orders to pay a poll tax because "preachers of the gospel" enjoyed tax-exempt status, the judge stated "that he would not recognize a Mormon elder as a preacher."[75]

The question of whether or not Mormonism constituted a genuine religion was thus much more than an academic or polemical argument for southerners. If they considered it a legitimate, though false, religion—along the lines of Roman Catholicism—then it and its members were guaranteed all the freedoms and benefits that other religions enjoyed under the First Amendment. If, however, Mormonism was an illicit scheme using religious forms and rhetoric as a cover for the accomplishment of darker, more sensual aims, then it was promised none of the constitutional protections of free exercise and instead deserved to be prosecuted as criminal and fraudulent. This line of reasoning was ultimately endorsed by the *Yorkville Enquirer*, which called for the annihilation of Mormonism on the grounds that it had forfeited all claims to religious liberty: "All religions are guaranteed by the Constitution, but whenever any system goes beyond common morality, it ceases to be a religion, and should be unceremoniously stopped."[76] One did not need to deal with the complicated question of how far religious freedom should go if, in fact, it was determined that religious freedom should not be extended at all.

Polygamy thus revealed the form, and to some degree extent, of southerners' commitment to religious freedom. Mormons, of course, argued that in denying their right to practice a fundamental requirement of their religion the rest of the nation had betrayed the spirit and letter of the First Amendment's free exercise clause. But most southerners, like the Supreme Court, separated religious belief from action; they genuinely defended the unlimited rights of the former, while making qualifications about the limits of the latter. The religious tolerance associated with free exercise did not dictate blanket acceptance, and southern Protestant critiques of Mormonism (and vice versa) were simply an indication of two rivals posturing within a competitive religious marketplace. When they admitted Mormonism's right to exist, however fraudulent they believed it to be, while ferociously attacking the Mormon practice of plural marriage, postbellum southerners acted in harmony with contemporary jurisprudence as established in the 1879 *Reynolds* case. They were on shakier constitutional and moral ground when state legislatures passed laws against the preaching of polygamy, or when mobs attacked missionaries whose personal behavior was beyond reproach and whose message contained nary a word of plural marriage. But even these situations had their own logic, with the reasoning that Mormonism was fundamentally an illicit, anti-Christian, and depraved scheme that entrapped virtuous women in polygamous harems. As such, Mormonism forfeited its claim to constitutional protections, and Mormon elders were agents of organized crime rather than ministers of the gospel. Throughout the second half of the nineteenth century, both critics and believers insepa-rably connected Mormonism with plural marriage. This meant, in the south-ern mind as well as the halls of Congress, statehouses, and courts, that institutional Mormonism was inherently criminal, and its voluntary adher-ents therefore deserved no more constitutional rights for their immoral and unlawful enterprise than did a horse thief or a rapist. Polygamy thus defined the limits of First Amendment free exercise rights even as it denied its prac-titioners the ability to claim those rights.

THE PARADOX OF SOUTHERN ANTIPOLYGAMY

Anti-Mormonism became a nexus in post-Reconstruction efforts to reunite the American republic, bringing together southerners with northerners, states with the federal government, Democrats with Republicans, and clergy and lay members of various Protestant denominations. The movement per-meated all levels of society, involving the White House, Congress, Supreme Court, state legislatures and courts, local law enforcement, ministers and churchwomen, and ordinary people participating in citizens' meetings or mobs. Indeed, the "Mormon Question" was a major topic of national discus-sion in the late 1870s and 1880s. Southerners actively participated in this conversation; many if not most came to support federal antipolygamy efforts and worked to erase the stain of polygamy nationally as well as in their own locales. In so doing, they joined a reform movement that only a few years earlier they had condemned as violating the cherished American traditions of religious freedom, popular sovereignty, and local rule. By the 1880s, south-erners, who previously would be hard pressed to say anything positive about the federal executive, had so warmed to the White House's leadership in what historian Sarah Barringer Gordon has dubbed "a second 'Reconstruc-tion' in the West" that they heartily endorsed the antipolygamy platform of not only Democrat Grover Cleveland, but also Republican presidents Hayes, Garfield, and Arthur.[77] Anti-Mormonism thus served to subsume regional and partisan identities by uniting southern Democrats with their erstwhile northern Republican foes in a common religious and national cause.

For an institution that never existed in the South, Mormon polygamy was remarkable in the passionate reactions it evoked from southerners and the ways in which it highlighted key elements of postbellum southern culture. In an era and a region obsessed with the virtue of womanhood, the purity of the home, and the Christian nurture of children, polygamy served as a clear example of what could happen if postbellum southerners abandoned any of their domestic responsibilities. The degradation of Mormon womanhood offered a stark contrast with the exalted status of the southern woman, and no effort—by husbands, fathers, brothers, churches, or the state—was too great to prevent lecherous Mormon missionaries from destroying the peace and morality of the Christian home. Even for poor, rural, or unchurched southerners whose homes did not conform exactly to the Victorian ideal, the duty of men to safeguard southern women was of ultimate concern in defining their own sense of honor. Furthermore, when southerners looked at Utah and viewed a distinct Mormon civilization based, in their collective mind, on polygamy, it provided a clear counterpoint to their own society founded on democratic and Christian ideals. Indeed, the antipolygamy crusade of the late 1870s and 1880s revealed the deeply Christian—and specifically evangelical Protestant—nature of the southern world. Southern churches may have stayed out of politics in a formal sense, but their overwhelming influence over virtually all elements of southern culture was unmistakable, and they unabashedly considered their hegemony to be a sign of their divine call to establish God's kingdom on earth.

A strong sense of localism had always imbued southerners' political thought, and their recent experiences in the Civil War and Reconstruction left most southerners bitter toward an activist federal government. Some sympathized with the Mormon plight, in an abstract or political if not moral sense, since they understood what it meant for the government, dominated by ideologues from a distant region, to extend its powerful arm into the private affairs of a proud people. The shared principles of popular sovereignty, local government, and states' rights made southerners and Mormons natural ideological and pragmatic allies against New England Republicans and their moral crusades. Historians have noted how the specter of race in this period erased class distinctions among white southerners and inspired many poor whites to act against their own economic interests in uniting with the Democratic planter elite to defeat interracial populism.[78] Similarly, southerners' horror with polygamy outweighed all other concerns, leading the majority among them to ally with northern reformers and Republicans in Washington in the national effort to stamp out polygamy and thus eradicate the second of barbarism's twin relics. Whereas white southerners had decried the imposition of federal power in their own local affairs only a few years earlier, by the mid-1880s most had come to embrace judicial activism and coercive federal measures against Mormons and their peculiar marital institution. Opponents of the first Reconstruction, white southerners now became agents and supporters of a second.

6

The Mormon Monster

Political and Religious Aspects of Southern Anti-Mormonism

"There are several plague spots upon our national body politic," wrote prominent Nashville Baptist newspaper editor Edgar E. Folk in 1900, "but one of the most terrible of the plague spots is what is known as Mormonism." Folk pulled no punches in launching his diatribe, entitled *The Mormon Monster*, which at nearly three hundred pages of text became one of the most substantial single works of anti-Mormon literature produced in the South. Mormonism, he continued, "is a travesty upon the name of religion, a stench in the nostrils of decency, a constantly running sore, an immense octopus reaching out its slimy tentacles and seeking to seize hold upon our religious, social and political institutions, an ugly and misshapen monster."[1]

Born in 1856 in Haywood County, Tennessee, Folk graduated from Wake Forest College and Southern Baptist Theological Seminary. In his early thirties, Folk assumed the editorship of the *Baptist and Reflector*, the major Baptist newspaper in Tennessee, a position he held for nearly three decades, from 1888 to 1917. From 1912 to 1914 he was president of the Tennessee Baptist Convention. In short, few men had greater influence over Baptist affairs and public opinion in late nineteenth- and early twentieth-century Tennessee than did Edgar Folk.[2] The forces of southern, and national, anti-Mormonism thus found a powerful ally when, in response to the election of LDS polygamist B. H. Roberts to the House of Representatives in 1898, Folk turned his attention westward to combat the evils of Mormonism. The Roberts case brought Mormonism back into the national spotlight and convinced many, including Folk, that the perceived Mormon capitulation to the federal legislation of the 1880s had only been a ruse, a clever trick played on the nation by scheming Mormon hierarchs who had sought—and achieved—the legitimacy and protections of statehood. Roberts's election revealed Mormonism for what it really was, a kind of fifth column that sought to undermine the Christian republic from within. Edgar Folk was one of many editors, clergymen, politicians, and reformers who were alarmed by the prospects of Mormonism's resurgence and who sprung into action at the turn of the century to defeat this resurrected leviathan. After taking a trip to Utah to assess the situation for himself, Folk returned to Nashville where he composed his expansive exposé, printing much of it serially in the *Baptist and Reflector* before publishing it as a book with a Chicago-based house that expedited nationwide distribution of his findings.

Folk recruited his friend George Lofton, who as chairman of the board of the Tennessee Baptist Convention had helped author an alarmist 1898 report about the advance of Mormonism in Tennessee, to write the introduction to *The Mormon Monster*.[3] Lofton penned an intense critique of Mormonism that articulated many of the deep suspicions and antipathies of the evangelical Protestant establishment. He spared no opprobrium in describing the religion of the Latter-day Saints, calling it a "stupendous humbug . . . a moral and spiritual enormity . . . an abnormal development and horrible deformity . . . a fraudulent revelation. . . . It incarnates every unclean beast of lust, guile, falsehood, murder, despotism and spiritual wickedness." Mormonism was "like a great Python" that "trails its slimy length" across the country and world, and whose venomous bite exceeded "the deepest debauchery, superstition and despotism known to Paganism, Mohammedanism or Medieval Papacy." While claiming to teach restored Christianity as outlined in the Bible, in truth the Mormon gospel was built on the "chief cornerstone" of polygamy and worshipped a God of "anthropomorphic licentiousness" who rewarded those who embraced plural marriage with a "celestial harem." Not only was Mormonism "theologically rotten and spiritually sterile," but it also featured "a politico-ecclesiasticism headed by an anti-Christian priesthood . . . in league with hell against all personal liberty and civil government outside of itself and grounded in the polygamous degradation of the human race." Heresy and theocracy rooted in polygamy—this, according to Lofton, was "the great moral octopus" that already had Utah in its clutches and threatened to spread its tentacles across the remainder of the Union unless aggressively and effectively checked.[4]

In the main body of the book, Folk built on the themes introduced by Lofton. He outlined the eighty-year history of Mormonism, characterizing it as "a story from beginning to end of imposture, of fraud, of quarrelings, of rebellion, of bloodshed, of deception, of theft, of murder. . . . It is the most shameful, the most dreadful, the most infamous history of any people on the face of the globe." Folk's real focus in *The Mormon Monster*, however, was not history per se so much as theology and politics. He dedicated several chapters to examining the intricacies of the Mormon belief system, with lengthy quotes from LDS scriptures, prophetic statements, and other sources. Following the example of other anti-Mormon writers, Folk sought to condemn Mormonism with its own words, exposing its teachings not just as wildly imaginative and nonsensical but as anti-Christian and genuinely dangerous. While other nineteenth-century authors would sometimes attribute a kind of evil genius to Mormon founder Joseph Smith, Folk saw in the early American prophet nothing inventive or creative. Instead, Folk portrayed Smith as a degenerate and derivative con artist whose religious system simply "borrowed the worst features of all religions, and all creeds," then wove "them into a conglomerate but compact mass of incongruous absurdities." Mormonism, rather than being the authentic new religious tradition celebrated by modern scholars such as Jan Shipps and Rodney Stark, was a complete farce: "It was born in the womb of imposture, nursed in the lap of fraud, rocked in the cradle of deception, clothed in the garments of superstition, fed on the milk of ignorance, and fattened on the strong meat of sensualism, despotism, fanaticism, crime, bloodshed, and rebellion." At every turn Folk found the religion to be little more than "a deification of lust, a glorification of sensualism" that represented "a shame and disgrace and an insult to any Christian community that it should rear its slimy head in." In short, in its theology, rituals, and daily practice, Mormonism perverted and subverted true Bible religion; it was therefore "not only un-Christian, but anti-Christian" to the core.[5]

In Folk's estimation, Mormonism was not only "a travesty on the name of religion, a foul blot on the escutcheon of Christianity"; it was also "the octopus of our political life" and distinctly "un-American." Along with being a threat to monogamous homes and the Christian religion, it constituted a menace to American democratic political institutions. If polygamy was the cornerstone of Mormon faith, then theocracy was its "fundamental principle." Folk saw a clear comparison between the politics of Mormon Utah and Tammany Hall, where the poor and ignorant masses were mobilized to vote "at the dictation of their leaders." The political machine was designed to get out the vote, not for the purpose of extending the privileges of democracy, but rather to maintain a stranglehold on all the power in the community. Mormon political might was even more ominous than that of Boss Tweed's ring, since power was centralized not in corrupt Democratic Party bosses but in a tyrannical priesthood hierarchy led by a prophet that professed to be God's mouthpiece on earth. Unlike Protestants who championed the separation of church and state, "the Mormon priesthood claim the right of control politically as well as religiously." The Mormon theocracy allegedly exercised "absolute political despotism" over Utah as well as bordering states such as Idaho, Wyoming, and Arizona, and sought to spread its dominion throughout the West and ultimately the entire nation, resting at nothing until it placed "its foul hand even upon the White House." Its theocratic political values and ambitions naturally brought Mormonism directly "into conflict with republican institutions" and made the Mormon question a political as much as religious one. Folk concluded that all "good, intelligent, law-abiding Christian citizens" should be made aware of this looming presence on their western frontier and be prepared to resist its steady onslaught.[6]

The Mormon Monster is a paradigmatic example of how southern anti-Mormonism went beyond the antipolygamy crusade to develop a full-bodied critique of Mormonism as a religious and political menace. Indeed, while polygamy almost always lay at the heart of anti-Mormon polemics, in the South as in the rest of the nation, authors such as Edgar Folk also examined the other aspects of Mormonism that contradicted their own ideals. (For a sense of the Mormons' reaction to the work of Folk and other anti-Mormons, see figure 6.1.) LDS doctrine and politics inevitably became the secondary targets of anti-Mormon ire, and together with polygamy made up a kind of unholy trinity that threatened the very foundations of Christian society in America. Reverend Martin L. Oswalt, a contemporary of Folk's

Figure 6.1 Cartoon presented to Southern States Mission president Ben E. Rich by his associates in the mission office. Edgar Folk comes from Nashville with notes from two weeks among the Mormons in Utah, replenishing the stock of another anti-Mormon author also spreading "mud, filth, and indecency." The Mormon missionary stands on a solid foundation of "scripture and reason," while the anti-Mormons trample "things not wanted" such as apostles and prophets, gifts of the Spirit, and various other biblical injunctions. *Southern Star* vol. 2 (Chattanooga: Southern States Mission, 1900), 87. Courtesy of L. Tom Perry Special Collections, Harold B. Lee Library, Brigham Young University, Provo, Utah.

who was one of the leaders of the anti-Mormon campaign in Mississippi, captured the multilevel threat posed by Mormonism when he wrote, "The system that [Joseph Smith] instituted, and left to curse the human race, has given the United States more trouble than all the other religious systems therein, and has been the cause of shedding much innocent blood. It is a foul blot on the fair escutcheon of our nation, a disgrace to the civilization of the nineteenth century, and a stench in the nostrils of Almighty God."[7] Mormonism, according to critics such as Folk and Oswalt, was offensive to all Americans who loved their country, their true (Protestant) religion, or their democratic liberties, and its survival jeopardized the preservation of all those institutions.

Southerners drew from all these elements to construct a picture of Mormonism as an institution and ideology that was foreign and fundamentally offensive to their conception of the good society. Their rhetorical invectives against Mormon theology and politics played an important supporting role in their attacks—both verbal and physical—on the Mormon immorality, rooted in its embrace of polygamy, that threatened southern homes and families. These theological and political elements did not in themselves lead southerners to violent retaliations against LDS missionaries, but they provided additional evidence that helped justify behaviors that were primarily constructed as a defense against Mormon licentiousness. Demonstrating the dangerously heterodox nature of Mormonism on questions of theology and politics further marginalized the religion and its members to the point at which violence and coercive legislation against it became not only tolerated but mandated.

"ONE OF THE FOULEST SORES UPON THE BODY POLITIC"

Some twenty years prior to the scandal regarding B. H. Roberts's election to the U.S. House of Representatives, southerners had a foretaste of what Mormon representation in Washington would look like. From 1872 to 1882, Utah's territorial delegate to Congress was George Q. Cannon, who in the late nineteenth century was the LDS Church's chief political strategist and thus a major target for the national press. Cannon was called as an apostle following the 1857 murder of Parley Pratt and went on to become a close counselor to four successive presidents of the church. He was also a leading polygamist, with a tally of five wives and thirty-two children. Following the 1879 *Reynolds v. U.S.* decision, Cannon denounced the verdict and defiantly proclaimed that Mormons would continue to practice polygamy as zealously as ever and that "they would be poltroons and cravens indeed if they would yield those principles to the dictate of a Supreme Court." He likened the Saints to Galileo, who despite the "heavy hand of the law" remained true to his principles; Mormons too, despite all opposition, "would stamp on the ground and say, 'Still we do believe in polygamy.'"[8]

In the crises related to secession, war, and Reconstruction, southern whites had insisted that their resistance to federal heavy-handedness was the ultimate act of loyalty to the founding principles of the nation, that they were defending the true spirit of the Constitution when the rest of the country (especially New England Republicans) had abandoned it. But they did not interpret Cannon's—and by extension all of Mormonism's—intransigence as an equally noble act of resistance against the unjust imposition of federal authority on local values, certainly not in the grand southern tradition of doing so. The possibility that Mormons were animated by the same arguments of local sovereignty fell on deaf ears in the South, especially as the Mormon question became increasingly intractable in the late 1870s and 1880s. Whereas postbellum southerners lionized their secessionist forebears as true patriots, they demonized Mormon resistance to federal antipolygamy law as unpatriotic, unlawful, and ultimately treasonous. For their part, Mormons regularly asserted their love of nation and loyalty to the government. John Morgan maintained that his fellow Saints "love and revere and respect" the Constitution and the flag.[9] Others pointed to the Saints' service in the Mexican-American War, the "raising of the stars and stripes" upon entering the Salt Lake Valley (which was still Mexican territory) in 1847, and, at the end of the century, fighting in the nation's battles in the Philippines.[10] Such sentiments, however, rang hollow in the ears of most southerners. While some, such as Senator Joseph Brown of Georgia, admitted that "the Mormons are not in rebellion against the Government of the United States in any legal acceptation of that term," others insisted on the very real possibility that "the Mormons are in deed disloyal to the Government," and therefore "ought to be dealt with summarily."[11] Support for the 1887 Edmunds-Tucker Act was widespread not only because the law strengthened the ability of the federal government to prosecute and punish polygamy, but also because it targeted what newspapers had called "that treasonable organization—the Mormon Church," by disincorporating the church and seizing most of its significant property holdings.[12]

Southerners understood that politics stood next to polygamy in defining the dangerous character of Mormonism. They may not have grasped all the dynamic intricacies between the LDS Church and federal government that lasted for much of the second half of the nineteenth century, but they understood on a basic level that Mormon political power facilitated the preservation and expansion of polygamy. The possibility of Mormons gaining any significant traction in local or state politics within the South was virtually nonexistent, given their small numbers in the region. What southerners feared, however, was an augmented Mormon political presence in the national government. With increased access to and representation in Washington, Mormons would exercise greater influence over federal policy, which would in turn not only allow them to protect their own interests but also potentially push their agenda on the rest of the nation. Particularly in the 1880s, southerners thus joined with voices from around the country in exposing Mormonism as a political—as well as moral—threat to the nation and American civilization. The *Alabama Christian Advocate* denounced Mormonism as "a crime of great enormity, hostile to our form of government, in deadly conflict with modern civilization, and in the last degree destructive to morals."[13] This echoed the words of a Connecticut minister who labeled Mormonism "the greatest delusion of modern times, a strong centralized power, hostile ever to our government, and a still greater foe to our civilization."[14] Reverend Richard Hartley told the Fourth Baptist Congress that "No man can be loyal to his country and loyal to Mormonism," and from Santa Fe, New Mexico, a writer declared that "So utterly un-American is the Mormon theory, that *it* or the great Republic must sooner or later go to the wall."[15]

The political theory that critics saw as dangerously "un-American" was called "theodemocracy" by Mormons. Proclaiming their allegiance to God in all human affairs while also maintaining a sincere faith in American republicanism, early Mormons, under the direction of founding prophet Joseph Smith, sought to create a sociopolitical order that combined the virtues of government by God and by the people. Rather than seeing theocracy and democracy as being inherently incompatible, Smith and his followers viewed them as complementary; indeed, many argued that they were inseparable and one could not be fully enacted without the other, that *theos* and *demos* were in fact part of an organic system of government that permeated not only earthly but also heavenly realms. To this end, inasmuch as Mormons contributed something resembling a distinctive political theory, particularly in the period from their settlement in Nauvoo, Illinois, until the abandonment of plural marriage in 1890, it was most succinctly captured in Joseph Smith's 1844 presidential campaign platform: "I go emphatically, virtuously, and humanely, for a theodemocracy, where God and the people hold the power to conduct the affairs of men in righteousness."[16]

An Illinois mob assassinated Smith before he could flesh out what exactly he meant by theodemocracy, let alone how it would be applied in the United States, but nineteenth-century Mormons continued to hold fast to the ideal. Brigham Young, for example, declared that "a theocratic government . . . is a republican government, and differs but little in form from our National, State, and Territorial Governments." The main distinction, he pointed out, was that in a theodemocracy the citizens "will recognize the will and dictation of the Almighty."[17] Whereas Young had sought to show the harmony between theocracy and republicanism, his successor John Taylor admitted that there was "a little difference" between the church's principles of government and democratic principles. Explicitly repudiating the notion that popular sovereignty expressed divine will, he stated, "I do not believe that the voice of the people is the voice of God. . . . The proper mode of government is this—God first speaks, and then the people have their action."[18] Further statements reinforced the notion that in a theodemocracy, God spoke and the people obeyed. Wilford Woodruff, fourth president of the Church, affirmed that theodemocratic government relied on both "the voice of God and the sanction of the people," a notion echoing an earlier statement by Apostle George A. Smith when he proclaimed, "Our system should be Theo-Democracy,—the voice of the people consenting to the voice of God."[19]

What Mormons called theodemocracy, however, non-Mormons saw simply as an autocratic theocracy. The southern press characterized the Mormon political system as "a little feudal despotism," an "absolutism" under the leadership of a "political monarch" who exercised "priestly tyranny" over the people.[20] To ensure unanimous submission, church leaders squelched "independent thought and free speech." Church members submitted all questions to the prophet, "whose ruling is accepted as the word of God, and therefore final." This system purportedly resulted in the repression of any independent thought or reason within the community and in turn stifled individual freedom.[21] To its critics, therefore, Mormon theodemocracy was anything but democratic. Rather, it was "a practical union of church and State" that assaulted "two of the main props of the Republic": religious freedom and freedom at the polls.[22] Edgar Folk, in *The Mormon Monster*, asserted that Mormonism constituted "a menace to our political institutions," and that theocracy, which he saw as "a fundamental principle of the Mormon creed," was in direct "conflict with republican institutions."[23] The African American Methodist minister L. M. Hagood warned that while the nation was worrying itself with the potential invasion of Roman Catholic immigrants, it already faced "a system growing up in our midst that will be much worse, if that is possible, than the Romish idea," for "Mormonism clamps the political, religious, and moral rights of its people in its own fists." Reverend Hagood recommended that the government pay less attention to "priest-ridden Ireland" and more attention to "home corruption" and the "liberty-destroying system" that had already taken root in the American West.[24]

Southerners cited reports of tyranny in Utah to support their argument that Mormonism was in fact a theocratic despotism in direct contradiction with American liberty. (Mormons countered, to no avail, that the country's real theocrats were the Protestants, who had been "trying for a century to get

God into our national constitution."[25]) In explaining why ordinary Mormons did not revolt against the system or flee the territory, the *Alabama Christian Advocate* gave anecdotal evidence of the tyrannical grip of the priesthood. One man reportedly was afraid to admit his loss of faith in Mormonism for fear that the bishop would take his land and leave his family to starve. Another said he was forced to "live a lie all the time" and compelled to vote the Mormon ticket at elections. A third Mormon man who sold his property to a "Gentile" was excommunicated and "publicly denounced as an enemy to his people."[26] Such stories filtered throughout the South and sometimes contributed to threats of violence against LDS missionaries. In February 1889, West Virginia's Clear Creek Literary Society published a letter in the local newspaper addressed to the missionaries stationed in the area. The letter complained of the oppressive treatment experienced by southern converts to Mormonism who had gathered to the West:

> You have held them as exiles in a Western land. You have treated them as slaves of a bonded faith. You have squandered their property, reduced them to want and required of them tithes and high taxes. . . . You have compelled infants to kill their own mothers because they attempted to escape from your territory. You keep constantly on the road spies and detectives to prevent your dissatis-fied people from leaving and exposing your crimes.

Shortly after the letter was printed, a public notice, signed "Vigil Committee," was posted warning that if the missionaries did not leave the county within twenty-four hours the committee would "hang them to a tree." When a mob with blackened faces approached the elders, they took the notice seriously and fled the locale.[27]

The most infamous example of Mormon tyranny in the West was the 1857 Mountain Meadows Massacre, the tragic event in which Mormon settlers in southern Utah, along with some local Paiutes, slaughtered some 120 emigrants—men, women, and children—in cold blood.[28] Southerners believed the massacre provided a useful illustration of what Mormon authority really looked like when allowed to go unchecked. The *Biblical Recorder*, North Carolina's major Baptist periodical, informed its readers about the "reign of terror all over Utah—the most amazing crimes, secret assassinations, public murders—until the culmination of wickedness was reached in the Mountain Meadows' Massacre." Such crimes could only be laid on the doorstep of the LDS Church hierarchy, who, it was implied, exercised exclusive control over the Utah Territory's political and law enforcement institutions.[29] These accusations regularly reached the ears of missionaries. In a letter written just a few months before he was killed at Cane Creek, John Gibbs wrote his friend and fellow missionary Joseph Morrell that whenever he took questions from a crowd, "it is Polygamy first," but as soon as "they dry up on that subject," his audience would then "fly to the Mountain Meadows Massacre." Gibbs lamented that he had to deal with "the maximum of such business," leaving the remainder of his time for only "the minimum of the true principles of the Gospel."[30] Some southerners cited Mountain Meadows in their violent threats against missionaries in the South. John Morgan received an undated, unsigned, rambling note acerbically asking if the Mormons "have quitt Murdring Gentile Emigrants and Robing them," and warning that if Morgan did not leave the vicinity, he would be lynched.[31] In August 1899, over forty years after the massacre, a mob in Sweetwater, Tennessee, threw eggs and rocks at two missionaries. The crowd was incited in part by a man who reportedly had a sister killed at Mountain Meadows.[32] In short, the massacre became a convenient illustration for southerners who believed that the fruits of Mormon political power were not only undemocratic but potentially murderous.

With southerners holding such a dim view of Mormon political theory and practice, it was no wonder that they joined with others around the country to oppose Utah's repeated efforts to gain statehood. In the wake of Reconstruction, during which the South had been divided into military districts by congressional Republicans, few postbellum Americans appreciated the merits of independent statehood more than white southerners, who believed their strong doctrine of states' rights was not only a proper reading of the Constitution but a necessary means of preserving local liberties against the distant rule of a tyrannical government in Washington. Some southerners, particularly those in places like the mountains of South Carolina where hostility to federal authority was at its peak, remembered their own experience with Reconstruction and were "disposed to sympathize with the Mormons on account of the unfriendly course of the Government."[33]

Such sympathies with the Mormon plight became progressively less popular as the antipolygamy campaign wore on. Southerners keenly followed the developments relating to Utah statehood. They fully understood, as did the Mormons, the implications of a federally administered area gaining the constitutional protections of a state. At times their fears of Utah statehood bordered on the sensational, but for the most part southerners expressed legitimate concerns about the repercussions of Mormon political power operating independent of federal supervision. As always, polygamy and politics were intricately entwined in their minds. A Memphis newspaper warned that "should Utah be admitted and allowed to retain her present institutions, poligamy [sic] should be for ever established by law in the United States." Furthermore, the presence of Mormon polygamists in other territories such as Idaho and Arizona meant that they too would "claim admission upon the same footing."[34] Since marriage and divorce law remained the preserve of the states, some feared that federal antipolygamy legislation and Supreme

Court decisions would effectively be rendered null and void once Congress granted Utah its coveted statehood. The diabolical conspiracy extended even further: once plural marriages were legalized in the new state of Utah, by virtue of the "full faith and credit" clause of the Constitution other states would be bound to recognize those marriages as legitimate, thus opening the door for polygamy to spread unchecked throughout the nation. Even when Utah's 1887 petition for statehood to Congress included a newly written constitution that explicitly outlawed polygamy, southerners were convinced that the move, which in fact was orchestrated largely by non-Mormons empowered by the disfranchisement of Mormon political leaders in the wake of the Edmunds-Tucker Act, was "only a trick." With their own state, the Mormons could "manage to evade the antipolygamy clause in their Constitution, or find some way to make it of none effect." Utah's 1887 petition was a "Trojan horse," they reckoned, and southerners successfully extolled Congress to reject it.[35] Just as polygamy revealed the limits of southerners' conceptions of religious freedom, it also determined the boundaries of how far they were willing to extend the blessings and privileges of the sacred cow of states' rights.

Denying Utah statehood was only a single battle in the broader conflict. If the Latter-day Saints could not gain the shelter of statehood in Utah, then it was believed that they would scout out some other area in which they could practice polygamy and ideally have it legalized so as to promote its expansion to the rest of the nation. Throughout the 1870s and 1880s rumors swirled about the imminent exodus of the Saints from Utah. Just as they had earlier left New York, Ohio, Missouri, and Illinois seeking freedom to practice their religion, now many southerners thought they saw the signs of another mass Mormon emigration. An Atlanta newspaper detailed Brigham Young's intentions of taking his followers to the Sandwich Islands. The paper wryly added that "if he keeps moving on till he lands in Asia, his polygamic institution will be in its original and congenial atmosphere."[36] A few years later, Mormons were rumored to be secretly planning a "general exodus" to New Mexico Territory. They were allegedly buying up large tracts of land there and had "an army of friendly co-operators in Washington," to be paid from the revenues of selling their property in Utah, who would secure the admission of New Mexico as a state, at which point the Mormons would "establish themselves where they cannot be again molested by the Federal powers."[37] Another set of reports centered on "mysterious outgoings from Utah" that pointed to an impending Mormon emigration to northern Mexico, where the Saints could escape the reach of the U.S. government and set up a base for importing female converts and exporting elders to spread their polygamous faith.[38] These rumors all had a kernel of truth to them, although their conclusions were overly grand. Brigham Young and subsequent church presidents did send out missionaries throughout the intermountain West, the Sandwich Islands, and northern Mexico with the dual purpose of preaching the gospel and establishing Mormon settlements. Any notions of picking up and moving the entire church from its haven in the mountain valleys of Utah were fleeting at best, and the plan was always to maintain Salt Lake City as the hub and surround it with satellite colonies wherever they could reasonably be sustained. The Mexican colonies in particular did provide safe harbor for LDS men and families fleeing the federal antipolygamy raids in Utah in the 1880s, but a serious plan to relocate the entire church there never existed.[39]

Connected with fears of Mormons achieving statehood or moving to a location outside the purview of the U.S. government were anxieties over the burgeoning growth of the Mormon empire, in spite of—or perhaps partly because of—all efforts to stop it. A few accounts saw Mormonism in decline, citing the steady influx of non-Mormons into Utah, punitive federal policies, and the self-destructive tendencies of a false superstition as evidence for the religion's imminent demise.[40] Most southerners were not so sanguine, however. The *Alabama Christian Advocate* dismissed reports of Mormonism's slow death as "a vain hope," and the *Christian Index* asserted that the Mormons were "rapidly increasing despite the Edmunds bill."[41] At the turn of the century, an article in the *Atlanta Constitution* observed that "the Mormon church is growing faster today than ever before," spurred on and represented by an ever-expanding number of new settlements, churches, and missionaries.[42] The documented growth of Mormonism translated into fears of Mormon territorial and political expansion. Numerous observers asserted that "political conquest" had been central to Mormonism since its inception.[43] Anxieties regarding Mormon expansion often took on something of a conspiratorial note, as writers warned that it was the "settled policy of the Mormons to control Utah and the adjacent Territories, and from there to conquer the United States, and, subsequently, the whole world."[44]

Black southerners as well as whites registered such concerns. The *Southwestern Christian Advocate*, the main organ of African American Methodists in the South, captured the panicky mood of many southerners who saw Mormonism as a spreading cancer that threatened to engulf the entire country. The *Advocate* reported that Mormonism, which originated only five decades earlier with a mere six original members, now had increased "in number, power and resources until it has secured control of a vast and attractive area of country" larger than New England, New Jersey, and Maryland combined. Mormonism could not properly be labeled the "infamy of Utah," since it controlled "the balance of power in Wyoming, Idaho and Arizona with a rapid influx in Colorado." Mormon ranks were being "steadily replenished" as a result of missionary labors throughout the United States (including the southern states) and abroad. Given its size and strength, an army of 150,000 men would be needed "to wipe this blot off from our civilization." If earnest measures were not immediately taken, then Mormonism would prove to be "a sleeping volcano whose future eruptions will not only submerge the adjacent Territories, but will flow down into the States, and thus bring the happy families of the American people face to face with an institution more cruel than the Inquisition and more loathsome than the smallpox."[45] The message to all southerners was clear: Mormonism was on the march, and efforts to stem the tide of its advance had been hitherto unsuccessful. Unchecked, it would leave untold horrors in its wake, undermining Christian families and decimating American republican institutions.

Prevailing opinion in the South dictated that Mormonism and Americanism were so fundamentally and diametrically opposed that they could not coexist together in the same political entity, as one was based on submission to theocratic priesthood authority and the other on democratic rights and individual liberties. As Reverend Martin L. Oswalt, the prominent Mississippi anti-Mormon, declared: "As long as [Mormonism] holds to Joseph Smith as its lawgiver, and stands upon his revelations as its foundations, it is to be regarded as an enemy to our civilization."[46] Either the Mormon polygamous theocracy would continue spreading its tentacles out from its nerve center in Salt Lake City, or the American republic would destroy the vile organism before it did any more damage. It was nothing less than a clash of civilizations within the boundaries of the nation.

"THE WORST DELUSION THAT HAS EVER BEEN PRACTICED"

On a Sunday morning in early February 1877, a Mormon convert discovered a roughly spelled notice at the gate of his property in northeastern Alabama. The note, addressed to LDS missionary James Lisonbee, claimed to be written on behalf of "an outraged People." It characterized Lisonbee's faith as being "the most deadly Engine that could be plied against civil and Religious liberty and the most dangerous to our Republic." But Mormonism's assault on the American republic was not its worst transgression, according to the note's author. Even more offensive was how Mormonism perverted true religion. As "the worst Delusion that has ever been practiced on a civilised People," Mormonism drew local citizens away from the true fold of Christ, substituting the Spirit of God for "Belzebub," and thereby leading people to commit "the unpardonable Sin." Those who could be tempted by such a delusion were never sincere Christians, it is true—they were attracted to Mormonism precisely because they secretly harbored "Lascivious designs" or a "hope for gain"—but "this solem mockery" had spread too far, and "the time had come when it should be stoped." Elder Lisonbee and his "deluded followers" were given ten days to leave the area; "a failure to comply," the note warned, "will be sufficient to lay waste and Deluge this country in Blood." Lisonbee promptly left the county, traveling south to preach to some relatives.[47]

If polygamy and politics lay at the heart of Mormonism's threat to the nation and society, its false religious teachings represented the greatest danger to people's souls. Opposition to Mormonism's unique doctrines emerged simultaneously with the development of its distinctive theology. The official published history of the movement's early years is replete with accounts of hostility from preachers and believers from a wide variety of contemporary churches, as well as those with no obvious church affiliation who simply found the new faith's claims to be outlandish. Indeed, the opening sentence of the history, dictated by Joseph Smith to scribes, indicates that its primary purpose was to counter "the many reports which have been put in circulation by evil-disposed and designing persons" who sought to "militate" against the character of the church and impede its "progress in the world."[48] Mormons explained the persecution they consistently encountered in the first seventy years of their corporate existence as manifestations of Satan's opposition to God's true church; as Mormon firebrand Jedediah M. Grant said, "We look for mobs, and the very scum of hell to boil over. . . . We expect the rage of all hell to be aimed at us to overthrow us."[49] Some modern scholars have taken up this view albeit in more academic terms, arguing that "the popular hostility that Mormonism engendered was, from first to last, rooted in—if not confined to—*religious challenges to Christian orthodoxy*, and its American Protestant variety in particular." In assessing the sources of nineteenth-century anti-Mormon hostility, Terryl Givens concluded, "even when the theological dimensions of conflict are not decisive, they are inescapable and present a constant feature in anti-Mormon antagonisms."[50]

Comments, or even tomes, disparaging Mormon doctrines did not necessarily violate southerners' commitment to the nation's founding ideal of religious freedom, particularly in a nineteenth-century context. Indeed, scathing attacks on the beliefs and practices of other groups represented a common feature of the hypercompetitive nineteenth-century American religious marketplace, with some of the most strident remarks coming from the internecine squabbles among various Protestant denominations. Of course, those outside the emergent Protestant mainstream—such as Catholics, Jews, Swedenborgians, spiritualists, and Mormons—received particularly strong doses of vituperation, but they were participants as well as victims in the intramural melee for religious ascendance, often dishing out nearly as much as they received. Particularly in the South, deviance from the religious norm opened up a group to pointed criticism. Postbellum southern polemics against the Latter-day Saint religious system typically concentrated on four areas (other than polygamy and theocracy): inventorying the list of "corrupt" LDS doctrinal teachings; dismissing Mormonism as a false or illegitimate religion; tracing the patterns of LDS missionary activity and expressing alarm at the growth of the church; and denigrating the quality of converts attracted to Mormonism. Major anti-Mormon books, such as Edgar Folk's *The Mormon Monster*, Martin Oswalt's *Pen Pictures of Mormonism*, and J. C. Thomas's *The Mistakes of Mormon and of Mormons*, contained all of these elements, whereas shorter works or individual detractors might focus their critiques on just one area.

Southern whites who mobbed Mormon missionaries frequently cited the elders' false teachings as a justification for their attack, although when pressed they could rarely provide details for what, beyond polygamy, was objectionable about the Latter-day Saints' faith. Some of the citizens of Habersham County, Georgia, gave Elder Joseph Keeler and his companion a notice advising them "not to pollute the air with your false doctrine" or to tell "your big Mormon lies," or else they would not escape "with all the skin on your backs."[51] A mob in Lawrence County, Tennessee, complained that the missionaries were "preaching false doctrine; doctrines that were got up by Joe Smith, and doctrines that are contrary to the laws of the U.S."[52] A convert in Buncombe County, North Carolina, found a notice wrapped in a Baptist newspaper telling the elders to leave the county, "as the citizens didn't want their false doctrines." On the outside of the envelope was drawn a gallows with a man hanging from it.[53] Southern anti-Mormons frequently indicated their distaste for what they variously called "Joe Smith's doctrine," "false doctrine," "rotten doctrine," and "d—rotten doctrine," but few could actually articulate any specific heterodox LDS teachings other than the principle of plural marriage.[54] John Morgan in particular complained of the persecution that southerners heaped on his faith although they remained "ignorant in regard to the doctrines" preached by LDS missionaries. He particularly lamented the "uninformed" character of those in positions of authority—"Congressmen, governors, legislators, and others of distinction and character"—who then spoke out and legislated against the Saints despite being "totally ignorant in regard to our views."[55]

Other southerners, however, particularly leaders in the evangelical denominations, were better able to elucidate precisely what about Mormon doctrine they found offensive. Since the beginning of the movement, many of Mormonism's most vocal opponents were former converts who had become disaffected and left the fold for one reason or another. Reverend Martin Luther Oswalt was one of this group. A Mississippi native, Oswalt joined the LDS Church in 1879 and moved a year later to Manassa, Colorado, where many other southern converts had also gathered. He remained in Manassa for three years, during which time he experienced multiple disappointments, as neither the settlement nor his coreligionists lived up to the grand vision he had imagined. Upon returning to Mississippi and reuniting with former friends and family, he admitted he had been one of "the dupes of fanaticism" but now wanted to be restored to his former life, including membership in the local Baptist church. Oswalt entered the ministry in December 1893 and was ordained some two and a half years later, serving as pastor in churches in Noxabee Hill and Evergreen, Mississippi. When LDS missionaries appeared in his community in 1895, a "tumult arose," and Oswalt determined to "warn the people against this pernicious evil." He lectured widely around the state on "the evils of Mormonism," and in 1899 published his exposé, *Pen Pictures of Mormonism.*[56]

Like most other anti-Mormon polemical works, Oswalt's book described LDS doctrine, especially some of its more esoteric teachings, with the hope of inoculating the southern public against the dreaded spiritual disease. Oswalt and other authors frequently quoted directly from LDS scriptures and other authoritative sources, including statements by church leaders, to lend their analysis an aura of authority and objectivity; much of their evidence was in fact authentic, though Mormons would debate their interpretations and the context of the sources cited. When placed against the widely accepted norms of nineteenth-century evangelical Protestantism, Mormonism emerged in *Pen Pictures* as an unfamiliar and un-Christian religion. Oswalt claimed, for instance, that Mormonism essentially "discards the Bible," accepting it as a historical account of God's dealings with past peoples, but denying its "binding force to the people of this age of the world." Correspondingly, he said, "Mormons attempt to rob Christ of the honor, the power, and the glory so justly due his holy name, and confer it all upon the man, Joseph Smith." By allegedly undercutting the eternal authority of the Bible and replacing Jesus Christ with Joseph Smith as the center of their worship, Mormons rejected the central tenets of historic Christianity. As if rejecting Christ and the Bible were not enough, Oswalt documented a list of other corrupt doctrines, including a "low and degrading" portrait of God (referring to Mormonism's anthropomorphizing of deity and the corresponding deification of humans), the concept of "polytheism" (due to Mormon teachings that many gods exist in the cosmos and that humans can become gods), and statements by some nineteenth-century LDS leaders that God has multiple wives and that "Jesus Christ was a polygamist, and that Mary and Martha and Mary Magdalene were his wives" (never official church doctrine, but speculated upon and asserted in writing by multiple church leaders). After rehearsing this litany of heresies from traditional Christianity, Oswalt wondered "that Mormons even attempt to cling to Christ at all," for their religious system in fact "has no connection whatever with the Christian religion."[57]

Other anti-Mormon publications presented a similar list of evidence for Mormon infidelity. Two publications by Methodist ministers—the Reverend Wildman Murphy's *What the Mormons Teach* and the Reverent J. C. Thomas's *The Mistakes of Mormon and of Mormons*—provided an overview of some of Mormonism's more controversial teachings. Each quoted from LDS sources on topics such as the plurality of gods, "a female deity," polygamy and celestial marriage, baptism for the dead, conceptions of the Godhead, the apostasy of the Christian churches, the Adam-God theory, and so forth.[58] A Macon, Georgia, newspaper summarized a recently published book exposing the esoteric rites and ceremonies conducted in LDS temples, mocking the sacred rituals that Mormons consider to be the apogee of their faith.[59] The women's missionary organization of the Methodist Episcopal Church South published a pamphlet entitled *The Menace of Mormonism*, in which they ridiculed the Book of Mormon as absurd and the LDS Articles of Faith as deceptive. The plurality of gods and polygamy—as practiced by God, Jesus, and ordinary Mormons—also received their usual mention.[60] A Methodist newspaper reporting on a Sabbath service in the Tabernacle in Salt Lake City reported that "the name of Joseph Smith was mentioned perhaps fifty times in the sermon while the name of Jesus did not fall on our ear more than once."[61]

Edgar Folk's *The Mormon Monster* provided perhaps southern literature's most lyrical, if overwrought, remonstrance against Mormon theology. Building on the common argument that Joseph Smith simply conceived of Mormonism by borrowing disparate components from the available religious landscape and then reconfiguring them in a single system, Folk asserted that in the process Smith had managed to bring together the worst of ancient and modern heresies:

> The truth is that Mormonism is a combination, or rather a conglomeration, of the literalism of Campbellism, the materialism of Fetishism, the sensualism of the Phallic worship, or Venus worship, the polygamy of Mohammedanism, the polytheism of Grecian Mythology, the theocracy of Judaism, the priestcraft of Catholicism, the despotism of Jesuitism, the self-righteousness of Pharisaism, the transmigration of souls of Buddhism, the cruelty of the worship of Juggernaut, the superstition of Confucianism, the degradation of women of heathenism, the mystic rites of Masonry, the hypnotism of mesmerism, the fanaticism of Dervishism, the salvation by works of Socinianism, the sacerdotalism of High Church Episcopalianism, and the political organization of Tammany Hall.[62]

The remarkable thing about Mormonism, by Folk's account, was not that it was a deeply flawed, even corrupt, religious system—it obviously had plenty of company on that score. What set Mormonism apart was the way it "borrowed the worst features of all religions, and all creeds," and then wove them "into a conglomerate but compact mass of incongruous absurdities." This amalgamation was not accomplished accidentally nor was it an honest mistake. In direct contrast to Joseph Smith's self-portrayal as a sincere seeker of truth, Folk assigned the founder of the faith nothing but the most malign intentions. Mormonism grew not out of a desire to restore lost Christianity, or, as Mormon historian Marvin Hill has argued, as a "quest for refuge" from the vagaries of American pluralism. Rather, the religion was a deceit from the beginning. As Folk maintained, Mormonism was "a colossal fraud, a mammoth sham, a gigantic humbug, a huge farce, which would be comical if it were not so tragical in its results."[63]

Folk's litany of Mormonism's vices thus combined two related but distinct categories of criticism: first, that Mormonism taught false doctrine; second, that Mormonism was an inherently false or illegitimate religion. Though the first charge was serious, flawed doctrine was a matter of degree. A southern Baptist like Folk might alternately condemn Methodism, Masonry, mesmerism, "Mohameddanism," and Mormonism, but clearly there was an ascending hierarchy of abuses relative to each case. Other Christian churches might be misguided, but they were not fundamentally fraudulent; note that in Folk's catalog of Mormonism's collective heresies, he did not mention Methodists or Presbyterians (but did include Episcopalians and Campbellites). The second charge, of conscious deceit and evil intent, was far more serious. Its Protestant critics often suggested that Mormonism had demonic origins. Methodist publications referred to the religion as "diabolical," and called Joseph Smith the "prince of deceivers," a title reserved in Christian scripture for the devil. The Atlanta-based *Christian Index* dubbed Mormonism "a cunningly devised fable," and remarked that "Satan has seldom if ever invented a more ingeniously contrived system for the subversion of souls."[64]

One of the most common tropes employed by anti-Mormon authors in discounting the religion was comparing it to Islam, which served as the paradigm of illegitimate and false religion for many nineteenth-century Americans.[65] A Methodist newspaper made clear the contrast between acceptable and unacceptable heterodoxies when stating that Mormonism was more like Islam, which was a "false religion," than it was like Catholicism, which was "distorted, but true."[66] The superficial similarities between Islam and Mormonism, or between Joseph Smith and "Mahomet," were simply too numerous—and too juicy—for critics to ignore. New Orleans' *Southwestern Christian Advocate* elucidated the parallels between the two religions. Both faiths were "planted in the desert," accepted the leadership of "a false prophet and a polygamous priesthood," taught that salvation depended upon "obedience to the orders of the Church" (and used the sword to enforce it), and promised that "the crimes and cruelty of the saints" would be rewarded with "the glories of heaven."[67] Other writers pointed to the new scripture, or "false Bible," delivered by the founders of each faith.[68] Anti-Mormon author Jennie Fowler Willing took the parallel even further, claiming in the subtitle of her book that Mormonism was in fact "the Moham-medanism of the West." In her opening pages, she emphasized that both systems were polygamous, offered the assurance of "a sensual, material heaven" for faithful believers, and used violence to gain converts and extend their power, all in the quest for "universal domination."[69]

If Mormon domination in the South would not be achieved through vio-lence, it could be gained, southerners feared, through the more subtle means of evangelization. Particularly alarming was when they converted previously active Protestant churchgoers. For instance, in 1882 the *Raleigh News and Observer* reported that LDS missionaries had "captured" a local church, gain-ing fifteen converts in one fell swoop, and that dozens of others had been similarly entrapped: "Great numbers are flocking to them from the regions around and about the mountain, to receive and hear their doctrines."[70] Even anti-Mormon mobs were not immune to the elders' wiles. In 1887, the *Charles-ton News & Courier* related the remarkable story of how a band of fifteen vigilantes, "masked and armed to the teeth," surrounded a house in Rich-mond County, Georgia, where Elder Samuel Spencer was staying. The mis-sionary appeared at the door and confidently began to speak to the assembled mob. After only five minutes of preaching, the newspaper reported, "every member of the Kuklux band was converted to the Mormon religion," and they left in peace. The correspondent, "ashamed" that the area's defenders turned out to be "such a party of cowardly men," now feared that "the whole upper section of this country is one mass of Mormons."[71]

Protestant denominations, which already struggled particularly in rural areas to attract regular churchgoers, naturally felt threatened by an active missionary force that intensified religious competition and stole away not only potential converts but also current church members. In Tennessee, the state Baptist convention grew worried as it considered the aggressiveness of Mormon missionizing compared with the relative laxity of Baptists' own efforts. The convention's annual meetings regularly included reports about the number of LDS missionaries in the state and how many converts they had achieved during the previous year. For example, according to their count, the Mormons baptized over twelve hundred Tennesseans in 1894 and 1895. (Internal reporting in the LDS Southern States Mission showed a much more modest 215 baptisms during the same two-year period.) Particularly galling, and indicative of long-term problems, was the fact that in 1895, Mormons had placed twice as many missionaries in Tennessee than did the

Baptists, this in a state where thirty-five county seats, and over 150 towns and cities in general, had no established Baptist church. This lack of Baptist presence, in the heart of the so-called "Bible Belt," translated into "near a hundred thousand homes without a copy of God's word," and "thousands of families in Tennessee, into whose homes no minister or Christian man has ever gone with the word of life." Conditions were thus ripe for the LDS Church to send its "false preachers" to the state, flooding Bible-poor regions with Mormon tracts and organizing branches that attracted even some Baptists. It was not too late to reverse the trend, but enough damage had been done that it would "take twenty years to counteract the evil they have already wrought in this State." The situation apparently failed to improve, as the convention's board (chaired by George Lofton, who would write the introduction to *The Mormon Monster*) complained in 1898 that "no denomination in this State is . . . half so deeply bent on propagandism as is the Mormon." In one region Mormons had preached more sermons, made more visits, and erected more meetinghouses than all the other churches combined. In 1899, the year before Folk published his book—in which he warned that "They are coming to *your* home, if they have not already been there"—the state Baptist convention officially resolved to "view with alarm the zeal evinced by Mormon missionaries in propagating their monstrous doctrines under the specious guise of religion." To combat the invasion, Baptist missionaries would circulate anti-Mormon literature, and pastors around the state "shall warn the masses from the pulpit against this pernicious system."[72]

While bemoaning the apparently bounteous harvest that Mormon missionaries were reaping in their southern field of labor, educated and well-to-do southerners took some comfort, and even pleasure, in what they perceived to be the low quality of converts that Mormonism attracted. Newspapers around the region reported on the poverty and marginal status of Mormon converts. The most common adjective used to describe the Latter-day Saint convert was "ignorant"—or, as Tennessee Methodist minister J. C. Thomas elaborated, "ignorant, deluded, fanatical, and foolish."[73] The *Yorkville Enquirer* disdainfully reported that Mormons had "proselyted a good many ignorant people here," and that the missionaries succeeded by "deluding the ignorant."[74] The *Alabama Baptist* perpetuated the stereotype, arguing that the elders "preach their most damnable 'isms' to simple-minded people," many of whom, "in the simplicity of their hearts, are led astray." The missionaries avoided the towns and cities, "where people have access to books, schools, and newspapers." Instead, they deliberately chose to concentrate their work "in the rural districts, in the piney woods, where the people are poor and illiterate, and confiding in their natures, and are not suspicious."[75] A national publication noted how Mormons enjoyed particular success among the "mountain whites," the majority of whom could neither read nor write, and who were "like children in their religious belief . . . extremely superstitious."[76] A Macon, Georgia, newspaper was "sorry to learn" that in one town "a few respectable, good citizens have been blinded into an acceptance" of Mormonism, but it still maintained that "as a rule," Mormon converts came from "among the illiterate and weak-minded."[77] The *New York Times*, reporting on the expansion of Mormonism in the South, shared the same view, saying that "the work of the proselyters has, almost without exception, been done in the mountain districts and localities removed from the influence of the enlightenment of cities or towns." Eschewing the respectable and educated population of the South, the missionaries allegedly made "captives of the weak" and gathered "great crowds of ill-smelling, unwashed outcasts."[78]

Mormons acknowledged the relative poverty of their converts, although they interpreted it as more of a virtue than a vice. A year before he was killed, John Gibbs wrote his wife from Tennessee, saying he had learned a simple lesson in preaching the gospel: "Keep away from the rich," as "they have no time to talk about the principles of the Gospel." Instead, missionaries should "go to the poor like the Saviour of old." There, among the humbler folk of the South, missionaries could expect to "get a bed and something (such as it is) to eat and a chance to preach the Gospel to them."[79] Elder John Harper, who labored in Wilkes County, North Carolina, did just as Gibbs suggested, teaching people who were "in hard circumstances." The Saints "were very poor," Harper recorded in his diary, and the food they provided for the missionaries was also "very poor," though it represented a generous gift of "the very best they had."[80] An 1884 circular to all elders in the Southern States Mission from the mission leadership admitted that "the Saints who come from the South, as a rule, are poor," and explained that one reason that southern converts who emigrated to the West were sent to southern Colorado, rather than Utah, was because land prices were cheaper there.[81] John Morgan, president of the Southern States Mission in the early 1880s, gave the most charitable assessment of the socioeconomic standing of southern converts when he told a reporter that the majority of newly baptized members were "small farmers, neither extremely rich or extremely poor. Nearly all can read or write, and bear a good reputation in their neighborhood."[82] Morgan perhaps exaggerated the point when, a month later, he told a congregation assembled in the Salt Lake Tabernacle that the average convert in the South came from "the middle classes," though his embellishment did not match that of a missionary who wrote in 1879 that southerners' hostility toward Mormon missionaries came because they converted the region's "best citizens."[83]

While some people expressed concern that the downtrodden citizens of the South appeared to be particularly vulnerable to the Mormons' machinations, others interpreted it as yet another piece of evidence attesting to the depravity of the Mormon system. According to this logic, if an organization or ideology could be judged by the quality of the people it attracted, then Mormonism was a very low religion indeed. Conversions to Mormonism were always a matter of concern, but they could be more easily explained, and even stomached, by the region's educated elite if it was the poor and ignorant folk of the rural South who were swept away. Delusion spread most effectively among those without education and far from not only the centers of learning but also the reach of organized churches and regular ministers. In this vacuum of cultural and religious authority, the ministry of LDS missionaries seemed genuine and the doctrines of Mormonism went unchallenged. When southerners who "knew better" looked at the complete picture, however, what they saw was a religion that at best corrupted the true gospel and at worst was a product of satanic influence that resembled Islam more than Christianity. That missionaries avoided urban centers and almost exclusively targeted those on the margins of southern white society provided further testimony that Mormonism failed to present itself as a legitimate and respectable religion. All things considered, the Mormon religious system appeared to many southerners to be "the worst of all" the "religious fads, fancies, and monstrosities" birthed in the nineteenth century.[84]

THE LIMITS OF TOLERANCE

Southerners were not completely immune from acknowledging some of the positive qualities of the Saints. Indeed, one of the struggles of the anti-Mormon movement in general was reconciling their typical portrayal of Mormons' complete depravity with the well-known fact that Latter-day Saints almost singlehandedly had transformed the valleys of the Great Basin, previously uninhabited by whites, into fertile farmland and had built a productive society on what had been considered desolation. Reports praising the well-ordered society in Utah challenged popular assumptions about Mormon backwardness, ignorance, and idleness. The *Alabama Baptist*, otherwise not known for its kindnesses toward the Saints, admitted (in an article entitled "Falsest of Prophets" that referred to Joseph Smith as a "second Mahomet") that "their signal good qualities are patience, perseverance, courage, and industry," a list that would have made any nineteenth-century western settler proud.[85] Similarly, in an otherwise unflattering portrayal of the Mormon kingdom in the West, the *Atlanta Daily Sun* praised the "industry and enterprise" exhibited by the Saints, admitting they had rendered the American public a great service by furnishing a comfortable and well-supplied halfway point for overland emigrants.[86] The *Richmond Christian*

Advocate marveled at the acoustics and design of the tabernacle in Salt Lake City, acclaiming "the intelligence of the Mormon architects" and suggesting that perhaps this signal accomplishment "exalts them above all others."[87] Senator Joseph Brown of Georgia noted in a speech on the Senate floor, during the height of congressional antipolygamy sentiment, that Mormons "are industrious, laborious, people; they are a thrifty people. No beggars or tramps are found in the street." The children and wives in polygamous marriages were well cared for, and until non-Mormons came to settle "neither prostitutes nor houses of ill-fame were known to any extent in the Territory."[88]

In some ways, Mormonism represented the ultimate tragedy for nineteenth-century southerners committed to American ideals such as rugged individualism and progress as well as Victorian Protestant values including thrift, temperance, and industry. Viewed through one lens, Mormons represented the western pioneer or Victorian moralist par excellence. They had opened up a vast swath of the West to American colonization and had developed agricultural and irrigation techniques that would make settlement in those lands not only possible but even profitable. They built a frontier society dedicated not to material greed or survival of the fittest but to the worship of God, to hard work and industry, and to the communal good. They established governmental and legal structures that echoed nineteenth-century American constitutional democracy and even extended suffrage to women long before most other states and territories.

The tragedy in southern eyes was that, in almost Newtonian fashion, for every virtue that Mormons displayed, they exhibited an equal or greater vice. The unforgiveable sin of polygamy counteracted any moral integrity the Mormons may have otherwise possessed. Furthermore, the government that Mormons had established in Utah certainly looked like American democracy, with a constitution, three branches of government, elected representatives, and local and territorial courts bound to upholding the law. The catch, as southerners insisted, was that Mormon government preserved the forms of democracy while denying its essential ingredient: free elections as the expression of individual conscience. In popular democratic theory, the voice of the people was the voice of God (*vox populi vox Dei*), but in the Mormon theodemocracy, God spoke through the leaders of the LDS Church, and the people were expected to concur. "Free" elections consisted of choosing to vote for Brigham Young, or electing between two Mormon candidates, both vetted by the church hierarchy. Utah politics was in fact significantly more complicated than that, particularly in the 1870s and 1880s as the anti-Mormon Liberal Party increasingly gained power with the disenfranchisement and criminal prosecutions of polygamists. Nevertheless, the image of the Mormon theocrat, in stark opposition to the American democrat, pervaded southern (and national) discourse about Mormons well into the early twentieth century. Their brand of religious politics, peculiar even considering the nineteenth-century Protestant quasi-establishment, marginalized Mormons and negated the otherwise positive contributions they had made to the expansion of the United States and the development of the West.

A similar dynamic existed in the religious sphere. Mormonism was born in the religious hothouse of Jacksonian America and displayed many of the traits common to nineteenth-century evangelicalism. The gospel preached by Mormon elders in the South and elsewhere was based on biblical texts and focused on faith in Jesus Christ, repentance, baptism for the remission of sins, obedience and righteousness, and justification and sanctification by the Holy Spirit. The religion encouraged adherence to a behavioral code that—other than a celebration of music and dancing—would have been embraced by most morally conservative Protestants. Saloons and brothels were conspicuously absent from Mormon communities (until, as Senator Brown pointed out, introduced by non-Mormons). Nevertheless, as *The Mormon Monster* and other anti-Mormon literature claimed, although "before the deceived masses the Mormon appears fairly evangelical," and while he "spells and pronounces some words correctly and often uses the same words that we do," in fact, Mormonism had completely corrupted the use and meaning of the gospel lexicon. The entire system was therefore "theologically rotten and spiritually sterile under a false conception of God and of human depravity."[89] Polygamy was only the most obvious evidence of the degeneracy of Mormon doctrine. At every turn, southern Protestants claimed, Mormons had degraded the Christian gospel and produced a truly damnable theology.

But however much southerners railed against Mormon peculiarities in politics and religion, in the end theocracy and theology were only background, contributing factors—not primary causes—to the violence that Mormon missionaries and converts received in the postbellum South. If Mormons had ever gathered enough population in any single southern town so as to threaten taking over a local government with its corresponding power and spoils, then it is conceivable that longtime residents might have rallied against Mormon intrusion on principally political grounds, as occurred in antebellum Ohio, Missouri, and Illinois. Southern whites had certainly demonstrated a willingness to defend by violent force their entitlement to political power during Reconstruction and the ensuing decades. The relatively small number of Latter-day Saints who ever accumulated in any given southern locale prevented politics from becoming an immediate trigger for conflict, but denunciations of Mormonism's theocratic tendencies remained a staple of southern anti-Mormon rhetoric throughout the period.

Religious differences were likewise a driving force behind southern anti-Mormonism. Even if they did not preach or spread plural marriage in the

South, LDS missionaries did provide religious competition for the more conventional evangelical denominations, who following the Civil War were often struggling to establish themselves particularly in rural areas. Anti-Mormon polemics delighted in revealing the more controversial doctrines of Mormonism. Yet with all the criticism of Mormon theology, particularly by southern churchmen and denominational newspapers, considerably more ink than blood was spilled over theological differences. A few mobs cited the Mormon religion itself as a motivating factor for their vigilantism, but they could rarely point to particular points of doctrine, other than polygamy, that were so offensive as to inspire violence. Exotic doctrines made it easier for opponents of Mormonism to marginalize the religion and portray its agents and believers as fundamentally "other," but heterodoxy was not the immediate precipitating cause of violence the way that fears over the practice of polygamy were. Indeed, as one newspaper argued, "intolerance of Mormonism at the south is based more upon hostility to the immoralities of polygamy than on opposition to a peculiar and unpopular faith." In other words, the "peculiarly unwelcome" reception that Mormon missionaries received in the South owed more to the southerners' abhorrence with the religion's practices than any objection to its particular beliefs.[90]

Postbellum southerners thus conformed to the broader pattern of nineteenth-century American religious tolerance, which allowed for considerable pluralism, but only up to a certain point. William Hutchison explained how "time and again," nineteenth-century Americans applied the pluralist ideals of the nation's founding to matters of strict belief, but "drew the line at what they perceived as socially threatening behavior." Thus polygamy, and fears surrounding it, precipitated social activism, legislation, and violence in ways that abstract theology concerning the nature of God never did, no matter how offensive the latter was to the defenders of religious orthodoxy. According to Hutchison, "this meant that if you were a cultural insider, you could be about as different as you wished in actual religious views. And it meant that if you were an outsider, acceptance depended to a large extent upon your willingness to adjust, to become assimilated, especially in matters of religious and general behavior."[91] This double standard resulted in an ideal of religious pluralism that was severely curtailed in practice. In a very real sense, in the nineteenth-century South the *vox populi* did become, and in many ways defined, *vox Dei*. Through formal democratic bodies such as Congress and state legislatures, civil society mechanisms such as the press, and informal and raw democratic expression via vigilantism, southerners dictated that Mormon polygamy, politics, and theology lay outside the realm of what was popularly sanctioned in a Christian society. These elements combined to make Mormonism not just false or even alien, but truly "monstrous."

7

Patterns and Context of Southern Anti-Mormon Violence

The hostility harbored by many postbellum southerners toward Mormons and Mormonism, stoked by fears of polygamy as well as political concerns and religious prejudice, manifested itself in everything from vitriolic pamphlets to coercive legislation to, most dramatically, violent abuses. The depths that mob violence reached are vividly captured in the Joseph Standing murder and Cane Creek massacre discussed earlier. However, anti-Mormon violence in the postbellum South was far more pervasive than those two cases, touching every former Confederate state and permeating the last quarter of the nineteenth century. Vigilantes, usually working in small groups, targeted hundreds of Latter-day Saints, some converts and sympathizers but especially missionaries, using coercive intimidation or violence to rid their communities of the Mormons' small but apparently menacing presence. In many of the more than three hundred documented cases violence was only threatened, while in other attempts it was unsuccessful, either because the targeted Mormons escaped or the mob demonstrated last-minute mercy or ineptitude. Nevertheless, in dozens of other episodes, Mormons were whipped, kidnapped, forcibly expelled from towns or even their own homes, and in a few instances killed. Property damage was also extensive, whether through arson, shootings, or confiscation. Anti-Mormon violence thus represented the most common sort of violence against religious minorities—black Christians excepted—in the postbellum South. With southern Latter-day Saints generally too scattered to mount an effective defense and local law enforcement generally unable or unwilling to protect them, Mormons in the late nineteenth-century South often found themselves subject to the capricious whims of mob law.

Latter-day Saints understandably interpreted the violence against them primarily as persecution born of religious bigotry. Though not without merit, this argument is ultimately insufficient in explaining the extent and nature of southern anti-Mormon violence, especially considering the substantial tolerance extended to other heterodox religious communities in the South

such as Jews and Catholics (see chapter 9). As previous chapters have demonstrated, postbellum southern anti-Mormonism was situated in a particular set of conflicts between Mormons and white southerners that were
embedded in deeper local, regional, and national contexts. Anti-Mormon
violence in the late nineteenth-century South was distinctive from its ante-
cedents in the antebellum North, conditioned by the dynamics specific to its
time and place. This chapter accordingly begins with a panoptic overview of
the violence against Mormons by non-Mormon southerners, including a
consideration of its geographic and historical setting as well as a description
of the many forms it took. The conflict will then be situated within the long
tradition of American vigilantism that retained a special hold in the postbellum South even as it was dying out in the rest of the country.

PATTERNS OF ANTI-MORMON VIOLENCE

No southern state was free from anti-Mormon violence in the last quarter of
the nineteenth century. Some, however, experienced more than their share
of intimidation, terror, and bloodshed. Of the fourteen states comprising the
Southern States Mission, Tennessee and Alabama were decidedly the most
violent, with significant hostilities also occurring in the Carolinas, Mississippi, Georgia, and Kentucky. West Virginia, Louisiana, Florida, Maryland,
Texas, and Arkansas, on the other hand, were relatively tame if not wholly
unscathed (see table 7.1).

   One feature that stands out in this geographic distribution is the lack of a
clear division between levels of violence in the "Upper South" states of Kentucky, Tennessee, Maryland, West Virginia, Virginia, and North Carolina,
and the "Lower" or "Deep South" states of South Carolina, Georgia, Alabama,
Mississippi, and Louisiana. (Arkansas straddles the geographic and cultural
boundary between Upper and Lower South, and Texas and Florida are generally considered outliers.) By contrast, studies of late nineteenth-century
racial violence, especially African American lynchings, have persuasively
demonstrated a regional divide. For instance, sociologists Stewart Tolnay
and E. M. Beck have shown that the top five lynching states from 1882 to
1930—Mississippi, Georgia, Louisiana, Alabama, and Florida—all came from
the Lower South. In addition, when including state-sponsored executions of
African Americans (sometimes called "legal lynchings"), Tolnay and Beck
conclude that "two-thirds of all black executions between 1882 and 1930
took place in the states of the Deep South."[1] Because the Upper-Lower South
distinction is so reliable, in general terms, in the study of lynching, the Mormon case emerges as an intriguing anomaly because the geographical divide
holds little or no explanatory power for understanding anti-Mormonism.

Table 7.1: Number of Cases of Anti-Mormon Violence per Southern State, 1876–1900

State	Number of Cases	% of Total Cases
Alabama	57	17.0
Arkansas	1	0.3
Florida	6	1.8
Georgia	28	8.3
Kentucky	18	5.4
Louisiana	5	1.5
Maryland	2	0.6
Mississippi	31	9.2
North Carolina	40	12.0
South Carolina	41	12.2
Tennessee	64	19.0
Texas	2	0.6
Virginia	24	7.1
West Virginia	7	2.1
State unknown	10	3.0
Total	336	100.1

Note: Statistics based on author's count. Data drawn primarily from SSMMH; other sources include various archival collections, missionary diaries, newspaper articles, and secondary literature. My data set represents only those cases that were documented and that I found in my research, and thus is most certainly an undercount. Some states (or years, in figure 7.1) may be relatively overrepresented because of the richness of the available source materials that chronicle the violence in a particular historical moment or place. Especially noteworthy on this score are the papers and journals of John Gibbs, LDSCA, which detail the anti-Mormon movement in west-central Tennessee in the years 1883 and 1884. While it is true that this was a particularly conflictive locale precipitated at least in part by the notable success enjoyed by Gibbs (as outlined in chapter 3), the day-by-day account provided by Gibbs reveals a number of relatively minor acts of intimidation and violence that I have included in my sample but that might not appear in the brief retrospective narratives that many other missionaries provided for LDS newspapers at the close of their missions, and which form the basis for much of the SSMMH.

The two leading states, Tennessee and Alabama, are prominent representatives of their respective subregions, while states that saw very little violence—West Virginia, Louisiana, Florida, Maryland, Texas, and Arkansas—are split between Upper and Lower South.

Unsurprisingly, the states most heavily proselytized by Mormon elders were those in which they received the most violence. Southern States Mission records suggest that the most thoroughly canvassed states were Tennessee, Alabama, Georgia, Mississippi, Kentucky, and the Carolinas; without exception those seven states recorded the highest number of anti-Mormon incidents. This explanation also holds true in the negative: those states that witnessed infrequent and spotty missionary activity, such as Louisiana, Arkansas, Maryland, and Texas, saw correspondingly low levels of violence.

Perhaps the most dramatic proof of this general phenomenon was Georgia. Climaxing with the Joseph Standing murder in 1879, Georgia gained partic- ular notoriety among the elders as virulently anti-Mormon, so much so that in 1890 LDS church officials pulled all missionaries from the state. They did not return until 1898, and in their eight-year absence, there was not a single reported instance of anti-Mormon violence throughout the entire state.[2]

Mormons offered their own explanation of what sparked anti-Mormon violence in a particular time and place. John Morgan theorized that prosely- tizing success and violence were directly correlated: "the more success we have in baptizing people, the more bitter the feeling manifested toward us by our opponents."[3] Elder Francis McDonald also conjectured on the relation- ship between converts and conflict in a letter from Paintsville, Kentucky: "As we keep adding to our numbers the spirit of persecution gets worse and worse."[4] As a case in point, Alphonso Snow related that in his initial labors in Tennessee during the summer of 1881, he and his traveling companion B. H. Roberts held six or seven meetings a week, with no converts and little resis- tance from community members. By early fall, however, the elders had begun baptizing converts, at which point "the people became enraged, and many threats were breathed against us." Notices appeared on trees and schoolhouses warning the missionaries to leave, including one signed by "Indignant Citizens" and addressed to "Most Infamous Scoundrel," which told the newly successful missionaries to "go, or we will hang you like dogs." Snow noted that the letter came from the son of a local Presbyterian minis- ter, some of whose flock had joined with the Mormons.[5] Similarly, members of a Georgia mob told their missionary victims that their primary offense was "going around breaking up churches," demonstrating how religious competition between Mormons and established Protestant congregations could precipitate conflict.[6] Direct causation is difficult to establish, but the correlation of successful LDS proselytizing and heightened anti-Mormon ac- tivity bears out in a number of identifiable cases, including the Standing and Cane Creek episodes.

Though southern anti-Mormon violence pervaded the last quarter of the nineteenth century, it concentrated in certain key time periods. No year passed without at least two documented cases of anti-Mormon violence somewhere in the South. Most years had a substantial number of episodes; indeed, during this period the South witnessed one instance of anti-Mormon vigilantism approximately every twenty-seven days. The heaviest years were the 1880s, spiking in 1884 and averaging almost twenty incidents per year. These levels dropped significantly during the 1890s before briefly rising again at the close of the century (see figure 7.1).

No single, generally applicable rule explains the timing of anti-Mormon violence. Even the spike in 1884, attributable in part to the flurry of hostility

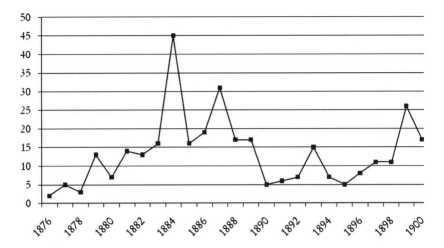

Figure 7.1 Number of Cases of Southern Anti-Mormon Violence per Year, 1876–1900. For information on sources, see table 7.1.

against John Gibbs and his associates leading up to the Cane Creek massacre in August of that year, eludes simple explanation, as it was an extremely violent year for elders throughout the Southern States Mission and not just in Tennessee. In general, however, the levels of violence in the South correlated relatively closely with the intensity of the national anti-Mormon, and specifically antipolygamy, campaign. The chronological trends in southern anti-Mormon violence demonstrate striking parallels to those in Jan Shipps's research analyzing American perceptions of Latter-day Saints from 1860 to 1960. Shipps found that while popular attitudes toward Mormons were consistently negative throughout the period from 1861 to 1895, "the lowest point in negative attitudes for the entire century occurred . . . between 1881 and 1885." According to Shipps, public opinion gradually improved from its nadir in the mid-1880s until the overall trend shifted toward favorable perceptions beginning in the mid-1890s.[7]

That the 1880s would be both the low point for the Mormon image in the American mind and the high point for violence against Mormons in the South is not surprising. Although the federal government had long been concerned about Mormon polygamy and the political and economic power of the LDS Church in Utah Territory, the nation became truly serious about putting an end to the "Mormon question" in the 1880s, illustrated most pointedly by the passage of the Edmunds Act in 1882 and the Edmunds-Tucker Act in 1887. Scholars have disagreed over whether it was Mormon politics or polygamy (or both) that was the main target of Congress and the courts, but polygamy was certainly the burning issue in the minds of most

Americans.[8] National opinion of the Mormons began to improve somewhat after LDS president Wilford Woodruff's 1890 announcement suspending the practice of plural marriage. Following the pattern, southern anti-Mormon violence experienced a sharp downturn at the same time, falling precipitously from 1889 to 1890 and remaining relatively low for several years. The violence rose sharply in 1899, corresponding with the national controversy surrounding B. H. Roberts's election to Congress. In general, the correlation holds true that violence against Mormons in the South reached its highest points during the years in which Mormonism sparked the greatest controversy throughout the nation, particularly during the antipolygamy campaign of the 1880s and again at the end of the century during the debates surrounding Roberts's election.

Violent episodes generally concentrated in the summer. The warmer months from March through September represented the high time for southern anti-Mormon violence—July was particularly explosive—whereas the autumn and winter months of October through February were typically calmer. This trend mirrors the pattern of racial violence in the South. Tolnay and Beck reveal that the vast majority of lynchings occurred in the summer months, while the winter months were considerably less violent.[9] Mormon elders recognized this pattern and offered their own explanations for why the summer was a particularly hot time for them. In August 1899 Donald Urie wrote his father saying, "This is the time of religious revivles, & this Southern blood when hot is hell, therefore we are keeping low till revivle time passes."[10] Similarly, in the days following the Cane Creek massacre (which transpired on a hot August day in 1884), Southern States Mission president John Morgan told a reporter that the elders had their greatest trouble with locals "in hot weather and during the season of revivals." After citing several examples of summertime violence, including the Joseph Standing murder, Morgan contemplated that the warm weather made people "seem more irritable." Revivals built up considerable excitement among the people and led them to "deeds of violence which they would not be guilty during the colder months and when the enthusiasm awakened by the revivals has passed away." As a matter of self-preservation, Morgan accordingly counseled the elders in the South "not to press the proselyting as vigorously" during the summer revival season.[11]

Evangelical Protestant revivals were indeed among the most highly anticipated events in the annual calendar of many southern communities. Though typically scheduled in July and August primarily because of the natural pause in the agricultural cycle between the planting and harvesting seasons, one observer suggested that the revivals were planned for "the height of the summer heat, possibly because at this season the emotional nature of individuals is more readily attuned to religious fervor." Revivals were the religious, social, and emotional climax of the year for most rural southerners, when individuals assured their commitment to Christ, either for the first time or in rededication, and community values were reinforced by the collective witnessing of individual professions of repentance and devotion. The power of the word was in full display, as was the cultural influence of the preachers and ministers who wielded it. Even backsliders and those who normally scoffed at evangelical mores were frequently drawn in by the magnetic pull of God's spirit working among the people. Revivalists carefully crafted their sermons to achieve the maximum emotional response, and the altar call provided a profound moment not only for the seeker of salvation but also for those who were validated and strengthened in their faith by seeing family members, friends, and neighbors experience spiritual rebirth. The most private and intimate struggles of the soul thus played out for all to see, and public rites such as mass baptisms capped the feverish pitch of the revival season.[12]

The *Deseret News*, commenting on the causes of the Cane Creek massacre, asserted that annual summer revivals were tools "used to inflame the multitude against the 'Mormons.' . . . Mobocracy is easily provoked by the rash and rabid revivalists."[13] Despite the LDS newspaper's claims, however, no compelling evidence suggests that any particular revival set off a wave of anti-Mormon violence anywhere in the South during this period. Indeed, the Mormons' attitudes toward the evangelical revival season—alternating between ridicule and fear—probably had as much to do with their own anti-Protestant prejudice as any concrete connection between revivalism and violence. Nevertheless, revivals reinforced the evangelical ethos of the southern mind and heart and represented the high point of in-group identification for southern evangelicals, creating the moment when the community had its greatest sense of differentiation from the outside world of the unconverted, or worse, the apostate. Mormon missionaries thus had good reason to be wary about proselytizing in the heat of the southern summer, with its combined proclivity for communal violence and revivalist enthusiasm.

TYPES OF ANTI-MORMON VIOLENCE

Violence against Mormons in the South took many forms. Most commonly, vigilantes forcibly drove missionaries from a neighborhood, town, county, or even state. Sometimes this expulsion was preceded by personal violence such as a beating or whipping. More often, however, it worked preemptively, with vigilantes roughing up the elders a bit and then releasing them without any significant bodily harm, but with the promise that if they returned they would not be treated so munificently. Although most proselytizing elders in the southern states received dire threats at some point, the situation never degenerated to the point at which it looked like the contemporaneous mass pogroms against Jews in eastern Europe, or even like the state-sponsored anti-Mormon campaign in Missouri in the late 1830s. Perhaps this was because the race question dominated southern culture to the near-exclusion of all else, or because Latter-day Saints in the South never possessed the same kind of political or economic power that they did (or threatened to) in antebellum Ohio, Missouri, and Illinois. Regardless, particularly in light of the southern African American experience, anti-Mormon violence could have been much worse. Although lethal force was not ruled out and even seemed to be the primary option if one listened to the anti-Mormons' belligerent rhetoric, most vigilantes defended their communities with less violent measures such as whipping, beating, tarring and feathering, and expelling—rather than killing—targeted offenders.

The most dramatic, and sometimes deadly, moments of southern anti-Mormon violence predictably involved gunfire. In approximately forty recorded instances in the late nineteenth century, white southerners, either as individuals or in groups, shot at Mormon elders or local church members. How many consciously intended to kill their targets, and how many simply wanted to scare them with a theatrical show of force, is impossible to determine. Only five of these shootings resulted in one or more deaths: the murders of Joseph Standing (1879), Alma Richards (1888), George Canova (1899), and John Dempsey (1900), and the Cane Creek massacre (1884), in which two missionaries and two Mormon converts were killed. Of these, only the Standing murder and the tragedy at Cane Creek were mob affairs clearly connected to the victims' religious identities. The others were murders performed by individual assailants, and it is unclear whether they were religiously motivated: Richards, a missionary working near the Mississippi-Alabama border, was murdered mysteriously one night, probably as part of a bungled robbery;[14] Canova, president of the LDS branch in Sanderson, Florida, was shot in the dark by an unknown attacker while returning home from a church conference (no one was apprehended, and no cause or motive was ever identified);[15] and although Dempsey was killed by his neighbor, a Campbellite preacher known for his "intense hatred" toward Mormons, the hostility between the two men seems to have been a long-standing personal rivalry, and the shooting was triggered by a conflict over the local school.[16] Even in the Cane Creek and Joseph Standing episodes, the respective mobs most likely intended to intimidate and even punish the offending elders but not necessarily to kill anyone. Nevertheless, it is remarkable that more Latter-day Saints were not killed, given the frequency of mob attacks, the fierce anti-Mormon spirit that pervaded so many southern communities, the prevalence of guns in the rural South, and the chance that any given conflict situation could spiral out of control.

On several occasions, mobs almost certainly did shoot to kill. For instance, in February 1884, while two missionaries sat in a church member's home in Jones County, Mississippi, an unknown shooter fired a pistol through a crack in the wall near the chimney, the bullet "passing unpleasantly close" to Elder William Crandall's head. Several more bullets followed at intervals throughout the night, "killing the dogs, knocking down the door, shooting boards off the side of the house, and tearing down the garden fence," but ultimately not harming anyone in the house.[17] Two elders in Georgia also barely missed being shot when members of an approaching gang, led by two Baptist ministers, fired at them with double-barreled shotguns, shredding the brush next to where the elders were standing but leaving them unscathed. That evening the same group of armed men hovered around the post office, waiting for the elders to come that way, swearing that it was their "avowed intention to murder them."[18] Perhaps the most remarkable failed murder attempt involved Elder John Alexander, laboring near Adairsville, Georgia. Three masked men each shot at him from within twenty feet: the first bullet went through his hat, the second through his open coat (grazing his watch chain), and the third missed him completely. Alexander passed out when the firing commenced, and his assailants left the scene, supposing he was dead.[19] Numerous other instances occurred in which elders were shot at but were luckily (or in their view, miraculously) unharmed.[20]

Sometimes the shooters hit their targets, but not fatally. In December 1887, three men assaulted Elders Milo Hendricks and John Tate near Irish Creek, Virginia. The attackers stopped the elders from going down one road, so they turned and proceeded down another path. The assailants took a shortcut through the woods and intercepted the missionaries again, at which point the elders spun around to go yet another way. As they turned their backs, one of the men fired his shotgun at them and then ran away. Both elders were hit in their legs, Tate receiving about sixteen shots and Hendricks eight. Five months later Tate still required the use of a cane to walk, and his injury precipitated his early release from his mission.[21] In 1885, Elders Wiley Cragun and F. A. Fraughton had just stopped for the night near the borders of the Catawba Indian reservation in South Carolina. As they settled in, an armed mob of twenty-five men materialized and demanded that they come out of the house. Cragun bolted for the back door "amid a shower of bullets," one of which struck him in the forehead and another in his face near the chin. Although neither wound proved to be serious, both were nearly fatal, and Cragun's chin in particular troubled him long after the shooting.[22] The assailants in all these shootings seemingly had murderous intent, and the elders escaped deadly harm by a matter of only feet or inches.

Most assaults on missionaries in the South, however, did not include gunplay. While these other attackers did not use potentially lethal force, they clearly intended to punish or expel the unwanted missionaries. Whipping or lashing was one of the most common punishments inflicted on Mormon elders. Mobs used hickory withes, halter straps, persimmon sprouts, doubled-over ropes, and bullwhips to administer their chastisements.[23] Some assailants preferred beating or clubbing the missionaries. While waiting for the ferry to cross the Cumberland River, Elder Richard Shipp was suddenly grabbed by several men. Forcing him to bend over a wagon and pinning him down by the neck, arms, and legs, they pummeled Shipp with an "oak barrel stave" fifteen to twenty times. When the missionary refused to answer their demand for him to leave the area and never return, they gave him another fifteen or twenty blows. The gang stopped only when the ferryman approached, and left a parting warning, in the name of "the citizens of this city," for Shipp not to come back. The missionary's body was "black and blue for several days," and he said he was "so sore I could scarcely move." Thankful that the beating was no worse, he chalked it up to being "one of the 'amusing incidents' of missionary life in the South."[24]

Hostile citizens frequently abducted elders from the homes of local church members and other friends, often with the express purpose of whipping them. In 1896, approximately a dozen vigilantes seized Elders R. E. Caldwell and Granville Pace from a house in Livingston Parish, Louisiana, where they had held a meeting. The masked men marched the elders five miles to the parish line, then administered thirty-six lashes to each before sending them out of the parish with a firm command never to return.[25] Other kidnappings ended relatively peacefully, though the elders were typically forced to leave the area. For instance, a mob of forty men, "all armed with shot guns and clubs," dragged Elder J. B. Reid and his companion out of a house. The group took the elders to the woods, where their captors pulled the missionaries' hair and thrust gun barrels into their faces. After some debate amongst the mob members, they decided to let the missionaries go unharmed, provided that they would leave the county. To ensure compliance, they escorted the elders to the train depot eight miles away and put them under a guard of twenty armed men until the train arrived. Reid recounted that he did not put up much of a fight to stay in the area; he later admitted, "If anybody was ever glad to see a train arrive I was."[26]

On multiple occasions a mob apprehended missionaries with the intention of doing them harm, but for various reasons did not follow through. A mob seized Elders Gordon Bills and Daniel Densley from their beds in Laurence County, Georgia, and carried them to a dense thicket where the vigilantes had made preparations to hang them, "ropes and suitable trees having been selected for their nefarious purposes." With the would-be lynching victims standing by, their abductors began arguing, and by the time they made up their mind to proceed, some friends of the missionaries arrived and frightened the gang so badly that they immediately fled the scene.[27] In Sumpter County, Alabama, Elder William Cowan and his companion had stopped at a home when over one hundred men converged on the site. They compelled the elders to go with them to an old church, making wild noises and threatening the missionaries all along the way. Once they arrived at the church, the mob debated for two hours about what to do with their captives; as Cowan recalled, "Some were in favor of shooting, others were for hanging and many other Christian acts." The mob opted in the end for humiliation and expulsion, forcing the elders to undress and then expelling them from the county. Twenty armed men escorted the elders through a rainstorm to the county line then set them free, promising that murder would be their fate if they ever came back.[28]

Although forced expulsions, whippings, beatings, and threatened murder represented the most common forms of violence suffered by LDS missionaries, southern mobs also used a number of other creative methods to harass, intimidate, and punish these unwelcome outsiders. For instance, Elder Charles Flake had a tub of two gallons of tar dumped over his head while waiting at a train depot in Mississippi.[29] Local citizens gave Elder Charles Bliss a glass of water "well seasoned" with croton oil, a strong natural purgative, as he delivered a public lecture at the courthouse in Columbus, Alabama.[30] Missionaries also endured showers of all manner of projectiles, including stones, rotten eggs, ice chunks, bricks, and chairs.[31]

Sometimes local regulators were not so brave as to confront their targets in person, and left intimidating notes instead. John Morgan, who served as a missionary in Georgia before becoming president of the Southern States Mission, received several such notes, including two particularly ominous examples. One featured a hand-drawn picture of a masked man standing next to what appears to be a Mormon elder hanging from a tree, with a caption reading, "A Charitable hint to Mormons" (see figure 7.2). The second was a handwritten note, addressed specifically to Morgan, with a sketch of two men with rifles shooting at another man in a suit (presumably Morgan). The scribbled notice accompanying the picture is barely coherent at points, but intensely purposeful nonetheless: "Runn Morgan . . . youd Better Gitt Away Thou Serpent of the Devil A Prophet of Hell." The note warned that unless Morgan and his converts hastened to leave the vicinity, "wee will hang you and shoot you five hundred Times" (see figure 7.3).[32] Morgan remained unmoved, as did most other missionaries who received similarly threatening notices.[33] Such notes professed to speak on behalf of the community and invoked the populist threat that "Judge Lynch" would handle the situation if

Figure 7.2 Hand-drawn illustration of a Mormon elder being hanged, labeled "A Charitable hint to Mormons." Undated note delivered to John Morgan while he served as a missionary in Georgia in the late 1870s. John Morgan Correspondence, 1863–1881. Courtesy of the Church History Library, The Church of Jesus Christ of Latter-day Saints, Salt Lake City, Utah.

the missionaries did not cease their teaching or leave the area. Vigilantes also posted threatening notices on the gates of local converts' homes, warning them "not to give food, shelter or other aid to any Mormon Elders, Priests, Prophets or Divines," nor to allow the elders to "hold any meetings, public or private."[34]

Another common form of violence was the destruction of Mormon property, particularly church meetinghouses or other places of worship. Arsonists reduced LDS church buildings to ashes in Tennessee, Alabama, West Virginia, South Carolina, and Kentucky, and dynamite was used to blow up a church in Georgia.[35] In Fleming County, Kentucky, the local citizens took an innovative approach, surrounding an LDS church with guards and then demolishing it with sledgehammers, saws, axes, and firearms. They said they tore down the church rather than burn it so that the Saints could not collect fire insurance to cover the damage.[36] On several occasions mobs became so irate with the Mormon presence in their communities that they destroyed local schoolhouses that the Saints used for their Sunday meetings.[37] In May 1883 a school in Wayne County, Tennessee, was burned down after LDS leaders announced it to be the site of the West Tennessee Conference's annual meetings. The presiding elders then asked a local member if they

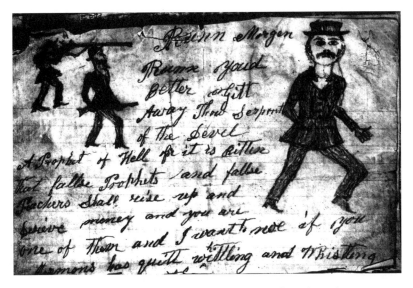

Figure 7.3 "Runn Morgan." Undated hand-written note delivered to John Morgan while he served as a missionary in Georgia in the late 1870s. The text reads in part: "Runn youd Better Gitt Away Thou Serpent of the Devil A Prophet of Hell for it is Bitter that fallse Prophets and fallse Teachers Shall rise up and Desieve [meney?] and you are one of them." John Morgan Correspondence, 1863–1881. Courtesy of the Church History Library, The Church of Jesus Christ of Latter-day Saints, Salt Lake City, Utah.

could use his mill for the meetings but he declined, citing fear that his property would end up in flames as well.[38]

Although most anti-Mormonism in the South was aimed at the missionaries, a significant amount of intimidation and violence targeted local residents who were either converts to the church or simply friendly toward it. The most notable example of this came in the months following the violence at Cane Creek, Tennessee, when mob law descended on the region and vigilantes drove all Mormon families and sympathizers from their homes. The Cane Creek case, though particularly poignant, was not singular. A few years earlier, at the same time as Joseph Standing's murder in northern Georgia, a wave of vigilantism targeted the small community of Latter-day Saints in Brasstown, North Carolina. In July 1879, local anti-Mormons dragged six men and women out of their homes and "cruelly whipped and clubbed them," ordering them to leave the state within four weeks or risk further violence and even death. Furthermore, the mob warned these Saints that if any of them gave shelter to the missionaries, "it should be at the risk of their lives." The Mormons acted quickly to leave the area, trying to sell their property but getting so little in return that they had virtually no money with which to emigrate west. Having thus been robbed by the "mobbers and their colleagues," at the end of the allotted four weeks they simply traveled across the Georgia state line and joined with the branch of the church in Fannin County until resources could be provided for them to move on. A missionary who observed the entire set of affairs noted that upon arriving in Georgia the exiles from North Carolina were "in a destitute condition; some have scarcely nothing."[39] The parallels to the Latter-day Saints' experiences in Missouri in the 1830s, when mobs violently drove them from their homes and forced them to bordering Illinois, were clear.

Sometimes vigilantes targeted individual Mormon families. Almost as soon as the J. R. and Jane Henson family of Decatur, Tennessee, accepted the teachings of the missionaries and joined the LDS Church, they became the subjects of repeated harassment and aggression beginning in April 1884. Two elders were holding a meeting at the Henson home when several local roughs, "being under the influence of liquor," tottered in and out of the meeting making abusive comments, scaring the women with a large black snake, throwing rocks at the house, yelling threats and insults, and occasionally wandering up to the preaching stand. They departed when the meeting ended, leaving frayed nerves but no real damage. The following Saturday, three of the same men returned to the Henson home, again "all intoxicated." Jane greeted them at the door, where they asked for her forgiveness and then queried where they could find J. R., supposedly to "make amends." She pointed them toward the field he was working in, but suspicious of their intentions she took a shorter route to warn her husband of their approach. When the three men found J. R., they apologized and chatted congenially for nearly an hour. As the conversation ended and J. R. turned to go to the house, however, one of them suddenly pulled out his pistol and fired three shots. The bullets missed, partly because Jane, who saw the man draw his gun, threw herself at the shooter as he pulled the trigger. The Hensons barricaded themselves in their home, and after their assailants left J. R. went to the sheriff and sought out a warrant. The sheriff arrested the three men and put them in jail, ending the immediate threat to the family. Nevertheless, the conflict between the Hensons and their neighbors escalated in early August, when a mob surrounded their home and began firing into it, wounding one of the daughters. The ruffians threatened to drag J. R. out of the house and kill him, but knowing the family possessed guns, none of the attackers seemed particularly eager to be the first one in the door, and they eventually dispersed. Before they left, however, they warned J. R. to leave the area within five days or they would come back and kill him. Not wanting to press his luck any further, especially after hearing about the deadly attack at Cane Creek the next day, J. R. fled the state and went to Jonesboro, Arkansas. His wife and children stayed behind, hoping things would settle down, but a month later, Jane received a note telling her to leave within ten days or her home would be burned down "with herself in the flames." She gathered her family and what few possessions she could, and left to join her husband.[40]

The attack on the Hensons and other Mormon families revealed one of the distinguishing characteristics of southern anti-Mormon vigilantism, namely that mobs were willing to target women and children as well as men. Southern racial violence overwhelmingly targeted black men, and the few female lynching victims were usually accused of murder or other violent crimes and attacked in the frenzy of mass mob action rather than the relative secrecy of small, private mobs.[41] However, what Sarah Gordon identified as the "erosion of sympathy" for Mormon women previously seen as "victims" of polygamy meant that when southern women joined with the Latter-day Saints, they forfeited their claim to virtuous womanhood that southern men were bound to protect.[42] This shift from victimhood to complicity made possible what otherwise would be nearly unthinkable: that white women would be subject to vigilante violence by southern men seeking to uphold feminine virtue and defend the sanctity of the Christian home. That joining a minority religion—not adultery or any criminal act—was these women's greatest transgression only accentuated the distinctiveness of the violence against them.

Even those southern Latter-day Saint converts who did not receive threats or outright violence by local vigilantes feared the repercussions of their new association. For example, the Dotson, Quinn, and Bagwell families all attended Bethlehem Baptist Church in Ackerman, Mississippi, and held various positions of some importance within the congregation. In 1880 eleven members of Bethlehem Baptist were "lost to the Mormon church," and in 1896 several others were removed from the congregation for being baptized as Latter-day Saints. In converting to Mormonism, these men and women consciously severed ties with their local community church and its attendant social networks that had played a central role in their families' lives for three generations. Many relatives of the LDS converts remained firmly ensconced at Bethlehem Baptist, and at least some disowned their Mormon family members. Although no evidence suggests that any of the converts ever received any violence or explicit threats from local community members, many elected to be baptized before dawn for fear of mob action.[43]

The experiences of these converts suggest that joining the LDS Church constituted, in many cases, a significant act of social disruption. Southern converts did not simply join a new church when they accepted baptism—they adopted an entirely new worldview and social position. Their membership in the most vilified of nineteenth-century American religions meant that they had chosen to alienate themselves from the religious and cultural orthodoxies of their upbringing. In becoming Mormon, these converts not only accepted a new faith but also intrinsically rejected at least part of their former faith commitments and social networks. While the explicit purpose of their Mormon baptism was to forsake sin and seek salvation, southern converts had implicitly renounced a key part of what it meant to be a southerner and thereby their position as a mainstream member of the community. In at least some sense, therefore, families like the Hensons and those in Brasstown, North Carolina, had exiled themselves even before the mobs forced them from their homes. Conversions to Mormonism disrupted individual lives, strained or broke family relationships, and threatened to unravel the fabric of communities around the South. Whether or not mobs actually called on them, Mormon converts were aware that vigilante action might be used against them. Knowing that their conversion transgressed the boundaries of the community, new members entered the Mormon faith braced for potentially violent repercussions to follow.

Anti-Mormons targeted not only Mormon missionaries and converts, but also anyone who overtly sympathized with them. In Overton County, Tennessee, a leading candidate for sheriff ultimately lost the election after his opponents heralded the fact that his daughter was a Mormon and he hosted the LDS missionaries in his home.[44] More dramatically, anti-Mormons repeatedly attacked William Metz, a prominent farmer in Calhoun County, West Virginia, who sheltered, supported, and championed the Mormon elders who evangelized in the community, although he never chose to join their church. Despite his efforts to protect them, vigilantes banished the missionaries from the county, after which point Metz's life became "one continual round of abuse and persecution." One night in early spring 1888, arsonists burned Metz's house and barn to the ground, he and his family barely escaping the blaze. Shortly after this attack, his abusers sent numerous letters and notices ordering him to leave the area and threatening further violence if he did not. Metz sold the farm he lived on, with its home and barn in ashes, and purchased another one several miles away. He visited his new home the night before he was scheduled to move in, and found it in flames as well. Following that he bought yet another piece of property but shortly thereafter "found only an ash heap" in place of the home, accompanied by yet another warning to leave. In addition, Metz's cattle were poisoned, his wells choked, and his fences torn down, all of which contributed to his financial ruin. His children received taunts and were scorned by former playmates, and his wife became "almost deranged" over the sustained persecution. The strong anti-Mormon sentiment in the area meant that even if Metz could identify the arsonists, they would never be prosecuted.[45]

Though most suffered in relative silence, not all Mormons and their friends played the role of passive victims of southern mobbing. In Lawrence County, Tennessee, the intercession of their local friends saved a number of missionaries from a serious beating (or potentially worse), with some of the women in particular giving the elders' would-be assailants a thorough "tongue-lashing." The missionaries actually had to restrain their protectors from "doing violence to the mob," who then chose to retreat rather than press the issue.[46] In Marshall County, Kentucky, about fifteen Mormon converts, defiant after repeated anti-Mormon activity in the area, shot back at an anti-Mormon mob that had fired "a fusillade of bullets" into a worship meeting.[47] Another remarkable example of resistance against anti-Mormon vigilantism occurred in northern Alabama in March 1886, where missionaries had recently made some converts. One night a "committee of citizens" surrounded the home of Hiram Harrison, who though not a member of the church frequently housed the elders. When the vigilantes did not find the missionaries, who were staying elsewhere that night, they notified Harrison that he must never again permit the elders to lodge at his home. Harrison did not take kindly to the threats leveled against him or his family, nor did he appreciate taking orders from a mob. The next morning he bought a gun and ammunition and scribbled out a note reading, "Come to our house another night and some of you will eat breakfast in hell next morning." The younger Harrison shot a pistol ball through the note and attached it to the gatepost of one of the men they suspected was part of the previous night's mob. No more trouble was reported at the Harrison home.[48]

Concerted and open resistance efforts like these were rare. Whereas African Americans in the South sometimes managed to ward off white aggression by arming themselves and forming self-defense organizations, Mormons rarely enjoyed the kind of numerical presence in any one locale that would allow them to organize an armed defense.[49] Mormons made for particularly vulnerable targets because they had so few allies; by the 1880s virtually the entire nation had turned against them, and they learned that no recourse could be found in courts, legislatures, or the executive branch, on both state and federal levels. Much like antiblack lynch mobs, anti-Mormon vigilantes knew they could act with relative impunity, and usually did not even bother to disguise themselves as they conducted their attacks. Furthermore, mob behavior was positively reinforced every time it successfully induced Mormon elders or converts to leave a community, thus legitimizing the logic that the ends of community preservation and harmony justified the means of extralegal action. Simply put, mobbing usually worked to purge an area of its unwanted Mormon presence, at least in the short-term.

ANTI-MORMONISM AND THE TRADITION OF SOUTHERN VIGILANTISM

The violence directed toward Mormons in the late-nineteenth-century South can be understood within the historical context of American, and especially southern, vigilantism. Violence as an effective means of conservative social control and community preservation was a long-standing tradition in the United States, stretching back to the colonial era. Public opinion in the eighteenth and nineteenth centuries generally supported limited vigilantism, especially when it was perceived as ultimately upholding the law and preserving social order.[50] Vigilantes targeted real lawbreakers such as horse thieves and outlaw bands, as well as "subversive" groups such as Mormons, Catholic, and Masons, whom they deemed to undermine democratic institutions or community values.[51] Although antagonists ultimately aimed to destroy these groups and their ideologies, their proximate objective was usually to rid the community of their potentially perilous influence. As Latter-day Saint missionaries and the gospel message they preached represented a challenge to southern beliefs and folkways, local citizens repeatedly summoned the time-honored tradition of vigilante activism to confront the threat.

No uniform profile fits all cases, but it is possible to describe, however imprecisely, the "typical" nineteenth-century vigilante movement. While some groups numbered in the thousands, most consisted of between a dozen and perhaps a few hundred members. Some bands appeared spontaneously, but many, particularly larger groups, were often extremely well organized, with a constitution or manifesto clearly stating their objectives. Most groups came together only temporarily and disbanded once they had accomplished their stated purpose; the Ku Klux Klan and other permanent and semipermanent organizations represented exceptions rather than the rule. Vigilantism characteristically sprouted where regular law enforcement was absent, too costly, or deemed ineffective (either in not enforcing the law, or because the law did not go far enough). By the late nineteenth century, vigilantism was primarily limited to rural areas, as towns and cities had developed increasingly professional and effective police forces that monopolized the use of violence to control the social order. Rather than being composed of the dregs of society, mobs often consisted of middling farmers or workers who had some stake in the community. The leadership of vigilante movements, especially the larger and more organized variety but sometimes smaller bands as well, was frequently made up of a cross-section of community elites who had a vested interest in maintaining the status quo and who used their influence to ensure that the violence would in the end preserve and reinforce, rather than disrupt and potentially overturn, the existing social order. Finally, mobs were almost always selective in their target groups. Social violence was not a spasmodic manifestation of irrational fury and fear but rather a calculated action designed to enhance the social, cultural, political, or economic standing of those who participated. While organizers often rallied the mobs with emotional pleas, and the act of violence itself was an intense emotional and psychological experience, at its root vigilantism was typically an ordered and reasoned phenomenon.[52]

Anti-Mormon vigilantism in the South followed these general patterns very closely. While southern mobs were more accustomed to combating racial, political, or criminal groups, they nevertheless followed well-established patterns of vigilantism in dealing with Mormon elders and converts. As noted previously, most Mormon missionaries studiously avoided large towns and cities, preferring to work among the humbler folk of the backwoods. This may have worked to their advantage in terms of proselytizing success—recall the abject failure of John Gibbs and William Jones on their speaking tour of southern cities in the summer of 1884—but it made them vulnerable to rural vigilantism. Though most missionaries had not actually broken any laws, many southerners deemed extralegal violence an appropriate response to the perceived Mormon threat.

In many instances local citizens held mass meetings and passed resolutions before taking any concrete action against LDS missionaries. These meetings had a democratic element to them, with open debate and votes taken prior to committing to any particular course of action. Meetings commonly ended with attendees passing a resolution urging the elders to leave the community and warning them of consequences if they did not. Those who punished or drove out Mormon elders frequently did so acting in the name of the community or the common good. For example, in York County, South Carolina, residents held an "indignation meeting" in 1882 during which they adopted resolutions demanding that the elders leave the region. No timetable was given, but the decree urged the missionaries to "depart in peace before the indignation of our people becomes uncontrollable and they do them bodily injury." The elders ignored the warning, as the area was one of the more fruitful proselytizing fields in the entire mission. Two years passed before leading citizens of the county called for another meeting, in August 1884, again commanding the elders to "vacate the state and to return no more among us." The meeting's resolution gave the missionaries five days to leave, and warned they would suffer "the consequences to disobedience," ominously concluding, "We are going to get rid of you."[53] York County, spurred on by citizens' meetings and its anti-Mormon newspaper, the *Yorkville Enquirer*, proved to be among the most virulently anti-Mormon counties in the South in the 1880s. The county was also among the most notorious sites of Ku Klux Klan activity during Reconstruction, suggesting at least a circumstantial link between anti-black and anti-Mormon vigilantism in certain locales.[54]

As in other cases of American vigilantism, many participants in anti-Mormon actions were notable for their social respectability. Mormons were often accosted by men who were little more than common ruffians, but in many other episodes the most esteemed institutions and members of society mobilized to oppose Mormonism, even endorsing outright violence if necessary. Anti-Mormon mobs originated in such reputable places as farmer's granges and local debating societies, and were often mobilized by "prominent citizens" who militated against Mormons in the name of civilization and refinement.[55] For instance, in 1886 Rufus Cobb, president of the local iron works and former governor of Alabama, led a mob of 150 men against a Mormon elder and threatened him with death if he continued to preach and hold public meetings.[56]

Over the years Latter-day Saints learned to be ambivalent regarding the role of government officials and law enforcement authorities. They knew that there were some officials—including a handful of judges, congressmen, and senators—who made genuine efforts to protect Mormon interests, or at least the rights of the minority, both on the local and national level.[57] In most instances, however, government and law enforcement officials tended to side with the anti-Mormons. Public authorities in several North Carolina towns, responding to requests by local clergymen, prohibited further Mormon meetings on the grounds that the preaching was illegal.[58] The mayor of Birmingham, Alabama, informed missionaries they would only be allowed to preach if they secured a letter from pastors of the local Baptist, Methodist, Episcopal, Catholic, and Jewish churches certifying their approval, suggesting that Mormons were seen as outsiders even where Catholics and Jews were considered acceptable community members.[59] City councils in Cocoa, Florida, and Savannah, Georgia, similarly refused permission for Mormon missionaries to hold their meetings within city limits or to sell their literature without a license (that would not be granted).[60] Public officials were thus often complicit in anti-Mormon vigilantism out of apathy, unwillingness to intervene, or sympathy with the cause. The leadership of the Southern States Mission frequently appealed to state authorities across the South to help enforce the law and bring vigilantes to justice. In most cases their pleas brought only cool indifference or at best elicited congenial but shallow statements of sympathy, often ending in the declaration that these were local matters that state officials had no authority over.[61] Only in 1903, after a quarter century of violence, did a federal court first try southerners accused of anti-Mormon vigilantism, in this case prominent residents of Hart County, Georgia, who had abducted and then lashed a pair of Mormon elders.[62] For the most part, Mormons in the late nineteenth-century South could count on either unresponsiveness or opposition from local elites and legal institutions.

Southern anti-Mormon vigilantism not only displayed many of the broad characteristics of southern extralegal violence, but also had the distinct influence of the region's signature vigilante group, the Ku Klux Klan. Indeed, many of those who attacked LDS missionaries clearly drew inspiration from, or were former members of, the Klan. On multiple occasions elders reported being assaulted by members of the "K.K.K.," "ku-klux," "Ku Klux combination," or "Ku Klux gang." Vigilantes wearing "the garb of the ku-klux" terrorized LDS church members in Tennessee, and a mob presided over by "an old Ku Klux leader" assaulted missionaries in South Carolina.[63] Reports following the Cane Creek massacre described the vigilantes who instituted mob rule in Hickman and Lewis Counties as wearing clothing reminiscent of the Klan.[64]

Strictly speaking, it is anachronistic to speak of Mormons being attacked by the Ku Klux Klan in the late 1870s or 1880s, as federal legislation and military enforcement had outlawed and effectively disbanded the paramilitary organization in the early 1870s. Vigilante violence persisted throughout the South, of course, often led by former Klan members, and the Klan became something of a generic brand for all southern vigilantism.[65] Federal authorities differentiated between "Klan" violence and anti-Mormon vigilantism in 1882, when an LDS family in Tennessee who had been subjected to what they dubbed a "Ku Klux outrage" went to a federal commissioner in Nashville seeking justice. Officials there referred the family to state officials for redress, sending the clear message that even if anti-Mormon depredations looked like Klan violence, and even if committed by men who had former Klan ties, such crimes did not qualify as federal offenses prosecutable under the provisions of the 1871 Ku Klux Klan Act.[66] Even though the actual organization technically no longer existed by the time major LDS missionary efforts in the South commenced, the Klan nevertheless left a "continuing legacy of violence" in the region, casting a long shadow that influenced vigilante actions against not just African Americans but also Mormons and other minority groups.[67]

The anti-Mormon campaign in the South thus followed the patterns of vigilantism in both its broadly American and distinctively southern forms. Many nineteenth-century Americans took from the American Revolution the lessons that violence was an effective means of securing social and political goals, and that violence could be morally positive when utilized to secure freedom, the sovereignty of the people, or some other greater good. Democratic ideology and violence were thus closely related in the republic's first century, and rioters often invoked the principles of majority rule and popular sovereignty to justify their actions as being within "the spirit of '76." When southerners organized to intimidate, punish, or even kill Mormons, they acted firmly within the tradition of early American vigilante justice. "Regulators" who assaulted Mormon missionaries and converts knew they worked outside the restraints of the law, but they considered their extralegal actions to be legitimate in maintaining social order, preserving Christian homes, and purging their communities of unwanted foreign elements. In the postbellum South, the voice of the people—at least those who claimed to act on behalf of the people—manifested itself in extralegal activity that super-seded regularly constituted law and government on behalf of the perceived common good.

In many ways, vigilantism reflected the deepest dilemmas that nine-teenth-century American democracy faced.[68] American society was founded on the guarantee, protection, and exercise of individual rights. As an inevi-table result of pluralism, however, the rights of various segments of the population were bound to clash at some point. Mormonism confronted nine-teenth-century Americans, including southerners, with profound challenges to their identity and conception of the good society. In their violent treat-ments of Mormon missionaries and converts, southern anti-Mormon vigi-lantes operated within the forms of extreme populist democracy while simultaneously violating key elements of the basic democratic principles of due process, minority rights, and the fundamental guarantees of life, liberty, and property. In undermining the rule of law and basic personal freedoms, anti-Mormon vigilantism too often crossed the line from community defense to the tyranny of the majority feared by democratic thinkers such as James Madison and Alexis de Tocqueville. Of course, participants in anti-Mormon mobs did not see themselves simply as mobs, but as legitimate (if extralegal) extensions of the pure will of the people, using violence to protect the citizenry—particularly its most vulnerable elements, such as women—from the forces of disruption and dissolution as embodied in the alien Mormon missionary. In a democratic country, vigilantism represented the democrati-zation of social violence. In a very real sense, then, southern vigilantes' response to the Mormon menace was a democratic one, but ultimately their violent denial of minority rights revealed one of the fundamental flaws of democracy, namely that the people may prey on the people in the name of the people.[69]

8

The Blood of Martyrs

Southern Anti-Mormonism and LDS Identity

On Sunday afternoon, August 24, 1884, a capacity crowd filled the tabernacle in Salt Lake City, with over seven thousand people packed into every seat and standing in the galleries. Top LDS Church dignitaries representing the leading priesthood quorums presided from the stand. The occasion was the memorial service for Elders John Gibbs and William Berry, the victims of the vigilante attack on the Conder home in Cane Creek, Tennessee, just two Sundays prior. The two missionaries, who had labored in relative obscurity in the backwoods of northwestern Tennessee, were now celebrated by Mormons as martyrs for the truth, joining the hallowed ranks of Joseph and Hyrum Smith, the early Christian apostles, and even Jesus himself. Readers of the church-owned *Deseret News* had followed every detail of the unfolding story in the fortnight since the news first reached the Salt Lake Valley. Now they came to hear their priesthood leaders pay tribute to the fallen elders.

In fact, the services that day had very little to do with Gibbs and Berry themselves; most of the speakers were acquainted with them only in death. An effort toward a personal touch was the custom-made floral arrangement lavishing the communion table, taken from the city's best gardens. It featured a crystalline cross and the victims' initials in white pansies set against carefully chosen flowers signifying death, resurrection, and martyrdom (see figure 8.1). The sermons themselves offered little by way of eulogy; rather, they rehearsed a narrative that had become a familiar refrain in the ears of nineteenth-century Mormons, particularly during the tumultuous decade of the 1880s. They were God's chosen people, and God's people had always suffered persecution and even martyrdom at the hands of evildoers. Latter-day Saints were key players in a cosmic battle between the forces of light and darkness. Casualties would come along the way, but ultimately God would exact vengeance on the wicked and vindicate the faithful remnant.

The speakers reminded the assembled crowd of the sharp boundary dividing the church from the outside world, and of the need for the Saints to remain

Figure 8.1 Photograph of tribute to Elders William Berry and John Gibbs, with floral arrangement resting on communion table in Salt Lake Tabernacle during the public funeral service for the missionaries killed at Cane Creek, Tennessee, August 1884. Courtesy of the Church History Library, The Church of Jesus Christ of Latter-day Saints, Salt Lake City, Utah.

faithful in the face of persecution. Joseph F. Smith, second counselor to John Taylor in the church's First Presidency and son of the martyred Hyrum Smith, reflected sadly "that men in the peaceful pursuit of their calling should be inhumanly butchered in this land of religious freedom." He lamented that a supposedly "enlightened nation" was in fact a place of darkness and violence for the Saints, but emphasized that they should respond to "crime and violence" with "moderation" and "charity," remembering that followers of Jesus had a "mission of peace on earth and good will toward men." Following Smith's bleak portrayal of the outside world, Angus M. Cannon, president of the Salt Lake Stake, instructed the congregation that they should teach their children that "it is better to lay down life willingly and gladly than to relinquish one principle of our revealed religion." John Morgan, president of the Southern States Mission, followed by asserting that all those "who fall to-day to establish religious liberty and in defense of the Kingdom of God . . . will go down to future generations as martyrs for the truth." Their sacrifices would not be in vain, as "the blood of the martyrs will be the seed of the Church as it ever has been." Wilford Woodruff, president of the Quorum of Twelve Apostles and future church president, further reminded the assemblage that true disciples of Christ would always receive persecution, and that just as Jesus and his apostles had suffered martyrdom, now it was the Latter-day Saints' turn. In life Elders Berry and Gibbs had followed the lead of

Peter and Paul in preaching the gospel to unbelieving and hostile crowds, and so it should come as no surprise that they would also follow them to a martyr's death.[1]

The memorial service was a powerful means of sharpening the Saints' identity in opposition to the outside world. The particular context of the murders was less important than the larger story they told and the purpose they played in reifying the division between the Saints and their persecutors. For those assembled in the tabernacle that Sunday afternoon in August 1884, and for all those Mormons who read or heard of repeated atrocities committed against missionaries throughout the region, anti-Mormon violence in the postbellum South took on an ahistorical and transcendent character employed in strengthening the enclave of the Saints and vilifying the outsider "Gentiles." The potent effect the Tennessee killings had on the collective Mormon mind was powerfully illustrated in the coming months, when Latter-day Saints throughout the intermountain West took up donations for the families of the "Tennessee Martyrs," collecting over $4,200 from October 1884 to May 1885.[2]

Despite lying on the geographical and demographic margins of the church, the South loomed prominently in the late nineteenth-century Mormon mind. The region represented a place where the conflict between the Saints and their antagonists assumed heightened visibility precisely because of the violent treatment of the elders, which they and church members back home easily translated into narratives of persecution and martyrdom. Mormon publications in Utah frequently reported on southern violence against missionaries, whether in regular reports from the field or increasingly formulaic accounts noting a missionary's safe return home after a series of hostile encounters. In particular, the 1879 murder of Elder Joseph Standing and the 1884 Cane Creek Massacre became landmarks in Mormons' self-image as the persecuted—and thus chosen—people of God. Generations after the event occurred, Latter-day Saints continued to memorialize their violent rejection in the South.[3] Such collective memory of persecution helped maintain the boundaries of the Mormon enclave by continually feeding an oppositional identity. This identity gained strength as the Latter-day Saints became convinced that they were the victims of a national conspiracy, rooted in Utah's non-Mormon population, spread nationally by the press, and headed by evangelical Protestant clergy around the country. Mormons saw the plot hatched by this alliance as not only infringing upon their constitutional rights of religious liberty but also threatening their very existence as a church and as a people. Thus, violence and other forms of resistance experienced in the church's southern hinterland considerably shaped Mormon identity in the western heartland.[4]

CONSTRUCTING A PERSECUTION NARRATIVE

On May 2, 1885, at the height of the national antipolygamy crusade, Latter-day Saints in Utah held a mass meeting to protest what they considered to be gross, and repeated, violations of their constitutional freedoms. Speakers included a number of Mormon luminaries who appealed to morality, justice, freedom, the Constitution, and the conscience of the American people in remonstrating against the 1882 Edmunds Act. Orson F. Whitney—a popular future apostle who had penned the inscription on Joseph Standing's monument in the Salt Lake Cemetery—read a "Declaration and Protest" addressed to the president and people of the United States and decrying "this crusade, which bears all the aspect of a religious persecution." Whitney asserted that polygamy was a central tenet of the Mormon religion, and defiantly proclaimed that "force may enslave the body, but it cannot convince the mind." Antipolygamy legislation, he argued, had nothing to do with enhancing the morality of the nation, but rather stemmed from "popular prejudice and religious interference." John T. Caine, Utah's territorial delegate to Congress, underscored Whitney's contentions, framing the entire record of the Latter-day Saint movement as "a history of persecution brought on by prejudice and religious bigotry." Asserting the loyalty of the Saints to the United States and the Constitution, Caine claimed that Mormon views on church and state were scarcely different than the nation's Puritan founders, and that the Saints had established a republican government, not a theocracy, upon settling their wilderness home in Utah. In recounting the nation's harsh treatment of the Saints, he found it "hard to believe that such outrages could be enacted in a land dedicated to liberty." America was providentially designed to "afford an asylum to the oppressed of all nations," not to be the agent of unjust and intolerant persecution.[5]

Nineteenth-century Mormons traced this persecution to their earliest history. The skepticism that greeted Joseph Smith's founding visions quickly transformed into individual opposition and eventually organized acts of hostility and violence. Smith's official personal history—serialized during his lifetime, published afterward as the *History of the Church*, and then excerpted for canonization in Mormon scripture—is replete with images of persecution; indeed, in only five verses (in the canonized version) describing the "sectarian" world's rejection of his vision of God the Father and Jesus Christ in 1820, Smith used the word "persecution" and its correlates eleven times. Smith reported that when rumors circulated that an angel had delivered golden plates to him, "the persecution became more bitter and severe than before," and soon became "so intolerable" that he was forced to move south to Pennsylvania. Relocation provided only a temporary respite. Smith had to hide the details of his continuing translation of the Book of Mormon and his repeated angelic manifestations, "owing to a spirit of persecution which had already manifested itself in the neighborhood. We had been threatened with being mobbed, from time to time, and this, too, by professors of religion."[6] After he moved his family and the church to Ohio, a mob brutally attacked the Mormon prophet on a cold night in March 1832, dragging him from his house, choking him into unconsciousness, stripping his clothes off, tearing at his naked flesh, trying to force poison in his mouth, and then tarring and feathering him.[7] The violence that dogged Smith's prophetic ministry for over a decade and a half climaxed in June 1844 in Carthage, Illinois, when a mob attacked the jail where he and three other prisoners were being held, killing Joseph and his brother Hyrum.

Though Smith was personally a lightning rod for hostility, his followers also attracted heated opposition. Wherever the Mormons went, from New York to Ohio, Missouri to Illinois, local residents saw them initially as a curiosity, then as a nuisance, and then as a threat that needed to be removed, by force if necessary. As in the postbellum South, anti-Mormon hostility always had a religious component to it, but actual mob violence erupted only when the conflict between Mormons and non-Mormons took on more concrete political, economic, and legal dimensions. The Missouri experience was particularly harsh, as angry settlers drove hundreds and then thousands of Mormons from their homes, first in 1833 and then again as part of the "Mormon War" of 1838, when local and Mormon militias actually faced each other in pitched battle. Mormons still remember Haun's Mill, where a mob killed nearly twenty Mormon men and boys who had waved the white flag of surrender, and Governor Lilburn Boggs's "extermination order," which legitimized and even ordered the forced expulsion of Mormons from Missouri in 1838, as the ultimate examples of the injustices that attended the early Saints' persecutions.[8] The Mormons' dire plight after being driven, once again, from their homes in Nauvoo, Illinois, inspired a temporary wave of national sympathy when the poignant scenes of forced homelessness and exodus were publicized by empathetic reformers such as Thomas Kane.[9] But the 1852 public announcement of plural marriage, and growing suspicions that the Mormons' "kingdom" in the West was in fact a theocracy hostile to the American republic, inspired a new wave of anti-Mormonism, this one national rather than local or state-based, which persisted for the remainder of the nineteenth century. The conflict between Latter-day Saints and the federal government peaked in 1857 with the Utah War (made worse by the Mountain Meadows Massacre), and then again in the 1880s with the height of antipolygamy prosecutions, known by Mormons as "the raid."

By the late nineteenth century, opposition had profoundly shaped Mormon identity, and the Saints had come to expect it. Even if they had not personally suffered in Missouri, Illinois, or Utah, persecution lay at the heart of stories that Mormons told about themselves. For instance, in 1887, reacting to the congressional debate over what became the Edmunds-Tucker Act, Mormon apologist R. W. Sloan recounted the Mormon narrative as one of "unmistakable traces of relentless persecution—of weary and worn mothers, starving babes at their breasts, the blood of fathers, brothers and husbands . . . the bitter sobs of the wife and mother among lone graves on trackless prairies."[10] Sloan's telling was maudlin, to be sure, but not without historical grounding. Nor was he alone in making persecution a central theme in the Latter-day Saint story. In a semi-canonical collection of discourses by Mormon leaders published in 1886, nearly half (nineteen out of forty) of the sermons featured the related themes of persecution, opposition, and outside hostility.[11] And John Nicholson's popular account of *The Martyrdom of Joseph Standing*—emerging from his conversations with fellow inmate Rudger Clawson as the two men served prison sentences for unlawful cohabitation and polygamy—used the missionary's murder in Georgia to critique the broader pattern of "unjust punishment and indignities" piled upon the Saints "in the vain attempt to crush religious convictions out of the hearts of a devoted people."[12] Rather than achieving its aim of eliminating Mormonism, in the long run violent anti-Mormonism only reinforced the Mormon sense of community by giving the Saints a shared history of enduring persecution. Vigilantism, though often effective in the short term, was ultimately counterproductive, strengthening rather than weakening the psychological and social boundaries of Mormonism. It produced what historian D. Michael Quinn has called "a siege mentality" within the nineteenth- (and twentieth-) century church, and provided assurances for the suffering Saints that God was on their side and would vindicate their sorrows.[13]

One of the primary vehicles for constructing this persecution narrative was the *Deseret News*, which served not only as the major newspaper in Utah Territory but also as one of the official organs of the church (non-Mormons in Utah typically opted for the *Salt Lake Tribune*). In addition to secular news, the paper reprinted sermons from church leaders, letters from missionaries laboring around the United States and abroad, various items of church-related business and news, and updates on the latest maneuvers of the church's many critics. Throughout the last quarter of the nineteenth century, the *Deseret News* regularly presented readers with news about missionary labors in the Southern States Mission. The articles they read, often consisting of published letters from missionaries in the field, included tales of opposition, hostile threats, and violence. The newspaper portrayed southern hostility in even more concentrated form by printing summary reports provided by groups of elders returning from their labors in the South. Particularly in the 1880s, the *Deseret News's* reports of returning missionaries became progressively more standardized. Most reports included the name and hometown of the missionary, dates and locales of his service, an often specific recounting of prejudice and violence encountered, and a general outline of successes (typically the number of baptisms and/or healings attributable to the elder). The increasingly formulaic recitations of violence suggest a kind of trope that was anticipated by elders in narrating their missionary experiences in the South. A few who had been victims of violence chose to focus on the more positive aspects of their work, but the majority dwelt, at times almost exclusively, on the violence, both reflecting and perpetuating an oppositional persecution mentality.

Two returned missionary reports provide representative samples of the genre. The first, from November 1884, came in the wake of the Cane Creek Massacre and reflected the heightened anxiety of the period. The article told of nine missionaries who had returned to Utah along with a company of eighty immigrants from the South, including over twenty "Cane Creek refugees" who were "compelled to flee before the murderous threats and persecution of the Tennessee mobocrats." The missionaries had been spread out across the mission, serving in Mississippi, Alabama, Tennessee, North Carolina, and Georgia. Even so, their experiences, as recorded in the newspaper, were remarkably similar. Each baptized a handful of converts, held dozens of meetings, and walked some four thousand miles during the course of their mission. The majority of each of their entries focused on the persecution they received. For instance, Elder W. H. Crandall "met with much opposition and some violence" in southern Mississippi, including being fired on by gunmen while at a local church member's home. Elder Joseph Belnap and his companion regularly went hungry after being refused food. On multiple occasions Belnap was "hunted by mobs," narrowly escaping one and talking another out of an intended punishment of a whipping followed by rubbing ashes and cayenne pepper into their backs. Elder J. A. Mower "met with all kinds of opposition" in Georgia. Local citizens posted "threatening placards" warning him and his companions to leave, and a rock-throwing crowd chased the missionaries from a meeting after rumors circulated that they were "baptizing their converts naked and taking the women to Utah to make slaves of them." Furthermore, local preachers stirred up hostility by telling their congregants that the Mormons caused a series of cyclones that had recently devastated the area. Elder Charles Call reported that "the opposition was bitter," Elder Joseph Morrell "met with almost incessant opposition and persecution," and Elder R. A. Crump "was subjected to considerable opposition" by "mobocrats" in Tennessee "generally led by sectarian preachers."[14]

Another article relating returned missionaries' experiences in March 1886 presented an even more discernable pattern. Though the details of the eight elders' reports varied, the formula remained largely the same: elder's name, hometown, location of mission, stories of persecution, healings, successful results (usually baptisms), and general impressions. Those missionaries who encountered the most opposition received the longest and most detailed entries; the shortest entry went to the one elder who declared that the Alabamans treated him "so much better than he expected that he feels it would be ungrateful in him to mention the unpleasant things he had to encounter." Otherwise, the range of encounters was familiar: Elder Wiley Cragun was shot in the forehead and jaw by a mob; Elder George Woodbury and his companion were taken out in the woods and given sixty lashes with persimmon sprouts; Elder John Bevan "was many times threatened by bigoted and lawless persons"; Elder Thomas Davis managed to escape receiving any violence, "though he had some 'close calls'"; Elder Willard Bingham was stymied by "the opposition of the sectarian preachers"; Elder Ormus Gates discovered that southerners were "greatly prejudiced against the Latter-day Saints"; and Elder Lyman Shepherd "was threatened many times" and only escaped thanks to "providential circumstances."[15]

Deseret News subscribers read hundreds of such accounts of southern hostility against Mormon missionaries and converts in the closing decades of the nineteenth century. Elders returning from other missions also recalled their experiences in the newspaper, but the opposition they received was noticeably less violent than missionaries in the Southern States Mission reported. The Southern States missionaries' accounts collectively reminded the Saints that the war between God and the devil was not only spiritual in nature, but had very real, tangible, and violent manifestations in the flesh. Mormons in the 1870s and 1880s did not need to be told that they were an embattled minority besieged by hostile forces. But southern anti-Mormonism, especially because the violence (actual or threatened) was so frequent and consistent, highlighted the fact that the battle was in the field, not just in the courts and legislative halls. While the antipolygamy crusade had devastating effects on the Mormon image nationally and ultimately threatened to destroy the church institutionally, the fact that almost every missionary who labored in the South during this period experienced some form of violent hostility, and that virtually every Mormon in Utah knew it, punctuated the conflict and let them know that their enemies were real and actively sought their destruction.

Mormons' persecution narratives maintained that they were innocent victims suffering persecution for Jesus's sake. They did not instigate the conflict—they were merely preaching the gospel and exercising their religious freedom—but they would courageously persevere in the face of persecution. They would even rejoice in opposition, knowing God would reward their suffering. This self-portrayal pertained to the whole body of the Saints, but it applied especially to those on the front lines of the conflict. Church leaders and publications extolled elders in the Southern States Mission as models of virtue, innocence, faith, and courage in the face of oppression. For instance, in a sermon shortly after the Cane Creek Massacre, George Q. Cannon, first counselor in the church's First Presidency, affirmed that "great sacrifices" were called for by followers of the gospel, possibly "even life itself." Elders Gibbs and Berry had passed the test, and as the latest martyrs for the truth they, along with their fellow laborers in the South, served as inspiration to other Saints who would also inevitably be persecuted for the gospel's sake.[16] In its first issue after receiving news of Cane Creek, the *Woman's Exponent*, an influential periodical that served as the public voice for Mormon women, bemoaned the fact that "the wicked still continue to persecute the Saints," and "seek the lives" of those "innocent, inoffensive, honest young men, sent to proclaim the glad tidings of salvation and seeking to bring souls to a knowledge of the truth."[17] In a public discourse about the progress of evangelization in the South, mission president John Morgan recognized that elders in the region "are called upon to pass through trying circumstances," and applauded them for their fortitude. He confidently proclaimed, "I do not remember of a single instance in which a young Elder flinched from the performance of his duty." Instead, they always stood ready to sacrifice "for the good of the cause, even to the risking of their lives."[18] Missionaries proved their mettle, and their sincere commitment to the truth, by persevering in the face of violent opposition. Or, as historian Laurence Moore framed it, "Bearing persecution became the distinctive badge of membership in the church."[19]

This lionizing of not only the fallen martyrs but also those who remained behind to continue God's work was fundamental in the creation of a historical continuum between the Saints of the late nineteenth century and their mythologized forebears who had suffered at the hands of hostile crowds in the antebellum era and even in early Christianity. John Morgan counted it a blessing for elders in the South to get the "experience" of persecution, "in order that they may know what their fathers know, and that they may be able to stand shoulder to shoulder with them."[20] He saw in the missionaries' rough treatment a dynamic similar to that experienced by earlier generations of Saints. "The same influence that fought and contended against the Latter-day Saints in the State of Missouri," Morgan told a congregation in the Salt Lake Tabernacle in 1880, and "the same influence that cried out nearly 2000 years ago 'crucify him, crucify him,' is still abroad in the land."[21] In his address at the funeral of Joseph Standing, senior apostle John Taylor lifted the significance of the missionary's murder beyond the particular historical setting of the American South by claiming that the animating spirit behind the murder was the same as that which led to Joseph Smith's assassination and Jesus's crucifixion.[22] The Southern States Mission's newspaper, the *Southern Star*, directly compared those who persecuted the Saints in the late nineteenth-century South with those who, under the influence of Satan, had always stood against God's righteous people and appointed messengers. Elder Warren Johnson said that the aphorism that "persecution is the heritage of the Saints" was so true that "it would not be wrong to call it Scripture."[23] Latter-day Saints thus found a rich array of historical analogies for their suffering, stretching from Abel to Paul to select Christian reformers of the "dark ages" who suffered death at the hands of religious bigots.[24]

Religious historian Jan Shipps offers a compelling argument about how early Latter-day Saints understood history and their place in it. Because Joseph Smith's earliest visionary experiences led him to disavow virtually all of post-apostolic Christian history as hopelessly corrupted—Mormons refer to the period from the death of the apostles, or at least the Council of Nicea, until Smith's First Vision in 1820 as the "Great Apostasy"—Mormons were left with "an enormous . . . lacuna in their religious history." The Latter-day Saints' religious history jumped over more than a millennium and a half of traditional Christian history to connect with the earliest generation of Christians who lived the true gospel before the church purportedly fell into darkness. As Latter-day Saints lived through a new series of sacred events, they realized that their activities mirrored those of the former day saints. They came to believe that they were reenacting the cosmic drama that God's chosen people had always participated in, whether it was the Israelites in the Exodus, Jesus in his ministry, or early Christians in taking the gospel to the known world. In Shipps's telling, early Mormons recovered this sacred past, and placed themselves in a new reliving of it, through a fourfold process similar to the one used by Christians in appropriating the history of the Israelites: *reiteration* of the sacred stories of the past; theological *reinterpretation* of that narrative in light of current revelation and eschatology; actual *recapitulation* of key events of the sacred past in a new time and place; and *ritual re-creation* of the narrative in a particular Mormon context.[25]

Although Shipps's analysis focuses primarily on the first generation of Latter-day Saints, her insights help explain the premium that Saints in the late nineteenth century placed on connecting their experiences to their mythic past, specifically in regards to persecution and martyrdom. Other Christians, of course, had a long history of saints and martyrs to emulate, but Mormons, with their rejection of most of Christian history, could not properly model themselves after those who lived and died for a presumably apostate faith. They found meaning and redemption in their suffering as they understood it to be a recapitulation of biblical persecutions.[26] The oppressive hand of American government and law enforcement was a reminder of Pharaoh's slavery or Roman tyranny, with all the brutality that underlay their maintenance and exercise of power. Bloodthirsty mobs acting at the behest of their religious leaders were reminiscent of those who sent Jesus to the cross. Those who rejected and sometimes assaulted the missionaries were contemporary manifestations of those who turned away the early apostles and eventually martyred them. Persecution and martyrdom became bodily reenactments of a sacred past that initiated the Saints into a chosen community of those called to suffer for the gospel's sake. If suffering was a prerequisite for celestial glory, then late nineteenth-century Saints had to show how they measured up to the persecutions of the early Christians, or more immediately, those who had persevered through the hardships of Missouri, Illinois, and the westward trek to Utah.

In a sermon delivered less than a month after the funeral for Elders Gibbs and Berry, George Q. Cannon articulated how the binding ties of persecution connected the Saints of the 1880s to their spiritual ancestors and witnessed to the divine nature of their work:

> The religion of our Lord and Savior was established at the cost of precious and it may be said inestimable blood and lives, and it has been the characteristic of truth in every age to be hated and to be opposed. If, therefore, we as Latter-day Saints are exposed to opposition and hostility,—having our names cast out as evil, and men thinking that they are doing God's service in killing us,—it is no more than men have endured in past generations for the truth, for that which is now recognized as the purest and most heavenly truth. It is with our generation as it was with the generation in which the Savior lived, and as it has been with all generations.[27]

The often violent anti-Mormonism of the late nineteenth-century South therefore provided not only a negative oppositional identity for the Saints but also gave them a positive sense of connection with a long-running sacred drama in which they now played a vital part. The handful of major incidents of violence dramatized the severity of the conflict and the murderous dedication of the opposition. The hundreds of more minor episodes, in which missionaries escaped the fate of Elders Standing and Gibbs, exposed the persistence of hostility while also demonstrating how Providence, in most cases, protected the Saints and prevented threats and attempted murders from becoming something worse.

Suffering, no matter how poignant, was not redemptive unless performed in the cause of truth. In order for the hardships they experienced to be meaningful, missionaries in the South had to believe that they were on God's side, that God was on theirs, and that they were faithful servants on a divine errand. This sense of providential purpose and security was pervasive among the elders. In a letter to another missionary, Elder Samuel Spencer recounted the organization of "a regular 'ku-klux' party" in Belair, Georgia, with members signing "a villainous manuscript declaring that we should be exterminated or put to death." The missionaries escaped, according to Spencer, only because of the protection of local church members and the intervention of a "higher power." He affirmed, "I do not know what our destiny will be but it cannot be more than the death of the body, and they cannot take my life unless God permits them to do so."[28] John Gibbs poignantly expressed this deep faith in providence in his letters home to his wife Louisa, especially in the months immediately leading up to his violent death in August 1884. In April he wrote, "Do not be alarmed or have any fears in regard my safety. Have faith and plead with our Father for my protection. . . . The Lord has protected me, and has the same with all the Elders, so we have no need to fear. . . . They cannot go any farther than God will allow them. . . . And if we are united and faithful He will not allow them to do anything at all." A month later, after escaping a scrape with some local citizens, Gibbs rejoiced that God had "quelled the mob, and allowed us to finish our labors." Just five days before being murdered, he reassured Louisa and encouraged her to trust in God: "We cannot tell what lies in the future, so all I can say is let the morrow take care of it self [sic], and we will await the final decision of the future developments."[29]

Of course, the future was not kind to John Gibbs, and critics might scoff that his assurance of divine protection was clearly misplaced. The faithful, on the other hand, remained confident that fallen elders such as Gibbs, Berry, and Standing each wore a martyr's crown and would be received triumphantly into God's glory.[30] Their deaths were part of a heavenly calculus that defied earthly arithmetic. God transformed negative experiences into positive outcomes, and the loss of each martyr resulted in a net gain for the church. Latter-day Saints understood that opposition bred success. The *Deseret News* reported that the missionaries were "sustained" by the fact that "persecution raises up for them friends and not infrequently causes converts to flock around them."[31] A missionary writing from Nashville provided firsthand testimony that "the more opposition, the better success attends the labors of the missionaries; the more sharp persecution from without, the more of a unity of spirit is seen among the Saints."[32] John Morgan understood the practical utility of opposition particularly well; though distressed with extreme acts of violence, in general he did not regret the elders being persecuted. "In the long run," he told the Saints, opposition resulted in "bringing the honest in heart . . . to a knowledge of the truth." Morgan even suggested that the fierceness of antagonism against the Saints served as a barometer for the future success of the movement—the more widespread the feeling of opposition, the better omen for Mormonism's growth and success.[33]

In their persecution narrative, late nineteenth-century Mormons asserted that they were a people of peace, and thus were not belligerents in a shared conflict but rather victims in a one-sided campaign. George Q. Cannon powerfully asserted the peaceful ideals of the Latter-day Saints by quoting a canonized 1833 revelation to Joseph Smith in which God urged the Saints to "renounce war and proclaim peace," and emphasizing that no matter what wrongs were done to them, "There is no room for revenge in the heart of a true Latter-day Saint." Cannon insisted that "we must be lovers of peace. . . . God designs that we shall be a peaceful people, a people who shall love and cultivate peace, a people who shall seek by every means in their power to avert war and to avert bloodshed, to proclaim peace, and to entreat people for peace." God did not, according to Cannon, "intend that the Latter-day Saints shall be a people shedding blood." Cannon surely spoke out of principled conviction, but he also spoke from a pragmatic recognition of the Saints' relative weakness. In 1884, when he gave his sermon, the Saints had no real means of defending themselves against their enemies, whether mobs in the South, Republicans (and increasingly Democrats) in Washington, or federal marshals in Utah. As Cannon acknowledged, "We cannot defend ourselves by earthly weapons. We are too feeble. We are not strong in numbers. We are not strong in wealth. We are not strong in worldly things." Lacking legitimate alternatives, seeking peace, or at least avoiding conflict, was the Saints' only viable option. The Saints did possess one advantage, however: God was on their side. No earthly power would protect them, but Cannon promised that God would fight the battles of his chosen people if they righteously relied on his power rather than their own.[34]

The notion that God would fight his people's battles could be expressed positively, as in Cannon's sermon, but in general the Mormons' rhetoric became increasingly angry during the last quarter of the nineteenth century as they speculated on the fury that God would surely unleash upon their enemies. In a missive to the Latter-day Saints in the South, urging them to remain faithful in the face of persecution, mission president Ben E. Rich declared that God "will bare His almighty and powerful arm in defense of His chosen ones, and the wicked and ungodly will feel the avenging hand of God, and shall be destroyed from the earth."[35] In this mode, God's support of the Saints appeared less as a defensive bulwark than as an offensive force. Not only would he protect the believers, but he would take retributive action against their oppressors. The "apocalyptic dualism" that historian Grant Underwood has identified in early Mormonism persisted into the late nineteenth century, with the ultimate salvation of the Saints and destruction of the wicked as two sides of the same coin. Nineteenth-century Latter-day Saints drank deeply from the waters of millennialism, with its promise of a miraculous culmination to history in which good triumphs over evil. The belief in a final, decisive victory, resulting in the annihilation of one's temporal foes, makes the suffering of the moment bearable, even embraceable, and is therefore attractive to many oppressed religious groups, Christian and otherwise.[36] By the same token, Latter-day Saints' expectation that the forces of evil would nearly triumph over righteousness in the endtimes immediately preceding Christ's Second Coming helped explain and give meaning to the opposition that beset them on all sides. Eschatology thus encountered and framed contemporary history, and Mormons warned that God would take vengeance on anyone who persecuted, much less martyred, his Saints.

Episodes of southern anti-Mormon violence elicited such sentiments from the Mormon faithful. Following Joseph Standing's murder, John Morgan publicly wished divine vengeance on Standing's killers. In a circular letter to the missionaries and church members in the Southern States Mission, he counseled the Saints not to seek recrimination, but only because "vengeance is mine and I will repay, saith the Lord." Because God would exact justice, Morgan reasoned with his fellow Saints, "we can afford to leave the assassins of Elder Standing in his hands." Three months later, increasingly frustrated with the sham trial of Standing's killers, Morgan concluded his published correspondence with the *Deseret News*, "May the day speedily come when God will put forth His hand to avenge their wrongs."[37] The *News* took up where Morgan left off, expressing in classic millennial terms that it did not matter whether the Saints' persecutors "ever receive from earthly courts or not the proper penalty for their inhuman deeds and violations." Malefactors' escape from justice would surely be only temporary, as they could not avoid falling "into the hands of the living God." At that moment of divine judgment, the wicked oppressors of the Saints would "vainly lament over their iniquities but will find no escape from the penalties of divine law nor the miseries of irrevocable doom."[38] After the Cane Creek Massacre, the *Deseret News* rebuked not only the actual murderers of Elders Gibbs and Berry but also the "lying priests" and the libelous anti-Mormon press who had "done [their] part in the slaughter." A seeming victory for the forces of darkness would eventually be swallowed up in God's perfect, and demanding, justice: "You cannot wash out the stain; you cannot worm yourselves out of the responsibility; you cannot escape the certain penalty for your malice and mendacity. As God lives, your judgment will be sure and just."[39]

These warnings, printed in Mormon letters and periodicals, were not principally intended for the general public but rather appealed to an internal Mormon audience, reinforcing Latter-day Saints' identity as the beleaguered but ultimately chosen people of God. Confident in divine judgment, late nineteenth-century Mormons could see themselves as innocent victims and heed George Cannon's call to eschew revenge, knowing that God would be the agent of their retribution. At every step, then, the Saints perceived their temporal powerlessness as a virtue, a testimony that they—like Jesus on the cross, the early Christians in Roman coliseums, or the early Mormons in Missouri jails—were despised for the gospel's sake. Their suffering was thus noble, righteous, and ultimately redemptive. The violent persecution of Mormons in the postbellum South, punctuated by Joseph Standing's murder and the massacre at Cane Creek, played a crucial role in constructing and reinforcing a persecution narrative that sustained, and was sustained by, the dualistic millennialism inherent in nineteenth-century Latter-day Saint faith.

BUILDING AN OPPOSITIONAL IDENTITY

On Sunday, August 24, 1879, John Taylor, who would be ordained as church president one year later, spoke to the congregation assembled in the Salt Lake Tabernacle. He contrasted the virtue of the Latter-day Saints with the corruption of "Gentile" society. Precisely because they stood for truth and adopted "a proper, consistent, upright, virtuous and honorable course," the Latter-day Saints would stand out in an impure and wicked world. Their distinctiveness would bring not only attention but also antagonism. Taylor peppered the congregation with a series of rhetorical questions: "Will they persecute you? Yes. Will they hate you? Yes. Will they rob you? Yes, and thank God for having the privilege."[40]

The persecution narrative crafted by nineteenth-century Mormons contributed to a broader identity that relied as much on who Latter-day Saints were not as who they were. For John Taylor and his fellow Saints, there always existed a "them" that sought to harm "us." "They" might variously be defined as mobs, the government, the press, non-Mormons in Utah, or the Protestant clergy; indeed, it made sense that "they" all conspired together in an unholy alliance against the Saints. Nineteenth-century Mormons were not entirely delusional or paranoid in thinking this way, as the anti-Mormon (or at least antipolygamy) crusade of the 1880s did bring together multiple segments of society in a loose alliance, and the Saints did in fact suffer at their hands. Mormons did have a tendency, however, to overstate the pervasiveness of hostility against them. For instance, a missionary writing home from Nashville complained, with at least some hyperbole, that "one cannot pass a bookstore without seeing in its windows scandalous stories about the 'Mormons,' and ridiculous illustrations, such as task-masters set over the 'Mormon' women in the fields."[41] Seeing enemies everywhere, and feeling assailed on all sides, became an essential element to Mormon identity in the 1880s. This pattern echoes what Michael Ignatieff has said about certain forms of contemporary ethnic nationalism, which "glances up at the Other only to confirm its difference. Then it looks down again and turns its gaze upon itself."[42] Rooted in both real and imagined anti-Mormon hostilities, a sense of opposition joined with self-chosen otherness in largely defining what it meant and felt like to be a Latter-day Saint in the late polygamy period. Antagonists could be seen everywhere the Mormons looked, but the

South, with its special combination of legislative, religious, and violent anti-Mormonism, loomed large in the Mormon oppositional imagination.

As Mormons reflected on the causes of southern hostility—the origins of which they always located external to the Saints themselves—they identified those groups who were at the root of the opposition, and thus were the agents of their persecution. In broader Mormon discourse, the national government, with its alleged abuses of constitutional guarantees of religious liberty, figured prominently. Following Cane Creek, George Q. Cannon observed that the time foreseen by earlier Mormon prophecies seemed to be "fast approaching," when the United States government would fail and the Latter-day Saints would be required to protect the freedoms embodied in the Constitution (which LDS revelation declared to be inspired by God). Since the current government officials clearly found themselves in conflict with the kingdom of God, Cannon surmised, "The time is drawing near when constitutional government will have to be maintained by some other hands than those who now profess to be its upholders."[43] In general, however, the Saints saw the failures of government officials in Washington as a contingent, secondary cause of their southern troubles, and they looked toward more immediate sources of southern anti-Mormonism.

Latter-day Saints commonly identified the press as an instigator of southern hostility. Although they did at times acknowledge examples of fair treatment from the non-Mormon press, far more often the Saints complained of "inaccuracies" regarding them and their religion in southern newspapers.[44] John Morgan observed that in the year 1879, for instance, "a spirit of persecution and mobocracy was prevalent throughout a great portion of the South, brought about, to a great extent, by inflammatory articles in the newspapers." According to Morgan, the many misrepresentations and denunciations in the southern newspapers resulted in "the mobbing of a number of the elders and the driving from their homes of quite a number" of convert families.[45] Several years later, the *Deseret News* provided only a slightly more positive assessment of the role of the southern press, saying that "while many journals do not openly applaud the application of mob violence to the 'Mormon' missionaries hundreds of them appear to be only too ready to wink at it and apologize for all those who resort to it."[46]

Mormons also pointed their collective finger at the non-Mormon population in Utah, especially the more caustic anti-Mormon component. John Morgan acknowledged that much of the difficulties encountered by elders in the South had their "foundation in Salt Lake City."[47] Following the murder of Elders Gibbs and Berry in Tennessee, and recalling the Joseph Standing incident five years previous, the *Deseret News* argued that southern anti-Mormon violence was "planted, watered and nourished by hands nearer home than Tennessee or Georgia." Both the press and anti-Mormons in Salt Lake had "stirred up the basest passions of lawless men by their foul calumnies of the Latter-day Saints," which were circulated throughout the nation in an effort to rally support for the antipolygamy campaign.[48] In recounting a recent series of mob actions against him and his companion, Elder Francis McDonald complained that "these lawless acts are traceable to writings of anti-Mormons and apostates from Utah." As proof of the connection between the anti-Mormon movements in Utah and the South, McDonald offered that he had seen "one of these mob preachers" carry anti-Mormon literature originating from Utah "under his arm to church the same as if it were the Bible."[49] The Saints later made similar claims as an explanation for the killings at Cane Creek.

As their rhetoric indicated, late nineteenth-century Mormons defined themselves first and foremost religiously. If they were essentially religious, then so was the perceived nature of opposition arrayed against them. Religious bigotry, not political or moral considerations, "guided the current of popular opinion and prejudice" against the Saints, and "wielded the venomous instincts of the rabble" in targeting LDS missionaries and converts.[50] Politicians, judges, and the press were unfriendly, to be sure, but Mormons saw their actions more as symptoms rather than as underlying causes. Latter-day Saints' principal frame of oppositional reference was religious competitors. With repeated instances of southern aggression in mind, Mormons especially resented Protestant clergy, for whom they blamed much of the antagonism that sparked anti-Mormon violence and whom they also identified as instigating and leading mobs against them on numerous occasions. John Morgan forcefully made the point when he argued in an 1880 address that "there would be but little said in relation to the work the Latter-day Saints are doing" in the South "but for the religious influence." He went on to underscore what he saw as the hypocrisy of the "orthodox" southern religious elite, claiming that "the worst treatment I have ever received at the hands of any class of men has been from men who can pray the longest prayers, preach the loudest sermons, and wear the longest face, and who profess to be going back to Abraham's bosom. . . . If we have difficulties they are to a greater or less extent caused by those who profess to believe in this Bible."[51] Mission president Ben E. Rich similarly concluded that most of the Mormons' trouble in the South "comes from the ministers." He impugned the clergy's Christian character, saying that "if they would remember the commandments of God and stop their lying and stop bearing false witness against their neighbors," the Mormons would be left unharmed.[52] Alphonso Snow, the son of fifth LDS president Lorenzo Snow and a missionary in Tennessee in the early 1880s, confirmed Morgan's and Rich's opinions, asserting that "never upon one occasion, when we took time to investigate, did we fail to trace the cause of these persecutions to a religious source."[53] In the Latter-day Saints' minds, Protestant clergy hypocritically complained of "heathen" persecution of

Christian missionaries abroad while overlooking and even countenancing violence against Mormon missionaries in the South (for one graphic example, see figure 8.2).

Missionaries in the South frequently complained about the overtly hostile stance adopted by the Protestant leadership. Contemporaneous accounts published in the *Deseret News* demonstrated that the clergy's opposition to the Mormons went far beyond theological disagreements or religious defenses against LDS proselytizing. Elder Matthias Cowley, later called into the church's Quorum of Twelve Apostles before being disciplined for his continuing practice of plural marriage after the church had suspended the practice, wrote that the opposition he experienced as a missionary in Tazewell County, Virginia, was "generally instigated by men professing great Christian piety."[54] Francis McDonald, laboring in Paintsville, Kentucky, was even more specific, noting that the local people had been "gulled by unprincipled

Figure 8.2 "A Sermon without Words." Christian clergymen request a battleship to retaliate against "the ungodly heathens [who] are persecuting our Christian missionaries in China" while overlooking mobs in the United States burning Mormon churches and beating and whipping Mormon missionaries. Cartoon from the *New York Truthseeker*, reproduced in *Southern Star* vol. 1 (Chattanooga: Southern States Mission, 1899), 408. Courtesy of L. Tom Perry Special Collections, Harold B. Lee Library, Brigham Young University, Provo, Utah.

preachers," with "two ministers, one a Methodist and the other a Baptist," leading the anti-Mormon mob that threatened his life.[55] The success of missionaries in the region of Roan Mountain in eastern Tennessee reportedly prompted persecution "instigated by religious ministers" who were motivated by "jealousy and hatred."[56] In South Carolina, a band of "regulators" accosted Elder Joseph Thorup and his companion, announcing that "the ministers of the neighborhood had decided that the 'Mormons' must go." When the elders ignored their threats and remained in the area, a preacher named Wright delivered a sermon denouncing the Mormons, "and urging the people to drive them out." The next day, Thorup was arrested and thrown in a vermin-infested prison cell, where he spent two nights before being released.[57] As late as 1900, missionaries in North Carolina reported that Christian preachers "say all manner of evil against our people" and "occasionally suggest mobocracy and lynch law."[58]

In missionary tracts as well as reports in the *Deseret News*, Latter-day Saints used their encounters in the South to sustain an identity separate from and built in opposition to traditional Protestantism. Ben Rich authored a number of tracts based on his experience as president of the Southern States Mission from 1898 to 1908. In "Two Letters to a Baptist Minister," Rich provided a bold defense of the faith in response to a pair of sermons preached by Reverend J. Whitcomb Brougher, pastor of First Baptist Church in Chattanooga, which Rich characterized as "tirades of falsehoods and misrepresentations from beginning to end; they were filled with much bitterness and hatred, and during one of his sermons he came as near advocating mob violence as he dared." Another tract authored by Rich, "A Friendly Discussion upon Religious Subjects," took the form of a conversation between a Tennessee lawyer, physician, and clergyman. The trio had begun a discussion about religion and politics, when an "attractive" and "genial" man named Charles Durant joined them. Durant, who initially identified himself as "a believer in religion" but concealed his Mormon identity, claimed that while following "the truth of the gospel of Christ . . . I often find myself opposed by ministers." As he presented a doctrinal exposition on the foundational principles of Mormonism, the preacher, included as a straw man, offered feeble objections that Durant easily swept aside. In due course, the other two men were convinced by the Mormon's beliefs. The doctor admitted that Durant's teachings were in perfect "accordance with Holy Writ," and the lawyer exclaimed, "I have heard more that appears reasonable from you, Mr. Durant, regarding religion than ever before in my life. . . . No one can find any fault with those doctrines." The tract simultaneously accomplished a number of objectives. It provided a triumphalist rendering of Mormonism, in which its doctrine was judged by supposedly objective and educated southerners as eminently logical and acceptable, not heretical and marginal. The minister's hostility to Durant's teachings appeared as unenlightened resistance to true Christianity. Rich thus inverted the typical anti-Mormon discourse, as the Mormon missionary in his narrative represented a progressive and reasonable Christianity for a modern age while the Protestant clergyman embodied a backward and regressive corruption of authentic religion. The self-evident truthfulness of Mormonism was highlighted through an agonistic discourse in which LDS theology and identity was distinguished in its sharp contrast with evangelical Protestantism.[59]

The Saints' oppositional identity was further constructed through autobiographies published late in life by men who had proselytized in the South during their youth. Though the pervasive campaign of violence against Mormon missionaries in the region had long since subsided, the South emerged in these autobiographies as a place of conflict between good and evil, true and false religion, and reminded a new generation that the general attitude of other religions toward Mormonism was one of animosity. In his self-published 1953 autobiography, *A Divinity Shapes Our Ends*, Thomas Cottam Romney (a great-uncle of 2008 presidential candidate Mitt Romney) wrote extensively about his missionary labors in Virginia. He claimed to "meet with some opposition, especially from the ministers," and related an incident in which two missionaries working just across the James River from him were "accosted" and struck in the face by a Protestant Sunday School superintendent.[60] Andrew Israelsen's autobiography chronicled a succession of mob actions against him during his mission in Alabama. In his "fourth mobbing scrape" in less than four months, in which the missionaries were threatened with death if they did not leave the county, Israelsen reported that the leader of the mob was a Baptist minister. Earlier, "the greatest Baptist preacher in that part of the country" had delivered a note to the family that had sheltered him and his companion saying that their house would be burned if they allowed the Mormons to hold meetings there. Soon after, another Baptist minister told the same family that "if you allow those Mormons to stay with you, a mob will be as numerous around your house some of these nights as those tobacco stalks are now."[61] Romney's and Israelsen's autobiographies would have had a limited readership outside of their immediate families, but together they illustrate how the nineteenth-century Mormon conflict with southern Protestants continued to shape and reinforce grassroots Latter-day Saint identity long after the actual violence had occurred.

For Latter-day Saints, the contest between themselves and Protestants, and society at large, was not simply a matter of competing earthly identities and ideologies. Mormons believed that their temporal conflict was part of a larger, and eternal, cosmic war between the forces of righteousness and the forces of evil. Though theirs was only one front in the larger battle, they believed their part of the fight was crucial to the overall effort to overthrow wickedness and establish the kingdom of God on the earth. Christ was at the helm, rallying and supporting his people in the fight. But this meant that the devil himself was on the other side of the line, leading his followers in an all-out onslaught to overcome the righteous and frustrate the works of God. Latter-day Saints therefore identified the ultimate motivating force behind southern hostility not just as religious competition, but as a satanic conspiracy against godly truth. Thomas Romney expressed the view that Satan was the prime mover behind southern anti-Mormonism in poetic verse: "So great the opposition/So fierce the devil's fight – /That we, the Mormon Elders,/Baptized late in the night."[62] Another missionary, Donald Urie, wrote home to his father that the missionaries across the South seemed to be encountering resistance almost simultaneously. Urie explained this coincidence of mission-wide hostility by pointing to otherworldly forces, saying that "Satan must have had a well organized secret service which burst forth all at once."[63] John Morgan also saw the opposition experienced by southern missionaries as inspired by the devil, who he supposed "is even more determined now than ever to put it into the hearts of wicked and bigoted men to oppose" the spread of Mormonism in the South.[64] From the Latter-day Saints' perspective, the forces of hell seemed to be arrayed against them. Rather than deflating their resolve, this belief instead reinforced a powerful sense of their own righteous purpose.

With its identity shaped in large part through antagonistic relations with both state power and other religious groups, late nineteenth-century Mormonism thus followed patterns demonstrated in many other modern religious enclave communities. Historian Emmanuel Sivan's comparative profile of these religious enclaves helps illuminate the processes behind the construction of the late nineteenth-century Mormon oppositional identity. According to Sivan, religious enclaves are created through the voluntary choice of their members, and are self-consciously defined against an outside culture, which with its "prestige, cultural hegemony, and access to governmental sanctions as well as to resources" constitutes a constant threat and temptation. The enclave, by definition a minority community, cannot guarantee the personal safety of its members, particularly as they interact with the outside. However, the community provides other rewards for fidelity in the face of opposition, including knowledge among its members that they are part of the chosen remnant resisting the onslaught of evil, as well as the ultimate promise of salvation. In order to retain and protect its members from the "polluted, contagious, [and] dangerous" outside world, the enclave constructs a "wall of virtue" that places "the oppressive and morally defiled outside society in sharp contrast to the community of virtuous insiders," thus separating Zion from Babylon. Maintaining the cohesion and purity of the enclave is accomplished through strict observance of behavioral standards, social practices encouraging and reinforcing the insider-outsider dynamic, and rhetorical posturing asserting the enclave as the chosen community of grace and the outside world as a persistent threat.[65] Literary scholar Regina Schwartz builds upon this notion by arguing that the group's identity is defined in negative terms—in other words, not only by who they are but also very much by who they are not: "those outsiders—so needed for the very self-definition of those inside the group—are also regarded as a threat to them."[66]

While the South provided a steady trickle of converts in the late nineteenth century, it played perhaps an even more important role in reinforcing the oppositional identity of Mormonism. Anti-Mormonism was not unique to the South, nor did anyone (other than perhaps missionaries in the Southern States Mission) believe that the South was the principal theater of conflict. What distinguished the South from all other regions of the country, or the world for that matter, was the persistence, even pervasiveness, of violence against the Mormons. The violence inflicted upon missionaries, converts, and Mormon sympathizers in the region transformed them into martyrs—or, if they survived, suffering saints—in the Mormon mind and solidified the persecution mentality that shaped the church's often-antagonistic relationship to the nation, to other faiths, and to its own dissenters. The impact of southern anti-Mormonism thus resonated far beyond the confines of Dixie. Narratives of violence, actual or threatened, emerging from the South provided concrete evidence of just how far the anti-Mormon forces would go in accomplishing their purposes. A number of circumstances combined to make the South unique in its approach to the Mormon problem, but the Saints did not feel compelled to dwell on the historical and sociological aspects of southern particularity. The distinctly violent approach that many southerners adopted in fighting Mormonism offered a valuable rhetorical tool for both elite and grassroots Mormons seeking to reinforce a powerful oppositional identity that originated in the church's early years and continued to define and sustain the Saints through the polygamy era and beyond. This collective defensive mentality was instrumental in steeling the resolve of the faithful and helping maintain the cohesion of the community in the face of concerted efforts to destroy it.

9

Religious Minorities and the Problem of Peculiar Peoplehood

Most studies of conflict in the postbellum South focus exclusively, and justifiably, on racial and political violence against African Americans and to some extent their white political allies. As the Mormon experience shows, the late nineteenth-century South could also be a hostile environment for religious outsiders. But Mormons were not the only religious minorities in the postbellum South, nor the only victims of violence. Although the total tally of violent episodes (including nonlethal attacks) was greater for Mormons than any other single religious minority group excepting black Christians, southerners killed dozens of Jews and Catholics in the last quarter of the century and perpetrated many other instances of lesser violence against them as well. This betrayal of religious tolerance provides unique insights into postbellum southern culture and the sometimes violent nature of the American experiment in religious pluralism.

The Mormon case offers an unambiguous example of religious violence, in that both instigators and victims saw religion as a central dimension of the conflict, even if other factors were also at work. In religious violence, the religious identity of the perpetrator or victim (or both), as expressed in belief and practice, becomes a principal motivating or triggering factor for violence and provides the primary discourse through which the respective parties understand their aggression or victimhood. Religious doctrine matters in religious violence, both in terms of unorthodox doctrines that spur hostility as well as certain theological orientations that allow and even call for violence against individuals or groups who are seen as ungodly or otherwise dangerous. Purely theological disputes have rarely led to violence in America, but competing theological commitments and doctrinal interpretations have frequently led to, or at least justified, the use of violence against those whose religious practices positioned them out of the mainstream. Religious violence has typically occurred when concrete social and cultural practices that are inspired by religious commitments are perceived to transgress accepted community norms.[1] The campaign against

Mormonism, and specifically polygamy, is a vivid example of this form of religious violence.

Limiting religious violence to this pure definition, however, misses many nuances of the other ways that religion also operates in violent settings. Beyond specific practices, religion also dictates or at least informs broad social, economic, political, and cultural orientations. It may not even be a specific religiously prescribed rite that draws opposition but rather a world-view that is shaped by the religious vision of certain religious outsiders. For example, the explicit involvement of black preachers in politics following emancipation was inspired by their notion of an undifferentiated "sacred cosmos," a cultural retention from West Africa that made no clear distinction between sacred and secular.[2] In the case of biracial southern Christianity, religion undergirded and sacralized competing approaches to political cul-ture. In other words, the pluralism within Christianity was the source of two diametrically opposed religious and political approaches. The "liberationist" Christianity of African American freedpeople, drawn largely from the Old Testament narrative of the exodus, clashed with the establishment Chris-tianity of the white evangelical Protestants, whose dominance over main-stream culture allowed them to enforce their own idiosyncratic version of a church-state separation, and who reacted violently when African Americans transgressed the boundaries they had constructed. While it would obscure as much as it clarifies to categorize white terrorist attacks on black churches and preacher-politicians as religious violence per se, it is important to con-sider the religious dimensions of violent episodes that are commonly catego-rized solely as political or racial.

Whereas African Americans, who sought political and economic independ-ence, and Mormons, who sought their own form of separation from Protes-tant America, consciously made religion a marker of their outsider status, Jews and Catholics generally sought an accommodation with American cul-ture by privatizing their religion. Violence against individual members of these religious minority groups in the South was triggered more by their eco-nomic and ethnic profiles than by competing religious doctrines, practices, or worldviews. Although anti-Semitism and anti-Catholicism operated as perva-sive cultural forces throughout this period, and arguably were strengthened with the rise of populist fears of foreign conspiracies in the late nineteenth century, they did not translate into widespread or systematic violence against Jews or Catholics in the South. These groups' conscious decisions to accul-turate as much as possible to the southern mainstream made them non-threatening on a local level even while many southerners raged against the broader international perils of the "Jewish conspiracy" or the "papist threat."

Identity-based violence is often difficult to categorize precisely because personal and even group identities are overlapping and shifting. Individuals might simultaneously operate in their various religious, political, ethnic, economic, and familial roles, and groups can be difficult to classify (e.g., are Jews a racial, ethnic, or religious group?). Historical actors' "real" motivations are often difficult to discern, particularly because many perpetrators will cloak their true intentions in a guise of religion in order to justify their actions with a deeper and more transcendent meaning.[3] Even seemingly clear-cut religious violence may also be shaped by other elements; in the Mormon case, for instance, religion overlapped with worldviews informed by honor, gender, and politics.

Examining cases of anti-Jewish and anti-Catholic violence alongside anti-Mormonism will help us to better understand not only the historical encounter of religious minorities in the postbellum South but also the multivalent dynamics of religion in a conflict setting. Religion played different roles in the ways that Mormons, Jews, and Catholics precipitated, experienced, and responded to southern violence as religious outsiders. What connected all their experiences was that the victims had been accused of sinning against the social order, and violence (actual and threatened) became the means of punishing the transgressors and impelling them to conform to southern cultural and religious orthodoxies. This concluding chapter briefly examines the respective experiences of Jews and Catholics in the New South, then posits the notion that the extent of religious violence suffered by Mormons, Catholics, and Jews directly related to the degree to which these various groups deployed their particular religious peoplehood.

ANTI-JEWISH VIOLENCE IN THE NEW SOUTH

Jews in the late nineteenth- and early twentieth-century South found themselves in an ambivalent position. On one hand, they hailed the South as a land of freedom and opportunity, far better than eastern Europe's pogroms or even the urban North's slums; one Jewish immigrant to the South openly celebrated the region as a "very good place to live."[4] Jews had a long history in the region, with some families tracing their southern roots back to the early colonial era and most having loyally supported the Confederacy. Most European Jews had little or no experience with agriculture, due to restrictive laws prohibiting Jewish land ownership, but they often came to the United States with substantial experience as middlemen in the exchange of goods. This skill set prepared them to fill an important economic niche as peddlers and store owners selling goods and extending credit to southern farmers. As a result, Jews nurtured and rose with the New South economy. Embracing the opportunities afforded them in their new homeland and conscientious not to stick out or give offense, Jews made cultural and religious adaptation a virtual article of faith. They not only became good Americans but also acculturated to specific regional mores and customs. As Jews made efforts to be indistinguishably southern, for the most part their Protestant neighbors, particularly in urban settings and in the middle and upper classes, received them as such.[5]

Nevertheless, Jews did not entirely escape anti-Semitic discrimination and even violence in the New South. A pervasive, typically dormant anti-Semitism clearly existed in southern culture, which was periodically exacerbated by bouts of xenophobia, nativism, and economic downturns. When southerners needed a scapegoat, they could draw on the usually latent symbols and attitudes of traditional anti-Semitism, including images of the merciless Christ-killer and the avaricious Shylock. Georgia populist Tom Watson most famously employed these images during his days of demagoguery, but the very fact that Watson's vitriolic rhetoric resonated so well with a certain segment of the southern populace suggests that the anti-Semitic themes he employed were neither new nor foreign to his listeners.[6] Of course, white southerners scapegoated Jews for their troubles much less frequently than they did African Americans. Jews also experienced far less overt prejudice and violence than they did in Europe, and overall were victims of fewer instances of vigilantism than were Latter-day Saints in the late nineteenth-century South. Notwithstanding their relative good fortunes, the threat of losing their tolerated and even integrated status constantly hung over their heads and occasionally became real. When Jews in the South acculturated to local customs so as to blend in with the majority, it was done partly out of a desire to be accepted but also out of real fear of the consequences of rejection. The documented violence against them was sporadic, but taken as a composite it casts a shadow on the fairly optimistic portrayal of southern Jewish life provided by some historians.[7] Though a relatively high degree of acceptance and tolerance typically characterized the daily interactions of most southern Jews with their Christian neighbors, discrimination and violence were realities that they could neither ignore nor altogether escape.

Most of the violence experienced by Jews in the South was connected to their roles as peddlers and merchants in the postbellum economy. Peddlers were robbed and sometimes killed, and store owners were robbed, intimidated, and expelled from town. The violence often assumed an explicitly anti-Semitic character, but Jews' assailants more typically targeted them not because of their particular religious identity but rather because they had cash in their pockets, wares in their carts, or credit extended to hopelessly indebted farmers. The violence displayed a distinct class component, as "respectable citizens" of the New South frequently condemned anti-Jewish violence performed by disgruntled farmers or simple ruffians; this differentiated it from anti-Mormon violence, the approval of which often cut across class lines. Economic grievances thus typically provided the trigger for violent acts against Jews that were then frequently aggravated or rationalized by appeals to anti-Semitic images and prejudices. Other than brief and localized stretches, however, the South never had a systematic and extended anti-Semitic campaign, even during the era of the Leo Frank lynching in 1915 and the concomitant rise of the second Ku Klux Klan, which marked the low point of southern Jewish-Gentile relations.

The anti-Jewish violence that did occur took a number of forms. Much of the violence was linked to robbery, though it sometimes turned lethal. For instance, in July 1887 "a number of negroes" broke into Jacob Simon's store in Breaux Bridge, Louisiana. They choked the merchant to death, then robbed the store and "made away with the booty."[8] On the very same day, Solomon Dreeben was robbed and murdered while peddling near Wylie, in northeast Texas.[9] Jewish peddlers who solitarily rambled through the southern countryside made attractive targets for thieves and other desperate men. For every documented instance of an assaulted or murdered peddler, there were surely at least an equal number who narrowly escaped harm, like B. M. Surasky, who overheard the family with whom he was staying overnight plotting against him but made his flight before they could carry out their plan.[10] Without the insulation of a surrounding community, individual Jews in rural areas and small towns were particularly exposed. However, in many of these instances of simple robberies, even those that resulted in murder, the victims' Jewish identity seemed to have been incidental rather than causal, and violence proved the exception to the cordial treatment that Jewish peddlers and merchants received most of the time.

Anti-Semitism often became more transparent in cases in which vigilantes attacked southern Jews for their strength rather than for their weakness. The economic power of Jewish merchants could lead to resentment among their competitors or other local residents, particularly their debtors. Jewish proprietors were culpable in their enemies' eyes not only as individual transgressors but also as visible agents of a largely invisible and impersonal system of economic injustice and oppression. For example, in the northeastern Louisiana parish of West Carroll, long-standing resentment against Simon Witkowski, "the leading merchant and richest man in the parish," finally turned into violence in early spring 1887, resulting in the death of one unidentified man and the driving of Witkowski from the area. The *American Hebrew* reported the alleged cause of the violence: "It was stated that Witkowski had ground down those who were indebted to him, and had pursued a very hard policy in dealing with them."[11] It was not just Simon Witkowski's individual business practices that drew the mob's ire but his personification of the image of the greedy and manipulative Jewish Shylock, who lined his pockets by stealing from honest farmers and workers who were left in a spiraling cycle of indebtedness and poverty.

Violence fueled by prejudicial and conspiratorial images failed to differentiate between individual merchants against whom indebted customers may have had legitimate complaints and others who were guilty of nothing more than being Jewish. Shortly after the Witkowski incident, 170 miles downriver in Avoyelles Parish, a mob of "wild young men" attacked a store owned by two Jewish merchants, Kahn and Bauer. The store had been "doing a fine business," which engendered some local jealousy. The assailants riddled the store and surrounding fence with bullets, then delivered a written warning to Kahn and Bauer that they must leave the parish or be killed. The mob posted additional proclamations claiming that "the people . . . wanted no more Jews among them, and therefore advised all Jews to leave the county by April, under penalty of death." To the vigilantes' surprise, the local populace, for whom they presumed to speak, rose up in support of the Jews. The parish's two newspapers called for the mob's apprehension and punishment, local citizens held a mass meeting to the same effect, and the governor was persuaded to offer a large reward for the perpetrators' conviction.[12] Though frustrated in achieving their end goal, the vigilantes revealed a prejudice common among at least some southerners that vilified the general population of "all Jews" and not just individual Jewish merchants.

Most of the organized agrarian violence against southern Jewish store owners occurred in the late 1880s and early 1890s, when increasingly hopeless conditions drove many small farmers to desperation. Agrarian protest movements did not give birth to anti-Semitism in the South or America more broadly, but they triggered long-standing prejudices and stereotypes that found resonance with large numbers of southerners beset by a radically changing set of social, cultural, and economic circumstances.[13] The most extensive campaign of violence against southern Jews was initiated by a group of "rural and small town anti-Semitic propagandists," mostly in Louisiana and Mississippi.[14] On an early Saturday afternoon in October 1889, a "large party of armed men" rode into the northeastern Louisiana city of Delhi, not far from where Simon Witkowski had been violently driven from town two years previous. The mob fired their pistols into the showcases and front windows of the Jewish-owned mercantile establishments in the town, discharging about fifty bullets into T. Hirsch's storefront window, smashing up the store of S. Blum & Co., and sending bricks through the windows of Karpe, Weil & Co. Threatening the Jewish store owners and "putting them in terror for their lives," the rioters "ordered them to leave the place" within the next twelve to fifteen hours, then rode away as fast as they had come. The townspeople immediately expressed their "general regret" over the incident, which probably protected the merchants from further harm. Local newspapers ascertained that the violence stemmed from the mortgages that the merchants held on many small farms in the area, and that "certain debtors in the neighborhood were banded together, to run their creditors away."[15]

Despite the general antipathy toward anti-Semitic vigilantism shown by the majority of "respectable" citizens of northeastern Louisiana, mob violence struck again. In mid-November, a store owned by Jews in Tompkins Bend, about fifty miles northeast of Delhi, was riddled with some fifty rifle shots in the middle of the night. A posted sign read: "No Jews after the 1st of January. A Delhi warning of fire and lead will make you leave." Vigilantes also shot up another store, Bernard & Bloch, and fired twenty rounds into the home of one of the store's proprietors, one bullet narrowly passing over the bed where his family lay in fear.[16] This attack was more explicitly anti-Semitic than the Delhi outrage, overtly identifying "Jews" and not just individual storeowners as the target. Although the people of East Carroll Parish denounced the assault on their Jewish neighbors, the purpose of the terrorist violence was fulfilled when some of the targeted merchants decided to give up their businesses and leave the area.[17]

As the 1890s dawned and the agricultural condition of the South reached its lowest point leading up to the depression of 1893, farmers in the Deep South lashed out in desperation. Their discontent gave rise to Whitecapping, a dirt farmer movement that scapegoated black tenant farmers and Jewish merchants and used violence against them to benefit local white farmers. Whitecaps targeted African American tenants on lands owned by Jewish merchants, driving them from their homes and affixing notices declaring: "This Jew place is not for sale or rent, but will be used hereafter as pasture." Regulators beat, whipped, and killed numerous blacks, and burned scores of tenant homes to the ground.[18] Vigilantes typically did not target individual Jews for direct violence but did force many from their homes and businesses; many Jewish merchants and landholders also suffered considerable economic losses because of the attacks against their black tenants and properties. In one case, farmers even threatened lawyers who represented Jews in court.[19] News of the Jews' expulsion reached the federal government, and U.S. Senator Donelson Caffery asked a friend in a letter why the Jews were "the subjects of extradition, not of a legal but of an actual kind?"[20] The Whitecap movement indicated how an ideology of victimization and retribution, drawing on a blend of anti-Semitism and traditional southern racism, could result in explosive violence.[21]

Economic hardship, class antagonism, and populist protest were the immediate causes of the agrarian violence that racked the Deep South and victimized many Jews in the late 1880s and early 1890s, but that violence was also situated in a much broader tradition of anti-Semitism in the United States and Europe rooted in both religious and economic prejudices. American Christians, including southern Protestants, held complex and sometimes contradictory religious attitudes toward Jews. Jews became both indirect and direct victims of nineteenth-century American Protestant triumphalism, including laws upholding the Christian Sabbath as the national day of rest; Bible readings, recitations of the Lord's Prayer, and the singing of Protestant hymns in public schools; explicit Christian references in official government discourse; missionary drives to convert Jews to Christianity; and a general dismissal of Judaism as a viable and respectable religious system in its own right, rather than as simply a precursor to Christianity.[22] Nineteenth-century religious sermons and popular novels often depicted Jews in unflattering terms, and many Jewish children had to endure taunts from schoolmates that they were "Christ-killers."[23]

When southern Jewish-Christian interactions are viewed as a whole, however, it is difficult to argue for a substantial religiously based anti-Semitism in the nineteenth century. Many southern evangelicals saw Jews as part of the great unsaved mass of humanity that needed conversion and redemption, but relatively few Jews recalled specific attempts to convert them personally. Seen as God's chosen people of the Old Testament, many southerners considered even nonobservant Jews to be religious authorities and often engaged itinerant Jewish peddlers in long, and respectful, religious discussions.[24] A number of southern Christian churches invited rabbis from Reform temples to give sermons or lessons on the Hebrew scriptures. As one observer of southern Jewry notes, "To rock-ribbed Baptists, [Jewish rabbis] seemed the very embodiment of the prophets themselves."[25] Although many of these relationships were patronizing and even condescending, it would be an overstatement to say that most nineteenth-century southerners saw Jews as some kind of demonic anti-Christian threat. Prejudicial Christian triumphalism did feed southern anti-Semitism, but the pervasiveness of evangelical Protestantism did not necessarily lead to conscious anti-Semitic feelings among most southern Christians, and strains of religious philo-Semitism were present alongside negative images of Jews as Christ-killers.

The second major source of anti-Semitism in the late nineteenth century was the stereotype of Jews as greedy, unproductive moneylenders. Like religious prejudices, however, this image was also complicated. Michael Dobkowski has described the duality of virtues and vices that "the Jew" personified for nineteenth-century Americans: on the one hand, he was resourceful and energetic in business, paralleling the best of Yankee America; on the other hand, "keenness might mean cunning; enterprise might shade into greed." National publications in late nineteenth-century America portrayed Jews as materialists who virtually worshipped profit and economic advantage, and looked at the world through "cash-register eyes."[26] In many ways the uneasiness that Americans felt toward Jews, who were disproportionately involved in mercantile activity, reflected their anxieties about the nation's new economy in which wealth was mysteriously produced (and hoarded) by industrialists and bankers rather than farmers and workers.

Even New South boosters who were energetic advocates of commercial enterprise were not entirely comfortable with the merits of a class of creditors who earned money based on economic concentration and who made profits, it seemed, based on the hard work of others. Despondent farmers throughout the Midwest and South, searching for an explanation for the never-ending cycles of debt and failure they suffered, often summoned up images of "the Jew" as merciless creditor, the Wall Street banker, or the international financier; in other words, as one historian has noted, "the epitome of the exploitative moneyed interests."[27] Individuals who believed they had been shortchanged on business transactions with Jewish lenders or merchants reverted to stereotypes to make sense of the situation. Alabaman Philip Pitts complained in his diary that he had received only forty-three of the fifty pounds of meat he had ordered from "Ernst Bros." He then remarked, "No Jew that I ever met with was honest. My Bible tells me 'A false ballance is an abomination to the Lord'–These Jews then must be an abomination to the Lord."[28] Such anti-Semitic attitudes were not unique to the South nor did they originate there. While the mass of southerners were generally neither more nor less anti-Semitic than other Americans in the period, the depressed agricultural and financial condition of the postbellum South allowed for scapegoat images of the Jew to be exploited by willing parties, such as Tom Watson and the Whitecaps, and then given a southern flavor as expressed in anti-Jewish vigilante violence.

The anti-Semitic violence that plagued rural Louisiana and Mississippi in the late nineteenth century struck a chord with Jews around the country. Due to his proximity in New Orleans, Rabbi Max Heller felt compelled to comment publicly about the tragedies. His response to the violence is intriguing, even surprising. Rather than issuing blanket condemnations of southern anti-Semitism, Heller offered a more measured response. He argued that the charge of "Antisemite" had been bandied about too lightly. Jewish circles in northern cities exaggerated the anti-Semitic content of southern violence, Heller maintained. He contrasted the vicious "Jew-hatred" of Germany and eastern Europe with the "lawless rowdyism" that Jews occasionally fell victim to in the South. A culture of vigilantism was not the same as epidemic anti-Semitism, and he assured his readers "how little these troubles mean as regards the general feeling in Louisiana towards the Jews." Heller's scrapbook for the period includes clippings from various newspapers describing anti-Semitic atrocities in Russia occurring at the same time as the anti-Jewish violence in northern Louisiana, clearly meaning to show by comparison how well Jews in America and particularly in the South really had it. Pointing to instances when the southern press denounced anti-Semitic violence, Heller extolled the "perfect harmony prevailing between Jew and Gentile" in the region.[29] Perhaps Heller was overly sanguine about the situation of Jews in the postbellum South, but he was certainly correct when he asserted that their treatment far excelled that of Jews in Russia or African Americans in the South.

Violent anti-Semitism in the postbellum South could have been much worse. One of the key factors differentiating southern Jews from other groups was their unique social and economic location, which led them to build relationships with the southern middle class, moving them away from the fringes of society and closer to the cultural center.[30] Although sometimes it was Jews' very success at integration and upward mobility that fueled new hostilities, particularly from frustrated poor farmers, in most times and places southern Jews were adept at being southern enough that their Jewishness was deemed by their neighbors to be either irrelevant or merely curious.[31] Overt anti-Semitism and violence would never be dominant themes in the southern Jewish experience like they were in fin de siècle Europe. Despite the broadly congenial contours of Jewish-Gentile relations in the New South, however, the episodic nature of southern anti-Jewish violence proved that no amount of integration and acculturation could guarantee Jews complete immunity from the capricious whims of southern vigilantes, particularly when disgruntled and debt-ridden farmers drew upon the anti-Semitic images and attitudes that existed but usually lay dormant in southern culture. In the end, Jews' integration in communities across the South did in fact reflect a wide degree of acceptance. However, the omnipresent threat and occasional reality of anti-Jewish violence in the New South demonstrated the precarious and limited nature of that acceptance.

THE CATHOLIC CASE

In the largest lynching in American history, a mass mob brutally slaughtered eleven Sicilian Catholic immigrants in New Orleans in 1891. The day before they were murdered, a jury had found the eleven men not guilty for the murder of the city's police chief, but the judge ordered them to be held in prison nonetheless. Indignant at the jury's verdict, a mob consisting of perhaps ten thousand people, including many of the city's leading citizens, converged on the prison and systematically hunted down each of the men. The travesty of justice, and the feeble response to it by Secretary of State James Blaine (a noted anti-Catholic), severed diplomatic relations between the United States and Italy for over a year, and some feared it would spark a war.[32]

More Catholics were lynched in the late nineteenth-century South than any other religious group (excepting black Christians), more than Mormons and Jews combined. From 1891 to 1901, at least nineteen Italians and twenty-four Mexicans—virtually all of whom we can assume were at least nominally

Catholic—fell to southern lynch mobs.[33] Anti-Catholic violence thus seems the perfect entryway to studying religion and violence in the postbellum South. What complicates the matter is that the mass mob that performed the New Orleans lynching was comprised largely of Irish and Italian Catholics, many of whom were community elites. Furthermore, the religion of both the perpetrators and victims is rarely if ever mentioned, let alone highlighted, in either contemporary sources or historical accounts of the lynchings; the violence is never referred to as "anti-Catholic," but rather as racist, nativist, xenophobic, and so forth. The fact that German, Irish, and French Catholics not only were immune to southern violence but also helped inflict it on Sicilian immigrants reveals that other factors—racial, economic, political, cultural, and otherwise—outweighed and even trumped religion in this case.[34] Just as their common Protestantism did not stop southern whites from lynching African Americans, their shared Catholicism did not prevent well-established French and Irish Catholics from being among the leading proponents of anti-Sicilian sentiment throughout Louisiana.[35] Therefore, historians and contemporary observers alike concur that the lynchings of these Sicilian, Italian, and Mexican Catholics had little or nothing to do with religion but reflected racial and ethnic prejudices stimulated by fears about labor and crime in southern communities. Religion was in fact present in these lynchings, but it was deeply buried, far more than in the anti-Mormon or even anti-Jewish episodes. The case of Catholics in the late nineteenth-century South demonstrates how religion can be subsumed in ethnic and racial identities, both by outsiders who see religion as one of a group of characteristics used to define a minority group's ethnicity or nationality, and by insiders who downplay religious difference in the effort to be accepted by the mainstream. Because anti-Mexican violence was more of a southwestern than strictly southern phenomenon, in this brief treatment I focus on Italian immigrants in the South, particularly in Louisiana.

Despite being largely obscured by other more prominent elements such as class, race, and ethnicity, religion operated as a factor in southern anti-Italian violence in two subtle ways. First, Catholicism was a key element in the constellation of traits that made up the racial-ethnic-national identity of Italians, particularly as that identity was constructed by Anglo-Saxon Protestants. That Italians were Catholic was simply understood, and the religious element of their national identity was taken for granted by late nineteenth-century southerners. Put another way, Americans knew that Italian immigrants were Catholic—and thus intimately connected in the Protestant mind to the ever-perilous papist threat—simply because they were Italian. Protestant Americans perceived Catholic immigrants as the advance guard of papal infiltration of American political institutions, and the Sicilian "Mafia" (such as those accused of killing the New Orleans police chief) as "willing tools of the priesthood."[36]

That was part of what made Italian (or Sicilian) immigrants marginal, dangerous, and Other, particularly in a nineteenth-century southern culture that was so deeply imbued with traditional Protestant images, values, attitudes, and fears.[37]

Second, the fact that race and ethnicity trumped religion in the discourse surrounding the Italian lynchings was largely a result of the conscious efforts of southern Catholics. The seemingly negligible impact of the lynching victims' Catholic identity speaks to the character of postbellum southern Catholicism. Like Jews, Catholics generally pursued a path of accommodation and integration with southern mainstream culture. Some aspects of their Catholic identity could not be compromised, and consequently garnered negative attention; for instance, priests and nuns, whose perceived deviance represented challenges to the social order rooted in traditional Victorian conceptions of family life and gender roles, personified Catholic otherness. In most ways, however, Catholics in the South made their religion a private affair and readily accommodated themselves to the prevailing cultural norms, with the hope that doing so would allow them to practice their religion unmolested.[38] Because southern Catholics did their best to fashion themselves as cultural insiders, their religious outsiderhood became less threatening and did not end up triggering explicitly anti-Catholic violence.

Catholic acculturation in the South took many forms. That Catholics accommodated to the southern culture of violence is apparent from their participation in the 1891 New Orleans mob. Catholics could also boast that they had diligently supported the Confederate cause, sending chaplains as well as soldiers to the front. One celebrated example was the Jesuit priest Darius Hubert, who seemed omnipresent in the great battles in Virginia, Pennsylvania, and Maryland; the bullet he received at Gettysburg was extracted and later placed in the New Orleans Confederate Memorial Hall.[39] Even more significantly, Catholics embraced the southern racial order. In the antebellum period they consistently defended slavery in principle, receiving praise from many leading southerners for not meddling with the "peculiar institution," as many northern evangelicals did.[40] By the late nineteenth century, southern Catholics had established segregated parishes for African Americans, a move that reflected at least tacit rejection of statements from the Vatican that set forth a relatively liberal policy encouraging racial integration.[41] Jesuit leaders in Georgia considered open relations with blacks "injurious to the social if not moral culture" of local Catholics, and discouraged any interracial efforts that would antagonize southerners to the harm of (white) Catholic interests.[42] In short, southern Catholics never overtly challenged the postbellum racial order, and most openly supported it. Through their ready participation in some of the key elements of southern society, including support for the Confederacy, the embrace of racial segregation, and even involvement in extralegal violence, southern Catholics repeatedly asserted their similarities rather than differences with their surrounding culture.

The thinness of Catholic community in most areas of the South—southern Louisiana being the exception—meant that parish life in its fullest sense was difficult if not impossible to maintain, which translated into a lapse in explicit devotional activity by many southern Catholics. Even where established parishes existed, the Catholic population was still too small to represent a significant force in local politics or culture. This lack of institutional strength combined with the widespread cultural accommodation of southern Catholics to make the church less like the ominous leviathan of paranoid anti-Catholic conspiratorial discourse and more like a small denomination struggling even to exercise spiritual power over its own adherents. To say that southern Catholics privatized their faith would be generous, as for many of them the church was largely irrelevant in the daily patterns of their lives. Priests and nuns assigned to the South—of which there were too few to serve the needs of the scattered Catholic populace—constantly bewailed the poor spiritual condition of their flock. In an 1887 letter, a Jesuit in Alabama wrote that particularly in the outlying areas Catholics "do not usually show off their faith in words, and still less in conduct." He lamented that most Alabama Catholics, typically "of the humbler and poorer class," were so "badly instructed" in the religion that they were "frequently not able to repel the attacks they had to encounter from the sophistry of the [Protestant] preachers." Isolated in communities that did not have a parish, and rarely visited by priests, southern Catholics had to "go to Protestant churches if they want to go to church at all."[43] In short, between their weak ties to the church and their ready acculturation to most aspects of southern society, Catholics in the South did not pose a sufficiently strong challenge to religious or cultural orthodoxies to inspire vigilante violence against them.

This did not mean that Catholics were accepted or loved by Protestant southerners. Anti-Catholicism remained a fixture in southern thought, but unlike the North—where nativist organizations like the American Protective Association sought to limit Catholic immigration and influence—anti-Catholicism in the New South existed almost exclusively on a rhetorical plane.[44] Southern Protestants widely shared the stock images of Catholics that had existed since the Reformation. Robert Lewis Bolton, who assumed duties as pastor of a Baptist church in New Orleans in 1909, reported that he was "surrounded with Catholics, who are just as ignorant and superstitious as any body found in the valley of the Ganges in India, or in Canton, China." Bolton complained of the "idolatry" and "immorality" of the city, specifically linking these traits to the Catholic majority.[45] Robert Parish, an itinerant Methodist preacher in Louisiana, similarly noted that the Catholics he met (and tried to convert) were "quite ignorant and supersticious."[46] While Bolton and Parish recapitulated standard depictions of the degraded and deluded Catholic masses, southern Methodist minister L. L. Pickett focused on the well-rehearsed evils of the apostate "popish system." In his fairly typical (if extended) anti-Catholic tract, Pickett covered such topics as infallibility, transubstantiation, relics and miracles, celibacy, the confessional, "bloodshed," temporal power, and education. He claimed that Roman Catholicism was "beyond a doubt . . . the greatest apostasy" in the world, and had "violated nearly if not every law of God." Although he worried about the ignorance, superstition, immorality, and poverty that Catholicism inevitably led to, he was most concerned about the political threat posed by Rome and its mindless devotees. Pickett argued that Catholics cared "only for the triumph of the Pope," and manipulated the American political system to achieve their ends of subverting republican government, crushing Protestantism, and gaining "universal *temporal* and spiritual sovereignty" for "the old man at Rome." The progress of Romanism in achieving its nefarious goals was driven primarily by the "rapid influx" of Catholics in the country, and the only way to protect Protestant America, including the South, was to restrict immigration and create stricter naturalization procedures.[47] The parallels to contemporaneous southern anti-Mormon rhetoric—the exposure of deviant sexuality, denunciation of false doctrines, and warning against theocratic power—are abundant.

While a certain degree of anti-Catholicism was inherent to Protestantism, it became increasingly powerful in the late nineteenth century as it associated with growing plainfolk fears of foreign hierarchy and conspiracy.[48] The culmination of this populist strain of southern anti-Catholicism came in the form of Tom Watson's diatribes against the impending dangers of growing Roman influence. In a tirade at the courthouse in Thomson, Georgia, Watson fumed that Catholicism stood for monarchy, superstition, idolatry, tyranny, bigotry, and the union of church and state, and militated against democracy, individual liberty, free speech, the free press, public schools, and marriage. He quoted Abraham Lincoln's famous declaration that "this Republic cannot exist half slave and half free," and applied it to his current struggle against Catholic tyranny: "As sure as you live, the autocratic principles of Popery, and the historic principles of Democracy and Republicanism, cannot travel the same track, going in opposite directions, without a collision and a tragedy."[49] Watson was more generous to individual Catholics, particularly "so long as they confined themselves to their so-called 'religion' as a form of worship" and not politics.[50] He noted that "individual Protestants coming in contact with individual Catholics found them to be average Americans," a telling statement rooted in Watson's southern experience.[51] In short, his fight was with "Romanism" on an international and political level, not necessarily with individual Catholics.

Watson's position was indicative of a larger trend: while anti-Catholicism was present at all levels of southern society and arguably even intensified from the 1890s to the 1910s, it was usually manifest as fear of the international, not local, Catholic menace. Good will toward local Catholics and fear of the shadowy Roman conspiracy often operated simultaneously in southern communities. In Greenville, South Carolina, Protestant civic and business leaders contributed toward the construction of a new Catholic church. While their generosity inspired gratitude among local Catholics, it also inspired virulent protests from nearby nativists who saw the church as a "fortification for the troops of an enemy."[52] In some places the dedication of a new Catholic church was seen as "interesting" and "novel," whereas in other communities Catholics had a difficult time even getting notices of their meeting time and place into the local newspaper.[53] In general, southern Protestants' treatment of their Catholic neighbors reflected elements both of standard anti-Catholic attitudes and a more welcoming and open approach toward coexistence in the community.

Southern Catholics did experience a certain amount of discrimination, but it was uneven and somewhat idiosyncratic in its application. The anti-Catholicism that pervaded the Protestant South rarely if ever translated into direct violence, and daily relationships between Protestants and Catholics were usually congenial. Although church leaders sometimes complained of the lack of devotion shown by the majority of southern Catholics, it was their collective understatement of faith that made the religion seem innocuous in a region that was otherwise suspicious of the Catholic presence in America. Like their Jewish counterparts, many Catholics found the South a hospitable home, especially as they muted their Catholic identity and emphasized what they had in common with their neighbors. While southern Catholics would remain religious outsiders and as such would always be at least somewhat uncomfortable in the evangelical Protestant South, they felt most at ease as they shaped themselves in the mainstream mold, downplaying their difference and portraying their faith as just one religious expression among many.

Perfectly capturing this sentiment, and explaining in part why Catholics-qua-Catholics did not become common targets of vigilante violence, is a letter from Sister Anne of Jesus, a nun at St. Vincent Academy in Shreveport, Louisiana. As a sign of hope that "little by little our holy religion will spread itself in this beautiful country," Sister Anne reported that Catholic churches were springing up "in almost every town where there is a railroad station." She then qualified her statement, acknowledging that "if the Catholic churches are arising on all sides, so are the Protestant ones, as well as the Jewish temples." Most striking was her conclusion about this abounding religious revival: "This is a very good sign, a sign people are worshipping God."[54] Hardly the language of conspiratorial exclusivity, these statements by Sister

Anne blended a sincere faith in Catholic triumphalism with the distinctly American notion of religious pluralism. So long as southern Catholics adhered to a privatized religion that seemed more like a Protestant denomination than an international conspiracy seeking to "throttle Republicanism, bruise freedom, crush Protestantism, control the press, shape legislation, direct our institutions, manipulate our national wealth, and enthrone the pope in our midst," they could be, and were, tolerated in the postbellum South.[55]

PECULIAR PEOPLES

The varying experiences of Mormons, Jews, and Catholics in the postbellum South speak to the complex and multiple ways in which religion operates in identity construction, social relations, and even political and economic structures. While religion did not operate in isolation in any of these cases— if indeed it ever does—it was a key element in the ways that each of these three groups situated themselves in the dominantly evangelical Protestant South. Anti-Mormonism offered the "purest" example of religious discrimination and violence, in that a direct challenge to southern religious and cultural orthodoxies by a self-defined religious group sparked opposition that ultimately led to hostile legislation and violence. While radical Mormon doctrines precipitated heated theological disputes both orally and in print, actual violence occurred only when the core Mormon principle and practice of polygamy came into direct conflict with an equally fundamental article of faith for southern white men, the need to defend the purity of Victorian womanhood. Rather than crumpling in the face of sustained hostility and violence, Mormons used it to reinforce their own oppositional identity by furthering their self-image as martyrs persecuted for the truth. Any conflict with non-Mormons they encountered (or precipitated) became proof that they were the chosen people of God besieged by the forces of evil, led predominantly by the Protestant clergy.

Religion was more muted in the Jewish case, as most anti-Jewish violence was not directly motivated by religious antagonism but rather by poor white farmers' frustration at indebtedness brought on by poor agricultural and economic conditions. Perpetrators of anti-Jewish violence sometimes rationalized their actions by drawing on traditional anti-Semitic images that emphasized the Jews' cultural and religion otherness. While religion did not motivate anti-Jewish violence in quite the same way that it did in the Mormon case, it remained a persistent element that allowed would-be anti-Semites to marginalize and even demonize Jews whom they originally found offensive for reasons other than their explicit religious identity. Jews responded to the violence by trying to accommodate as much as possible to southern norms. They pointed to their Reform religious practices, which did indeed have strong resemblances to (and even borrowings from) Protestant worship, as proof that they were not the Christ-killers and Shylocks of legend but rather good, God-fearing southerners who wanted and deserved inclusion.

Southern Catholics pursued a strategy similar to that of their Jewish neighbors, adopting an accommodationist stance toward their surrounding culture. More than their coreligionists in the urban North, southern Catholics strove to downplay religious difference and elevate cultural similarities; like southern Jews, their relatively thin numbers (except in southern Louisiana) made ghettoization virtually impossible. Religion still played a key role in whites' imposition of allegedly inherent traits of inferiority on marginalized groups such as Sicilians and Mexicans. However, religious difference was essentially subsumed in and reduced to those ethnic and national differences, insomuch that their religious identity was not even mentioned when nominal Catholics became lynching victims. While Catholicism survived and even grew in the South during this period, in most ways it was effectively neutralized as a significant category of difference, both by antagonists and by Catholics themselves. So long as Catholics spoke and acted like southerners, muffled their explicit religious distinctions as much as possible, and generally conformed to a pluralist denominational and political model, Catholic growth in the postbellum South represented less of a conspiratorial threat of foreign invasion than simply an innocuous novelty.

What differentiated Catholics, Jews, and Mormons from Protestant America, and largely what explained their status as cultural and religious outsiders, was that they were not simply denominations but rather peoples. Their peoplehood was construed as both a positive and negative identity. That is, while there remained variation and pluralism within each group, individual members still understood themselves as constituents of a larger people, defined both by who and what they were, and who and what they were not. No matter how acculturated or even assimilated they would become, Mormons, Catholics, and Jews would never be fully part of the Protestant mainstream. Each group saw themselves united by a common culture, history, tradition, and (less so in the Catholic case) kinship. These common traits transcended political boundaries and ran deeper than theological affinities—peoplehood was more visceral than geographic, political, or intellectual.

For instance, within decades of Joseph Smith's founding revelations, late nineteenth-century Mormons already had constructed a shared history, a common theological language, distinctive marital and family practices, and an organic vision of the social, political, and economic aspects of their ideal society. Mormons reinforced and sharpened these positive identity traits by setting themselves in opposition to mainstream American Protestantism and

Protestant America. Latter-day Saints viewed themselves not just as a new American church or another voice added to the cacophony of frontier religious movements but as God's chosen people.[56] Non-Mormons also recognized that Mormonism went beyond Protestantism's traditional denominational character, and some even assigned physiognomic particularity to Latter-day Saints and suggested that Mormons constituted a "new race."[57] Jews and Catholics similarly had deep ties that bound members of the group to one another and gave them a sense of peoplehood that existed simultaneously with, and in some cases supplanted, other personal and group identities. Their peoplehood was rooted in their respective theological visions—Jews as God's ancient covenant people, Catholics as the universal body of Christ—and it took form in distinctive cultural, social, and political characteristics.

Particularly in nineteenth-century America, the unique peoplehood of each of these three groups was an unavoidable and unshakeable fact. When Americans spoke of a Baptist or a Methodist, they spoke only of religious affiliation, but when they referred to a Jew or a Mormon, there was not only an inference of their being exotic and alien, but also an impression that they constituted religious nations that were ultimately unassimilable in the American nation. While Jews and Mormons often protested that they could in fact be fully patriotic Americans while retaining their religious and ethnic particularity, they agreed on the fundamental notion that being Jewish or Mormon was in the blood, an essential part of who a person was from the moment of his or her birth (or, for Mormon converts, spiritual rebirth). Catholics had a different notion of peoplehood, one that relied primarily on the conception of spiritual communion with the universal church. "Catholic," then, was not a designation of *ethnos* in the way that "Jew" and "Mormon" were, but rather represented a universal (catholic) peoplehood subdivided by national inheritances—thus, Irish Catholic, Italian Catholic, German Catholic, and so forth. Of course, a person's national and religious identities were often assumed to be conflated to the point of being indistinguishable—Italians were Catholic by virtue of being Italian, Englishmen were Protestant, Turks were Muslim, and so forth. These religious-national identities had remarkable staying power among many immigrant communities well into the twentieth century and even persist today.[58]

An outsider group's relationship to the mainstream (white Protestant) American nation was thus largely dictated by how they understood and deployed their peoplehood. That in turn determined to a large degree the likelihood of their becoming potential targets of violence. Sometimes, particularly in cases of racial conflict, the choice was imposed (or taken away) by the majority—even after emancipation, whites confined African Americans to their racial identity and never allowed them to fully integrate into the mainstream. Groups who escaped the confining strictures of the biracial order had more options available to them. In the South, Catholics and Jews both downplayed the distinctive aspects of their peoplehood, asserting in a variety of ways their acceptance of dominant southern attitudes, norms, and practices. They retained the fundamental aspects of their religious beliefs and rituals while minimizing or casting aside other cultural traits that would have been offensive to the southern way. In self-identifying both as southerners and Jews or Catholics, they insisted that there would be no conflict between their loyalties to their religion and their region.

Nineteenth-century Mormons, on the other hand, consciously elevated their Mormon peoplehood and spurned—or at least diminished—their affinities with all others. To be sure, even in the midst of their conflict with federal, state, and territorial governments most Latter-day Saints remained patriotic Americans, believing that God had established the United States and inspired the Founding Fathers as they drafted the Constitution and Bill of Rights.[59] Arguably, because most Latter-day Saints were of Anglo-American or northern European ancestry they could have integrated into the American mainstream much easier than most Jews or Catholics, who increasingly in the late nineteenth century came from the "darker" nations of southern and eastern Europe. But Mormons' primary commitment was to the kingdom of God, and to expanding the church in preparation for the advent of Christ's millennial reign on the earth. Nationality of birth, at least in theory, was rendered all but meaningless—those baptized into the church were adopted into the House of Israel, all others were Gentiles, and the Mormon mission was to spread their new Israel throughout the whole earth. For those who joined the church, any aspects of national, regional, or ethnic culture that clashed with Mormon doctrine and practice would have to be discarded or at least minimized. Utah was a melting pot of converts from around the world, and once they gathered to Zion they were no longer considered Britons or Scandinavians or even Americans but rather Latter-day Saints and members of the kingdom of God on earth.

Reality, of course, did not always match the vision, and individuals retained many of the customs and prejudices of their native cultures. Furthermore, Mormonism was profoundly shaped by its American setting, and appropriated many traits of its cultural environment. Nevertheless, Latter-day Saints remained remarkably committed to the idea that they were a holy nation drawn out of the world and chosen by God. Their distinctive cultural practices—most notably plural marriage—were markers of their chosenness, much as circumcision was the token of the Abrahamic covenant. Polygamy was an essential part of what set apart the Mormon people beginning in the 1850s, and became increasingly so as the church and its members were persecuted for their commitment to "the Principle," whether or not they actually practiced it personally. In this way ordinary Mormons were like Civil War–era southerners who fought and died for the principles of slavery and states' rights, even if they did not themselves own slaves. Just as antebellum southerners' sense of what made them a people was so different from contemporary northerners' that the clash of cultures culminated in a bloody civil war, so did Mormon and southern commitments to competing visions of peoplehood contribute to violent conflict in the last quarter of the century. Their elevated sense of peoplehood, in addition to the transiency of their ministries, does much to explain why LDS missionaries in the South, in contrast to many Jewish rabbis and Catholic priests who settled permanently in the region, made only token efforts in deference to local customs and were in turn so often expelled by local citizens who did not want such self-conscious and unrepentant difference to contaminate their communities.

The general pattern that emerges from these cases is that violence in the postbellum South usually followed those outsiders who disrupted or sinned against the social order, particularly in ways that seriously undermined the foundations of society as conceived by white evangelical southerners. The threat became even more acute when religious outsiders sought to spread their dangerous heterodoxies through aggressive proselytization. Jews' and Catholics' accommodation to cultural norms did not necessarily earn them full insider status, but it did help them gain acceptance in their daily interactions with most fellow southerners. On the other hand, southerners perceived the Mormon confluence of religion and politics to be a threat to American disestablishment—although even as they criticized Mormon "theocracy," nineteenth-century evangelicals were blind to the many ways that they had created their own form of a religious establishment to instrumentalize their vision of social and political godliness. Even more, the alternative marriage practices promulgated by Mormons struck at the heart of southerners' conceptions of a good society. In particular, the itinerant Mormon missionary, envisioned in the southern mind as a depraved seducer, mounted a direct challenge to white men's claims of protecting the sanctity of womanhood, and thus undermined the hierarchy they maintained as a necessary part of a patriarchal and honor-bound society. Polygamy did in fact represent a substantial challenge to the traditional model of monogamous marriage widely accepted in Victorian America, and so to a certain extent southerners were right to judge the practice as potentially disruptive to foundational social norms. Southern Protestants joined their counterparts in the North and West in mobilizing the press, Congress, and the courts to defeat the Mormon menace. Not satisfied with only discourse or even coercive legislation, southern men grabbed whips and guns to drive the dangerous seducers out of their communities.

Vigilantism against religious minorities illustrates how the Ku Klux Klan and its associated terrorist organizations continued to cast a long shadow over the South even after being officially disbanded in the early 1870s. Anti-Mormon and anti-Jewish mobs often wore the same garb, invoked the same rhetoric, employed the same tactics, and even involved some of the same participants as did the Klan. Even after the umbrella organization was broken up by federal law enforcement, its component parts (especially individual members) did not forget the lessons they had learned in Reconstruction—namely, that terrorist violence can be remarkably effective, especially when conducted against a minority group with few allies and little political influence. The terrorist campaigns of the Reconstruction Klan thus had ramifications far beyond its few years of formal existence. Thousands of southern white men had fine-tuned the art of violent intimidation, and they translated those skills into defending their communities or their individual interests against a wide variety of perceived threats, not just blacks and Republicans. Although vigilantism was by no means a purely or originally southern phenomenon, as a culturally acceptable tradition it tenaciously held on in the South even as it waned in other parts of the country in the decades after the Civil War. Extralegal violence, southerners knew, could be put to use against not only racial but also religious minorities, particularly those who transgressed cherished cultural norms.

A NEW ERA

In 1915, Leo Frank was lynched in Marietta, Georgia, climaxing a wave of anti-Semitic hysteria that swept the South. That same year, in a mysterious ceremony on Stone Mountain in Georgia, the Ku Klux Klan was revived. The Klan identified Jews and Catholics as groups that southern—and American—society needed to be saved from, but there was no mention of Mormons. Indeed, following the public relations fiasco surrounding the Reed Smoot hearings in the first decade of the new century, the LDS Church officially—and definitively—abandoned polygamy and retreated from its ambitions of establishing a political kingdom of God. Echoing the acculturative tactics of nineteenth-century Catholics and Jews, Latter-day Saints came to look less like a distinctive people and more like a respectable denomination.

As many of its nineteenth-century detractors feared, Mormonism not only survived the national antipolygamy campaign but thrived in the century that followed. Though interrupted in the first half of the twentieth century by two world wars and the economic depression of the 1930s, Mormon missionaries continued to carry their message of the restored gospel to people throughout the United States and around the world. The LDS Church reached the one million member mark in 1947, the two million member mark sixteen years later, and three million by the early 1970s. Accelerated growth, based on both convert baptisms and natural growth through birth, reached the point by the late twentieth century that the church was adding one million members approximately every three years.[60] This explosive increase has been both reflected and fueled by LDS Church growth in the modern American South. Twelve of fourteen southern states (excepting only Louisiana and West Virginia) saw the number of LDS adherents increase by at least 70 percent from 1980 to 2000; in six of those states the LDS population more than doubled. This rate of growth outstripped that of Mormonism in the United States as a whole during that time period (58%), although the number of Mormons per capita remained lower in the South (ranging from 3.6 to 7.5 per 1,000) than nationwide (15 per 1,000). At the dawn of the new millennium, over half a million Latter-day Saints—approximately one in eight of all American Mormons—lived in the South.[61] This small explosion in the southern Mormon population, especially remarkable given the church's diminutive presence in the South at the turn of the twentieth century, was due not only to convert baptisms but also what Jan Shipps calls the "scattering of the gathered," referring to the Mormon diaspora from the intermountain West to the rest of the country in the mid-to-late twentieth century.[62] Of the 130 LDS temples in operation as of late 2009, 14 were in the American South (including four in Texas), all of which were built after 1980.[63]

Though anti-Mormon violence in the South ebbed with the death of polygamy, anti-Mormon sentiment has not. Indeed, the LDS Church's remarkable expansion inside America's Bible Belt has reignited the historical antagonism between Mormonism and southern evangelical Protestantism. The Southern Baptist Convention developed a number of programs beginning in the 1980s designed to inoculate their members from LDS missionary incursions and to spread the word that Mormonism was a dangerous and un-Christian cult. Echoing the language of late nineteenth-century anti-Mormons such as Edgar Folk, a 1998 book by the director of the SBC's Interfaith Witness Division titled *Mormonism Unmasked* promised to "lift the veil from one of the greatest deceptions in the history of religion," and Southern Baptist leaders openly referred to Mormonism as "a counterfeit Christianity."[64] In 1998, the SBC adopted a counter-offensive strategy, holding its annual convention in Salt Lake City. Accompanied by a media blitz, some three thousand Baptists volunteered for a door-to-door evangelization campaign in the very heart of Mormonism, an effort that accomplished more by way of symbolic meaning than the number of souls saved.[65]

In a stunning reversal that speaks to America's twentieth-century transformational movement toward true pluralism, Mormons now walk the halls of power in Washington, as do Jews, Catholics, and African Americans. The 111th Congress that convened in January 2009 included five Mormons in the

Senate—including majority leader Harry Reid—and nine in the House of Representatives. Mitt Romney challenged for the 2008 Republican presidential nomination and seems poised to run again in 2012. Mormons currently hold major positions as leaders in business, higher education, science, the military, sports, the arts, and entertainment. Indeed, as historians Leonard Arrington and Davis Bitton noted in their survey of Mormon history, by the early twentieth century "the Mormons were more American than most Americans." This mainstreaming was only accomplished once they had learned "the practical limits of religious life in America" and traded in their commitment to plural marriage and theodemocracy—and the resultant defiance of American legal, political, cultural, and religious norms—for "patriotism, respect for the law, love of the Constitution, and obedience to political authority."[66]

Mormon peoplehood persists, though in muted and chastened form compared to the robust version that challenged nineteenth-century orthodoxies and inspired violence. Anti-Mormonism in the South has similarly been tempered as a result of changes within both Mormonism and the region. Mormons and southerners alike became more fully integrated into the mainstream of twentieth-century America as they gave up certain distinguishing peculiarities, whether polygamy and the political kingdom of God or vigilantism and Jim Crow. And despite the continuing wariness and even enmity with which Mormons and southern evangelicals view each other, in the political sphere they have once again become strange bedfellows, joining forces in the nation's culture wars. Once persecuted for their distinctive views on marriage and sexuality by a coalition of evangelical Protestants and reformers organized under the aegis of the Republican Party, in the early twenty-first century Mormons have allied with southern religious conservatives and Republican politicians in an effort to preserve "traditional marriage" from those who wish to expand its definition by an appeal to constitutional rights and freedoms.

The nation's founders would have been astonished—if not horrified—to see their words summoned in defense of polygamy or same-sex marriage. But once they enshrined the language of individual rights in the Declaration of Independence and Bill of Rights, they let the genie out of the bottle. The runaway logic of liberalism allowed all kinds of groups excluded in the Founders' original formulation—women, blacks, the propertyless—and groups whose claims as political communities they could not have envisioned— Mormons, homosexuals—to demand full inclusion and insist on constitutional protections to express fully their cultural identities within the American polity. Certainly, the reality of Madison's feared tyranny of the majority still shadows us, and extralegal violence has plagued our American democracy from the beginning, with victims ranging from Elijah Lovejoy to

Leo Frank, Joseph Standing to Matthew Shepard. Even given the persistence of hate crimes against newly demonized groups, progress has nevertheless been made from an era in which the ascendant will of "the people" was all too commonly enforced by lash, rope, and trigger. The remarkable trajectory taken by Mormons in the past century and a half, from vilification to integration, suggests the expansiveness of America's accommodative power in dealing with staggering pluralism. But this accommodation is often a story of compulsory transformation: for Mormons and many other minorities, inclusion has come only after a lengthy process of negotiation and compromise, with many individuals and communities forced to shrug off some of their more radical—and at one time essential—behavioral practices and ideological claims in order to earn the privileges of belonging. At each juncture, certain claims of minority rights have been renounced even as others have been realized. The boundaries of American tolerance have enlarged considerably but unevenly in the century since the end of the nation's anti-Mormon crusade, shaped as much by the paths that have foreclosed as those that have opened.

Abbreviations Used in Notes

BYU	L. Tom Perry Special Collections Library, Harold B. Library, Brigham Young University, Provo, UT
D&C	*The Doctrine and Covenants of the Church of Jesus Christ of Latter-day Saints Containing Revelations Given to Joseph Smith, the Prophet, with Some Additions By His Successors in the Presidency of the Church* (Salt Lake City, UT: Church of Jesus Christ of Latter-day Saints, 1981)
Drew	Methodist Library, United Methodist Archives Center, Drew University, Madison, NJ
LDSCA	Archives of the Church of Jesus Christ of Latter-day Saints, Salt Lake City, UT
LLMVC	Lower Louisiana and Mississippi Valley Collection, Hill Memorial Library, Louisiana State University, Baton Rouge
Loyola	Special Collections & Archives, J. Edgar & Louise S. Monroe Library, Loyola University, New Orleans, LA
Princeton	Department of Rare Books and Special Collections, Princeton University Library, Princeton, NJ
SHC	Southern Historical Collection, Louis Round Wilson Library, University of North Carolina at Chapel Hill
SSMMH	Southern States Mission Manuscript History, in Archives of the Church of Jesus Christ of Latter-day Saints, Salt Lake City, UT
U of U	Manuscript Division, J. Willard Marriott Library, University of Utah, Salt Lake City

NEWSPAPERS AND PERIODICALS

Alabama Baptist (Selma to 1885, Montgomery from 1886)
Alabama Christian Advocate (Birmingham)
Atlanta (Daily) Constitution
American Hebrew (New York)
American Israelite (Cincinnati)
Arkansas Intelligencer (Van Buren)

Baptist and Reflector (Nashville)
Biblical Recorder (Raleigh, NC)
Christian Advocate (New York)
Christian Index (Atlanta)
Commercial Appeal (Memphis, TN)
The Contributor (Salt Lake City, UT)
Daily American (Nashville)
Daily Herald (Columbia, TN)
Daily Picayune (New Orleans)
Daily Sun (Atlanta)
Deseret (Evening) News (Salt Lake City, UT)
Georgia Weekly Telegraph and Georgia Journal & Messenger
   (Macon)
Hickman (TN) Pioneer
Hinds County Gazette (Raymond, MS)
Improvement Era (Salt Lake City, UT)
The Latter-day Saints' Millennial Star (London)
LDS Church News (Salt Lake City, UT)
Nashville Banner
New Mississippian (Jackson)
New York Times
News and Courier (Charleston, SC)
News and Observer (Raleigh, NC)
Public Opinion (New York)
Richland Beacon (Rayville, LA)
Richmond (VA) Christian Advocate
Salt Lake Tribune
Southern Star (Chattanooga, TN)
Southwestern Christian Advocate (New Orleans)
St. Louis Christian Advocate
Tennessee Baptist (Memphis, TN)
Times and Seasons (Nauvoo, IL)
Washington Post
Weekly American (Nashville)
Woman's Exponent (Salt Lake City, UT)
Woodstock Letters (Woodstock, MD)
Yorkville (SC) Enquirer

Notes

CHAPTER 1

1. Parley P. Pratt, *Autobiography of Parley P. Pratt*, ed. Parley P. Pratt Jr. (Salt Lake City, UT: Deseret Book, 1985), 402, 409. An expanded version of this treatment of Pratt's murder will appear in Patrick Q. Mason, "Honor, the Unwritten Law, and Extralegal Violence: Contextualizing Parley Pratt's Murder," in *Parley P. Pratt and the Making of Mormonism*, ed. Gregory Armstrong, Matthew J. Grow, and Dennis Siler (Norman, OK: Arthur Clark, forthcoming, 2011).

2. The details of Pratt's murder appear in multiple sources, the most complete of which is Steven Pratt, "Eleanor McLean and the Murder of Parley P. Pratt," *BYU Studies* 15 (1975): 1–27; quote on 16. The most extensive single primary source on the murder is from Eleanor, who either witnessed firsthand or had immediately related to her the events. Her sixty-two-page handwritten testimonial is Eleanor J. McComb, "Account of the death of Parley P. Pratt, ca. 1857," LDSCA.

3. "Murder of Parley P. Pratt," *The Latter-day Saints' Millennial Star* 19 (July 4, 1857): 417; see also Orson Pratt, "Biographical Sketch of Parley P. Pratt," *Millennial Star* 19 (July 4, 1857): 421–25.

4. See "Martyrs to the Truth," *Deseret News*, December 29, 1888; Preston Nibley, *Stalwarts of Mormonism* (Salt Lake City: Deseret Book, 1954), 135; Alexander B. Morrison, *The Dawning of a Brighter Day: The Church in Black Africa* (Salt Lake City: Deseret Book, 1990), 69; and Susan Easton Black, *Who's Who in the Doctrine and Covenants* (Salt Lake City: Bookcraft, 1997), 234.

5. "Tragical," *Arkansas Intelligencer*, May 15, 1857.

6. Bertram Wyatt-Brown, *Southern Honor: Ethics and Behavior in the Old South* (New York: Oxford University Press, 1982). See also Richard E. Nisbett and Dov Cohen, *Culture of Honor: The Psychology of Violence in the South* (New York: Westview Press, 1996); Kenneth S. Greenberg, *Honor and Slavery: Lies, Duels, Noses, Masks, Dressing as a Woman, Gifts, Strangers, Humanitarianism, Death, Slave Rebellions, the Proslavery Argument, Baseball, Hunting, and Gambling in the Old South* (Princeton, NJ: Princeton University Press, 1996); and Wyatt-Brown, *The Shaping of Southern Culture: Honor, Grace, and War, 1760s–1890s* (Chapel Hill: University of North Carolina Press, 2001), the appendix of which is a broadly comparative essay on the recent historiography on honor.

7. Quoted in Richard Maxwell Brown, "Western Violence: Structure, Values, Myth," *Western Historical Quarterly* 24 (Feb. 1993): 15. See also Brown, *No Duty to Retreat: Violence and Values in American History and Society* (New York: Oxford University Press, 1991).

8. Wyatt-Brown, *Southern Honor*, 305–6.

9. Hendrik Hartog, "Lawyering, Husbands' Rights, and 'the Unwritten Law' in Nineteenth-Century America," *Journal of American History* 84 (June 1997): 67–96; Robert M. Ireland, "The Libertine Must Die: Sexual Dishonor and the Unwritten Law in the Nineteenth-Century United States," *Journal of Social History* 23 (Autumn 1989): 27–44. On domestic violence as a means of social control, see Laura F. Edwards, "Law, Domestic Violence, and the Limits of Patriarchal Authority in the Antebellum South," *Journal of Southern History* 65 (Nov. 1999): 733–70; and David Peterson, "Wife Beating: An American Tradition," *Journal of Interdisciplinary History* 23 (Summer 1992): 97–118.

10. Richard Maxwell Brown, *Strain of Violence: Historical Studies of American Violence and Vigilantism* (New York: Oxford University Press, 1975), quotes from vii.

11. Wyatt-Brown, *Southern Honor*, 306.

12. David Brion Davis, "Some Themes of Counter-Subversion: An Analysis of Anti-Masonic, Anti-Catholic, and Anti-Mormon Literature," in *From Homicide to Slavery: Studies in American Culture* (New York: Oxford University Press, 1986), 137–54.

13. Terryl L. Givens, *The Viper on the Hearth: Mormons, Myths, and the Construction of Heresy* (New York: Oxford University Press, 1997). While recognizing the importance of nonreligious factors, and the necessity for anti-Mormons to frame their principal objections in those terms, Givens still privileges theology as the "inescapable" and "constant feature in anti-Mormon antagonisms" (8).

14. William R. Hutchison, *Religious Pluralism in America: The Contentious History of a Founding Ideal* (New Haven, CT: Yale University Press, 2003), 32.

15. D&C 1:30.

16. Gregory Pingree, "'The Biggest Whorehouse in the World': Representations of Plural Marriage in Nineteenth-Century America," *Western Humanities Review* 50 (Fall 1996): 213–14, 226. See also Craig L. Foster, "Victorian Pornographic Imagery in Anti-Mormon Literature," *Journal of Mormon History* 19 (Spring 1993): 115–32.

17. "Killed Girl, Then Himself," *Washington Post*, September 2, 1899; "Mob Shoots a Young Woman," *New York Times*, September 3, 1899. The *Times* lists the farmer's name as Burton Vinson.

18. Michael Feldberg, *The Turbulent Era: Riot and Disorder in Jacksonian America* (New York: Oxford University Press, 1980), 90–91.

19. Abraham Lincoln, "The Perpetuation of Our Political Institutions: Address to the Young Men's Lyceum of Springfield, Illinois," in Lincoln, *Speeches and Writings, 1832-1858: Speeches, Letters, and Miscellaneous Writings, the Lincoln-Douglas Debates* (New York: Literary Classics of the United States, distributed by Viking Press, 1989), 29.

20. David Grimsted, "Rioting in Its Jacksonian Setting," *American Historical Review* 77 (April 1972): 397. See also Brown, *Strain of Violence*, 62.

21. William M. Newman and Peter L. Halvorson, *Atlas of American Religion: The Denominational Era, 1776–1990* (Walnut Creek, CA: AltaMira Press, 2000), 73–75. For a graphic representation of church growth in the South during this era, see Edwin Scott Gaustad and Philip L. Barlow, *New Historical Atlas of Religion in America* (New York: Oxford University Press, 2001), 81–82, 225–27. See also Henry K. Carroll, *The Religious Forces of the United States: Enumerated, Classified, and Described on the Basis of the Government Census of 1890* (New York: Christian Literature, 1893).

22. Christine Leigh Heyrman, *Southern Cross: The Beginnings of the Bible Belt* (New York: Knopf, 1997).

23. Edward L. Ayers, *The Promise of the New South: Life After Reconstruction* (New York: Oxford University Press, 1992), 160.

24. On the use of violence as a political tool in the South during the late 1860s and 1870s, see Nicholas Lemann, *Redemption: The Last Battle of the Civil War* (New York: Farrar, Straus and Giroux, 2006); Steven Hahn, *A Nation under Our Feet: Black Political Struggles in the Rural South from Slavery to the Great Migration* (Cambridge, MA: Belknap Press of Harvard University Press, 2003), chap. 6; Christopher Waldrep, "The Politics of Language: The Ku Klux Klan in Reconstruction," in *Warm Ashes: Issues in Southern History at the Dawn of the Twenty-First Century*, ed. Winfred B. Moore Jr., Kyle S. Sinisi, and David H. White Jr. (Columbia: University of South Carolina Press, 2003), 138-54; Jerry L. West, *The Reconstruction Ku Klux Klan in York County, South Carolina, 1865-1877* (Jefferson, NC: McFarland, 2002); Michael W. Fitzgerald, "Extralegal Violence and the Planter Class: The Ku Klux Klan in the Alabama Black Belt During Reconstruction," in *Local Matters: Race, Crime, and Justice in the Nineteenth-Century South*, ed. Christopher Waldrep and Donald G. Nieman (Athens: University of Georgia Press, 2001), 155-71; Gilles Vandal, *Rethinking Southern Violence: Homicides in Post-Civil War Louisiana, 1866-1884* (Columbus: Ohio State University Press, 2000); Kenneth C. Barnes, *Who Killed John Clayton? Political Violence and the Emergence of the New South, 1861-1893* (Durham, NC: Duke University Press, 1998); Allen W. Trelease, *White Terror: The Ku Klux Klan Conspiracy and Southern Reconstruction* (Baton Rouge: Louisiana State University Press, 1995); Eric Foner, *Reconstruction, 1863-1877: America's Unfinished Revolution* (New York: Harper & Row, 1988); and George C. Rable, *But There Was No Peace: The Role of Violence in the Politics of Reconstruction* (Athens: University of Georgia Press, 1984).

25. W. Fitzhugh Brundage, *Lynching in the New South: Georgia and Virginia, 1880-1930* (Urbana: University of Illinois Press, 1993), 8. See also C. Vann Woodward, *Origins of the New South, 1877-1913* (Baton Rouge: Louisiana State University Press, 1971), 351-52. For a comparative analysis of lynching across different regions of the country, see Michael J. Pfeifer, *Rough Justice: Lynching and American Society, 1874-1947* (Urbana: University of Illinois Press, 2004). Other recent works on lynching include Crystal Nicole Feimster, *Southern Horrors: Women and the Politics of Rape and Lynching* (Cambridge, MA: Harvard University Press, 2009); Bruce E. Baker, *This Mob Will Surely Take My Life: Lynchings in the Carolinas, 1871-1947* (London: Hambledon Continuum, 2009); Amy Louise Wood, *Lynching and Spectacle: Witnessing Racial Violence in America, 1890-1940* (Chapel Hill: University of North Carolina Press, 2009); Margaret Vandiver, *Lethal Punishment: Lynchings and Legal Executions in the South* (New Brunswick, NJ: Rutgers University Press, 2006); William D. Carrigan, *The Making of a Lynching Culture: Violence and Vigilantism in Central Texas, 1836-1916* (Urbana: University of Illinois Press, 2004); Christopher Waldrep, *The Many Faces of Judge Lynch: Extralegal Violence and Punishment in America* (New York: Palgrave Macmillan, 2002); Philip Dray, *At the Hands of Persons Unknown: The Lynching of Black America* (New York: Random House, 2002); W. Fitzhugh Brundage, ed., *Under Sentence of Death: Lynching in the South* (Chapel Hill: University of North Carolina Press, 1997); and Stewart E. Tolnay and E. M. Beck, *A Festival of Violence: An Analysis of Southern Lynchings, 1882-1930* (Urbana: University of Illinois Press, 1995).

26. Tolnay and Beck, *A Festival of Violence*, 17; Brundage, *Lynching in the New South*, 8. The NAACP recorded 2,522 blacks lynched in the United States from 1889 through 1918. See *Thirty Years of Lynching in the United States, 1889–1918* (New York: National Association for the Advancement of Colored People, 1919), 7. Another source, the Tuskegee Institute records, documents 3,417 lynchings of blacks and 1,291 of whites from 1882 to 1944; see Dray, *At the Hands of Persons Unknown*, viii.

27. See George C. Wright, *Racial Violence in Kentucky, 1865–1940: Lynchings, Mob Rule, and "Legal Lynchings"* (Baton Rouge: Louisiana State Press University, 1990), 3.

28. See Woodward, *Origins of the New South*, 351. For a detailed statistical analysis of lynching, see Tolnay and Beck, *A Festival of Violence*.

29. Woodward, *Origins of the New South*, 158–59. Edward Ayers concurs, saying that the New South was "a notoriously violent place," with homicide rates easily "the highest in the country [and] among the highest in the world." Ayers, *Promise of the New South*, 155. See also Edward L. Ayers, *Vengeance and Justice: Crime and Punishment in the 19th-Century American South* (New York: Oxford University Press, 1984).

30. Leonard J. Arrington, "Mormon Beginnings in the American South," unpublished paper, Task Papers in LDS History, no. 9 (Salt Lake City: Historical Department of the Church of Jesus Christ of Latter-day Saints, 1976); LaMar C. Berrett, "History of the Southern States Mission, 1831–1861" (M.A. thesis, Brigham Young University, 1960).

31. Brigham Young considered sending missionaries back to the South as early as 1867. He was dissuaded in part by John D. Lee—who labored as a missionary in Kentucky and Tennessee in 1839 before becoming one of the masterminds behind the 1857 Mountain Meadows Massacre—who said that "unexperienced Boys would do but litle good amoung those Southerners; men of experience would do More good." Lee diary entry, April 30, 1867, in Robert Glass Cleland and Juanita Brooks, eds., *A Mormon Chronicle: The Diaries of John D. Lee, 1848–1876*, vol. 2 (Salt Lake City: University of Utah Press, 1983), 69, original spelling and capitalization preserved.

32. See SSMMH; and Heather M. Seferovich, "History of the LDS Southern States Mission, 1875–1898" (M.A. thesis, Brigham Young University, 1996).

33. See Tolnay and Beck, *A Festival of Violence*, 96–97; Ayers, *Vengeance and Justice*, 255–56. Only two passing mentions of Mormonism appear in Samuel S. Hill, ed., *Religion*, vol. 1 of *The New Encyclopedia of Southern Culture*, ed. Charles Reagan Wilson (Chapel Hill: University of North Carolina Press, 2006).

34. See Daniel Liestman, "'We Have Found What We Have Been Looking For!' The Creation of the Mormon Religious Enclave among the Catawba, 1883–1920," *South Carolina Historical Magazine* 103 (July 2002): 226–46; David Buice, "'All Alone and None to Cheer Me': The Southern States Mission Diary of J. Golden Kimball," *Dialogue: A Journal of Mormon Thought* 24 (Spring 1991): 35–54; Austin E. Fife, "Virginia Folkways from a Mormon Journal," *Western Folklore Quarterly* 9 (Oct. 1950): 348–58; Fife, "Folkways of a Mormon Missionary in Virginia," *Southern Folklore Quarterly* 16 (June 1952): 92–123. Two M.A. theses have chronicled LDS missionary labors in the nineteenth-century South; see Berrett, "History of the Southern States Mission," and Seferovich, "History of the LDS Southern States Mission." See also Mary Ella Reed Engel, "Praying with One Eye Open: A Gendered Interpretation of Mormon Joseph Standing's Murder in Appalachian Georgia" (Ph.D. diss., University of Georgia, 2009).

35. In addition to missionary diaries and letters, newspapers from Utah and around the South chronicled much of the Mormon missionary activity in the South and provided detailed coverage of much of the conflict between the LDS elders and local citizens. Many of these news clippings and other primary source accounts have been compiled into the SSMMH.

36. R. Laurence Moore, *Religious Outsiders and the Making of Americans* (New York: Oxford University Press, 1986), xiii.

37. On the culture of southern violence, see Sheldon Hackney, "Southern Violence," *American Historical Review* 74 (Feb. 1969): 906-25; Brown, *Strain of Violence*; Dickson D. Bruce, *Violence and Culture in the Antebellum South* (Austin: University of Texas Press, 1979); Elliot J. Gorn, "'Gouge and Bite, Pull Hair and Scratch': The Social Significance of Fighting in the Southern Backcountry," *American Historical Review* 90 (Feb. 1985): 18-43; and Ted Ownby, *Subduing Satan: Religion, Recreation, and Manhood in the Rural South, 1865-1920* (Chapel Hill: University of North Carolina Press, 1990).

38. For instance, I share my title with a number of contemporary works from around the nation. See George Whitfield Phillips, *The Mormon Menace: A Discourse before the New West Education Commission* (Worcestor, MA: n.p. 1885); Samuel Fallows and Helen M. Fallows, *The Mormon Menace* (Chicago: Woman's Temperance Publishing Association, 1903); [John D. Lee,] *The Mormon Menace: Being the Confession of John Doyle Lee, Danite, an Official Assassin of the Mormon Church under the Late Brigham Young*, Introduction by Alfred Henry Lewis (New York: Home Protection Publishing Co., 1905); and *The Menace of Mormonism* (Nashville: Home Department Woman's Missionary Council, M. E. Church, South, 1914), in Pamphlets Collection, Drew.

39. Eliza R. Snow Smith, *Biography and Family Record of Lorenzo Snow* (Salt Lake City: Deseret News, 1884), 424.

40. John Morgan, "Discourse by Elder John Morgan," in *Journal of Discourses by President John Taylor, His Counsellors, the Twelve Apostles, and Others*, vol. 23 (London: Latter-day Saints' Book Depot, 1883), 41.

41. Sarah Barringer Gordon, *The Mormon Question: Polygamy and Constitutional Conflict in Nineteenth-Century America* (Chapel Hill: University of North Carolina Press, 2001).

42. R. W. Sloan, *The Great Contest: The Chief Advocates of Anti-Mormon Measures Reviewed By their Speeches in the House of Representatives . . .* (Salt Lake City: n.p., 1887), 1, 4, 10.

43. See circular letter from John Morgan and B. H. Roberts to the Presidents of Conferences and Traveling Elders in the Southern States Mission, ca. early 1884, in John Henry Gibbs Collection, BYU; letter from B. H. Roberts to Joseph Morrell, August 23, 1884, in Joseph Morrell Correspondence, 1883-1906, LDSCA; circular letter from Ben E. Rich to the Elders of the Southern States Mission, July 2, 1898, in Benjamin Erastus Rich Correspondence, 1881-1908, LDSCA.

44. SSMMH, February 8, 1882.

45. SSMMH, February 18, 1889.

46. See Moore, *Religious Outsiders*, 35.

47. Givens, *Viper on the Hearth*; Gordon, *The Mormon Question*.

48. "Mormons in the South," *Public Opinion* 28 (Jan.-June 1900): 114.

49. The classic historical analysis of the LDS Church's racial policy is Lester E. Bush, "Mormonism's Negro Doctrine: An Historical Overview," *Dialogue: A Journal of Mormon Thought* 8 (Spring 1973): 11–68. See also Newell G. Bringhurst, *Saints, Slaves, and Blacks: The Changing Place of Black People within Mormonism* (Westport, CT: Greenwood Press, 1981); Bush and Armand L. Mauss, eds., *Neither White nor Black: Mormon Scholars Confront the Race Issue in a Universal Church* (Salt Lake City: Signature Books, 1984); Mauss, *All Abraham's Children: Changing Mormon Conceptions of Race and Lineage* (Urbana: University of Illinois Press, 2003); Newell G. Bringhurst and Darron T. Smith, eds., *Black and Mormon* (Urbana: University of Illinois Press, 2004). The church's statement extending the priesthood to all faithful male members was canonized as Official Declaration No. 2 in D&C. For a broader treatment of how nineteenth-century Americans used biblical narratives in justifying racism, see Stephen R. Haynes, *Noah's Curse: The Biblical Justification of American Slavery* (New York: Oxford University Press, 2002).

50. Donald G. Mathews, "Lynching Is Part of the Religion of Our People: Faith in the Christian South," in *Religion in the American South: Protestants and Others in History and Culture*, ed. Beth Barton Schweiger and Mathews (Chapel Hill: University of North Carolina Press, 2004), 153–94; Orlando Patterson, *Rituals of Blood: Consequences of Slavery in Two American Centuries* (Washington, DC: Civitas/Counterpoint, 1998); Ownby, *Subduing Satan*; Paul Harvey, *Freedom's Coming: Religious Culture and the Shaping of the South from the Civil War through the Civil Rights Era* (Chapel Hill: University of North Carolina Press, 2005); Hahn, *A Nation under Our Feet*; Edward J. Blum and W. Scott Poole, eds., *Vale of Tears: New Essays on Religion and Reconstruction* (Macon: Mercer University Press, 2005). Despite this recent literature, virtually no mention of the connection of religion and violence, or even the Ku Klux Klan, is made in Hill, *Religion*.

51. The most insightful examination of the subject is Gene A. Sessions, "Myth, Mormonism, and Murder in the South," *South Atlantic Quarterly* 75 (Spring 1976): 212–25. I concur with much of Sessions' analysis, which is perceptive albeit brief. Berrett, "History of the Southern States Mission," and Seferovich, "History of the LDS Southern States Mission," both address anti-Mormonism, but their insights are preliminary and unpublished. The most extensive published examinations of southern anti-Mormon violence have come from William W. Hatch. *There Is No Law . . . : A History of Mormon Civil Relations in the Southern States, 1865–1905* (New York: Vantage Press, 1968), is a helpful introduction to the subject, though somewhat limited in historical analysis. Hatch builds on his earlier work in *When Push Came to Shove: Mormon Martyrs in an Unrelenting Bible Belt, 1831–1923* (Portland, OR: Inkwater Press, 2005), where he includes the antebellum period and adds a lengthy, and flawed, section on the impact of the Mountain Meadows Massacre on southern anti-Mormonism. On individual incidents, see Marshall Wingfield, "Tennessee's Mormon Massacre," *Tennessee Historical Quarterly* 17 (Mar. 1958): 19–36; and Ken Driggs, "'There Is No Law in Georgia for Mormons': The Joseph Standing Murder Case of 1879," *Georgia Historical Quarterly* 73 (Winter 1989): 745–72.

CHAPTER 2

1. "Last Letter from Elder Joseph Standing," *Deseret Evening News*, August 5, 1879.

2. There are two extended treatments of Standing's murder in secondary literature: Ken Driggs, "'There is No Law in Georgia for Mormons': The Joseph Standing Murder Case of 1879," *Georgia Historical Quarterly* 73 (Winter 1989): 745-72; and William Whitridge Hatch, *There Is No Law . . . : A History of Mormon Civil Relations in the Southern States, 1865-1905* (New York: Vintage Press, 1968), chap. 3. See also Hatch, *When Push Came to Shove: Mormon Martyrs in an Unrelenting Bible Belt, 1821-1923* (Portland, OR: Inkwater Press, 2005), chap. 7. See also Mary Ella Reed Engel, "Praying with One Eye Open: A Gendered Interpretation of Mormon Joseph Standing's Murder in Appalachian Georgia" (Ph.D. diss., University of Georgia, 2009).

3. Driggs, "There is No Law in Georgia," 750.

4. See the register to the Rudger Clawson Papers, U of U; Sarah Barringer Gordon, *The Mormon Question: Polygamy and Constitutional Conflict in Nineteenth-Century America* (Chapel Hill: University of North Carolina Press, 2002), 157; John Nicholson, *The Martyrdom of Joseph Standing; or, the Murder of a "Mormon" Missionary* (Grantsville, UT: LDS Archive Publishers, 1997), 7-8; and Driggs, "There is No Law in Georgia," 751-52. For additional insight into Clawson's character, as well as the broader culture of Latter-day Saints during the polygamy prosecutions of the 1880s, see Stan Larson, ed., *Prisoner for Polygamy: The Memoirs and Letters of Rudger Clawson at the Utah Territorial Penitentiary, 1884-87* (Urbana: University of Illinois Press, 1993).

5. Rudger Clawson, *Memoirs of the Life of Rudger Clawson, Written by Himself* (unpublished typescript, 1926), 44-45, in Clawson Papers. Both Driggs and Hatch state that it was men who came to the door and turned the elders away. Nicholson comes closest to identifying the family, but does so only as "J-----." See Nicholson, *Martyrdom*, 13-14. William Kaneaster confirmed that there was anti-Mormon mob activity in April and May of that year, which set local members on edge. Kaneaster reported that one convert, a Brother Loggins, stopped his son and daughter from going to school for fear the mob would apprehend them while on the road. William Kaneaster, "The Martyrdom of Joseph Standing," LDSCA, 3.

6. See Clawson, *Memoirs*, 44. See also Nicholson, *Martyrdom*, 13-14, which reports that upon being rejected at the house, Clawson thought to himself, "This is the fulfillment of Joseph's dream."

7. Nicholson, *Martyrdom*, 15-16; also see Clawson, *Memoirs*, 51.

8. "The Murder of Joseph Standing," *Deseret Evening News*, August 1, 1879; Nicholson, *Martyrdom*, 24-25; and Clawson, *Memoirs*, 48-49. Nicholson reports that when Standing asked under what authority the posse acted, he was greeted by a cocked revolver in the face (19).

9. Gordon, *The Mormon Question*, 122; for broader context, see all of chapter 3. *Reynolds v. United States*, 98 U.S. 145 (1878); the case was argued in November 1878 and decided in May 1879. George Reynolds, former private secretary to Brigham Young, was the first person convicted under the federal antibigamy law of 1862. He offered to serve as a test case in the church leadership's strategy to challenge the constitutionality of antipolygamy legislation in the courts. Reynolds was sentenced to two years' imprisonment and a $500 fine. See "The Convicted Mormons," *New York Times*, June 19, 1879. See also Edwin Brown Firmage and Richard Collin Mangrum, *Zion in the Courts: A Legal History of the Church of Jesus Christ of Latter-day Saints, 1830-1900* (Urbana: University of Illinois Press, 1988), 151-59.

10. "Anti-Mormon Manifesto," *Deseret Evening News*, August 9, 1879; "The Question of Mormon Rights," *New York Times*, August 13, 1879; "No Way of Stopping Mormons," *New York Times*, August 30, 1879. For an optimistic LDS interpretation of these events, see "Latter-day Lights," *Atlanta Daily Constitution*, October 31, 1879.

11. This exchange of letters, sent on June 12 and 21, respectively, was reprinted several times after Standing's murder, first in "Another Martyr for the Truth," *Deseret Evening News*, July 22, 1879; see also "The Mormon Feud," *Atlanta Daily Constitution*, August 5, 1879. On Colquitt, see "Gov. Colquitt," *Richmond Christian Advocate*, July 24, 1879; "Wise Tactics," ibid., July 31, 1879.

12. "The Murder of Joseph Standing," *Deseret Evening News*, August 1, 1879. Nicholson's account of Fawcett's threat reads slightly different, but with the same effect: "I want you men to understand that I am the captain of this party, and that if we ever again find you in this part of the country we will hang you by the neck like dogs." Nicholson, *Martyrdom*, 27.

13. Clawson, *Memoirs*, 51; "Told to Go Free," *Atlanta Daily Constitution*, October 23, 1879. Early reports agree that the mob's original intent was not to kill, but rather to give the elders a "handsome thrashing" and send them out of town; see "The Murder of Elder Standing," *New York Times*, July 24, 1879; "The Dead Mormon," *Atlanta Daily Constitution*, July 25, 1879. See also "Bad Law and Good," *Deseret Evening News*, November 3, 1879.

14. "The Murder of Joseph Standing," *Deseret Evening News*, August 1, 1879; Clawson, *Memoirs*, 52–53. The moment just before the shooting is a matter of some controversy. As quoted here, Clawson's early statements indicate that Standing was fired upon after grabbing a pistol from a guard, pointing it at his captors, and demanding their surrender. Later on, Clawson changed his story somewhat, saying that Standing "jumped to his feet, turned to face the horsemen, clapped his hands firmly together, and . . . said in a commanding voice, 'Surrender.'" Here Clawson asserts that to his "certain knowledge" Standing was unarmed, and that "he had never carried arms in the mission field," right up to his death. Clawson, *Memoirs*, 52, 54; also given in Nicholson, *Martyrdom*, 27. The earliest accounts of the murder all say that Standing had by some means seized a pistol from one of his captors. In addition to the *Deseret News* story cited above, see "A Mormon Elder Murdered," *New York Times*, July 22, 1879; and "Put to Death," *Atlanta Daily Constitution*, July 22, 1879. A third version of the story emerged, saying that Standing was shot after adamantly refusing to be whipped, which "infuriated the mob." See "The Murder of Elder Standing," *New York Times*, July 24, 1879. Although Standing had previously expressed his wish to die rather than be whipped, there is no evidence that the mob actually tried to whip him before he was shot. Although verification is impossible, Clawson's alternative version of the story—that Standing simply clapped his hands together—seems to have been invented to help protect the character of the fallen missionary and to undermine the mob's claim that they fired in self-defense. See also Larson, *Prisoner for Polygamy*, 134 n. 5.

15. Clawson, *Memoirs*, 53–55; "The Murder of Joseph Standing," *Deseret Evening News*, August 1, 1879; Nicholson, *Martyrdom*, 28–31.

16. "The Murder of Joseph Standing," *Deseret Evening News*, August 1, 1879; "Another Martyr for the Truth," *Deseret Evening News*, July 22, 1879; Nicholson, *Martyrdom*, 31–42; Hatch, 49–50.

17. Clawson, *Memoirs*, 57–59; Nicholson, *Martyrdom*, 42–49; "Told to Go Free," *Atlanta Daily Constitution*, October 23, 1879. Clawson surmised that the shots that disfigured Standing's face and neck must have been fired from point-blank range, as his skin was "powder-burnt." Nicholson, *Martyrdom*, 43. Local resident William Kaneaster said of the wound, "The mob had shot him the second time with a double barrel shot gun, one load where the first shot and the other just above. It was done at close range. . . . The two holes in his forehead was about large enough to turn a man's thumb around in without touching the fractured parts." Kaneaster, "The Martyrdom of Joseph Standing," 5. The twelve men identified by the coroner's jury were David D. Nations, Jasper N. Nations, A. S. Smith, David Smith, Benjamin Clark, William Nations, Andrew Bradley, James Fawcett (or Faucett), Hugh Blair, Joseph Nations, Jefferson Hunter, and Mack McClure. The statement by the coroner's jury is reprinted in multiple places, including "The Murder of Joseph Standing," *Deseret Evening News*, August 1, 1879.

18. Letter from Elder Francis McDonald to Elder John Nicholson, in SSMMH, August 4, 1879.

19. Letter reprinted in "Death of Elder Standing," *Deseret Evening News*, July 23, 1879.

20. D&C 115:6. The origin of the doctrine of the gathering was a revelation to Joseph Smith in December 1830 calling the Latter-day Saints to gather to Ohio (see D&C 37).

21. For a discussion of nineteenth-century Mormon millennialist beliefs and attitudes, see Grant Underwood, *The Millenarian World of Early Mormonism* (Urbana: University of Illinois Press, 1993).

22. This phenomenon is not entirely unique to Mormonism. See Emmanuel Sivan, "The Enclave Culture," in *Strong Religion: The Rise of Fundamentalisms around the World*, ed. Gabriel A. Almond, R. Scott Appleby, and Emmanuel Sivan (Chicago: University of Chicago Press, 2003), 23–89.

23. "The Murder of Joseph Standing," *Deseret Evening News*, August 1, 1879.

24. "Another Martyr for the Truth," ibid., July 22, 1879.

25. "The Murder of Joseph Standing," ibid., August 1, 1879.

26. "The Murderers of Elder Joseph Standing on Trial," ibid., October 28, 1879.

27. "Resolutions of Respect and Condolence on the Death of Elder Joseph Standing," ibid., August 4, 1879.

28. "Where the Guilt Lies," ibid., August 11, 1879; "Georgia Assassins Arrested," ibid., August 14, 1879.

29. The best analyses of this anti-Mormon literature from the second half of the nineteenth century are Terryl Givens, *The Viper on the Hearth: Mormons, Myths, and the Construction of Heresy* (New York: Oxford University Press, 1997), esp. chaps. 6–7; and Gordon, *The Mormon Question*, chap. 1.

30. "Mormonism Shaken," *New York Times*, August 14, 1879. John Morgan contended that there was a direct connection between the anti-Mormon machine in Salt Lake City and Standing's murder. While Morgan is generally a trustworthy source, there is no corroborating evidence of this particular claim. See typescript of interview with unidentified newspaper reporter, titled "Another Mormon Elder Shot!" (newspaper unknown) August 20, 1884; in John Hamilton Morgan Papers, U of U.

31. "Sons of Ishmael," *Atlanta Daily Constitution*, August 1, 1879; "Brigham's Dead Saint," ibid., July 23, 1879; "The Dead Mormon," ibid., July 25, 1879; "The Standing Killing," ibid., July 26, 1879; "Georgia's Mormon Murder," ibid., July 27, 1879; "Mormonism and the Remedy," ibid., August 23, 1879.

32. "Murder of a Mormon," *Christian Index*, July 31, 1879.

33. Reprinted in "The Standing Killing," *Atlanta Daily Constitution*, July 26, 1879.

34. Reprinted in "Mormonism and the Remedy," ibid., August 23, 1879.

35. "The Mormon Feud," ibid., August 5, 1879.

36. See ibid.; "In Brigham's Bosom," ibid., August 7, 1879; "Georgia Assassins Arrested," *Deseret Evening News*, August 14, 1879. There were some accusations that Mormon elders did preach polygamy in the South, but these claims were usually couched in general terms, such as the suggestion that the missionaries existed primarily "for the purpose of preaching their polygamic creed." "Brigham's Dead Saint," *Atlanta Daily Constitution*, July 23, 1879.

37. "A Lustful Lout," *Atlanta Daily Constitution*, August 24, 1879.

38. "The Mormon Feud," ibid., August 5, 1879.

39. Kaneaster, "The Martyrdom of Joseph Standing." Rudger Clawson publicly defended Standing's integrity and character in "A Calumny Refuted," *Deseret News*, September 17, 1879.

40. Driggs, "There Is No Law in Georgia for Mormons," 764. The Elledge family had given shelter to missionaries previously, and turned away a mob of seventy-five men at gunpoint on May 1, 1879. Kaneaster, "The Martyrdom of Joseph Standing," 2–3.

41. "Told to Go Free," *Atlanta Daily Constitution*, October 23, 1879.

42. "The Murderers of Elder Joseph Standing on Trial," *Deseret Evening News*, October 28, 1879. Nicholson reports that the sheriff was in fact ambivalent on the point of hunting the men who killed Standing. According to the story told by the deputy, the sheriff told him, "The man they murdered was only a 'Mormon,' and it doesn't matter about the perpetrators being brought to justice." Based on this account, it was the deputy who was responsible for seeing that the alleged murderers be brought to justice, despite public threats and the sheriff's apathy. See Nicholson, *Martyrdom*, 59–61; "The Murder of Elder Standing," *New York Times*, July 24, 1879.

43. Quoted in Driggs, "There is No Law in Georgia," 765.

44. "The Murderers of Elder Joseph Standing on Trial," *Deseret Evening News*, October 28, 1879; Nicholson, *Martyrdom*, 63; "Told to Go Free," *Atlanta Daily Constitution*, October 23, 1879. As early as six days after the murder, the *New York Herald* suggested that "no jury will think for a moment of convicting" the killers; reprinted in "Georgia's Mormon Murder," *Atlanta Daily Constitution*, July 27, 1879.

45. "The Murderers of Elder Joseph Standing on Trial," *Deseret Evening News*, October 28, 1879; Nicholson, *Martyrdom*, 69–75; Driggs, "There Is No Law in Georgia for Mormons," 765–768. See also "Told to Go Free," *Atlanta Daily Constitution*, October 23, 1879; "Criminals and Their Offenses," *New York Times*, October 26, 1879.

46. "The Murderers of Elder Joseph Standing on Trial," *Deseret Evening News*, October 28, 1879.

47. "Told to Go Free," *Atlanta Daily Constitution*, October 23, 1879; "The Indignant Mormons," ibid., October 28, 1879.

48. See Driggs, "There Is No Law in Georgia for Mormons," 769.

49. Standing's murder and his monument have been employed in recent years by activists in Utah pushing for a state law banning hate crimes. See Mike Cronin, "Young Activist Channels Passion," *Salt Lake Tribune*, December 6, 2004.

CHAPTER 3

1. John Gibbs was just shy of thirty years old when he was called as a missionary to the Southern States Mission in 1883. He was given a specific assignment to proselytize the rural counties of northwest Tennessee. He married Louisa Obray in 1874 in Salt Lake City, and together they had three children. Biographical information in John Henry Gibbs Collection, BYU.

2. "Notice," unsigned and undated [May 4, 1884, Cane Creek, TN], in Gibbs Collection; original spelling and punctuation preserved. In addition to keeping the original note, Gibbs copied it into his journal, with slight changes to some of the syntax; see "Notice to Mormons," in Gibbs journal (Feb.–Mar. 1883, 1884), in Gibbs Collection.

3. "An Interesting Experience," *Deseret Evening News*, May 21, 1884; letter from John Gibbs to Louisa Gibbs, May 14, 1884, in Gibbs Collection.

4. Gibbs journal, May 8, 1884, in Gibbs Collection.

5. After preaching in Indian Creek, Tennessee, Gibbs reported, "They would not let me go off alone, and on foot. So they furnished me a fine horse and saddle. So now I am a <u>Big Preacher</u>. . . . The big preachers are using my name from the pulpits. But dare not meet me, I am getting quite a favorite with a great many of the church members, they all want me to preach." Letter from John Gibbs to Louisa Gibbs, September 18, 1883, in ibid.

6. Letter from John Gibbs to Louisa Gibbs, no date or place [ca. June/July 1884], in ibid.

7. On the national anti-Mormon crusade in the courts and in Congress, see Sarah Barringer Gordon, *The Mormon Question: Polygamy and Constitutional Conflict in Nineteenth-Century America* (Chapel Hill: University of North Carolina Press, 2002). On the Mormon reaction, and rhetorical defenses of plural marriage, see David J. Whittaker, "Early Mormon Polygamy Defenses," *Journal of Mormon History* 11 (1984): 43–63; Davis Bitton, *The Ritualization of Mormon History and Other Essays* (Urbana: University of Illinois Press, 1994), 34–53.

8. Letter from John Gibbs to Louisa Gibbs, June 7, 1884, in Gibbs Collection. All other letters from John Gibbs to Louisa Gibbs, on dates noted, in Gibbs Collection. The notebook Gibbs used during his lecture tour was filled with extensive lecture notes on the subject of polygamy, including a fifteen-point vindication of the institution based on the standard Mormon defense that the First Amendment protected both belief in and practice of plural marriage. John Gibbs mission notebook, in ibid. On the general Mormon strategy of defending polygamy based on the First Amendment, see Gordon, *Mormon Question*, esp. chaps. 3–4; and Bitton, "Polygamy Defended," 38–41.

9. Letter from John Gibbs to Louisa Gibbs, June 17, 1884, in Gibbs Collection.

10. Letter from John Gibbs to Louisa Gibbs, August 5, 1884, in ibid.; letter from John Gibbs to Louisa Gibbs, July 18, 1884, in ibid..

11. Letter from W. E. Robison, W. H. Robinson, H. Thompson, and Wm. S. Berry to John Gibbs, June 25, 1884, in ibid. William Berry, also laboring in the region,

recorded in his journal a handful of confrontations with local citizens, including a minister who denounced the Latter-day Saints as "wolves in sheeps clothing and false prophets," and a lawyer who "started on me about the people of Utah and polygamy." William Shanks Berry Journal, June 1 and 6, July 23, 1884, LDSCA.

12. Letter from John Gibbs to Louisa Gibbs, August 5, 1884, in Gibbs Collection.

13. Gibbs had earlier written, "Do not be alarmed or have any fears in regard my safety. Have faith and plead with our Father for my protection. I have been in some rough storms, and where the waters have been up very high, but the Lord has protected me, and has the same with all the Elders, so we have no need to fear. . . . [Our enemies] cannot go any farther than God will allow them. . . . And if we are united and faithful He will not allow them to do anything at all." Letter from John Gibbs to Louisa Gibbs, April 21, 1884, in ibid.

14. William Berry's journal contains daily entries from his arrival in Cane Creek on August 5 until his last entry on Friday, August 8, none of which give any intimation of local hostilities.

15. My retelling of the events of August 10, 1884, draws on a combination of five primary and secondary sources, which together represent the best available narratives of the affair. Although they differ in some points, one is able to get the best possible estimate of what probably happened by piecing them all together. See John Nicholson, *The Tennessee Massacre and Its Causes; or, The Utah Conspiracy* (Grantsville, UT: Archive Publishers, 2000); B. H. Roberts, "The Tennessee Massacre," *Contributor* (Oct. 1884): 16–23; Marshall Wingfield, "Tennessee's Mormon Massacre," *Tennessee Historical Quarterly* 17 (Mar. 1958): 19–36; B. H. Roberts, *A Comprehensive History of The Church of Jesus Christ of Latter-day Saints* (Provo, UT: Brigham Young University Press, 1965), vol. 6, chap. 158; and B. H. Roberts, *The Autobiography of B. H. Roberts*, ed. Gary James Bergera (Salt Lake City, UT: Signature Books, 1990), chap. 17. Spelling in many nineteenth-century sources was notoriously inconsistent, so I have gone with the most common renditions of names and places.

16. "The Tennessee Tragedy," *Deseret Evening News*, September 13, 1884.

17. See "An Atrocious Deed," ibid., August 12, 1884; "Horrible Butchery," *Daily American*, August 12, 1884; "Murder of Mormons," *Nashville Banner*, August 12, 1884; "More About the Murders in Tennessee," *Deseret Evening News*, August 13, 1884; "The Lewis County Butchery," *Daily American*, August 13, 1884; and "Murdered by Masked Men," *New York Times*, August 13, 1884. Willis Robison, one of the missionaries serving in the area at the time, later reminisced that the press accounts in the immediate wake of the episode "were very conflicting. One statement was that all were dead, another assumed the fact that only one or two were killed, and the others were hid in the woods, but desperately wounded. In fact no two rumors seemed to agree." In Robison, "An Unpublished Letter on the Tennessee Massacre," *Improvement Era* 2 (Nov. 1898): 3.

18. Telegram John Morgan to Elders B. H. Roberts or Golding [sic] Kimball, August 12, 1884; telegram from James Jack to B. H. Roberts, August 12 or 13, 1884, in Telegrams, 1884, LDSCA.

19. Robison, "An Unpublished Letter"; also see Roberts, *Autobiography*, 146–47.

20. A non-Mormon who was recruited for the retrieval job later described the experience as "the worse job I ever got into," due to the summer heat and the condition of the bodies that had laid in temporary graves for six days. Donald M. Axleroad, "Cane

Creek Violence Took Four Lives in 1884," *Daily Herald*, March 26, 1964; reprinted in Jill K. Garrett, comp., *Historical Sketches of Hickman County, Tennessee* (n.p., 1978), 72–74.

21. Roberts, "The Tennessee Massacre," 22–23.

22. "More About the Murders in Tennessee," *Deseret Evening News*, August 13, 1884.

23. "The Lewis County Butchery," *Daily American*, August 13, 1884.

24. "The Murdered Mormon Elders," *New York Times*, August 14, 1884.

25. "The Murdered Mormons," ibid., August 23, 1884; "The Mormon Murder," *Nashville Banner*, August 23, 1884. William B. Bate was a native Tennessean, a Civil War general, and a lifelong southern Democrat who was elected to two terms as Governor of Tennessee beginning in 1882 (serving 1883–87), and was then elected to the U.S. Senate, where he held a seat until his death in 1905. See Robert Sobel and John Raimo, *Biographical Directory of the Governors of the United States, 1789–1978*, vol. 4 (Westport, CT: Meckler Books, 1978), 1487–88. Eli H. Murray, a Kentucky native, was a general in the Union Army, and was appointed as territorial governor of Utah by Rutherford Hayes in 1880. Immediately upon his appointment, Murray commenced a bitter anti-Mormon campaign that lasted throughout his six years as governor and spread beyond Utah's borders to influence national policy, particularly in antipolygamy legislation. See Miriam B. Murphy, "Territorial Governors (Utah Territory)," in *Utah History Encyclopedia*, ed. Allan Kent Powell (Salt Lake City: University of Utah Press, 1994), 549; and Thomas A. McMullin and David Walker, *Biographical Directory of American Territorial Governors* (Westport, CT: Meckler, 1984), 306–7.

26. ". . . Against Mormonism" (title incomplete), *Nashville Banner*, September 6, 1884.

27. See "A Badly Scared Detective," *Daily American*, September 3, 1884; "Not Cheerful for Detectives," *New York Times*, September 3, 1884.

28. "An Infamy and a Crime," *Deseret Evening News*, September 8, 1884.

29. "The Tennessee Mormon Slayers," *New York Times*, September 8, 1884.

30. "The Mormons," *Nashville Banner*, October 17, 1884. For other descriptions of the vigilantes' clothing, see Bergera, *Autobiography*, 139; "The Mormons," *Daily American*, August 21, 1884; and Nicholson, *The Tennessee Massacre*, 9.

31. "Not Cheerful for Detectives," *New York Times*, September 3, 1884. See Richard Maxwell Brown, *Strain of Violence: Historical Studies of American Violence and Vigilantism* (New York: Oxford University Press, 1975), esp. chap. 4. See also chapter 7 herein.

32. "The Mormons," *Nashville Banner*, September 25, 1884; "An Anti-Mormon Crusade," *New York Times*, September 25, 1884; "All Quiet in Lewis," *Hickman Pioneer*, September 26, 1884; "Mormon Converts Alarmed," *New York Times*, September 29, 1884.

33. "Forcing the Mormons Out," *New York Times*, October 3, 1884; "Mormons Immigrating," *Daily American*, October 3, 1884; Marise P. Lightfoot and Evelyn B. Shackelford, comp., *Maury County Neighbors: Records of Giles, Lewis, and Marshall Counties, Tennessee* (Mt. Pleasant, TN: n.p., 1967), 155.

34. Quotes from "Horrible Butchery," *Daily American*, August 12, 1884; "Murdered by Masked Men," *New York Times*, August 13, 1884. See also "Murder of Mormons," *Nashville Banner*, August 12, 1884; [missing title], ibid., August 13, 1884; "The

Mormon Murder," ibid., August 23, 1884; Lightfoot and Shackelford, *Maury County Neighbors*, 149–56.

35. "Terrible Tragedy," *Hickman Pioneer*, August 15, 1884.

36. See Lightfoot and Shackelford, *Maury County Neighbors*, 154.

37. "Account of Baptisms Etc. in the North West Tennessee Conference and scattered branches South – Recorded by Elder John H. Gibbs," Gibbs Collection. Information on the division of the conference, along with membership statistics, from SSMMH.

38. "The Tennessee Tragedy," *Deseret Evening News*, September 13, 1884.

39. "Account of Missionary Labors," in Gibbs journal (Feb.-Mar. 1883, 1884), Gibbs Collection. Gibbs had baptized a total of only fifteen in the twelve months of his mission until then.

40. See "Account of Baptisms," in ibid.; and "The Tragedy in Tennessee," *Deseret Evening News*, August 16, 1884.

41. Undated entry, and "Notice" (undated), in Gibbs journal (Feb.-Mar. 1883, 1884), in Gibbs Collection.

42. Circular letter, "To the Presidents of Conferences and Traveling Elders in the Southern States Mission," from John Morgan and B. H. Roberts, undated (ca. Jan.-early Feb. 1884), in ibid.

43. See letters from John Gibbs to Louisa Gibbs, June 26, 1883 and undated (ca. Feb. 1884), in ibid.

44. "The Mormon Murder," *Nashville Banner*, August 23, 1884.

45. Gibbs wrote his wife, with a certain tone of disdain, that "there have been several [missionaries] gone home lately, they could not stand persecution etc." He proudly affirmed, "I do not want to come home one minute before my time." Letter from John Gibbs to Louisa Gibbs, May 2, 1884, in Gibbs Collection.

46. "The Mormons," *Daily American*, August 21, 1884.

47. See "The Mormon Murders," *Nashville Banner*, August 14, 1884; "The Mormon Trouble," *Daily American*, August 19, 1884; "The Murdered Mormon Elders," *New York Times*, August 20, 1884.

48. "Mormonism," *Daily American*, August 25, 1884; also reprinted in "Mormonism," *Tennessee Baptist*, October 4, 1884.

49. "The Mormon Trouble," *Daily American*, August 19, 1884.

50. "What Shall Be Done with Mormons," ibid., August 18, 1884.

51. Lightfoot and Shackelford, *Maury County Neighbors*, 152–56.

52. Letter from John Gibbs to Louisa Gibbs, January 28, 1884, in Gibbs Collection. Gibbs wrote that the man "struggled with the young woman, threw her down, lifted her clothes and accomplished his wicked desires."

53. Letter from John Gibbs to Louisa Gibbs (pages missing, no place or date), in ibid.

54. Letter from John Gibbs to Joseph Morrell, January 10, 1884, in Joseph Morrell Correspondence, LDSCA.

55. Robison, "Unpublished Letter," 6.

56. "The Mormon Murders," *Nashville Banner*, August 14, 1884.

57. "The Mormon Trouble," *Daily American*, August, 1884.

58. For biographical information on William Berry, see "The Martyred Elder, W. S. Berry," *Deseret Evening News*, August 18, 1884. Genealogical information accessed

on www.familysearch.org suggests that Berry had a total of three wives, but only two at any one time. He married Rebecca Beck (d. 1903) in 1860; Diantha Allen (d. 1873) in 1864; and Lovinia Sylvester (d. 1955) in 1874.

59. In several letters to his wife, John Gibbs mentioned his desire to enter into plural marriage when he returned home, even asking her if she could "stand the pressure after I come home to be again separated for a year or so from me for Polygamy? (in jail)." Letter from John Gibbs to Louisa Gibbs, July 25, 1883, in Gibbs Collection.

60. Circular letter, "To the Presidents of Conferences and Traveling Elders in the Southern States Mission," from John Morgan and B. H. Roberts, [ca. January-early February 1884,] in ibid. See also "Justifying Assassination," *Deseret Evening News*, August 21, 1884.

61. "The Massacre and Its Apologists," *Deseret Evening News*, August 26, 1884; also see circular letter, "To the Presidents of Conferences," in Gibbs Collection.

62. "More About the Murders in Tennessee," *Deseret Evening News*, August 13, 1884.

63. "The Blood of the Martyrs," *Latter-day Saints' Millennial Star* (September 15, 1884): 586. For other articles blaming the clergy and the press, see "The Late Massacre in Tennessee," *Deseret Evening News*, August 19, 1884; "Resolutions of Respect," ibid., August 22, 1884; "Honoring the Martyrs," ibid., August 25, 1884; "The Massacre and Its Apologists," ibid., August 26, 1884; "Accessories before the Fact," ibid., September 8, 1884.

64. Nicholson, *The Tennessee Massacre*; quotes from pp. 6, 59, 16, 14. Mormon apologist R. W. Sloan similarly described the conspiratorial workings of "the Loyal League, in Utah—a secret organization whose members are pledged to secure rule of the Territory by the minority." This league allegedly included lawyers, lobbyists, and leaders from various sectors of Utah's non-Mormon community. See Sloan, *The Great Contest: The Chief Advocates of Anti-Mormon Measures Reviewed . . .* (Salt Lake City: n.p., 1887), 6-7.

65. The bishop's statements had supposedly been confirmed to him as "the will of the Most High" from a vision of the martyred Joseph Smith, complete with "blood-red spots and livid wounds where the bullets of the cursed Gentiles had entered his sainted body." The entire "Red Hot Address" is reprinted in Nicholson, *The Tennessee Massacre*, 70-74.

66. The president of the Juab Stake in 1884 was William Paxman, and the bishops over the four wards in the stake were William Warner, David Udall, John Haws, and Niels Aagaard. Information provided by Jeffrey O. Johnson, LDS Church History Library, in private e-mail correspondence with the author, June 30, 2004. Johnson also reported that there was no specifically designated Juab ward or branch. The claim about a washout was part of a refutation of the "Red Hot Address" made in a letter to the editor of the *Deseret News* from George Teasdale, a resident of Juab County, dated March 18, 1884, and reprinted in Nicholson, *The Tennessee Massacre*, 75-76.

67. No details are known about this "Parson Vandever," and I have only found him in Mormon sources. The 1880 Lewis County census lists two Vandeveer family heads, J. H. (age 54, wife and one daughter) and Allen W. (age 35, wife and seven children). See *1880 Census–Lewis County*, trans. Byron Sistler (Nashville: Tennessee State Library and Archives, 1998). In his *Comprehensive History of the Church*,

compiled years later in 1930, B. H. Roberts suggested that the "Red Hot Address" was the last straw in what he characterized as a "Special Period of Anti-'Mormon' Misrepresentation" that led up to the Tennessee massacre. Roberts, *Comprehensive History of the Church*, 89.

68. "The Tennessee Tragedy," *Deseret Evening News*, September 13, 1884.

69. Nicholson, *The Tennessee Massacre*, 32.

70. An undated entry near the end of one of John Gibbs's mission journals, with the heading of "Dialogue between a Mormon Preacher and two Reverand [sic] Divines, named respectively, Vandever & Henson of the Baptist and Methodist faith," describes a hostile encounter on the street in which the two Protestant ministers warned the unnamed missionary to leave town. John Gibbs journal (Feb.–Mar. 1883 and 1884), in Gibbs Collection. J. D. Westbrook, who joined the LDS Church in Cane Creek and then migrated to Utah shortly before the massacre, stated that David Hinson "was a local preacher, of the Methodist persuasion," who lived only about seven miles from the Conder farm. "The Tragedy in Tennessee in Interesting Particulars," *Deseret Evening News*, August 16, 1884. Non-Mormon sources do not mention Hinson being a preacher of any kind. Instead, they describe him as "a respectable citizen"; "a well-to-do farmer"; and "a well-known citizen and distinguished for his daring courage and good marksmanship. He was a jovial man, and liked by all who knew him." *Daily American*, August 12, 1884; *Nashville Banner*, August 12, 1884; *Hickman Pioneer*, August 15, 1884.

71. "The Tennessee Tragedy," *Deseret Evening News*, September 13, 1884.

72. "The Mormon Trouble," *Daily American*, August 19, 1884.

73. "The Heroic Victims of the Cane Creek Tragedy," *Deseret Evening News*, August 27, 1884.

74. "Murdered by Masked Men," *New York Times*, August 13, 1884; also see "The Mormon Trouble," *Daily American*, August 19, 1884.

75. "Terrible Tragedy," *Hickman Pioneer*, August 15, 1884; "The Mormon Murders," *Nashville Banner*, August 18, 1884; "Matters in Hickman," *Weekly American*, September 4, 1884. See also Lightfoot and Shackelford, *Maury County Neighbors*, 154.

76. See "The Tennessee Mormon Slayers," *New York Times*, September 8, 1884; "The Mormon Murders," *Nashville Banner*, August 18, 1884; "The Murdered Mormon Elders," *New York Times*, August 14, 1884.

77. "The Mormons," *Hickman Pioneer*, October 24, 1884; also see "The Mormon Murders," *Nashville Banner*, October 25, 1884. Mormons were thrilled with Bateman's charge to the jury, and saw him as a lone sympathetic voice. One LDS publication was so taken with the judge that it launched into poetic adulation: "the brave and manly words of Judge Bateman ring out clearly and distinctly as the chime of church bells on the frosty air of a winter's morning." "Judge Bateman's Charge," *The Latter-day Saints' Millennial Star*, December 22, 1884.

78. "Mormonism," *Daily American*, August 25, 1884.

79. "An Act to define and punish the crime of teaching polygamous doctrines and principles, and of persuading persons to embrace the same," Chap. 151 of *Acts of the State of Tennessee*, Forty-Fourth General Assembly, 262–63. See also "To define and suppress the teaching of polygamy," Senate Bill No. 65, *Senate Journal of the Forty-Fourth General Assembly of the State of Tennessee*, 137, 358–359. The law was repealed as part of a widespread revision of the state penal code; see *Public Acts and*

Resolutions of the State of Tennessee Passed by the Ninety-sixth General Assembly, First Regular Session (1989), chap. 591 sec. 1.

80. "To prohibit the teaching of polygamous doctrines in this State," Senate Bill No. 23, *Senate Journal of the Forty-Fifth General Assembly of the State of Tennessee*, 115, 168. See also "Mormons in Tennessee," *New York Times*, January 12, 1887.

81. See letter from John Morgan to Pres. John Taylor, May 18, 1885, in Morgan Papers; and SSMMH, 13 May, 13 July, and August 5, 1885.

82. "Bloody 'Mormon Massacre' on Cane Creek," Nashville newspaper clipping dated July 1, 1931, reprinted in Garrett, *Historical Sketches of Hickman County*, 74–77.

CHAPTER 4

Portions of chapters 4 and 5 also appear in Patrick Q. Mason, "Opposition to Polygamy in the Postbellum South," *Journal of Southern History* 76:3 (Aug. 2010): 541-78.

1. Leslie M. Mann, "Deviltry of Mormons," *(Tucson, AZ) Star*, February 8, 1889; quoted in SSMMH, February 8, 1889.

2. "Through Utah," *St. Louis Christian Advocate*, September 17, 1879. The Chicago *Times-Herald* noted that in the South, Mormonism was "considered identical with polygamy." Quoted in "The South and the Mormons," *Atlanta Constitution*, August 9, 1899.

3. "General Denominational News," *Christian Index*, December 19, 1878.

4. See Edwin Brown Firmage and Richard Collin Mangrum, *Zion in the Courts: A Legal History of the Church of Jesus Christ of Latter-day Saints, 1830-1900* (Urbana: University of Illinois Press, 1988), chap. 6; *Reynolds v. United States*, 98 U.S. 145 (1879); Sarah Barringer Gordon, *The Mormon Question: Polygamy and Constitutional Conflict in Nineteenth-Century America* (Chapel Hill: University of North Carolina Press, 2002), chaps. 3-4.

5. Rutherford B. Hayes, "Third Annual Message," in *A Compilation of the Messages and Papers of the Presidents, 1789-1897*, comp. James D. Richardson ([Washington, D.C.]: Published by Authority of Congress, 1899), 7:559-60. On Hayes's antipolygamy commitments, see also Gordon, *The Mormon Question*, 150.

6. Hayes, "Fourth Annual Message," in Richardson, *Compilation of the Messages and Papers of the Presidents*, 7:606.

7. Incidentally, Rudger Clawson, who witnessed Joseph Standing's murder in 1879, was the first person convicted under the terms of the Edmunds Act.

8. "Anti-Mormon Manifesto," *Deseret Evening News*, August 9, 1879; "The Question of Mormon Rights," *New York Times*, August 13, 1879; "No Way of Stopping Mormons," ibid., August 30, 1879.

9. James Garfield, "Inaugural Address," in Richardson, *Compilation of the Messages and Papers of the Presidents*, 8:11.

10. Chester Arthur, "First Annual Message," in ibid.; "Third Annual Message," ibid., 8:184.

11. Grover Cleveland, "First Annual Message," in ibid., 8:361-62; see also "Fourth Annual Message," ibid., 8:794. In 1891 Congress did officially exclude polygamists from immigrating to the United States, but it never acted on the earlier recommendations to target Mormon converts per se. See *The Statutes at Large of the United States of America* (Washington: Government Printing Office, 1891), 26:1084.

12. Untitled, *Christian Index*, August 3, 1882. See also "The Uprising against Mormonism," *Christian Advocate*, February 9, 1882.

13. Rev. L. M. Hagood, "Mormonism," *Southwestern Christian Advocate*, June 8, 1882. For a northern Baptist parallel, see Rev. T. A. K. Gessler, "The Mormon Question," *Proceedings of the Fourth Baptist Congress, Held in the City of New-York, Nov. 1885* (New York: Century, 1886), 18.

14. "Mormon Polygamy," *Alabama Christian Advocate*, November 21, 1881. See also Rev. John S. Porter, "The Suppression of Polygamy," *Christian Advocate*, January 19, 1882; *A Sermon by the Rev. Dr. Newman, Pastor of the Metropolitan Methodist Church, on Plural Marriage, to Which Is Added an Answer by Elder Orson Pratt* (Salt Lake City: Deseret News Office, 1870), 10.

15. Jennie Fowler Willing, *On American Soil, or Mormonism the Mohammedanism of the West* (Louisville: Pickett Publishing, 1906), 15, 24.

16. "Mormonism," *Tennessee Baptist*, October 4, 1884.

17. "The Durability of Mormonism," *Christian Advocate*, January 19, 1882.

18. "Loves of the Saints," *Georgia Weekly Telegraph and Georgia Journal & Messenger*, November 14, 1871.

19. Willing, *On American Soil*, 82.

20. Rev. Wildman Murphy, *What the Mormons Teach* (New York: Eaton & Mains, 1894), 12. See also Charles Fowler, *Missionary Work in the Mormon Empire* (New York: The Rindge Missionary Literature Department, n.d. [1903?]), 4; and *The Menace of Mormonism* (Nashville: Home Department Woman's Missionary Council, M. E. Church, South, 1914), 4–5.

21. "Mormonism in the East," *Christian Index*, March 31, 1887.

22. Willing, *On American Soil*, 15–16.

23. "Converts to Mormonism," *New York Times*, February 15, 1884.

24. Untitled, *Southwestern Christian Advocate*, July 26, 1883.

25. "Secular Editorials," *Christian Index*, April 10, 1879. See also untitled, *News and Observer*, July 20, 1881; "Mormon Polygamy," *Alabama Christian Advocate*, November 21, 1881; "The Mormons at Work in West Virginia," *Daily Picayune*, August 21, 1889; and "Mormon Dangers," ibid., March 24, 1889.

26. Untitled, *Christian Advocate*, June 17, 1886. See also "Growing Faster Than Ever," *Atlanta Constitution*, March 27, 1901.

27. "Loves of the Saints," *Georgia Weekly Telegraph and Georgia Journal & Messenger*, November 14, 1871; see also "Mormon Dangers," *Daily Picayune*, March 24, 1889.

28. "Mormon Polygamy," *Alabama Christian Advocate*, November 21, 1881.

29. "The Mormons Amongst Us," *News and Observer*, January 25, 1881.

30. "Mormons Distributed," *Commercial Appeal*, October 27, 1897.

31. "Work of Mormons Near Columbus," *Atlanta Constitution*, February 10, 1900; "Mormons Are Gathering in Georgia Town," ibid., April 18, 1900; "The Mormons at Our Gates," ibid., April 18, 1900; "Mormon Elders at Dahlonega," ibid., April 25, 1900; "Mormon Elders Preaching Here," ibid., September 9, 1900.

32. "Mormonism in the South," *New York Times*, February 1 and 2, 1889. See also SSMMH, February 8, 1889.

33. "Letter from Hickory Grove, *Yorkville Enquirer*, September 25, 1889; "Is a Community Safe When Mormon Elders Are Allowed to Inhabit It?" *Alabama Baptist*,

November 17, 1887; "False Teachers Dangerous and Should Not Be Heard," *Alabama Christian Advocate*, June 8, 1881.

34. Clarence E. Cowley, "At a Baptist Church," *Southern Star*, vol. 1 (Chattanooga, TN: Southern States Mission, 1899), 333.

35. Rev. M. L. Oswalt, *Pen Pictures of Mormonism* (Philadelphia: American Baptist Publication Society, 1899), 8. Another southern observer argued that missionaries "work upon the weak minded and fanatical and only make converts by destroying the peace of the family." Bill Arp, "Arp on the Mormons," *Atlanta Constitution*, August 13, 1899.

36. "The Course to Pursue," *Atlanta Constitution*, February 16, 1900.

37. Quoted in SSMMH, July 22, 1883; "Mormonism in Georgia," *(Ogden, UT) Daily Herald*, quoted in SSMMH, August 16, 1883. See also "Mormon Dangers," *Daily Picayune*, March 24, 1889.

38. Quoted in SSMMH, March 13, 1886.

39. Willing, *On American Soil*, 76.

40. Rumors of Mormon polygamy in the South included stories that a man in York County, South Carolina, took two additional wives after converting to Mormonism; that missionaries in Chilton County, Alabama, "began to practice what they preached" before being found out by the county officers; and that converts in central Mississippi were engaged in a "disgraceful scandal" involving "licentious practices . . . [that] are in keeping with doctrines that the elders have been preaching recently in secret meetings." *News & Courier*, July 23, 1887; *Alabama Christian Advocate*, December 6, 1882; Oswalt, *Pen Pictures of Mormonism*, 93.

41. *Alabama Baptist*, July 3, 1879.

42. See Martha Hodes, *White Women, Black Men: Illicit Sex in the Nineteenth-Century South* (New Haven, CT: Yale University Press, 1997); and Diane Miller Sommerville, *Rape and Race in the Nineteenth-Century South* (Chapel Hill: University of North Carolina Press, 2004).

43. Quote from Jacquelyn Dowd Hall, *Revolt Against Chivalry: Jessie Daniel Ames and the Women's Campaign Against Lynching* (New York: Columbia University Press, 1979), 147–48. The concept of the "rape complex" is discussed in W. J. Cash, *The Mind of the South* (New York: Knopf, 1941; new ed., Vintage Books, 1991), 114–17. For recent overviews of black resistance to lynching, see Christopher Waldrep, *African Americans Confront Lynching: Strategies of Resistance from the Civil War to the Civil Rights Era* (Lanham, MD: Rowman & Littlefield Publishers, 2009); and Paula Giddings, *Ida: A Sword among Lions: Ida B. Wells and the Campaign against Lynching* (New York: Amistad, 2008). On southern manhood, its conceptions of the virtue of white womanhood, and the relationship of the myth of the black rapist to southern violence, see also Bertram Wyatt-Brown, *Southern Honor: Ethics and Behavior in the Old South* (New York: Oxford University Press, 1982); Joel Williamson, *A Rage for Order: Black/White Relations in the American South Since Emancipation* (New York: Oxford University Press, 1986), chap. 3; Brundage, *Lynching in the New South*, 58–72; Tolnay and Beck, *A Festival of Violence*, 46–50, 96; Gail Bederman, *Manliness & Civilization: A Cultural History of Gender and Race in the United States, 1880–1917* (Chicago: University of Chicago Press, 1995), esp. chaps. 2 and 4; Glenda Elizabeth Gilmore, *Gender & Jim Crow: Women and the Politics of White Supremacy in North Carolina, 1896–1920* (Chapel Hill: University of North Carolina Press, 1996), chaps. 3–4; Martha Hodes,

White Women, Black Men; Laura F. Edwards, *Gendered Strife & Confusion: The Political Culture of Reconstruction* (Urbana: University of Illinois Press, 1997), chaps. 5–6; Wyatt-Brown, *The Shaping of Southern Culture: Honor, Grace, and War, 1760s–1890s* (Chapel Hill: University of North Carolina Press, 2001); Philip Dray, *At the Hands of Persons Unknown: The Lynching of Black America* (New York: Random House, 2002), esp. chap. 3; Sommerville, *Rape and Race in the Nineteenth-Century South*; and Crystal Nicole Feimster, *Southern Horrors: Women and the Politics of Rape and Lynching* (Cambridge, MA: Harvard University Press, 2009).

44. Quoted in Williamson, *A Rage for Order*, 84.

45. "Mormonism," *Alabama Baptist*, June 19, 1879.

46. "Mormonism," *Tennessee Baptist*, October 4, 1884.

47. Quoted in "Sentiment of the Press," *Southern Star*, vol. 1 (Chattanooga, TN: Southern States Mission, 1899), 285.

48. "The Danger to Which It Leads," *Atlanta Constitution*, July 29, 1899.

49. New Orleans' *Daily Picayune* offered an intriguing alternative interpretation to the relationship of Mormons' whiteness and violence against them. Reflecting lingering bitterness over federal protection of African Americans during Reconstruction, the *Picayune* argued that the federal government did not protect LDS missionaries in the South precisely because of their white skins. The newspaper suggested that if the Mormons wanted the federal government on their side, they should actively proselytize blacks, thus playing the race card in their favor and trying to gain shelter under the Fourteenth Amendment. "The Mormons and the Fourteenth Amendment," *Daily Picayune*, July 28, 1887. On Mormon racial identity and otherness, see also Givens, *Viper on the Hearth*, chap. 7.

50. "Morgan, the Mormon," *Georgia Weekly Telegraph, Journal & Messenger*, November 18, 1881.

51. "Converts to Mormonism," *New York Times*, February 15, 1884; "Mormon Success in the South," ibid., January 22, 1885.

52. "The Mormon Feud," *Daily Constitution*, August 5, 1879.

53. Reprinted in SSMMH, March 8, 1886.

54. "Mormonism Reviving," *Yorkville Enquirer*, November 10, 1886.

55. "From Mountain Creek," *Alabama Baptist*, July 3, 1879. See also Rev. J. C. Thomas, *The Mistakes of Mormon and of Mormons: A Lecture* (Nashville: Publishing House of the Methodist Episcopal Church, South, 1899), 5.

56. "McLaurin Attacks Mormons," *Atlanta Constitution*, January 4, 1900; see also "A Menace to Liberty," *Southern Star*, vol. 2 (Chattanooga, TN: Southern States Mission, 1900), 74.

57. For examples of arrests, see SSMMH, May 13, 1885; August 5, 1887.

58. "The Mormons on Matrimony," *Georgia Weekly Telegraph and Georgia Journal & Messenger*, January 31, 1871.

59. "Loves of the Saints," ibid., November 14, 1871.

60. See "A Mormon Episode," ibid., August 19, 1873.

61. Untitled, ibid., April 11, 1871.

62. "Mormonism among the Poor," ibid., September 16, 1870.

63. Fowler, *Missionary Work in the Mormon Empire*, 4.

64. Grace Greenwood, "Mormon Women," *Hinds County Gazette*, January 3, 1872; "The Mormon Women," *Georgia Weekly Telegraph and Georgia Journal & Messenger*, October 3, 1876.

65. "Letter from Hickory Grove," *Yorkville Enquirer*, September 25, 1889.

66. *Alabama Baptist*, November 3, 1881. In late nineteenth-century popular fiction, plural wives were commonly portrayed as being under a special kind of bondage, and were sometimes even described as being white slaves; see Givens, *Viper on the Hearth*, 146–49.

67. Willing, *On American Soil*, 22, 41, 75. See also "Mormonism," *Tennessee Baptist*, October 4, 1884.

68. Rev. G. L. Thompson, "The Mormon Problem," *Christian Advocate*, January 28, 1886. See also "Are Full of Fight," *Richmond Planet*, February 10, 1900.

69. "Polygamy," *Georgia Weekly Telegraph and Georgia Journal & Messenger*, March 13, 1873.

70. Mrs. O. J. Squires, "Salt Lake City and Mormonism," *Christian Advocate*, September 10, 1885; untitled, ibid., December 2, 1886. See also Peggy Pascoe, *Relations of Rescue: The Search for Female Moral Authority in the American West, 1874–1939* (New York: Oxford University Press, 1990).

71. "Mormon Polygamy," *Alabama Christian Advocate*, November 21, 1881.

72. Untitled, *News and Observer*, July 20, 1881.

73. "Among the Mormons," *St. Louis Christian Advocate*, November 8, 1876.

74. William Kirby, *Mormonism Exposed and Refuted, or True and False Religion Contrasted: Forty-Years' Experience and Observation among the Mormons* (Nashville: Gospel Advocate Publishing, 1893), 245 and chap. 18; see also *The Menace of Mormonism*, 3.

75. "Way-Notes from the Occident," *Baptist*, January 4, 1879. See also "Blackmailing the Mormons," *Georgia Weekly Telegraph and Georgia Journal & Messenger*, September 6, 1870.

76. Oswalt, *Pen Pictures of Mormonism*, 90; "Mormonism among the Poor," *Georgia Weekly Telegraph and Georgia Journal & Messenger*, September 6, 1870.

77. Willing, *On American Soil*, 15.

78. Francis MacDonald, "The History and Journal of Francis MacDonald—1851–1887," LDSCA, 33–34.

79. Quoted in SSMMH, December 23, 1881.

80. "The Mormons at Work in West Virginia," *Daily Picayune*, August 21, 1889.

81. Rev. A. J. Frost, "The Scriptural Law of Divorce," *Tennessee Baptist*, September 20, 1884.

82. Rev. A. J. Frost, "The Scriptural Law of Divorce," ibid., October 25, 1884. A number of other Christians similarly interpreted polygamy as one of many (though among the most serious) of challenges to marriage in America, using the controversy surrounding Mormon plural marriage as an opportunity to address "the Divorce question." See Rev. D. W. McKinney, response to Gessler, "The Mormon Question," 21; and untitled, *Christian Advocate*, October 18, 1883.

83. See *A Sermon by the Rev. Dr. Newman*, 3; Joseph E. Brown, *Polygamy in Utah and New England Contrasted: Speech of Hon. Joseph E. Brown of Georgia, Delivered in the Senate of the United States, Tuesday, May 27, 1884* (Washington, DC: n.p., 1884); "Answers to Inquiries," *Christian Advocate*, November 11, 1886.

84. Rev. A. J. Frost, "The Scriptural Law of Divorce," *Tennessee Baptist*, October 4, 1884.

85. "Ingersoll Reviewed," *Alabama Christian Advocate*, December 28, 1881.

86. Untitled, *News and Observer*, July 20, 1881.

87. Horace M. Du Bose, *Life and Memories of Rev. J. D. Barbee* (Nashville: Publishing House of the Methodist Episcopal Church South, 1906), 125; "Memoirs," *Journal of the Ninety-Second Session of the Tennessee Annual Conference of the Methodist Episcopal Church, South* (Nashville: Publishing House of the Methodist Episcopal Church, South, 1905), 55–65.

88. SSMMH, July 21, 1884.

89. Ibid., September 8, 1881. Mormons blamed the passage of the Edmunds Bill in part on the "false priests" of Protestantism. "The Edmunds Bill," *The Contributor* (April 3, 1882): 212-13.

90. SSMMH, September 4, 1880.

91. Typescript of John Morgan Journal, July 31, 1881, in John Hamilton Morgan Papers, U of U; letter from John Morgan to Pres. John Taylor, August 11, 1881, ibid.

92. SSMMH, September 3, 1881.

93. "Steps to Blot Out Mormonism," *Christian Advocate*, January 26, 1882.

94. "Mormonism in Earnest," *Alabama Baptist*, August 28, 1879.

95. "Antipolygamy Meeting in Washington," *Christian Advocate*, February 23, 1882.

96. "Mormonism," *Alabama Christian Advocate*, February 15, 1882.

97. "Mormon Polygamy," ibid., November 21, 1881.

98. *Alabama Baptist*, Aug 15, 1878; "The Problem of Mormonism," ibid., October 3, 1878; "Mormonism Doomed," ibid. February 13, 1879.

99. "Mormonism," ibid., December 28, 1881.

100. "The Mormon Question," *Southwestern Christian Advocate*, February 2, 1882.

101. "Mormonism Neither Dead Nor Dying," *Alabama Christian Advocate*, July 26, 1882.

102. *Alabama Baptist*, March 2, 1882.

CHAPTER 5

1. "Religious News and Notes," *Richmond Christian Advocate*, May 15, 1879. See also "More about the Mormons," *Christian Index*, February 20, 1879; untitled, *Georgia Weekly Telegraph and Georgia Journal & Messenger*, January 21, 1879.

2. "Mormonism Still Flourishing," *Georgia Weekly Telegraph and Georgia Journal & Messenger*, October 22, 1880.

3. Untitled, *Alabama Christian Advocate*, September 27, 1882.

4. David W. Blight, *Race and Reunion: The Civil War in American Memory* (Cambridge, MA: Belknap Press of Harvard University Press, 2001). See also Edward J. Blum, *Reforging the White Republic: Race, Religion, and American Nationalism, 1865-1898* (Baton Rouge: Louisiana State University Press, 2005); Nina Silber, *The Romance of Reunion: Northerners and the South, 1865-1900* (Chapel Hill: University of North Carolina Press, 1993).

5. "Is a Community Safe When Mormon Elders are Allowed to Inhabit It?" *Alabama Baptist*, November 17, 1887.

6. "Mormonism Reviving," *Yorkville Enquirer*, November 10, 1886.

7. "The Mormon Plague," ibid., September 29, 1886.

8. Quoted in SSMMH, December 31, 1885.

9. Quoted in ibid., April 7, 1884.

10. John Morgan, "Discourse by Elder John Morgan," in *Journal of Discourses*, vol. 21 (London: Latter-day Saints' Book Depot, 1881), 180.

11. "Uphold the Constitution," *Southern Star*, vol. 1 (Chattanooga: Southern States Mission, 1899), 293–94.

12. "Gov. Candler's Appeal," ibid., 285. About a week after giving his speech against mob violence, Governor Candler personally met with Southern States Mission president Ben E. Rich. As a result of the interview, "The Mormon leader found in Governor Candler one thoroughly out of sympathy with mob law and every outrage resulting from the banding together of any body of men for the purpose of avenging a real or imaginary wrong." "Mormon Leader Visits Candler," *Atlanta Constitution*, August 8, 1899.

13. "The Danger to Which It Leads," *Atlanta Constitution*, July 29, 1899.

14. *Speeches of Hon. Risden T. Bennett, of North Carolina, in the House of Representatives, Wednesday, January 12, and Thursday, February 17, 1887, against the Edmunds-Tucker Anti-Mormon Bill* (Washington, D.C.: n.p., 1887).

15. "The Mormon Elders," *Atlanta Constitution*, June 15, 1883.

16. *Alabama Baptist*, August 28, 1884. For a similar view among northern Methodists, see "The Uprising against Mormonism," *Christian Advocate*, February 9, 1882.

17. Rev. M. L. Oswalt, *Pen Pictures of Mormonism* (Philadelphia: American Baptist Publication Society, 1899), 95.

18. "The Problem of Mormonism," *Alabama Baptist*, October 3, 1878.

19. "Mormonism Neither Dead Nor Dying," *Alabama Christian Advocate*, July 26, 1882; "Mormon Polygamy," ibid., November 21, 1881. For a parallel view among northern Methodists, see "Missionary Concert Notes for May, 1882," *Christian Advocate*, April 13, 1882; untitled, ibid., October 26, 1882; "The Utah Educational Work," ibid., February 8, 1883; "A Voice from Utah," ibid., October 9, 1884; Rev. G. L. Thompson, "The Mormon Problem," ibid., January 28, 1886.

20. Joseph E. Brown, *The Mormon Question: Speech of Hon. Joseph E. Brown, of Georgia, in the Senate of the United States, Friday, January 11, 1884* ([Washington, D.C.]: n.p., 1884), 23–24.

21. Joseph Brown, *Polygamy in Utah and New England Contrasted: Speech of Hon. Joseph E. Brown of Georgia, Delivered in the Senate of the United States, Tuesday, May 27, 1884* (Washington, D.C.: n.p., 1884), 25. For the text of Beecher's speech, see "Toleration or the Sword?" *Deseret News*, December 12, 1883. See also "The Christian World," *Christian Advocate*, March 13, 1886.

22. "Mormonism in Earnest," *Alabama Baptist*, August 28, 1879.

23. "Is a Community Safe When Mormon Elders Are Allowed to Inhabit It?" *Alabama Baptist*, November 17, 1887; see also "From Mountain Creek," *Alabama Baptist*, July 3, 1879.

24. *25th Anniversary of the Tennessee Baptist Convention Held with Union City Baptist Church, October 11, 12 and 13, 1899* (Paris, TN: Wear's Printing Works, [1899?]), 27.

25. "Leaflet on Mormonism," *Baptist and Reflector*, October 10, 1899.

26. "Mormonism," *Alabama Christian Advocate*, December 28, 1881.

27. "The Oneida Community," *Christian Index*, September 11, 1879.

28. Untitled, *News and Observer*, July 20, 1881.

29. SSMMH, September 3, 1881. The contemporary Georgia statutes against "polygamy or bigamy" are in John C. Reed, *A Handbook of Georgia Criminal Law and Procedure* (Macon: J. W. Burke, 1873), 52–53. The prescribed punishment for polygamy in Georgia was two to four years' imprisonment and labor for previously married persons and one to three years' imprisonment and labor for previously single persons.

30. Untitled, *News and Observer*, March 9, 1886. See chap. 58 sec. 2505 in *The Revised Code of the Statute Laws of the State of Mississippi* (Jackson: Alcorn & Fisher, 1871), 554.

31. SSMMH, August 5, 1888.

32. "Mormon Polygamy," *Alabama Christian Advocate*, November 21, 1881.

33. "Mormonism," ibid., February 15, 1882. See also "General Denominational News," *Christian Index*, December 19, 1878.

34. "The Mormons," *Hinds County Gazette*, September 26, 1877.

35. Sarah Barringer Gordon, *The Mormon Question: Polygamy and Constitutional Conflict in Nineteenth-Century America* (Chapel Hill: University of North Carolina Press, 2002), 57–58.

36. Ibid., 82.

37. "Voice from the Southern States," *Deseret News*, April 19, 1882.

38. At the end of the nineteenth century, Southern States Mission president Ben E. Rich said that he preferred "reconstruction" to the mob: "We met our government in the courts of our land, our cause was also lost, and now let the days of reconstruction take place with us; let our cause be handled by statesmen, instead of being settled by mob violence." "President Rich in Georgia," *Southern Star* (1899), 293.

39. See David Buice, "A Stench in the Nostrils of Honest Men: Southern Democrats and the Edmunds Act of 1882," *Dialogue: A Journal of Mormon Thought* 21 (Autumn 1988): 100–103; Gaines M. Foster, *Moral Reconstruction: Christian Lobbyists and the Federal Legislation of Morality, 1865–1920* (Chapel Hill: University of North Carolina Press, 2002), 60–62.

40. Untitled, *Christian Index*, August 3, 1882.

41. Brown, *Polygamy in Utah and New England Contrasted*, 5.

42. Brown, *The Mormon Question*, 2, 17.

43. Brown, *Polygamy in Utah and New England Contrasted*, 17–23.

44. Ibid., 30–31. In the 1887 debate leading up to the Edmunds-Tucker Act, North Carolina Democrat Risden Bennett similarly compared federal anti-Mormon policies with Radical Reconstruction. See *Speeches of Hon. Risden T. Bennett*, 12.

45. John Randolph Tucker, *Polygamy: Speech of Hon. John Randolph Tucker, of Virginia, in the House of Representatives, Tuesday, March 14, 1882* (Washington, D.C.: n.p., 1882), 3, 6–7.

46. Prominent southern opponents of the 1882 Edmunds Bill in the Senate included Joseph Brown (Georgia), Wilkinson Call (Florida), George G. Vest (Missouri), and John T. Morgan (Alabama). See Buice, "A Stench in the Nostrils," 105–7; M. Paul Holsinger, "Senator George Graham Vest and the 'Menace' of Mormonism, 1882–1887," *Missouri Historical Review* 65 (Oct. 1970): 23–36.

47. Foster, *Moral Reconstruction*, 60–62.

48. "Passage of the Bill," *Deseret News*, January 26, 1887. The biblical reference is Matthew 19:5, or Mark 10:8. For a Mormon critique of the change in Tucker's stance from 1882 to 1887 (and his arguments more generally), see R. W. Sloan, *The Great*

Contest: The Chief Advocates of Anti-Mormon Measures Reviewed . . . (Salt Lake City: n.p., 1887).

49. See Foster, *Moral Reconstruction*, 63–64. Many of the southern Democrats who voted against the Edmunds Act—such as Missouri's George Vest, Florida's Wilkinson Call, and Alabama's John T. Morgan—continued their opposition to the Edmunds-Tucker Act. See Holsinger, "Senator George Graham Vest."

50. See Kathleen Flake, *The Politics of Religious Identity: The Seating of Senator Reed Smoot, Mormon Apostle* (Chapel Hill: University of North Carolina Press, 2004); and Michael Harold Paulos, *The Mormon Church on Trial: Transcript of the Reed Smoot Hearings* (Salt Lake City: Signature Books, 2008). See also D. Michael Quinn, "LDS Church Authority and New Plural Marriages, 1890-1904," *Dialogue: A Journal of Mormon Thought* 18 (Spring 1985): 9-104; B. Carmon Hardy, *Solemn Covenant: The Mormon Polygamous Passage* (Urbana: University of Illinois Press, 1992); and Richard S. Van Wagoner, *Mormon Polygamy: A History* (Salt Lake City: Signature Books, 1992), esp. chap. 15. Anti-Mormons were quick to seize on the disparity between the announced suspension of plural marriage and the practice continued in secret. For southern responses, see Rev. Wildman Murphy, *What the Mormons Teach* (New York: Eaton and Mains, 1894), 12; Fowler, *Missionary Work in the Mormon Empire*, 4; and *The Menace of Mormonism* (Nashville: Home Department Woman's Missionary Council, M. E. Church, South, 1914), 4-5.

51. Willing, *On American Soil*, 5-6, 82; *The Menace of Mormonism*, 8; Resolution on Mormonism by the General Conference of the Methodist Episcopal Church, 1912, at Drew.

52. For other treatments of this general Progressive orientation in the South, see Ted Ownby, *Subduing Satan: Religion, Recreation, and Manhood in the Rural South, 1865–1920* (Chapel Hill: University of North Carolina Press, 1990), chaps. 9-10; William A. Link, *The Paradox of Southern Progressivism, 1880-1930* (Chapel Hill: University of North Carolina Press, 1992); and Beth Barton Schweiger, *The Gospel Working Up: Progress and the Pulpit in Nineteenth-Century Virginia* (New York: Oxford University Press, 2000).

53. Richard J. Carwardine, *Evangelicals and Politics in Antebellum America* (New Haven, CT: Yale University Press, 1993), 321-22; Kurt O. Berends, "Confederate Sacrifice and the 'Redemption' of the South," in Beth Barton Schweiger and Donald G. Mathews, eds., *Religion in the American South: Protestants and Others in History and Culture* (Chapel Hill: University of North Carolina Press, 2004), 99-124; Randall M. Miller, Harry S. Stout, and Charles Reagan Wilson, eds., *Religion and the American Civil War* (New York: Oxford University Press, 1998); Charles Reagan Wilson, *Baptized in Blood: The Religion of the Lost Cause, 1865-1920* (Athens: University of Georgia Press, 1980); Rufus B. Spain, *At Ease in Zion: A Social History of Southern Baptists, 1865-1900* (Nashville: Vanderbilt University Press, 1967), chap. 1; Daniel W. Stowell, *Rebuilding Zion: The Religious Reconstruction of the South, 1863-1877* (New York: Oxford University Press, 1998), chap. 9; Foster, *Moral Reconstruction*; Joe Creech, *Righteous Indignation: Religion and the Populist Revolution* (Urbana: University of Illinois Press, 2006), 34-36 and passim.

54. "Political Preaching," *Christian Index*, December 5, 1878.

55. "About Voting," ibid., April 10, 1879, emphasis in original.

56. "Wise Tactics," *Richmond Christian Advocate*, July 31, 1879.

57. Untitled, *News and Observer*, July 20, 1881.

58. Brown, *Polygamy in Utah and New England Contrasted*, 4–5, 31. Brown's fears about the restrictions of political liberties based solely on religious belief materialized in Idaho, where an 1885 territorial statute disenfranchising all Mormons (even monogamous ones) was upheld by the United States Supreme Court in the 1890 case *Davis v. Beason*. See Edwin Brown Firmage and Richard Collin Mangrum, *Zion in the Courts: A Legal History of the Church of Jesus Christ of Latter-day Saints, 1830-1900* (Urbana: University of Illinois Press, 1988), 233-35.

59. See untitled, *Southwestern Christian Advocate*, July 3, 1884.

60. SSMMH, August 29, 1879.

61. Quoted in "Sentiments of the Press," *Southern Star*, vol. 1 (1899), 285.

62. Untitled, *News and Observer*, July 20, 1881.

63. "Through Utah," *St. Louis Christian Advocate*, September 17, 1879.

64. "Mormonism Reviving," *Yorkville Enquirer*, November 10, 1886.

65. "Mormonism Doomed," *Alabama Baptist*, February 13, 1879.

66. Quoted in SSMMH, August 28, 1884.

67. "An Act to define and punish the crime of teaching polygamous doctrines and principles, and of persuading persons to embrace the same," Chap. 151 of *Acts of the State of Tennessee, Forty-Fourth General Assembly*, 262-63.

68. "Murder of a Mormon," *Christian Index*, July 31, 1879.

69. "Falsest of Prophets," *Alabama Baptist*, June 10, 1886; "Mormonism," ibid., June 19, 1879.

70. "The Evil of Mormonism," ibid., April 22, 1886.

71. Ibid., March 2, 1882.

72. "The Course to Pursue," *Atlanta Constitution*, February 16, 1900. The *Constitution* also resorted to sectional rivalries in characterizing the illegitimacy of Mormonism, one of its writers calling the religion "another child born of New England fanaticism, where all the devilish things originate." Bill Arp, "Arp on the Mormons," ibid., August 13, 1899.

73. "Mormonism among the Poor," *Georgia Weekly Telegraph and Georgia Journal & Messenger*, September 6, 1870; "Missionary Concert Notes for May, 1882," *Christian Advocate*, April 13, 1882.

74. "Mormonism Reviving," *Yorkville Enquirer*, November 10, 1886.

75. "Will Have to Pay Tax," *Atlanta Constitution*, August 17, 1899.

76. "The Mormon Plague," *Yorkville Enquirer*, September 29, 1886.

77. Gordon, *The Mormon Question*, 144. For southern endorsements of presidential antipolygamy policies, see "Mormon Problem," *Hinds County Gazette*, March, 30, 1881; "Mormonism," *Alabama Christian Advocate*, December 28, 1881; "The Mormon Question," *Southwestern Christian Advocate*, February 2, 1882; "Mormonism Neither Dead Nor Dying," *Alabama Christian Advocate*, July 26, 1882; and "The Mormons Blasted," *New Mississippian*, March 24, 1885.

78. The classic expression of this is C. Vann Woodward, *Origins of the New South, 1877-1913* (Baton Rouge: Louisiana State University Press, 1971).

CHAPTER 6

1. Edgar E. Folk, *The Mormon Monster—or, The Story of Mormonism* (Chicago: Fleming H. Revell, 1900), 11.

2. See Albert W. Wardin Jr., *Tennessee Baptists: A Comprehensive History, 1779-1999* (Brentwood, TN: Executive Board of the Tennessee Baptist Convention, 1999), 245-47.

3. See *24th Anniversary of the Tennessee Baptist Convention Held with Athens Baptist Church, October 13-15, 1898* (Paris, TN: Wear's Printing Works, n.d. [1898?]), 18.

4. George A. Lofton, Introduction to Folk, *The Mormon Monster*, 6-8.

5. Folk, *The Mormon Monster*, 106-7, 272-73, 276. See Jan Shipps, *Mormonism: The Story of a New Religious Tradition* (Urbana: University of Illinois Press, 1985); Rodney Stark, *The Rise of Mormonism*, ed. Reid L. Neilson (New York: Columbia University Press, 2005).

6. Folk, *The Mormon Monster*, 273, 279-84.

7. Rev. M. L. Oswalt, *Pen Pictures of Mormonism* (Philadelphia: American Baptist Publication Society, 1899), 15.

8. Untitled, *Georgia Weekly Telegraph and Georgia Journal & Messenger*, January 21, 1879. For a sympathetic portrayal of Cannon, see Davis Bitton, *George Q. Cannon: A Biography* (Salt Lake City, UT: Deseret Book, 1999).

9. John Morgan, "Discourse by Elder John Morgan," in *Journal of Discourses*, 26 vols. (London: Latter-day Saints' Book Depot, 1854-86), 21:185.

10. Ben E. Rich, "Two Letters to a Baptist Minister," in *Tracts from Southern States Mission* (ca. 1900), Western Americana Collection, Princeton, 12.

11. Joseph E. Brown, *Polygamy in Utah and New England Contrasted: Speech of Hon. Joseph E. Brown of Georgia, Delivered in the Senate of the United States, Tuesday, May 27, 1884* (Washington, D.C.: n.p., 1884), 26; "What the Mormons are Doing," *Georgia Weekly Telegraph and Georgia Journal & Messenger*, June 25, 1878.

12. Untitled, *Christian Advocate*, June 17, 1886.

13. "Mormonism," *Alabama Christian Advocate*, February 15, 1882.

14. Rev. G. L. Thompson, "The Mormon Problem," *Christian Advocate*, January 28, 1886.

15. Rev. Richard Hartley, response to Rev. T. A. K. Gessler, in *Proceedings of the Fourth Baptist Congress, Held in the City of New-York, Nov. 1885* (New York: Century, 1886), 20; "Mormonism versus the Nation," *Christian Advocate*, December 27, 1883.

16. Joseph Smith Jr., "The Globe," *Times and Seasons* 5:510 (April 15, 1844). This article, a response to an eastern newspaper editor, was in fact ghostwritten by Smith's close associate William W. Phelps. This practice was common for Smith's published statements. See Samual Brown, "The Translator and Ghostwriter: Joseph Smith and W. W. Phelps," *Journal of Mormon History* 34:1 (Winter 2008): 50.

17. Brigham Young, "Human and Divine Government," in *Journal of Discourses*, 6:342.

18. John Taylor, "Union - Human and Divine Government, etc.," *Journal of Discourses*, 9:9-10. Note that these remarks came in the context of the beginning of the American Civil War; Brigham Young was still president of the LDS Church, and Taylor was a member of the Quorum of Twelve Apostles at the time. Southern newspapers noted Taylor's feisty defense of Mormon institutions, particularly polygamy: "He is a pronounced polygamist, and will do everything to defend and preserve this barbarous relic of the olden time." "Mormonism Still Flourishing," *Georgia Weekly Telegraph, Journal & Messenger*, October 22, 1880.

19. Wilford Woodruff, Joseph F. Smith, and Moses Thatcher, "Epistle of the General Superintendency; To the Officers and Members of the Young Men's Mutual

Improvement Associations throughout Zion," *Contributor* (June 9, 1888): 305; "Conclusion of President Young's Trip to Sanpete," *Deseret News*, July 26, 1865.

20. Untitled, *Alabama Baptist*, April 22, 1886; Gessler, *Proceedings of the Fourth Baptist Congress*, 18; Jennie Fowler Willing, *On American Soil, or Mormonism the Mohammedanism of the West* (Louisville: Pickett Publishing, 1906), 83; "The Mormons," *Hinds County Gazette*, September 26, 1877.

21. Oswalt, *Pen Pictures of Mormonism*, 81.

22. Willing, *On American Soil*, 84.

23. Folk, *The Mormon Monster*, 279–81.

24. Rev. L. M. Hagood, "Mormonism," *Southwestern Christian Advocate*, June 8, 1882.

25. Charles Ellis, "Mormons and Mormonism," in *Tracts from Southern States Mission*, 14. See also R. W. Sloan, *The Great Contest: The Chief Advocates of Anti-Mormon Measures Reviewed . . .* (Salt Lake City: n.p., 1887), 4–5.

26. Untitled, *Alabama Christian Advocate*, April 5, 1882; see also "Among the Mormons," *St. Louis Christian Advocate*, November 8, 1876.

27. Elder Bur Geoise, "In West Virginia," *Deseret News* April 10, 1889.

28. The most recent treatment is Ronald W. Walker, Richard E. Turley, and Glen M. Leonard, *Massacre at Mountain Meadows: An American Tragedy* (New York: Oxford University Press, 2008). See also Juanita M. Brooks, *The Mountain Meadows Massacre* (Norman: University of Oklahoma Press, 1970); and Will Bagley, *Blood of the Prophets: Brigham Young and the Mountain Meadows Massacre* (Norman: University of Oklahoma Press, 2002).

29. Rev. M. W. Montgomery, "Some Doctrines of Mormonism," *Biblical Recorder*, July 11, 1888. See also Rev. J. C. Thomas, *The Mistakes of Mormon and of Mormons: A Lecture* (Nashville: Publishing House of the Methodist Episcopal Church, South, 1899), 26–28.

30. Letter from John H. Gibbs to Joseph Morrell, January 10, 1884, in Joseph Morrell Correspondence, 1883–1906, LDSCA; original capitalization preserved.

31. Note [no author, date, or place], John Morgan Correspondence, 1863–1881, LDSCA; original spelling and capitalization preserved.

32. SSMMH, August 5, 1899.

33. "Mormon Success in the South," *New York Times*, January 22, 1885.

34. "Way-Notes from the Occident," *Baptist*, January 4, 1879.

35. Untitled, *Christian Index*, July 21, 1887; see also "The Last Trick of the Mormon Leaders," *Christian Advocate*, September 22, 1887.

36. "The Wane of Mormonism," *Atlanta Daily Sun*, June 14, 1871. The Sandwich Island rumors reappeared several years later; see untitled, *Christian Advocate*, February 11, 1886.

37. "A New Mormon Scheme," *Georgia Weekly Telegraph and Georgia Journal & Messenger*, April 18, 1876.

38. "The Mormons," ibid., December 23, 1879; untitled, *Christian Advocate*, August 27, 1885.

39. See Thomas Cottam Romney, *The Mormon Colonies in Mexico* (Salt Lake City: University of Utah Press, 2005).

40. See "The Wane of Mormonism," *Atlanta Daily Sun*, June 14, 1871; "The Mormon Women," *Georgia Weekly Telegraph and Georgia Journal & Messenger*, October 3, 1876.

41. "Mormonism," *Alabama Christian Advocate*, December 28, 1881; untitled, *Christian Index*, July 27, 1882. See also "Mormonism Neither Dead Nor Dying," *Alabama Christian Advocate*, July 26, 1882.

42. "Growing Faster Than Ever," *Atlanta Constitution*, March 27, 1901. A contemporaneous Mormon tract suggested that evangelical Protestants were less concerned with polygamy than they were with "the steady growth of the Mormon church." Ellis, "Mormons and Mormonism," 23.

43. Oswalt, *Pen Pictures of Mormonism*, 11–12.

44. Willing, *On American Soil*, 5; see also *The Menace of Mormonism* (Nashville: Home Department Woman's Missionary Council, M.E. Church, South, 1914), 6–7.

45. "The Growth of Mormonism," *Southwestern Christian Advocate*, January 12, 1882; "The Mormon Question," ibid., February 2, 1882; Rev. L. M. Hagood, "Mormonism," ibid., June 8, 1882. Concerning the size of the Mormon empire, just after the turn of the twentieth century Charles Fowler calculated that the area in the United States "brought under Mormon dictation" was "more than ten times as large as all the New England States, nearly twice as large as the thirteen original States, lacking but a trifle of being as large as all the Confederate States, including Texas. . . . [This area] may yet support more than five hundred million [people.]" Charles Fowler, *Missionary Work in the Mormon Empire* (New York: The Rindge Missionary Literature Department, n.d. [1903?]), 6–7.

46. Oswalt, *Pen Pictures of Mormonism*, 17.

47. "Coppy of a Notice found at the Gate of Bro D.R.," James Thompson Lisonbee Correspondence, February 13, 1877, LDSCA; original spelling and capitalization preserved.

48. [Joseph Smith, Jr.,] *History of the Church of Jesus Christ of Latter-day Saints - Period I. History of Joseph Smith, the Prophet, by Himself*, 2nd ed., rev. (Salt Lake City, UT: Deseret Book, 1980), 1. The first five chapters of Joseph Smith's history have been canonized by the LDS Church and appear as "Joseph Smith-History" in *The Pearl of Great Price: A Selection from the Revelations, Translations, and Narrations of Joseph Smith, First Prophet, Seer, and Revelator to the Church of Jesus Christ of Latter-day Saints* (Salt Lake City, UT: Church of Jesus Christ of Latter-day Saints, 1989).

49. Jedediah M. Grant, "Uniformity," *Journal of Discourses*, 1:348.

50. Terryl L. Givens, *The Latter-day Saint Experience in America* (Westport, CT: Greenwood Press, 2004), 59–60, emphasis in original; Givens, *Viper on the Hearth: Mormons, Myths, and the Construction of Heresy* (New York: Oxford University Press, 1997), 8.

51. SSMMH, December 23, 1881.

52. Ibid., June 23, 1884.

53. Ibid., November 24, 1886.

54. Ibid., August 19, 1884; September 11, 1886; March 4, 1885; October 9, 1889.

55. John Morgan, "Discourse by Elder John Morgan," *Journal of Discourses*, 21:179; John Morgan, "Discourse by Elder John Morgan," ibid., 23:40–41.

56. Oswalt, *Pen Pictures of Mormonism*, 5–8; George W. Lasher, *The Ministerial Directory of the Baptist Churches* (Oxford, OH: Ministerial Directory, 1899), 545. A parallel story is found in William Kirby's life. He encountered Mormon missionaries in England as a young married man around 1853, and was soon baptized. He sailed to America and crossed the plains to Utah, but eventually became disenchanted and

left Utah and the church, spending the rest of his life writing on religious subjects (he was editor of the *Bible Investigator* in Doniphan, Kansas) and ultimately publishing the lengthy anti-Mormon book *Mormonism Exposed and Refuted, or True and False Religion Contrasted: Forty Years' Experience and Observation among the Mormons* (Nashville: Gospel Advocate Publishing, 1893).

57. Oswalt, *Pen Pictures of Mormonism*, 23, 25, 28, 74, 77.

58. Rev. Wildman Murphy, *What the Mormons Teach* (New York: Eaton & Mains, [ca. 1900–04]); and Thomas, *The Mistakes of Mormons and of Mormons*.

59. "The Mormons," *Georgia Weekly Telegraph and Georgia Journal & Messenger*, May 31, 1870.

60. *The Menace of Mormonism*, 2–5; see also Fowler, *Missionary Work in the Mormon Empire*, 4.

61. "Among the Mormons," *St. Louis Christian Advocate*, November 8,1876.

62. Folk, *The Mormon Monster*, 272–73.

63. Ibid., 273; Marvin S. Hill, *Quest for Refuge: The Mormon Flight from American Pluralism* (Salt Lake City, UT: Signature Books, 1989).

64. "Answers to Inquiries," *Christian Advocate*, September 15, 1887; "The Founder of Mormonism the Prince of Deceivers," ibid., August 26, 1886; "A Mormon in Atlanta," *Christian Index*, November 20, 1879. The devil is referred to as a deceiver in Revelation 12:9.

65. On American perceptions of Islam, see Thomas S. Kidd, *American Christians and Islam: Evangelical Culture and Muslims from the Colonial Period to the Age of Terrorism* (Princeton, NJ: Princeton University Press, 2008); and Timothy Marr, *The Cultural Roots of American Islamicism* (New York: Cambridge University Press, 2006). On the Mormonism-Islam comparison, see J. Spencer Fluhman, "An 'American Mohamet': Joseph Smith, Muhammad, and the Problem of Prophets in Antebellum America," *Journal of Mormon History* 34 (Summer 2008): 23–45; Marr, *Cultural Roots of American Islamicism*, chap. 4; Givens, *Viper on the Hearth*, 130–37; Arnold Green, "Joseph Smith, an American Muhammad? An Essay on the Perils of Historical Analogy," *Dialogue: A Journal of Mormon Thought* 6 (Spring 1971): 46–58.

66. Untitled, *Christian Advocate* May 24, 1883.

67. Untitled, *Southwestern Christian Advocate*, May 10, 1877.

68. Fowler, *Missionary Work in the Mormon Empire*, 4.

69. Willing, *On American Soil*, 4. See also Kirby, *Mormonism Exposed and Refuted*, 223.

70. "The Mormons Amongst Us," *News and Observer*, January. 1881; "Among the Mormons," ibid., March 12, 1882.

71. "A Plague Spot in Georgia," *News & Courier*, July 28, 1887. See also SSMMH, July 26, 1887.

72. *Tennessee Baptist Convention, Fifteenth Annual Session, Held with the Baptist Church at Humboldt, Tennessee, October 17, 18, 19, 1889* (Nashville: Board of Missions and Sunday Schools, [1889]), 22; *Tennessee Baptist Convention 20th Session, Held in Edgefield Baptist Church, Nashville, October 17–20, 1894* (Memphis: Press of Wills & Crumpton, [1894]), 15; *Tennessee Baptist Convention. 21st Anniversary. Held with Mossy Creek Baptist Church, Mossy Creek, October 16–18, 1895* (Nashville: Marshall & Bruce, [1895]), 11, 17, 20; *Tennessee Baptist Convention. 22d Anniversary, Held with Paris Baptist Church, October 14–16, 1896* (Memphis: Wills & Crumpton, [1896]), 9–10; *24th*

Anniversary of the Tennessee Baptist Convention Held with Athens Baptist Church, October 13-15, 1898 (Paris, TN: Wear's Printing Works, [1898]), 18; *25th Anniversary of the Tennessee Baptist Convention Held with Union City Baptist Church, October 11, 12 and 13, 1899* (Paris, TN: Wear's Printing Works, [1899]), 27; Folk, *The Mormon Monster*, 12. For LDS reports on the number of baptisms in the South, see Southern States Mission Manuscript History. For a history of the Tennessee Baptist Convention, see Wardin, *Tennessee Baptists*. Episcopalian bishop Warren A. Candler similarly complained in 1899 that there were more Mormon elders at work in Georgia than either Presbyterian pastors or Episcopal rectors. "Bishop Candler's Statement," *Atlanta Constitution*, August 17, 1899. The editors of the *Atlanta Constitution* called for greater efforts by the Protestant churches in preaching in rural areas, so as to counter the progress made among "the ignorant and poor" by Mormons. "The Course to Pursue," ibid., February 16, 1900.

73. Thomas, *The Mistakes of Mormon and of Mormons*, 5.

74. "Letter from Hickory Grove," *Yorkville Enquirer*, September 25, 1889. See also "The Mormon Plague," ibid., September 29, 1886; "Mormon Success in the South," *New York Times*, January 22, 1885; "Mormons in Tennessee," ibid., January 12, 1887.

75. "Mormonism," *Alabama Baptist*, June 19, 1879. See also "From Mountain Creek," ibid., July 3, 1879; "Mormonism in Earnest," ibid., August 28, 1879; and "Is a Community Safe When Mormon Elders Are Allowed to Inhabit It?" *Alabama Baptist*, November 17, 1887. The irony of a Baptist publication critiquing the Mormon focus on rural areas is that most Southern Baptist churches were themselves rural. In 1916, 20,000 of 24,500 Southern Baptist Convention churches were rural. Wayne Flynt, "Churches, Country," in Samuel S. Hill, *Religion*, vol. 1 in *The New Encyclopedia of Southern Culture*, ed. Charles Reagan Wilson (Chapel Hill: University of North Carolina Press, 2006), 52.

76. "Mormons in the South," *Public Opinion* 28 (Jan.-June 1900): 113.

77. "Mormonism in North Georgia," *Georgia Weekly Telegraph, Journal & Messenger*, August 5, 1881.

78. "Mormonism in the South," *New York Times*, February 1, 1889.

79. Letter from John Gibbs to Louisa Gibbs, July 11, 1883, in John Henry Gibbs Collection, BYU.

80. Diary of John C. Harper, 1887-1888, typescript, Princeton, 5.

81. Circular letter, "To the Presidents of Conferences and Traveling Elders in the Southern States Mission," from John Morgan and B. H. Roberts, Chattanooga, TN, no date (ca. early 1884), in Gibbs Collection.

82. "Morgan, the Mormon," *Georgia Weekly Telegraph, Journal & Messenger*, November 18, 1881.

83. "Discourse by Elder John Morgan" (1883), 43; "Correspondence," *Deseret News*, December 10, 1879.

84. Lofton, Introduction, 5-6.

85. "Falsest of Prophets," *Alabama Baptist*, June 10, 1886.

86. "The Wane of Mormonism," *Atlanta Daily Sun*, June 14, 1871.

87. Untitled, *Richmond Christian Advocate*, August 28, 1884.

88. Brown, *Polygamy in Utah and New England Contrasted*, 9.

89. Lofton, Introduction, 7.

90. "The South and the Mormons," *Atlanta Constitution*, August 9, 1899.

91. William R. Hutchison, *Religious Pluralism in America: The Contentious History of a Founding Ideal* (New Haven, CT: Yale University Press, 2003), 57-58.

CHAPTER 7

1. See Stewart E. Tolnay and E. M. Beck, *A Festival of Violence: An Analysis of Southern Lynchings, 1882-1930* (Urbana: University of Illinois Press, 1995), 100-101. Tolnay and Beck use the categories of "Deep South" and "Border South," including Florida in the latter. Because of problematic sources, they do not include Texas, Virginia, or Arkansas in their analysis. Another key study comparing Upper and Lower South lynching is W. Fitzhugh Brundage, *Lynching in the New South: Georgia and Virginia, 1880-1930* (Urbana: University of Illinois Press, 1993). According to Brundage's count, from 1880 to 1930 Georgia had 460 victims of lynch mobs (441 black and 19 white), whereas Virginia had 86 (70 black and 16 white). Scholars generally agree that the most profitable analysis of southern violence occurs on the substate rather than state level; thus, Tolnay and Beck analyze violence on the county level, whereas Brundage divides his two states into subregions.

2. See SSMMH, March 1898. A similar pattern followed in Kentucky, where elders were "obliged to leave . . . on account of hostile sentiment" in 1883 or 1884. Ibid., April 18, 1884. No documented instances of violence occurred during their absence, but the hostility resumed following their return a few years later. See ibid., August 11, 1887; February 10, 1888; November 23, 1889; December 1890.

3. John Morgan, "Discourse by Elder John Morgan," in *Journal of Discourses by President John Taylor, His Counsellors, the Twelve Apostles, and Others*, vol. 23 (London: Latter-day Saints' Book Depot, 1883), 40.

4. "Mobocracy in the South," *Deseret News*, September 17, 1879.

5. Eliza R. Snow Smith, *Biography and Family Record of Lorenzo Snow* (Salt Lake City, UT: Deseret News, 1884), 423-24.

6. "Mobbing in Georgia," *Southern Star*, vol. 1 (Chattanooga, TN: Southern States Mission, 1899), 284.

7. Jan Shipps, "From Satyr to Saint: American Perceptions of the Mormons, 1860-1960," in *Sojourner in the Promised Land: Forty Years among the Mormons* (Urbana: University of Illinois Press, 2000), 51-97, quote from 64.

8. Jan Shipps argues that polygamy was used as a "bludgeon to destroy the temporal power of the church." Ibid., 65-66. Klaus Hansen similarly posits that the antipolygamy legislation was the most convenient way to strike at the Mormon ecclesiastical-political hierarchy, whereas Edward Lyman asserts that the Mormon practice of plural marriage was in fact the primary reason for Utah's repeated denial for statehood. See Klaus J. Hansen, *Quest for Empire: The Political Kingdom of God and the Council of Fifty in Mormon History* (Lincoln: University of Nebraska Press, 1974); Edward Leo Lyman, *Political Deliverance: The Mormon Quest for Utah Statehood* (Urbana: University of Illinois Press, 1986). For an analysis of nineteenth-century anti-Mormon literature focusing primarily on polygamy, see Terryl L. Givens, *The Viper on the Hearth: Mormons, Myths, and the Construction of Heresy* (New York: Oxford University Press, 1997), esp. chaps. 6-7; and Sarah Barringer Gordon, *The Mormon Question: Polygamy and Constitutional Conflict in Nineteenth-Century America* (Chapel Hill: University of North Carolina Press, 2002), chap. 1. Recent scholarship suggests

that polygamy and theocracy were seen by Americans as two sides of the same coin, and it was the LDS hierarchy's unrepublican form of monopolistic control over all areas of Mormon life that Congress and the courts sought to overthrow. Gordon, *The Mormon Question*, is the best and most thorough example of this new scholarship; see also Gaines M. Foster, *Moral Reconstruction: Christian Lobbyists and the Federal Legislation of Morality, 1865-1920* (Chapel Hill: University of North Carolina Press, 2002), 54-68.

9. See Tolnay and Beck, *A Festival of Violence*, 33.

10. Letter from Donald Urie to John Urie, August 22, 1899, in John Urie Correspondence, 1891-1899, LDSCA, original spelling preserved.

11. Typescript of interview with unidentified newspaper reporter, August 20, 1884, in John Hamilton Morgan Papers, U of U.

12. Ted Ownby, *Subduing Satan: Religion, Recreation, and Manhood in the Rural South, 1865-1920* (Chapel Hill: University of North Carolina Press, 1990), chap. 8; quote from 145.

13. "More about the Murders in Tennessee," *Deseret News*, August 20, 1884.

14. See SSMMH, August 2, 1888.

15. See ibid., June 5, 1899.

16. LDS church sources claimed that Thomas Clark, the Campbellite preacher, was angry when Dempsey closed a local schoolhouse by order of the school board. "Mormon Murdered in Cold Blood," *Southern Star*, vol. 2 (Chattanooga, TN: Southern States Mission, 1900), 354. A *New York Times* article said that Dempsey and Clark had been "enemies for months," originating in a snub of the preacher's daughter for a public school teaching position. According to this report, the two men came to blows, and Dempsey threw a hatchet at the minister (not mentioned in the LDS sources), who responded by shooting Dempsey twice with a shotgun. "Clergyman Kills a Man," *New York Times*, August 18, 1900.

17. SSMMH, November 18, 1884.

18. Ibid., 28 February. and March 4, 1882.

19. Ibid., June 1, 1883.

20. See ibid., February 10, 1882; November 16, 1882; February 10, 1887; March 15, 1888. Sometimes the attackers simply demonstrated ineptitude in wielding their weapons. For instance, one member of a Tennessee mob accidentally shot a fellow mob member in the leg, "quite seriously wounding him." Ibid., February 14, 1885.

21. Ibid., December 23, 1887.

22. Ibid., May 25, 1885.

23. See ibid., July 31, 1879; May 27, 1893; July 24, 1884; August 17, 1884; July 14, 1893; March 8, 1896; March 23 or 25, 1898; "Elders Mobbed and Whipped," *Deseret News*, August 5, 1893.

24. SSMMH, February 10, 1888. For similar episodes, see ibid., March 30, 1888, August 27, 1899; "Mormon Elder Assaulted," *Atlanta Constitution*, September 3, 1899.

25. SSMMH, December 5, 1896.

26. Ibid., April 11, 1889; see also ibid., December 8, 1896.

27. Ibid., October 1, 1880.

28. Ibid., June 28, 1886.

29. Ibid., May 16, 1884.

30. Ibid., April 12, 1880.

31. See ibid., July 9, 1884; October 22, 1885; February 21, 1888; January 20, 1893; December 13, 1896; March 1898; August 5, 1899; and September 28, 1899; "Egged the Mormon Elders," *Atlanta Constitution*, August 7, 1899.

32. Both notices in John Morgan Correspondence, 1863–1881, LDSCA.

33. See SSMMH, December 12, 1881; September 5, 1883; November 18, 1884; November 24, 1886; and January 13, 1887.

34. J. Warren Johnson, "Persecution a Saint's Heritage," *Southern Star*, vol. 1 (1899), 109; see also George H. Emery, "A Sample Mob," ibid., 205.

35. On arsons, see "An Interesting Experience," *Deseret Evening News*, May 21, 1884; SSMMH, May 4, 1882; June 25, 1884; December 23, 1884; August 11, 1895; July 4, 1897; and December 1, 1898. On dynamite, see "Mormon Church Was Destroyed," *Atlanta Constitution*, November 4, 1908; "Owner of Wrecked Church Now Fears More Dynamite," *Atlanta Constitution*, November 10, 1908.

36. SSMMH, July 20, 1899; "Kentucky Mob Cuts Down Mormon Church," *Atlanta Constitution*, August 5, 1899.

37. See SSMMH, June 26, 1884; October 17, 1887; and December 1893.

38. Ibid., May 27, 1883.

39. Ibid., August 29, 1879; see also July 20, 1879.

40. Ibid., April 19, May 21, August 9, and September 10, 1884.

41. See Brundage, *Lynching in the New South*, 80.

42. Gordon, *The Mormon Question*, 149 and all of chap. 5.

43. See Elizabeth Buckner Rester, "A History of Bethlehem Baptist Church" (July 1994), online at www.rootsweb.com/~mschocta/BethlehemChurch.html (accessed October 7, 2009); and interview of Lena Lillian Quinn Later by Matthew Mason, May 1, 2004, Sandy, UT. The Dotsons, Quinns, and Bagwells are all part of my personal ancestry. In another example, "five members of one church were expelled from the body for having embraced the doctrines of Brigham Young." "Shameless Effrontery of the Mormons," *Atlanta Constitution*, May 14, 1888.

44. Z. N. Decker, "Public Officers Not Friends of Mormons," *Southern Star*, vol. 2 (1900), 152.

45. SSMMH, April 20, 1888. For other examples of vigilantism against Mormon sympathizers, see ibid., October 17, 1887; and "Forcing the Mormons Out," *New York Times*, October 3, 1884.

46. SSMMH, June 23, 1884.

47. "Bullets Fired at Mormons," *Atlanta Constitution*, June 17, 1902.

48. SSMMH, March 8, 1886.

49. On black self-defense, see Nicholas Lemann, *Redemption: The Last Battle of the Civil War* (New York: Farrar, Straus and Giroux, 2006); Christopher B. Strain, *Pure Fire: Self-Defense as Activism in the Civil Rights Era* (Athens: University of Georgia Press, 2005); Lance E. Hill, *The Deacons for Defense: Armed Resistance and the Civil Rights Movement* (Chapel Hill: University of North Carolina Press, 2004); Steven Hahn, *A Nation Under Our Feet: Black Political Struggles in the Rural South from Slavery to the Great Migration* (Cambridge, MA: The Belknap Press of Harvard University Press, 2003), chap. 6; Eric Foner, *Reconstruction: America's Unfinished Revolution, 1863–1877* (New York: Harper & Row, 1988), 283–84; Herbert Shapiro, *White Violence and Black Response: From Reconstruction to Montgomery* (Amherst: University of Massachusetts Press, 1988); Thomas Holt, *Black over White: Negro Political Leadership*

in South Carolina during Reconstruction (Urbana: University of Illinois Press, 1977), 31-32; Allen W. Trelease, *White Terror: The Ku Klux Klan Conspiracy and Southern Reconstruction* (Baton Rouge: Louisiana State University Press, 1971).

50. See Richard Maxwell Brown, *Strain of Violence: Historical Studies of American Violence and Vigilantism* (New York: Oxford University Press, 1975), esp. chap. 4. For works tracing the vigilante tradition in Revolutionary and early America, see Paul A. Gilje, *Rioting in America* (Bloomington: Indiana University Press, 1996); Michael Feldberg, *The Turbulent Era: Riot and Disorder in Jacksonian America* (New York: Oxford University Press, 1980); David Grimsted, "Rioting in Its Jacksonian Setting," *American Historical Review* 77 (April 1972): 361-97; Gordon S. Wood, *The Creation of the American Republic, 1776-1787* (Chapel Hill: University of North Carolina Press, 1969), 319-21.

51. See David Brion Davis, "Some Themes of Counter-Subversion: An Analysis of Anti-Masonic, Anti-Catholic, and Anti-Mormon Literature," *The Mississippi Valley Historical Review* 47 (Sept. 1960): 205-24; reprinted in David, *From Homicide to Slavery: Studies in American Culture* (New York: Oxford University Press, 1986), 137-54. See also Mark W. Cannon, "The Crusades against the Masons, Catholics, and Mormons: Separate Waves of a Common Current," *Brigham Young University Studies* 3 (Winter 1961): 23-40.

52. See Brown, *Strain of Violence*, esp. chap. 4; Grimsted, "Rioting in Its Jacksonian Setting"; Feldberg, *The Turbulent Era*; Gilje, *Rioting in America*; Brundage, *Lynching in the New South*; Tolnay and Beck, *A Festival of Violence*; Michael J. Pfeifer, *Rough Justice: Lynching and American Society, 1874-1947* (Urbana: University of Illinois Press, 2004); and Gilles Vandal, *Rethinking Southern Violence: Homicides in Post-Civil War Louisiana, 1866–1884* (Columbus: Ohio State University, Press, 2000). See also E. P. Thompson, "The Moral Economy of the English Crowd in the Eighteenth Century," *Past and Present* 50 (Feb. 1971): 76-136; and Natalie Zemon Davis, "The Rites of Violence: Religious Riot in Sixteenth-Century France," *Past and Present* 59 (May 1973): 51-91.

53. SSMMH, August 21, 1882 and August 1884. For similar examples, see ibid., June 12, 1878, and October 6, 1886.

54. York County had nine documented episodes of anti-Mormon violence in the 1880s, the most of any single county in the South, according to my count. For the Ku Klux Klan in York County, see Jerry Lee West, *The Reconstruction Ku Klux Klan in York County, South Carolina, 1865-1877* (Jefferson, NC: McFarland, 2002); Trelease, *White Terror*, 362.

55. See SSMMH, December 23, 1881; April 18, 1882; September 25, 1882; and *Alabama Baptist*, April 27, 1882. Historians have demonstrated how social and economic elites often participated in and led vigilante groups. See Brundage, *Lynching in the New South*, 38; and Brown, *Strain of Violence*, 120.

56. SSMMH, September 23, 1886. Rufus Cobb is described as "a perfect exemplar of a New South Democrat." See Robert David Ward, "Rufus W. Cobb, 1878-1882," in *Alabama Governors: A Political History of the State*, ed. Samuel L. Webb and Margaret E. Armbrester (Tuscaloosa: University of Alabama Press, 2001), 107.

57. See SSMMH, January 4, 1879; October 10, 1879; February 28, 1882; October 17, 1882; November 23, 1882; May 21, 1884; October 26, 1884; July 13, 1885; July 31, 1892; December 13, 1896; April 24, 1897.

58. "Mormons in the South," *Public Opinion* 28 (Jan.–June 1900): 114.

59. "Mayor Drennen to Mormons," *Atlanta Constitution*, October 6, 1899.

60. L. A. Stevenson, "A City Councilman Objects," *Southern Star*, vol. 1 (1899), 206; "Shut Down on the Mormons," *Atlanta Constitution*, October 7, 1900; "Mormons Leaving the South," *New York Times*, November 3, 1901. A Baptist delegation unsuccessfully lobbied the South Carolina legislature to pass a law designed to "extirpate" Mormon elders from the state, in the name of seeking to "save them from having the mob violence that some sister states have lately had in trying to rid themselves of this sect." "Mormon Church in Carolina," *Atlanta Constitution*, December 22, 1899.

61. See SSMMH, November 26, 1884; December 1889; November 1896; December 5, 1896; George H. Emery, "A Sample Mob," *Southern Star*, vol. 1 (1899), 205; "Mormons Visit the Governor," *Atlanta Constitution*, October 5, 1901. One notable exception to this pattern of indifference was Georgia Governor Allen Candler's appeal for the citizens of his state to put an end to mob violence, and his personal meeting with Southern States Mission president Ben E. Rich. See "Gov. Candler's Appeal," and "President Rich in Georgia," *Southern Star*, vol. 1 (1899), 285, 293.

62. See "Mormon Elders in the Hands of a Mob," *Atlanta Constitution*, October 2, 1901; "Mormons Leaving the South," *New York Times*, November 3, 1901; "Want Big Pay for Lashes," *Atlanta Constitution*, March 2, 1902; "Elders Asking Heavy Damages," ibid., September 30, 1903.

63. SSMMH, June 12, 1878; November 16, 1882; October 31, 1884; May 23, 1885; June 13, 1887; June 17, 1887; "Ku-Klux Doings," *Deseret News*, July 6, 1887; and typescript of Morgan journal, in Morgan Papers, October 1, 1877 and November 14, 1877. See also handwritten note to "Elder Morgan" from "K.K.K.," in Morgan Correspondence.

64. See *Nashville Banner*, August 21, 1884 and October 17, 1884.

65. See Foner, *Reconstruction*, 454–59; Trelease, *White Terror*, chaps. 24–25.

66. SSMMH, November 16, 1882. The Klan Act of 1871 outlawed conspiracies "to deprive citizens of the right to vote, hold office, serve on juries, and enjoy the equal protection of the laws." Foner, *Reconstruction*, 454–455. The record does not make it clear, but the Mormon family likely made their case under the last provision (equal protection). In general, by 1882 the Klan Act was only intermittently enforced, even in the case of depredations against African Americans.

67. Quote from Trelease, *White Terror*, 420.

68. See Grimsted, "Rioting in Its Jacksonian Setting," 397.

69. See Patrick Q. Mason, "Traditions of Violence: Early Mormon and Anti-Mormon Conflict in Its American Setting," in *Archive of Restoration Culture Summer Fellows' Papers, 2000-2002*, ed. Richard Lyman Bushman (Provo, UT: Joseph Fielding Smith Institute for Latter-day Saint History at Brigham Young University, 2005), 163–85. Thanks to Richard Bushman for helping formulate these ideas.

CHAPTER 8

1. "Honoring the Martyrs," *Deseret News*, August 25, 1884.

2. "Record of Donations to Tennessee Martyrs," ledger book, LDSCA. This amount is approximately $100,000 in current values.

3. For instance, in 1952 LDS church president David O. McKay offered the dedicatory prayer over a new monument to Joseph Standing in Varnell Station, Georgia. See "Church of Jesus Christ of Latter-day Saints Southern States Mission Conference and Joseph Standing Monument Dedication, May 3-4, 1952," in LDSCA. Additionally, the Cane Creek Massacre was prominently recalled in an official LDS church publication at the time of the dedication of the church's Nashville temple. See David F. Boone, "1884 Slayings Recall Bitter Time," *LDS Church News*, January 8, 2000.

4. For a parallel argument, see Gene A. Sessions, "Myth, Mormonism, and Murder in the South," *South Atlantic Quarterly* 75 (Spring 1976): 212–25.

5. John Irvine, [comp.,] *"Mormon" Protest against Injustice: An Appeal for Constitutional and Religious Liberty* (Salt Lake City: Jos. Hyrum Parry, 1885), 6–24. Missionaries in the South often repeated this theme, expressing surprise that persecution came in spite of "the American Constitution, which allows all men everywhere the right to worship God according to the dictates of his own conscience." J. Warren Johnson, "Persecution a Saint's Heritage," *Southern Star*, vol. 1 (Chattanooga, TN: Southern States Mission, 1899), 109. See also "Mobbing in Georgia," ibid., 284.

6. Joseph Smith-History 1:21–25, 60–61, 74–75, in *The Pearl of Great Price: A Selection from the Revelations, Translations, and Narrations of Joseph Smith, First Prophet, Seer, and Revelator to the Church of Jesus Christ of Latter-day Saints* (Salt Lake City, UT: Church of Jesus Christ of Latter-day Saints, 1989). The phrases used by Smith to describe the initial opposition to his revelations include "great contempt," "great deal of prejudice," "great persecution," "the most bitter persecution and reviling," "ridiculed," "hated and persecuted," and "reviling me."

7. See Richard L. Bushman, with the assistance of Jed Woodworth, *Joseph Smith: Rough Stone Rolling* (New York: Alfred A. Knopf, 2005), 178–80; Leonard J. Arrington and Davis Bitton, *The Mormon Experience: A History of the Latter-day Saints* (Urbana: University of Illinois Press, 1992), 44–45.

8. Arrington and Bitton, *The Mormon Experience*, chap. 3, provides an excellent overview of the causes and different types of early persecution against the Latter-day Saints. The chapter dedicated to the Missouri period in the LDS Church's official history book used in Sunday School classes focuses almost exclusively on anti-Mormon violence, emphasizing Governor Boggs's extermination and Haun's Mill. *Our Heritage: A Brief History of The Church of Jesus Christ of Latter-day Saints* (Salt Lake City: The Church of Jesus Christ of Latter-day Saints, 1996), chap. 4.

9. Matthew J. Grow, *"Liberty to the Downtrodden": Thomas L. Kane, Romantic Reformer* (New Haven, CT: Yale University Press, 2009), chap. 5.

10. R. W. Sloan, *The Great Contest: The Chief Advocates of Anti-Mormon Measures Reviewed . . .* (Salt Lake City: n.p., 1887), 9.

11. See *Journal of Discourses by President John Taylor, His Counselors, the Twelve Apostles, and Others*, vol. 26 (London: Latter-day Saints' Book Depot, 1886).

12. John Nicholson, *The Martyrdom of Joseph Standing; or, the Murder of a "Mormon" Missionary* (Grantsville, UT: LDS Archive Publishers, 1997), 158. Nicholson dedicated seventy-two pages to the narrative of Standing's murder, and eighty-one pages to an "appendix" relating conditions in the Utah Penitentiary and providing individual biographies of those incarcerated there under the Edmunds Act.

13. D. Michael Quinn, *The Mormon Hierarchy: Origins of Power* (Salt Lake City: Signature Books, 1994), 93. On this phenomenon more broadly, see also David

Grimsted, "Rioting in Its Jacksonian Setting," *American Historical Review* 77 (April 1972): 389-394; and Catherine Wessinger, ed., *Millennialism, Persecution, and Violence: Historical Cases* (Syracuse, NY: Syracuse University Press, 2000), 17-18.

14. "The Spirit of Mobocracy," *Deseret News*, November 26, 1884.

15. "Proselyting in the South," *Deseret News (Weekly)*, March 10, 1886.

16. "Discourse by Prest. George Q. Cannon," *Deseret News*, September 24, 1884.

17. "Sad Occurrences," *Woman's Exponent*, August 15, 1884. See also "Mobocracy in the South," *Deseret News*, November 30, 1887; "Persecution and Misrepresentation," ibid., July 27, 1887.

18. John Morgan, "Discourse by Elder John Morgan," in *Journal of Discourses* vol. 23 (London: Latter-day Saints' Book Depot, 1883), 39. See also "Minutes," *Deseret News*, October 22, 1879; "Correspondence," ibid., December 10, 1879; "The Work in the Southern States," ibid., November 23, 1881; "Joys of Mormon Elders," ibid., August 18, 1900.

19. R. Laurence Moore, *Religious Outsiders and the Making of Americans* (New York: Oxford University Press, 1986), 34.

20. "Discourse by Elder John Morgan" (1883), 39.

21. John Morgan, "Discourse by Elder John Morgan," in *Journal of Discourses*, vol. 21 (London: Latter-day Saints' Book Depot, 1881), 186. See also "The Murderers of Elder Joseph Standing on Trial," *Deseret News*, October 28, 1879.

22. "Remarks by Prest. John Taylor," *Deseret News*, August 13, 1879.

23. J. Warren Johnson, "Persecution a Saint's Heritage," *Southern Star*, vol. 1 (1899), 109. See also "Albermarle Mobbing," and Ben E. Rich, "Saints of the Sunny South," *Southern Star*, vol. 2 (Chattanooga, TN: Southern States Mission, 1900), 134 and 414.

24. "Persecution Always Wrong," *Deseret News*, October 28, 1894; Sloan, *The Great Contest*, 3; "Mobocracy in the South," *Deseret News*, November 30, 1887.

25. Jan Shipps, *Mormonism: The Story of a New Religious Tradition* (Urbana: University of Illinois Press, 1985), 51-54.

26. R. W. Sloan, for instance, argued that "the parallel is perfect" between Mormon resistance to federal authority and early Christians' survival in the face of Roman persecution. Sloan, *The Great Contest*, 4.

27. "Discourse of Prest. George Q. Cannon," *Deseret News*, September 24, 1884.

28. "Ku-Klux Doings," ibid., July 6, 1887.

29. Letters from John Gibbs to Louisa Gibbs, April 21, 1884, May 14, 1884, and August 5, 1884, in John Henry Gibbs Collection, BYU.

30. See J. H. Ward, *Stanzas on the Death of Elder Joseph Standing*, in LDSCA.

31. "Persecution and Misrepresentation," *Deseret News*, September 27, 1887.

32. "Voice from the Southern States," ibid., April 19, 1882.

33. "Discourse by Elder John Morgan" (1883), 39-40.

34. "Discourse by Prest. George Q. Cannon," *Deseret News*, September 24, 1884. On historical ideas and practices of peace within Mormonism, see Patrick Q. Mason, "The Possibilities of Mormon Peacebuilding," *Dialogue: A Journal of Mormon Thought* 37 (Spring 2004): 12-45; Grant Underwood, "Pacifism and Mormonism: A Study in Ambiguity," in *Proclaim Peace: Christian Pacifism from Unexpected Quarters*, ed. Theron F. Schlabach and Richard T. Hughes (Urbana: University of Illinois Press, 1997), 139-56; Ronald W. Walker, "Sheaves, Bucklers, and the State: Mormon

Leaders Respond to the Dilemmas of War," *Sunstone* 7 (July/August 1982): 43–56; and D. Michael Quinn, "The Mormon Church and the Spanish-American War: An End to Selective Pacifism," *Pacific Historical Review* 43 (August 1974): 342–66.

35. Ben E. Rich, "Saints of the Sunny South," *Southern Star*, vol. 2 (1900), 414.

36. Grant Underwood, *The Millenarian World of Early Mormonism* (Urbana: University of Illinois Press, 1999), 46–51; see also Gabriel A. Almond, R. Scott Appleby, and Emmanuel Sivan, *Strong Religion: The Rise of Fundamentalisms around the World* (Chicago: University of Chicago Press, 2003), 96–97, 104.

37. Circular letter to the Elders and Saints in the Southern States Mission, from John Morgan, July 23, 1879, in John Hamilton Morgan Papers, U of U; "Correspondence," *Deseret News*, October 28, 1879.

38. "Murderers Encouraged," *Deseret News*, October 29, 1879.

39. "More about the Murders in Tennessee," ibid., August 20, 1884.

40. "Remarks by Prest. John Taylor," ibid., October 22, 1879. See also Clarence E. Cowley, "At a Baptist Church," *Southern Star*, vol. 1 (1899), 333; and Ben E. Rich, "Saints of the Sunny South," *Southern Star*, vol. 2 (1900), 414.

41. "Voice from the Southern States," *Deseret News*, April 19, 1882.

42. Michael Ignatieff, *The Warrior's Honor: Ethnic War and the Modern Conscience* (New York: Viking, 1998), 52.

43. "Discourse by Prest. George Q. Cannon," *Deseret News*, September 24, 1884.

44. "The Work in the Southern States," ibid., November 23, 1881. For an example of the Mormon press praising the objectivity of non-Mormon reporting, see "A Consistent View," ibid., August 27, 1884.

45. "Discourse by Elder John Morgan" (1881), 180.

46. "Persecution and Misrepresentation," *Deseret News*, July 27, 1887.

47. "Discourse by Elder John Morgan" (1883), 44.

48. "More about the Murders in Tennessee," *Deseret News*, August 20, 1884.

49. "Mobocracy in the South," ibid., September 17, 1879.

50. "Correspondence," ibid., October 28, 1879.

51. "Discourse by Elder John Morgan" (1881), 186.

52. Quoted in Sessions, "Myth, Mormonism, and Murder in the South," 224.

53. Eliza R. Snow Smith, *Biography and Family Record of Lorenzo Snow* (Salt Lake City: Deseret News Company, 1884), 424.

54. "Correspondence," *Deseret News*, December 10, 1879.

55. "Mobocracy in the South," ibid., September 17, 1879.

56. "Home from the South," ibid., August 12, 1885.

57. "Missionaries Maltreated," ibid., July 20, 1887.

58. "Joys of Mormon Elders," ibid., August 18, 1900.

59. Benjamin E. Rich, "Two Letters to a Baptist Minister," introduction; and "A Friendly Discussion upon Religious Subjects," in *Tracts from Southern States Mission* (ca. 1900), Princeton, 2, 7, 9, 12.

60. Thomas Cottam Romney, *A Divinity Shapes Our Ends: As Seen in My Life Story* (n.p.: Thomas Cottam Romney, 1953), 70.

61. Andrew M. Israelsen, *Utah Pioneering: An Autobiography* (Salt Lake City: Deseret News Press, 1938), 61, 64, 70. During his mission, Israelsen wrote home, "We meet much opposition from the pulpit. The preaching of the pious ministers is all turned to stirring up the people to anger against the Latter-day Saints. They tell all

the lies that tongue can tell. One minister told his congregation that he believed the Mormons killed President Garfield." SSMMH, June 26, 1884.

62. Romney, *A Divinity Shapes Our Ends*, 87.

63. Letter from Donald Urie to John Urie, August 22, 1899, in John Urie Correspondence, 1891–1899, LDSCA.

64. "Discourse by Elder John Morgan" (1883), 46–47.

65. Almond, Appleby, and Sivan, *Strong Religion*, chap. 1; quotes from 33–34, 36.

66. Regina M. Schwartz, *The Curse of Cain: The Violent Legacy of Monotheism* (Chicago: University of Chicago Press, 1997), 5.

CHAPTER 9

Portions of this chapter first appeared in Patrick Q. Mason, "Anti-Jewish Violence in the New South," *Southern Jewish History* 8 (2005): 77–119.

1. See William R. Hutchison, *Religious Pluralism in America: The Contentious History of a Founding Ideal* (New Haven, CT: Yale University Press, 2003).

2. See Mechal Sobel, *Trabelin' On: The Slave Journey to an Afro-Baptist Faith* (Westport, CT: Greenwood Press, 1979); and Samuel S. Hill, *One Name but Several Faces: Variety in Popular Christian Denominations in Southern History* (Athens: University of Georgia Press, 1996), 36–38.

3. Recent examples of this can be found in conflicts in the former Yugoslavia, Northern Ireland, and India. See Michael A. Sells, *The Bridge Betrayed: Religion and Genocide in Bosnia* (Berkeley: University of California Press, 1996); Sudhir Kakar, *The Colors of Violence: Cultural Identities, Religion, and Conflict* (Chicago: University of Chicago Press, 1996); Stanley J. Tambiah, *Leveling Crowds: Ethnonationalist Conflicts and Collective Violence in South Asia* (Berkeley: University of California Press, 1996); R. Scott Appleby, *The Ambivalence of the Sacred: Religion, Violence, and Reconciliation* (Lanham, MD: Rowman & Littlefield Publishers, 2000); and Mark Juergensmeyer, *Terror in the Mind of God: The Global Rise of Religious Violence*, 3rd ed., rev. and updated (Berkeley: University of California Press, 2003), esp. chap. 1.

4. Quoted in Robert A. Rockaway, "'I Feel as if Newly Born': Immigrant Letters to the Industrial Removal Office," *American Jewish Archives* 45 (Fall/Winter 1993): 169–70.

5. On the role of Jews in the economy, see Stephen J. Whitfield, "Commercial Passions: The Southern Jew as Businessman," *American Jewish History* 71 (Mar. 1982): 342–57.

6. C. Vann Woodward, *Tom Watson: Agrarian Rebel* (New York: Rinehart, 1938), chap. 23.

7. See Howard N. Rabinowitz, "Nativism, Bigotry, and Anti-Semitism in the South," *American Jewish History* 77 (Mar. 1988): 437–51.

8. "Domestic News," *American Hebrew*, August 5, 1887.

9. "Domestic News," ibid., August 12, 1887.

10. Arnold Shankman, ed., "Jewish Life in Aiken, S.C.: Childhood Memories of Esther Surasky Pinck," *SJHS Newsletter* (Mar. 1982): 2.

11. "Anti-Semites in Louisiana," *American Hebrew*, April 1, 1887.

12. Ibid.; and "The Louisiana Outrage," *American Israelite*, June 17, 1887.

13. See Michael N. Dobkowski, *The Tarnished Dream: The Basis of American Anti-Semitism* (Westport, CT: Greenwood Press, 1979), 6. See also Walter Nugent, *The Tolerant Populists: Kansas, Populism, and Nativism* (Chicago: University of Chicago Press, 1963); and John Higham, *Send These to Me: Jews and Other Immigrants in Urban America* (New York: Atheneum, 1975), chap. 7. Other historians have argued for a stronger link between the Populist movement and anti-Semitism. See Oscar Handlin, "How U.S. Anti-Semitism Really Began: Its Grass-Roots Source in the 90's," *Commentary* 11 (June 1951): 541–48; Richard Hofstadter, *The Age of Reform: From Bryan to FDR* (New York: Knopf, 1955), 78–80; Victor C. Ferkiss, "Populist Influences on American Fascism," *Western Political Quarterly* 10 (June 1957): 350–73.

14. David A. Gerber, "Anti-Semitism and Jewish-Gentile Relations in American Historiography and the American Past," in *Anti-Semitism in American History*, ed. David A. Gerber (Urbana: University of Illinois Press, 1986), 30. See also Higham, *Send These to Me*, 123–24.

15. "Mobbing Merchants," *American Israelite*, October 31, 1899; "Trouble in Delhi," *Richland Beacon*, November 2, 1889; "The Delhi Trouble," ibid., November 2, 1889.

16. "The Louisiana Outrages," *American Israelite*, November 21, 1889.

17. "Notes," ibid., January 23, 1890.

18. William F. Holmes, "Whitecapping: Anti-Semitism in the Populist Era," *American Jewish Historical Quarterly* 63 (Mar. 1974): 249.

19. See ibid., 251, 259.

20. Typescript letter from Donelson Caffery to Harry [no last name], November 23, 1893, from letter file book, vol. 6, 105, Caffery (Donelson and Family) Papers, LLMVC.

21. For an example of political violence that combined anti-black and anti-Jewish sentiments, see Daniel R. Weinfeld, "Samuel Fleishman: Tragedy in Reconstruction-Era Florida," *Southern Jewish History* 8 (2005): 31–76.

22. See Benny Kraut, "Jewish Survival in Protestant America," in *Minority Faiths and the American Protestant Mainstream*, ed. Jonathan D. Sarna (Urbana: University of Illinois Press, 1998), 40–41.

23. Robert Rockaway and Arnon Gutfeld, "Demonic Images of the Jew in the Nineteenth Century United States," *American Jewish History* 89 (Dec. 2001): 356, 375; Dinnerstein, *Uneasy at Home*, 89.

24. Leonard Rogoff, *Homelands: Southern Jewish Identity in Durham and Chapel Hill, North Carolina* (Tuscaloosa: University of Alabama Press, 2001), 85–88.

25. Eli N. Evans, *The Provincials: A Personal History of Jews in the South*, rev. ed. (New York: Free Press, 1997), 49. See also Malcolm H. Stern, "The Role of the Rabbi in the South," in *"Turn to the South": Essays on Southern Jewry*, ed. Nathan M. Kaganoff and Melvin I. Urofsky (Charlottesville: University Press of Virginia, 1979), 21–32.

26. Dobkowski, *Tarnished Dream*, 79, 94.

27. Louise A. Mayo, *The Ambivalent Image: Nineteenth-Century America's Perception of the Jew* (Rutherford, NJ: Fairleigh Dickinson University Press, 1988), 128. See also Leonard Dinnerstein, *Antisemitism in America* (New York: Oxford University Press, 1994), 49; Dinnerstein, *Uneasy at Home: Antisemitism and the American Jewish Experience* (New York: Columbia University Press, 1987), 91; and Myron Berman, *Richmond's Jewry, 1769-1976: Shabbat in Shockoe* (Charlottesville: University Press of Virginia, 1979), 247.

28. Philip H. Pitts Diary, Alabama, typescript, vol. 2 (1882–1884), SHC, 44; original spelling preserved.

29. Bobbie Malone, *Rabbi Max Heller: Reformer, Zionist, Southerner, 1860-1929* (Tuscaloosa: University of Alabama Press, 1997), 47–48.

30. See Steven Hertzberg, *Strangers within the Gate City: The Jews of Atlanta, 1845-1915* (Philadelphia: The Jewish Publication Society of America, 1978), 155–56.

31. Despite Jewish merchants' alliances with the southern middle class and aspirations for full acceptance, southern elites consistently barred Jews from certain elements of high society. See Gerber, "Anti-Semitism and Jewish-Gentile Relations," 27; and Wendy Lowe Besmann, *A Separate Circle: Jewish Life in Knoxville, Tennessee* (Knoxville: University of Tennessee Press, 2001), 51.

32. See Richard Gambino, *Vendetta: A True Story of the Worst Lynching in America, the Mass Murder of Italian-Americans in New Orleans in 1891, the Vicious Motivations Behind It, and the Tragic Repercussions That Linger to This Day* (Toronto: Guernica, 1998); Barbara Botein, "The Hennessy Case: An Episode in Anti-Italian Nativism," *Louisiana History* 20 (Summer 1979): 261–79; John V. Baiamonte Jr., "'Who Killa de Chief' Revisited: The Hennessey Assassination and Its Aftermath, 1890–1991," *Louisiana History* 33 (Spring 1992): 117–46; Marco Rimanelli and Sheryl L. Postman, eds., *The 1891 New Orleans Lynching and U.S.-Italian Relations: A Look Back* (New York: Peter Lang, 1992); and Louise Reynes Edwards-Simpson, "Sicilian Immigration to New Orleans, 1870-1910: Ethnicity, Race, and Social Position in the New South" (Ph.D. diss., University of Minnesota, 1996).

33. See Edward F. Haas, "Guns, Goats, and Italians: The Tallulah Lynching of 1899," *North Louisiana Historical Association Journal* 13 (Spring and Summer 1982): 45–58; Peter Vellon, "A Darker Past: The Development of Italian American Racial Consciousness, 1886-1920," (Ph.D. diss., City University of New York, 2003), 63, 84, and chaps. 1–2; William D. Carrigan and Clive Webb, "*Muerto por Unos Desconocidos* (Killed by Persons Unknown): Mob Violence against Blacks and Mexicans," in *Beyond Black and White: Race, Ethnicity, and Gender in the U.S. South and Southwest*, ed. Stephanie Cole and Alison M. Parker (College Station: Texas A&M University Press for the University of Texas at Arlington, 2004), 35–74; William D. Carrigan, *The Making of a Lynching Culture: Violence and Vigilantism in Central Texas, 1836-1916* (Urbana: University of Illinois Press, 2004), chap. 1. Precisely because religion is not mentioned in the sources, it is difficult to determine in a definitive way that individual Sicilian or Mexican lynching victims were Catholic. I am admittedly making broadly generalized assumptions about their religious identity as tied to their national origins.

34. On the racial status and social location of Italian immigrants, see Thomas A. Guglielmo, *White on Arrival: Italians, Race, Color, and Power in Chicago, 1890-1945* (New York: Oxford University Press, 2003); Jennifer Guglielmo and Salvatore Salerno, eds., *Are Italians White? How Race is Made in America* (New York: Routledge, 2003); Vellon, "A Darker Past"; David A. J. Richards, *Italian Americans: The Racializing of an Ethnic Identity* (New York: New York University Press, 1999); Matthew Frye Jacobson, *Whiteness of a Different Color: European Immigrants and the Alchemy of Race* (Cambridge, MA: Harvard University Press, 1998), 56–62; Edwards-Simpson, "Sicilian Immigration to New Orleans."

35. On conflict between various ethnic groups within American Catholicism, see Michael Doorley, "Irish Catholics and French Creoles: Ethnic Struggles within

the Catholic Church in New Orleans, 1835-1920," *Catholic Historical Review* 87 (Jan. 2001): 37-54; Jay P. Dolan, *The American Catholic Experience: A History from Colonial Times to the Present* (Notre Dame, IN: University of Notre Dame Press, 1992), 201-3, 237; Robert Anthony Orsi, *The Madonna of 115th Street: Faith and Community in Italian Harlem, 1880-1950* (New Haven: Yale University Press, 1985), 16-17, 55-57, 199; Richard Gambino, *Blood of My Blood: The Dilemma of the Italian-Americans* (Garden City, NY: Doubleday, 1974), 214-18; Silvano M. Tomasi, "The Ethnic Church and the Integration of Italian Immigrants in the United States," in *The Italian Experience in the United States*, ed. Silvano M. Tomasi and Madeline H. Engel (Staten Island, NY: Center for Migration Studies, 1970), 163-94.

36. Quoted in Andrew Rolle, *The Italian Americans: Troubled Roots* (New York: Free Press, 1980), 157. See also Donald L. Kinzer, *An Episode in Anti-Catholicism: The American Protective Association* (Seattle: University of Washington Press, 1964), 16.

37. See Peter R. D'Agostino, *Rome in America: Transnational Catholic Ideology from the Risorgimento to Fascism* (Chapel Hill: University of North Carolina Press, 2004). See also Jenny Franchot, *Roads to Rome: The Antebellum Protestant Encounter with Catholicism* (Berkeley: University of California Press, 1994); Michael Schwartz, *The Persistent Prejudice: Anti-Catholicism in America* (Huntington, IN: Our Sunday Visitor, 1984).

38. See Michael J. McNally, "A Peculiar Institution: Catholic Parish Life and the Pastoral Mission to Blacks in the Southeast, 1850-1980," *U.S. Catholic Historian* 5 (Winter 1986): 69-70.

39. Michael Kenny, S.J., "Jesuits in Our Southland, 1566-1946," unpublished typescript (1946), in Loyola University Special Collections, New Orleans. See also John T. McGreevy, *Catholicism and American Freedom: A History* (New York: W. W. Norton, 2003), chap. 3; Randall M. Miller, "Catholic Religion, Irish Ethnicity, and the Civil War," in *Religion and the American Civil War*, ed. Miller, Harry S. Stout, and Charles Reagan Wilson (New York: Oxford University Press, 1998), 261-96.

40. See McGreevy, *Catholicism and American Freedom*, chap. 2; Randall M. Miller and Jon L. Wakelyn, eds., *Catholics in the Old South: Essays on Church and Culture* (Macon, GA: Mercer University Press, 1999 [1983]); John C. Bowes, "Glory in Gloom: Abram J. Ryan, Southern Catholicism, and the Lost Cause" (Ph.D. diss., Saint Louis University, 1996), chap. 2.

41. See Dolores Egger Labbe, *Jim Crow Comes to Church: The Establishment of Segregated Catholic Parishes in South Louisiana* (New York: Arno Press, 1978 [1971]); Bowes, "Glory in Gloom," chap. 3. On Vatican pronouncements regarding African Americans and race, see McGreevy, *Catholicism and American Freedom*, 55. In the late nineteenth century the Josephite order was created to minister to African Americans. See Stephen J. Ochs, *Desegregating the Altar: The Josephites and the Struggle for Black Priests, 1871-1960* (Baton Rouge: Louisiana State University Press, 1990).

42. Kenny, "Jesuits in Our Southland," 142.

43. A. B. Friend, S.J., "Alabama," in *Woodstock Letters: A Record of the Current Events and Historical Notes Connected with the Colleges and Missions of the Soc. of Jesus in North and South America* vol. 17 (1888): 55-58.

44. See Kinzer, *An Episode in Anti-Catholicism*; John Higham, *Strangers in the Land: Patterns of American Nativism, 1860-1925* (New Brunswick, NJ: Rutgers University Press, 1992), chaps. 3-4.

45. Letters from Robert Lewis Bolton to Mrs. Compton, November 6, 1909 and June 17, 1910, in Robert Lewis Bolton Papers, SHC.

46. Robert T. Parish diary, September 30, 1861, LLMVC; original spelling preserved.

47. Rev. L. L. Pickett, *The Danger Signal; or, a Shot at the Foe* (Nashville: Publishing House of the M. E. Church, South, 1891), 3, 275, 277, 282, 301.

48. See Joe Creech, *Righteous Indignation: Religion and the Populist Revolution* (Urbana: University of Illinois Press, 2006).

49. "Address by Hon. Thomas E. Watson in the Court House in the City of Thomson, Georgia, 10:00 A.M., February 12th, 1916," typescript, in Thomas Edward Watson Papers, SHC, 14, 25–26. See Woodward, *Tom Watson*, chap. 22, which characterizes Watson's anti-Catholic writings as "a curious mixture of erudition and sensationalism bordering upon the pathological" (420).

50. "Editorial Notes and Clippings," *Watson's Magazine* (no date), in Watson Papers.

51. "Where the American" (no date or publication info), in ibid.

52. Quoted in Walter Edgar, *South Carolina: A History* (Columbia: University of South Carolina Press, 1998), 421. Protestant community leaders in Yazoo City, Mississippi, also helped rebuild a local Catholic church after it burned down. Richard Oliver Grow, S.T.D., comp., *Catholicity in Mississippi* (Natchez, MS: Hope Haven Press, 1939), 180–81. Similar shows of interreligious solidarity had occurred in the antebellum South. See John R. Dichtl, *Frontiers of Faith: Bringing Catholicism to the West in the Early Republic* (Lexington: University Press of Kentucky, 2008), 98–99.

53. For positive reviews of church dedications, see "Selma, Ala. How It Came to Be: Its Subsequent History Jesuit Residence & Church, from 1880 to 1931" (no pub. info), in Special Collections, Loyola University, New Orleans; numerous articles on front page about dedication of St. Joseph's church, *Atlanta Constitution*, November 15, 1903; "Dedication of St. Joseph's Church with Impressive Ceremonials," *Macon Telegraph*, November 15, 1903. For the more negative experience, see Rev. Albert Biever, S.J., typescript memoir, in Special Collections, Loyola University, 262.

54. Letter from Sister Anne of Jesus to Marie Joseph, December 18, 1888, in Sister Dorothea Olga McCants, Daughter of the Cross, *With Valor They Serve: A Sequel to They Came to Louisiana* (Baton Rouge, LA: Claitor's Publishing Division, 1975).

55. Pickett, *Danger Signal*, 275.

56. A February 1831 revelation to Joseph Smith (D&C 42:9) told the Latter-day Saints that "ye may be my [God's] people and I will be your God." On the notion of Mormon peoplehood, see Charles L. Cohen, "The Construction of the Mormon People," *Journal of Mormon History* 32 (Spring 2006): 25–64; Dean L. May, "Mormons," in *Mormons and Mormonism: An Introduction to an American World Religion*, ed. Eric A. Eliason (Urbana: University of Illinois Press, 2001), 47–75; Patricia Nelson Limerick, "Peace Initiative: Using the Mormons to Rethink Culture and Ethnicity in American History," *Journal of Mormon History* 21 (Fall 1995): 1–29; Jan Shipps, *Mormonism: The Story of a New Religious Tradition* (Urbana: University of Illinois Press, 1985); Jan Shipps, "Making Saints: In the Early Days and the Latter Days," in *Contemporary Mormonism: Social Science Perspectives*, ed. Marie Cornwall, Tim B. Heaton, and Lawrence A. Young (Urbana: University of Illinois Press, 1994), 64–83.

57. See Terryl L. Givens, *The Viper on the Hearth: Mormons, Myths, and the Construction of Heresy* (New York: Oxford University Press, 1997), 137. See also Davis Bitton and Gary L. Bunker, "Phrenology Among the Mormons," *Dialogue: A Journal of Mormon Thought* 9 (Spring 1974): 43–61.

58. See Orsi, *The Madonna of 115th Street*; Jon Gjerde, *The Minds of the West: Ethnocultural Evolution in the Rural Middle West, 1830-1917* (Chapel Hill: University of North Carolina Press, 1997).

59. See D&C 101:77, 80.

60. "Growth of the Church," http://newsroom.lds.org/ldsnewsroom/eng/background-information/growth-of-the-church (accessed November 23, 2009).

61. Statistics from Association of Religion Data Archives, http://www.thearda.com/mapsReports/reports/selectState.asp (accessed October 21, 2009). For questions about LDS church membership numbers, see John Dart, "Counting Mormons: Study Says LDS Numbers Inflated," *Christian Century*, August 21, 2007.

62. Jan Shipps, "The Scattering of the Gathered and the Gathering of the Scattered: The Mid-Twentieth Century Mormon Diaspora," in *Sojourner in the Promised Land: Forty Years among the Mormons* (Urbana: University of Illinois Press, 2000), 258-77.

63. "Temples of the Church of Jesus Christ of Latter-day Saints," http://www.ldschurchtemples.com/temples/ (accessed November 23, 2009).

64. Neil J. Young, "Southern Baptists v. the Mormons," December 19, 2007, http://www.slate.com/id/2180391/ (accessed November 23, 2009); R. Philip Roberts with Tal Davis and Sandra Tanner, *Mormonism Unmasked: Confronting the Contradictions between Mormon Beliefs and True Christianity* (Nashville: Broadman & Holman, 1998).

65. John W. Kennedy, "Southern Baptists Take Up the Mormon Challenge," *Christianity Today*, June 15, 1998. See also Jan Shipps, "Media Coverage of the Southern Baptist Convention in Salt Lake City," in *Sojourner in the Promised Land*, 143-54.

66. Leonard J. Arrington and Davis Bitton, *The Mormon Experience: A History of the Latter-day Saints*, 2nd ed. (Urbana: University of Illinois Press, 1992), 184.

Index

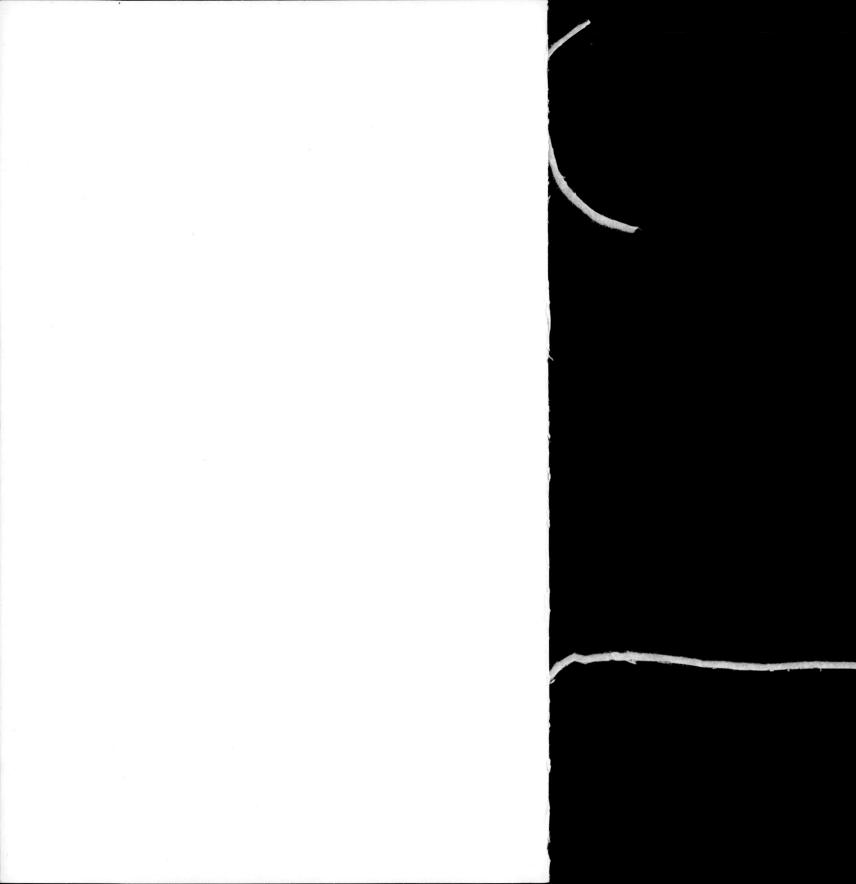